ROMANTIC INDIANS

Romantic Indians

Native Americans, British Literature, and Transatlantic Culture 1756–1830

TIM FULFORD

OXFORD
UNIVERSITY PRESS

OXFORD

UNIVERSITY PRESS

Great Clarendon Street, Oxford OX2 6DP

Oxford University Press is a department of the University of Oxford.
It furthers the University's objective of excellence in research, scholarship,
and education by publishing worldwide in

Oxford New York

Auckland Cape Town Dar es Salaam Hong Kong Karachi
Kuala Lumpur Madrid Melbourne Mexico City Nairobi
New Delhi Shanghai Taipei Toronto

With offices in

Argentina Austria Brazil Chile Czech Republic France Greece
Guatemala Hungary Italy Japan Poland Portugal Singapore
South Korea Switzerland Thailand Turkey Ukraine Vietnam

Oxford is a registered trademark of Oxford University Press
in the UK and in certain other countries

Published in the United States
by Oxford University Press Inc., New York

© Tim Fulford 2006

The moral rights of the author have been asserted
Database right Oxford University Press (maker)

First published 2006

British Library Cataloguing in Publication Data

Data available

Library of Congress Cataloging in Publication Data

Fulford, Tim, 1962–
Romantic Indians : native Americans, British literature, and transatlantic culture,
1756–1830 / Tim Fulford.
p. cm.
Includes bibliographical references and index.
ISBN–13: 978–0–19–927337–9 (acid-free paper)
ISBN–10: 0–19–927337–5 (acid-free paper)
1. English literature—18th century—History and criticism.   2. Indians in literature.   3. English
literature—19th century—History and criticism.   4. English literature—American influences.
5. Romanticism—Great Britain.   I. TItle.
PR448.I536F85 2006
820.9'897—dc22   2005029755

Typeset by Laserwords Private Limited, Chennai, India
Printed in Great Britain
on acid-free paper by
Biddles Ltd., King's Lynn, Norfolk

ISBN 0–19–927337–5   978–0–19–927337–9

1 3 5 7 9 10 8 6 4 2

ACKNOWLEDGEMENTS

For advice and help I am grateful to Alan Bewell, Carol Bolton, Dick Ellis, Marilyn Gaull, Richard Gravil, Anthony Harding, Kevin Hutchings, Gary Kelly, Peter J. Kitson, Morton D. Paley, Seamus Perry, Lynda Pratt, Stephanie Pratt, Fiona Robertson, Nicholas Roe, Fiona Stafford, Anya Taylor, Nicki Trott and Marina Warner. I have benefited especially from the suggestions and publications of Astrid Wind. Debbie Lee fostered the project through many vagaries and read the manuscript with sensitivity: I owe more to her support than I can say here.

The Arts and Humanities Research Board provided a grant enabling me to take a semester's research leave.

Some of the material that appears here was published, in earlier form, in *Symbiosis*, 2 (1998) and in N. Trott and S. Perry (eds.), *1800: The New Lyrical Ballads* (Basingstoke and New York: Palgrave, 2001). I am grateful to the editors for permission to incorporate it.

Derby Museum and Gallery kindly gave permission to reproduce on the dustjacket Joseph Wright's 1785 painting 'The Widow of an Indian Chief Watching the Arms of her Deceased Husband'.

Contents

Abbreviations

Adair   James Adair, *The History of the American Indians; Particularly Those Nations Adjoining to the Mississippi, East and West Florida, Georgia, South and North Carolina, and Virginia* (London, 1775)

Bartram   William Bartram, *Travels through North and South Carolina, Georgia, East and West Florida, The Cherokee Country . . . together with Observations on the Manners of the Indians* (London, 1791)

BPW   George Gordon, Lord Byron, *The Complete Poetical Works*, ed. Jerome McGann, 7 vols. (Oxford, 1980–86)

Carver   Jonathan Carver, *Travels through the Interior Parts of North America, in the Years 1766, 1767, and 1768* (London, 1778)

CL   *The Collected Letters of Samuel Taylor Coleridge*, ed. E. L. Griggs, 6 vols. (Oxford, 1956–71)

CN   *The Notebooks of S. T. Coleridge*, ed. Kathleen Coburn, 5 vols. (London and Princeton, NJ, 1957–2002)

CPW   Samuel Taylor Coleridge, *Poetical Works*, ed. J. C. C. Mays, 3 vols. (Princeton, NJ, 2001)

Hearne   Samuel Hearne, *A Journey from Prince of Wales's Fort in Hudson's Bay to the Northern Ocean 1769, 1770, 1771, 1772* (1795), ed. J. B. Tyrell (Toronto, 1911 [facs. rpt. New York, 1968])

LB   W. Wordsworth and S. T. Coleridge, *Lyrical Ballads 1798*, ed. W. J. B. Owen, 2nd edn. (Oxford, 1969)

Lects 1795   S. T. Coleridge, *Lectures 1795 on Politics and Religion*, ed. L. Patton and P. Mann (London and Princeton, NJ, 1971)

Norton   *The Journal of Major John Norton 1816*, ed. Carl F. Klinck and James J. Talman (Toronto, 1970)

Prelude   William Wordsworth, *The Prelude, 1799, 1805, 1850*, ed. Jonathan Wordsworth, M. H. Abrams, Stephen Gill (New York and London, 1979)

Southey   *Robert Southey: Poetical Works 1793–1810*, gen. ed. Lynda Pratt,
                 5 vols. (London, 2004)

WPW   *The Poetical Works of William Wordsworth*, ed. E. de Selincourt
                 and Helen Darbishire, 5 vols. (Oxford, 1940–49)

PART I

FACTUAL WRITING

1

Romantic Indians and their Inventors

JOHN NORTON

On 11 December 1804, the gentlefolk of the Bath and West of England Society welcomed a new honorary member—Captain John Norton. 'Tall, muscular and well-proportioned; his countenance fine & intelligent', Norton rose to his feet and delivered a 'most appropriate' speech of thanks.[1] After a smattering of applause, the polite company gathered round and chatted with their guest. Then they entreated him to sit for his portrait.

On the face of it, this was an evening like many others in Bath's social season: decorous, orderly; the British gentry engaged in one of the rituals by which they identified people as 'one of us'. And so it was, but with one difference. Norton, though educated in Edinburgh and fluent in French, was no ordinary British gentleman. Also known as Teyoninhokarawen, he was a chief of the Mohawks, a powerful leader of one of the principal tribes of the Iroquois (or Six Nation) alliance which had until 1784 been the strongest military power in North America.[2] A valued ally rather than a colonized subject, Norton would go on to lead British and Indian soldiers against the US in the war of 1812.

What does Teyoninhokarawen's reception in Bath tell us about relationships between Britons and Native Americans at the start of the nineteenth century? That the British gentry were culturally open-minded and prepared to welcome a foreigner so long as he acted with

[1] As described in the *Bath Chronicle*, Thursday 20 December 1804.

[2] The Iroquois were, for eighty years, the most powerful group in North America. An alliance of five (then six) nations (Seneca, Cayuga, Onondaga, Oneida, Mohawk and Tuscarora), they held the territory between French Canada and the New England colonies, and had vast experience at playing each white colony against the other, in return for trade goods. The Mohawks were cultivated by (and intermarried with) British officials; their power was diminished, however, and Iroquois unity broken, by the War of Independence, after which the Six Nations lost territory and independence.

what they called decorum and propriety? Perhaps. That they knew how to reward a token 'white man's Indian' for adopting their codes and furthering their beliefs? More likely. Teyoninhokarawen not only fought for the British (and gained promotion to major as a consequence) but, tutored by leading evangelical William Wilberforce, translated the Gospel of St John into the Mohawk language.

Yet there was another reason why Teyoninhokarawen was accepted—a reason that will be one of my concerns in this book. Teyoninhokarawen was welcomed because, under his gentle manners, his hosts hoped to discover the body and mind of a 'savage'—a man of nature, untouched, for good and ill, by civilization. He was embraced in Britain's sedate shires because North American Indians, portrayed in picture after picture, book after book, already seemed fascinatingly fierce and thrillingly sublime. So when he reached London it was to have a safe taste of Indian 'savagery' that fashionable ladies and gentlemen invited him to tea. Here is Romantic poet Thomas Campbell's account of one of these tea parties:

There is a Mohawk Indian in town, who whoops the war-whoop to ladies in drawing-rooms, and is the reigning rage of the town this season. He is an arch dog, and palms a number of old Scotch tunes (he was educated in the woods by a Scotchwoman), for Indian opera airs, on his discerning audience. Rogers the poet, somebody told me, being one of the spectators of this wonder, at hearing of proposals for the whoop, was seen to shrink with a look of inexpressible horror, and hide himself behind a sofa.[3]

For Campbell, Teyoninhokarawen was not authentically 'savage' enough. He seemed too British to be believably a member of a 'primitive' people: his Indianness must be a sham. Teyoninhokarawen had his own way of responding to such views. When an enquirer who thought him too cultured to be a real Indian asked 'How will you relish returning to the savages of your own country?' he replied 'I shall not experience so great a change in my society as you imagine, for I find there are savages in this country also'.

Campbell's anecdote is at the expense not just of Teyoninhokarawen but of a fellow Romantic poet—the banker Samuel Rogers. It serves to remind us just how popular was the cult of the American 'Indian' with the Romantics. And it hints at some of the reasons for that cult: the

[3] Letter of 25 April 1805; *Life and Letters of Thomas Campbell*, ed. William Beattie, 3 vols. (London, 1849), II, 51.

warrior-Indian and his 'savage' culture were imagined as the opposites of gentlemanly British writers and of the culture of domesticity to which their writing contributed. Campbell's humour exploits conventional oppositions between savage and civilized, frontier and metropolis, primitive and polite, warrior and poet. In London, the Mohawk is out of place: his bodily sublimity loses its power. In the fashionable drawing room the war-cry curdles the blood only of the most timid of poets; its force is absorbed by that most domestic of eighteenth-century inventions—the comfortably and reassuringly padded sofa. It is no coincidence that one of the era's most popular poems was William Cowper's *The Task* (1784), a poem in which civilization is symbolized by the sofa. In that work Cowper defined gentlemanliness in terms of tamed and cosseted bodies, and for that very reason remained both fascinated by bodies that suffered at others' hands or were subject to the forces of nature. For Cowper and others, Indians' bodies were the most fascinating of all because, more than any other people, they lived at one with nature. Autochthonous, 'primitive', they also seemed fierce, excessive, cruel and superstitious—characteristics that could not easily be reconciled with Teyoninhokarawen's gentility but that made them both horrible and desirable.

If Campbell's anecdote pokes fun at Rogers' timid unease, it is not without anxiety of its own, an anxiety that emerges from the discrepancy between the literary stereotype of the Indian and conditions on the early nineteenth-century frontier. To Campbell, Teyoninhokarawen's 'Scotch' opera airs made him a fraudulent mimic of white settlers. The primitive authenticity of Indian song was undermined by the Mohawk's colonial education—he was conditioned by the export of the vogue for Scottish ballads to the wildwood. Or he was an imposter, and not really Indian at all. But Campbell was ignorant: in the North American contact-zone between whites and Indians, cross-cultural partnerships and mixed-race children were not uncommon. Whites captured by Indians often became assimilated to tribal society; traders and trappers married Indian women; some British women, conversely, wed Indian 'braves'.[4] Norton said his father was a Cherokee, who, as a boy, was adopted by a British soldier and came to Scotland. Norton himself was probably born in Scotland, his mother white; he returned to Canada

---

[4] On the assimilation of captured white women see Christopher Castiglia, *Bound and Determined: Captivity, Culture-Crossing, and White Womanhood from Mary Rowlandson to Patty Hearst* (Chicago, 1995).

in the British army, became for a while a schoolmaster then a trader, and was adopted by the Mohawks. Teyoninhokarawen's Scots songs were not frauds but the fruits of a hybrid culture arising from colonial encounters.[5] They were the cultural products of a transatlantic exchange, its basis economic, which Indianized parts of British culture even as it anglicized aspects of Native American society. This two-way process was not equal—greater wealth and power came to lie on the British (and latterly the US) side, but nor was it the institutionalized exploitation of that other transatlantic exchange of people—the slave trade. And if it did not involve a transfer of humans on the scale of the black Atlantic, it did produce a greater number of close relationships and a higher degree of cultural mingling—marriages, offspring, friendships, with a resultant flourishing of hybrid social practices and cultural forms. One effect of this was that, of all the peoples encountered as a result of colonial expansion, it was Native Americans whom Britons first represented as complex fellow-humans rather than stereotypical Others (long before they became able to represent Africans and East Indians in anything but simplistic terms). Norton, in effect, was an embodiment of a 'red' Atlantic—one that flourished as the black Atlantic was being brought into existence, a transatlantic culture built from colonial encounter but predicated not on the exploitation of mass labour but on military alliance and economic advantage.

Before 1800 American Indians were not colonial subjects in theory or practice. They were independent peoples whose wealth (in land and furs) Britain desired to greater and lesser degrees. So did the newly independent US colonists. Individual Britons entered alliances with Indians, fought alongside them, lived among them if they were allowed to do so. Often Indians did allow it, seeing political and economic advantage in doing so, or choosing to adopt white asylum seekers into their society, or assimilating captives to replace their own dead relatives. The resultant hybrid culture was the fruit of an exchange not simply an effect of colonial subjugation, an exchange in which Indians possessed choice, power and agency (albeit an increasingly unequal exchange, especially as the US grew more powerful and more land-hungry once liberated from British rule).

Teyoninhokarawen understood the nature of this exchange of which he was himself a product. He was no naive primitive exhibiting himself as a spectacle but a skilled negotiator, who had acquired influence in

---

[5] See Carl F. Klinck's 'Biographical Introduction' in *Norton*.

his tribe because of his hybrid identity and consequent adeptness as an international diplomat. He sang and whooped the war-whoop for the same reason he made speeches—to win influential hearts and minds to his cause. He was an emissary who followed many predecessors who had previously crossed the Atlantic to represent their Nations to the British. He was, in effect, the latest in a diplomatic tradition that began in the early eighteenth century, when the 'Indian kings' were received at Queen Anne's court. Norton's mission was to get from the British government deeds giving title to the land the Iroquois had been granted after fighting on the British side in the War of Independence. He spoke at Bath of the Mohawks' need for help in farming this land; he waited in government offices, pressing ministers to honour their pledges. And when he got no satisfaction, he called the influential gentlemen he had met in drawing rooms to lobby on his behalf.

WALTER SCOTT

On a spring day in 1809 Walter Scott took down a book from his library shelf. Opening it towards the beginning, he read this statement by his fellow countryman Hugh Blair: 'an American chief, at this day, harangues at the head of his tribe, in a more bold metaphorical style, than a modern European would adventure to use in an Epic poem'.[6] Then he turned from Blair's prose to the verse that it introduced—the Song of Fingal, supposedly authored by Ossian, the Highland bard. Scott knew, of course, that this ancient poem was actually the modern production of his fellow antiquarian, James Macpherson. Blair's prose also told him that the romanticization of the Highlanders (which Macpherson had inaugurated) had, from the start, portrayed ancient Scots in the image of modern Indians. This portrayal seemed credible enough: after all, the eminent Edinburgh philosopher David Hume suggested Macpherson should travel among the Chikkasah, so that they might civilize him, while historian Adam Ferguson declared that in the American tribes we 'behold, as in a mirrour, the features of our progenitors'.[7] Then, in 1783, Joseph Ritson had taken the argument a step further. Indians, he'd claimed in his *Historical Essay on the Origin and Progress of National*

---

[6] *A Critical Dissertation on the Poems of Ossian, the Son of Fingal* (London, 1763), 2.
[7] Adam Ferguson, *An Essay on the History of Civil Society*, 6th edn. (London, 1793), 133.

Song, were the most representative tribal people still living. Warriors and
hunters, rustic and patriarchal, they flourished in the vast wilderness, as
the Scottish clans had once flourished. Their poetry was oral and sublime,
an immediate expression of the 'simplicity of the remotest periods' and
the gallantry of 'ancient heroes'.[8] It was the epitome of the songs
and ballads that Ritson wished to revive from Britain's own unlettered
rural past.

Scott knew Ritson's work; he knew, therefore, that the border ballads
came from a culture like that of the Indians. He made the comparison
himself in his collection *Minstrelsy of the Scottish Border* when he noted
that the English used 'to raise a cry, similar to the Indian war-whoop'
when they pursued the marauding Scots.[9] He had encountered Indian
songs in magazines, newspapers, and in the accounts written by some
of the many Scots who had emigrated to America and gone to live
with tribes. Scott had read *The History of the American Indians* by
James Adair, an Ulster Scot whose admiration of Cherokee warriors'
songs reflected forty years' experience of living among the Indians
of the south.[10] Scott also knew of the MacGillivrays—clan chiefs of
Strath Nairn near Inverness, who had adapted so well to life among
the Creeks of Alabama that Alexander had become the tribe's principal
leader, negotiating treaties with George Washington that resisted white
settlement from the new state of Georgia. Such men seemed living proof
of the cultural kinship of Scottish clan and Indian tribe—a matter of
similar traditions and practices.

In Scotland those traditions and practices were increasingly confined
to the past after the defeat of clan power in 1745 and the subsequent
clearing of the Highlands. It was left to Scots poets to lament their loss
and/or to find imaginary stages on which they could still be played out.
In 1809 Thomas Campbell, responding to his encounter with Norton,
found such a stage in America. His verse romance *Gertrude of Wyoming*

---

[8] Joseph Ritson, *A Historical Essay on ... National Song* in *A Select Collection of
English Songs*, 3 vols. (London, 1783), I, ii-iii.

[9] Scott's comment appears in the preface to 'The Fray of Suport. An Ancient Border
Gathering Song from Tradition,' in *Minstrelsy of the Scottish Border: consisting of historical
and romantic ballads, collected in the southern counties of Scotland; with a few of modern
date*, 3 vols. (Kelso, 1802), I.

[10] *Adair*. In his verse romance *Rokeby*, Scott included a footnote citing Adair, and
likening his hero's determination to 'the patience, abstinence, and ingenuity exerted by
the North-American Indians when in pursuit of plunder or vengeance'. See note 25 to
the poem (on p. 391 of *The Poetical Works of Sir Walter Scott*, ed. J. Logie Robertson
(London, 1926)).

depicted heroic Indian warriors who fought hand-to-hand to protect innocent white women from the English imperialists and their corrupt allies. This was to take a highly idealized view of Indian warrior-codes. It was also, implicitly, to place a romanticized revival of Scottish clan values against the colonialist culture of contemporary England—as if Campbell was displacing to America Highland resentment over Scotland's colonization within Georgian Britain. Thus Indians came to bear the marks of a residual Scottish nationalism.

When Walter Scott pulled Ossian's poems from his shelf that day in 1809, he had a purpose in mind. He too would write a poem about the ancient Scots, and so he did, as the inheritor of the romanticization of the clans that Ossian had begun and that Campbell had just transplanted to America. The poem that Scott composed appeared in 1810 as *The Lady of the Lake*. Set in an imagined Highlands of the medieval past, it idealized a hunter and warrior, brave and chivalrous, and a wilderness landscape, bleak and mountainous. The poem was a popular success and helped establish Scott as one of the young guns of the new and fashionable Romantic school of writing. And it appealed beyond Scotland, indeed, beyond British shores, as a letter that Scott received in 1814, from his brother in Canada, reveals:

Yesterday morning Captain Norton, the chief of the Five Nations, left. I had the pleasure to be his intimate acquaintance, and he is a man who makes you almost wish to be an Indian chief. What do you think of a man speaking the language of about twelve Indian nations, English, French, German, and Spanish, all well, being in possession of all modern literature, having read with delight your Lady of the Lake, and translated the same, together with the Scriptures, into Mohawk—having written a history of the five nations, and a journal of his own travels, now in London ready for publication, and being at the same time an Indian chief, living as they do and following all their fashions. For, brother, you ask doth he paint himself, scalp, etc. etc? I answer yea, he doth; and with the most polished manner of civilized life, he would not disdain to partake of the blood of his enemy at the banquet of sacrifice. Yet I admire and love the man, and would cheerfully give fifty guineas that you could see him for one half-hour. He is afraid that the *Edinburgh Review* will be hard on his book. I promised to write to you to have it reviewed in the *Quarterly*. It surely is a strange circumstance that an Indian chief should produce a literary child.[11]

Scott's brother would have been less incredulous and more admiring had he known about the many Native Americans who crossed Indian

---

[11] *Familiar Letters of Sir Walter Scott*, 2 vols. (Edinburgh, 1894), I, 344.

and Scottish cultures in this way. Many of these men also wrote in English; several translated the gospels into Indian languages. Few, however, read and translated Scott. Yet it is not surprising that Norton did so; after all, Scott's imaginary Highlanders showed the presence of Romantic Indians in their literary ancestry and Norton was himself an Edinburgh-educated part-Scot. In translating *The Lady of the Lake* he was in effect turning Adam Ferguson's dictum on its head: in the Scottish past Native Americans could contemplate their own present. They could do so because that past, as shaped by literature, was already partly Native American. Both Norton and Scott, that is to say, were adapting for their own purposes a prior romanticization of Indians, were manipulating a discourse founded on Britons' reading of themselves by analogy with Indians—and vice versa. Norton had a dual purpose in manipulating this discourse. First, he wanted to empower his people in the white people's codes, knowing that the Mohawks were now too reduced by disease, defeat, and drunkenness, and too hemmed in by white settlers, to defend their interests otherwise. And so he translated the gospel to give Mohawks a moral code for a future that would inevitably involve interaction with white society. And he translated Scott to remind them that many Britons revered the warrior and clan ethics for which Mohawks had long stood. In addition, he wanted to unsettle the prejudices of Britons who assumed Indians to be innately savage. By writing in English he could undermine the fantasy that made it easy for Britons to ignore Indian claims for political justice—the fantasy that Indians were brave and honourable but also simple and primitive, best treated as red children by their white fathers. The letter Scott received from his brother demonstrates exactly how Norton was able to do so: because he was an author with a sophisticated understanding of the British periodical press, he could not be dismissed simply because he painted himself, scalped and drank the blood of his enemies (staple motifs of the stereotype of the Indian as an inherently ferocious and bestial savage).

In his original literary work, Norton undermined stereotypes still further. In his narrative of his 1809–10 travels in the Cherokee country, he adopted a style whose Latinate diction and disinterested tone positioned him as a British gentleman:

After sunset, coming to a rivulet which I recognized, I kindled a fire, and having collected a sufficient quantity of wood, and spread my blanket by the lively blaze, which softened the frosty air, I supped heartily on bread, parched meal and venison. My horse in the meantime feeding freely on the surrounding herbage.

The Moon shone brightly, some flying clouds at times slightly interrupting her beams. Having finished my repast, I lighted my pipe, and passed the time in contemplating the effects of man's restless ambition; desolating the earth instead of enjoying it in peace. Even in these parts, long ere the thirst of riches or dominion could tempt the warrior, the vain glory of outdoing his fellows in feats of arms constantly incited him to seek the destruction of his species. Happy those people, should they now take warning from the ambition of others, and peaceable and numerous! I lay down to rest; and about midnight awaking, I found myself covered with snow, and the fire nearly extinguished: I arose, drew together the embers, and adding more fuel, raised such a blaze that I soon found myself very comfortable. At the dawn of day, I saddled my horse, and taking such a direction as I thought would bring me into the road, I proceeded.[12]

Here Norton adopts the quintessential Romantic pose that Scott (after Wordsworth) patented and that Byron adapted. He is a lonely traveller, enabled by his solitariness to contemplate in nature the futility of human ambition (which is reduced to pettiness by the sublime landscape). And since the 'thirst of riches or dominion' was a white, rather than Indian, vice, he here criticizes the land- and wealth-grabbing habits of the apparently civilized Anglos. He appears as a man who has seen the vanity of human wishes (the whole passage echoes Samuel Johnson's famous disquisition on the subject when finding himself alone in the Scottish Highlands).[13] He is worldly-wise but not cynical, a man, as it were, naked on the heath, contented to bivouac alone in the snow because he no longer lusts for the baubles for which most men (especially white men) compete.

Throughout his journal, Norton employs the Romantic motifs made available to him by a British literary tradition in which idealized Indians had played a formative role. And he does so for the benefit of white people, to the extent that his journal was written for a British readership. Norton's purpose was not simply educative, moreover. He undertook his travels in an effort to gauge the state of Indian nations across North America. His epic journey was intended to foster a pan-Indian consensus, to renew old alliances and forge new ones in reply to white encroachment on Indian land. In Britain's former colony, the now independent states used division within and between tribes to take territory piecemeal. A united front would restrict this process. Long

---

[12] 22 November 1809, near a place called Titsohhellengh. *Norton*: 108–19.

[13] *The Works of Samuel Johnson*, gen. ed. John H. Middendorf (New Haven, 1958–), vol. IX, 40–1.

an ally of the British, Norton may have intended his journal to revive
waning British support for the Indian alliance in which, before and
during the War of 1812, Iroquois, Shawnee and Cherokee warriors had
made common cause, with Tecumseh and Norton himself prominent
leaders, against the US. If so, then Norton's journal and the figure
of the Romantic Indian he manipulated in its pages had the political
purpose of reminding Britons that their Indian allies were people of
pride, valour, honour and wisdom, whom it was worth helping resist
US settlers' 'thirst of . . . dominion'.

This is a book about the views that Britons, colonists and North
American Indians took of each other during a period in which these
people were in a closer and more fateful relationship than ever before
or since. It is, therefore, also a book about exploration, empire, and the
forms of representation that exploration and empire gave rise to—in
particular the form we have come to call Romanticism, in which 'Indians'
appear everywhere.[14] It is not too much to say that Romanticism would
not have taken the form it did without the complex and ambiguous image
of Indians that so intrigued both the writers and their readers. Most of the
poets of the Romantic canon wrote about Native Americans—not least
Wordsworth and Coleridge; so did many whom we have only recently
brought back to attention—including Bowles, Hemans, and Barbauld.
Yet Indians' formative role in the aesthetics and politics of Romanticism
has rarely been considered. I aim to bring that formative role to our
attention, to show that the images of native peoples that Romantic
writers received from colonial administrators, politicians, explorers, and
soldiers helped shape not only these writers' idealizations of 'savages' and
tribal life but also their depictions of nature, religion, and rural society.

I began with the stories of Norton and Scott because they highlight so
many of the issues that I have written this book to investigate. What do
their stories tell us? That Romantic Indians were not real—they were
cultural types—constructed figures conjured up in the pages of authors
or played out as roles on stages (albeit the stage might be a London
drawing room or a learned society in Bath). They tell us that both white

[14] Terminology is difficult and there are objectors to every term for the peoples who
lived in America before white colonists arrived. Accordingly, I have chosen to use several,
so as to indicate my awareness that none is a completely accepted term. I use 'Indians'
most often, because that term was universally used in the period I am discussing, but I
also employ 'Native Americans', 'Indigenous Americans', and 'First Nations'.

people and Indian people contributed to the invention and modification of these cultural types—that these types accrued considerable power over hearts and minds and affected cultural forms that ostensibly had little to do with them. They tell us that Romantic Indians were more or less stereotypical—at their crudest they were clichéd examples of noble or ignoble savagery but at their most complex they were ambiguous, uncanny, disturbing. They tell us that Romantic Indians conditioned views of real Indians on both sides of the Atlantic, in some instances influencing policy decisions of colonial officials. And they tell us that they gave some Indians opportunities to represent themselves in terms likely to be powerful for whites but simultaneously restrictive for the Indians themselves—and that for this very reason these representations sometimes had to be resisted.

To understand Romantic Indians we need to investigate several discourses, discourses that are sometimes intertwined, sometimes mutually reflective, sometimes parallel, sometimes opposed. These narratives do not necessarily end in unity—and this book reflects as much in its divided structure. I examine whites' representations of Indians, based on a period of intense and intimate contact in a wide variety of contact situations. I also examine Indians' representations of themselves and of whites—in English. And I explore a number of representations made from in-between by people of mixed white/Indian ancestry and by people of one ancestry who crossed to the other side—whites who grew into adulthood as Indians, Indians who lived in white society for extended periods.

All these representations were made in a period of close imperial engagement. At the root of them are things real people did to and with each other in real places within the context of colonial struggle. These deeds generated factual narratives—histories, speeches, travel accounts, ethnographies, natural histories, captivity narratives, and autobiographies. And these narratives fed the fictions written—mostly—back in cities, often by authors who had never met Indians. These factual and fictional narratives returned to the frontier and were taken up by whites and—sometimes—Indians, who adapted and/or challenged them for their own purposes in a colonial context. Sometimes, as in the case of Norton and many other Indians who came to Britain, these fictions were taken up and used by Indians back at the imperial centre with disconcerting effects on whites.

How to structure an investigation of these discourses? I considered interspersing chapters on white writers' Romantic Indians among chapters on the works of mixed-race writers and of Indians. By so doing I hoped to replicate in the structure of this book the transatlantic process of import/export it describes and thus avoid suggesting on a formal level the idea that I attack on a conceptual level—the idea that Romantic Indians were simply the creation of a unified organic literary movement. However, I have finally chosen not to do so—mostly because the hybrid and Indian writers whom I examine came later than the white writers, and were in some case directly responding to them, while influencing each other. Interspersing discussion of them among discussions of the earlier white writers would create chronological confusion and obscure patterns of development. So I have instead placed the writers into British-based and American-based groups, each in a separate section, so that their communal similarities emerge clearly while contrasts with each other and with other groups remain apparent. I am aware, however, that there are risks in this structure: readers should take note that I do not wish formally to reify a supposed innate racial division between white and Indian that it is in fact one of my intentions to question. Nor do I intend my structure to endorse the assumption that Romanticism is a self-consistent body of thought, with its own internal logic and organic development from within a purely British context. I want to show, instead, both that Romanticism in Britain consisted of various, not always similar, responses to the foreign and that it was exploited, modified, challenged at the time by voices from elsewhere—sometimes these voices were enabled as well as limited by Romanticism. Accordingly I have included a number of chapters on Indian writers who were, in fact, of mixed ancestry and upbringing, and some on Indians who were, by birth, wholly white. I hope these chapters on writers who crossed cultures and moved back and forth across the Atlantic will reveal exactly how the white/Indian contrast was deconstructed, as the question of which side the author wrote from was reframed.

To help orient the reader, I have placed at the beginning several chapters that look at the complex history of colonial interaction and at the factual accounts that emerged from that interaction. These chapters constitute the first section of the book, devoted to factual writing, and are then followed by a section on fictional accounts written from Britain, before I turn to the accounts of Native American writers. By means of this tripartite structure I hope to establish what went on, and what was written about what went on, before investigating (and weighing the impact of) more fictional and literary responses.

But the most basic questions of all for such a study, the questions I turn to consider now, are which white people and which Indians should be explored, at which time and why.

WHICH WHITES?

The story of Romantic Indians I tell here is principally a British/Indian one. Why? There were, after all, many Romantic portraits of Indian people made in the independent US. But these portraits have been extensively studied; less has been said about the different trajectory of British/Indian depictions.[15] It is that trajectory I shall follow: accordingly, the reader will find little here on the work of Fenimore Cooper, Longfellow, and Irving (save to show how their Indians are indebted to the work of British Romantics) but much on the writing of Southey, Hemans, Wordsworth, and Campbell. My contention is that the cultural fruits of interaction between Britons and Native Americans have been somewhat neglected by post-colonial scholars, who have been occupied in excavating writings from the East Indian and African colonies and their legacies. Neither the history nor the literary history of the British in America has received the attention it deserves from the present generation of critics in Britain;[16] and while discussions of Native American writers of this period do exist, they often reflect current US desires to understand the post-independence history of US/Indian relations, although this history was often interwoven with the distinct, but related, history of British/Indian relations. One ends up with a different view of the literature and culture of the period 1756–1830, on both sides of the Atlantic, if one construes it in relation to the intense and turbulent relationship that developed between Britons, Indians and their offspring. It is my intention to arrive at that different view in this book.

---

[15] But see Carolyn Thomas Foreman, *Indians Abroad 1493–1938* (Norman, OK, 1943), Nancy Moore Goslee, 'Hemans's "Red Indians": Reading Stereotypes', in *Romanticism, Race and Imperial Culture 1780–1834*, eds. Alan Richardson and Sonia Hofkosh (Bloomington, IN, 1996), Astrid Wind, ' "Adieu to all": the Dying Indian at the Turn of the Eighteenth Century', *Symbiosis*, 2/1 (1998), 39–55.

[16] Notable exceptions include David Murray, whose *Forked Tongues: Speech, Writing, and Representation in North American Indian Texts* (London, 1991) is the groundbreaking account of Native American writers, and John Sugden, whose magisterial biography *Tecumseh: A Life* (New York, 1998) explores British–Indian relations, post 1786, in great detail.

WHICH INDIANS?

The 'Indians' discussed in these pages are those with whom the vast majority of interactions occurred—the people who lived east of the Mississippi. Although Alexander Mackenzie travelled to the Pacific shore in 1793 and Lewis and Clark followed in 1805, meeting 'western Indians', it was not for another two decades that accounts of the Great Plains tribes and of the coastal people of the Northwest began to appear in number. Printed descriptions of the Blackfeet and Sioux, the tribes whose nomadic society was based on buffalo hunting, would, after the 1840s, help establish the Wild West mythology that still conditions popular impressions of Indians today. But in the eighteenth and early nineteenth centuries it was the eastern woodlands, Great Lakes and Ohio Valley tribes that whites dealt with. In (what became) New York State the Iroquois were, for eighty years, the most powerful group in North America. An alliance of five (then six) nations (Seneca, Cayuga, Onondaga, Oneida, Mohawk and Tuscarora), they held the territory between French Canada and the New England colonies, and had vast experience at playing each white colony against the other, in return for trade goods. They hunted deer, bear, and beaver for subsistence and for the fur trade. So did their traditional enemies the Ojibwa (Anishinabeg), called at the time variously Chippewa, Mississauga, and Saulteaux. Both groups, however, also practised settled agriculture, hoeing fields for corn, beans, and squash. The Ojibwa belonged to the northern group, Algonquinian, separated by language from their Iroquois rivals. Both groups were changed by hundreds of years of contact with whites. They intermarried, converted to Catholicism and Anglicanism, fought alongside the French and British, grew dependent on manufactures, took to drinking alcohol, died of whitefolk's diseases in debilitating numbers. They promoted to influence in their councils those who had influence over the incomers, sometimes altering the gendered power-structure of their society in the process—among the Ojibwa young women who married fur traders gained prominence because they could gain trading advantages; among the Iroquois the relatives of Molly Brant, the wife of British agent William Johnson, became chiefs.

In the south the principal groups with whom whites engaged were the Cherokees, Creeks (Muskogee), and Choctaws. Intermarriage was common: by 1800 hundreds of Cherokees and Creeks were children of white traders. In response to US calls for Indians to become civilized, the Cherokees established a white-style agriculture, building barns, using slaves. They adopted new forms of government; they invented a written form of their language.

After the US victories in the War of Independence and in the War of 1812, pressure from settlers would bring the southern tribes into almost constant warfare with white immigrants. It would also bring more westerly tribes into white consciousness. Shawnees, Fox, Sauk, Delawares, and Miamis, for example, were by 1808 forming alliances to protect their lands in and to the west of the Ohio valley. The Shawnee leader Tecumseh was revered (at least after his defeat and death) for the qualities that whites most admired about Indians—oratory, bravery, dignity, leadership.

Such are the Native Americans who dominate this book. They were not the only tribes known to whites. Others on the East Coast had, by the eighteenth century, been almost destroyed. The Pequots and Mohegans survived in a few fragmented bands. By 1830 some of the other nations, still flourishing in 1756 and 1782, had been reduced by war, sickness, and alcoholism to a similar state of broken near-destitution; the Great Lakes Ojibwa had lost their military power and ceded most of their lands. Many were left demoralized, unable to maintain their traditional culture. North America was no longer primarily a Native American continent. Yet Indians did not, as the self-serving US myth suggested they must, die out. They survived, adapting old and acquiring new methods. One of the stories this book tells is how, adapting white discourse for their own purposes, they began to do so.

AT WHICH TIME AND WHY?

Why study precisely this period of British/Indian relationships? Why argue that it was between 1756–1830 that Romantic Indians flourished? Because it was at this time that the generic and idealized noble savages that Dryden called 'Indians' in *The Indian Queen* (1664) were replaced by the complex, ambivalent, detailed portraits found in Southey's 'Songs of the American Indians' (1799). This change was not an isolated coincidence but the result of a development in Britons' knowledge of and feelings about Indians: in the second half of the eighteenth century far more depictions appeared and of a very different kind from the skimpy classically-derived pictures of earlier years in works such as *The Indian Queen*. Indians became complex mixtures, in British eyes, of courage and ferocity, heroism and primitivism, honour and savagery, oratory and superstition, stoicism and violence, nature and bestiality, orality and simplicity, dignity and drunkenness. They appeared with a new, ethnographic level of detail: text after text told Britons how Indians lived, what they wore, what they believed, how they made war—and love, how they died. This occurred because of the particular history of America in the second half of the eighteenth century. From 1756 to 1763 the Seven Years' (French/Indian) War gave Britain a large territorial empire and brought Britons in vastly increased numbers onto the American continent. Although British settlers had lived beside, and fought with and against, Indians almost since the first colonization, it was not until this war that the European powers employed Native Americans wholesale to assist in their battles. As a result, more British soldiers and colonists encountered native peoples in close circumstances than ever before. They found themselves fighting alongside—or in direct opposition to—Indian warriors and even, in some cases, adopting their methods of warfare. By virtue of their victories in the war, the British gained new authority over Florida and Canada, allowing them to push their colony south and westward into contact with previously unexploited Indians. By 1775, close on 50,000 Britons had moved beyond the Appalachians. Thus settlers and traders met, and learnt the lifestyles of, peoples who had been unknown to them just a few decades before. Many adapted their own white ways to Indian society, living not only on the margins of Indian villages as traders, not only among Indians, but effectively as Indians—at least for some of the time. Their experiences, like those of the soldiers, were to make their way back to Britain in tales, notes, and journals. Twenty per cent of the texts published in Britain about North America between 1640 and 1760 appeared in the 1750s, and the most arresting parts of these texts—speeches, songs, torture stories—were excerpted in the newspapers, journals, and magazines that were now beginning to flourish. What resulted, as Linda Colley argues,[17] was not just an increase in the amount of information but an alteration in its kind. It was now less commercially oriented and more centred on the human-interest narratives that arose when Britons encountered Indians face to face, and lived, loved, and died among them.

---

[17] Linda Colley, *Captives: Britain, Empire and the World 1600–1850* (London, 2003), 173–4.

The Seven Years' War was followed by the War of Independence, by further wars in the East Indies, by wars with revolutionary and Napoleonic France and, from 1812 to 1814, a further war with the US. Involvement in colonial conflict, and a consequent intensification of contact with indigenous people, became a basic condition of the new imperial Britain and, consequently, a matter of pressing concern to its people. Britons were forced—as they heard of massacres committed on native people in their name, and as they found their relatives dying at native people's hands—to question what their nation's role, as a colonizing nation, should be with regard to Indians. Should Britain use them on its side in battle? Should it leave them free of exploitation? Should it honour their prior ownership of territory? Should it trade with them or conquer them? The *London Magazine*, for example, printed in 1758 an article purporting to be the speech of the 'chief of Mikmaki'—an article born of the contact produced by the war in Quebec. While this speech is a white ventriloquism of Indian responses to colonialism, it is nevertheless based on an actual encounter that was striking enough to make Britons question their imperial rule and its effects. However authentic it was, it posed sufficient questions to the conscience for at least one Briton, Samuel Johnson, to adapt it into a stinging indictment of empire in general and Britain's treatment of Native Americans in particular. In his journal *The Idler*, Johnson created a fictional Indian to voice this indictment, which remains one of the most powerful anti-colonialist statements ever written:

'My children' (said he) 'I have often heard from men hoary with long life, that there was a time when our ancestors were absolute lords of the wood, the meadows, and the lakes, wherever the eye can reach or the foot can pass. They fished and hunted, feasted and danced, and when they were weary lay down under the first thicket, without danger and without fear. They changed their habitations as the seasons required, convenience prompted, or curiosity allured them, and sometimes gathered the fruits of the mountain, and sometimes sported in canoes along the coast.

Many years and ages are supposed to have been thus passed in plenty and security; when at last, a new race of men entered our country from the great ocean. They inclosed themselves in habitations of stone, which our ancestors could neither enter by violence, nor destroy by fire. They issued from these fastnesses, sometimes covered like the armadillo with shells, from which the lance rebounded on the striker, and sometimes carried by mighty beasts which had never been seen in our vales or forests, of such strength and swiftness, that flight and opposition were vain alike. Those invaders ranged over the continent, slaughtering in their rage those that resisted, and those that submitted, in their mirth. Of those that remained, some were buried in caverns, and condemned to dig metals for their masters; some were employed in tilling the ground, of which foreign tyrants devour the produce; and when the sword and the mines have destroyed the natives, they supply their place by human beings of another colour, brought from some distant country to perish here under toil and torture.

Some there are who boast their humanity, and content themselves to seize our chaces and fisheries, who drive us from every track of ground where fertility and pleasantness invite them to settle, and make no war upon us except when we intrude upon our own lands.

Others pretend to have purchased a right of residence and tyranny; but surely the insolence of such bargains is more offensive than the avowed and open dominion of force. What reward can induce the possessor of a country to admit a stranger more powerful than himself? Fraud or terror must operate in such contracts; either they promised protection which they never have afforded, or instruction which they never imparted. We hoped to be secured by their favour from some other evil, or to learn the arts of Europe, by which we might be able to secure ourselves. Their power they have never exerted in our defence, and their arts they have studiously concealed from us. Their treaties are only to deceive, and their traffick only to defraud us. They have a written law among them, of which they boast as derived from him who made the earth and sea, and by which they profess to believe that man will be made happy when life shall forsake him. Why is not this law communicated to us? It is concealed because it is violated. For how can they preach it to an Indian nation, when I am told that one of its first precepts forbids them to do to others what they would not that others should do to them.

But the time perhaps is now approaching when the pride of usurpation shall be crushed, and the cruelties of invasion shall be revenged. The sons of rapacity have now drawn their swords upon each other, and referred their claims to the decision of war; let us look unconcerned upon the slaughter, and remember that the death of every European delivers the country from a tyrant and a robber; for what is the claim of either nation, but the claim of the vulture to the leveret, of the tiger to the faun? Let them that continue to dispute their title to regions which they cannot people, to purchase by danger and blood the empty dignity of dominion over mountains which they will never climb, and rivers which they will never pass. Let us endeavour, in the mean time, to learn their discipline, and to forge their weapons; and when they shall be weakened with mutual slaughter, let us rush down upon them, force their remains to take shelter in their ships, and reign once more in our native country.'[18]

Johnson gives his fictional Indian all the passionate vehemence and authoritative style at his command: the Native American acts as a

---

[18] Samuel Johnson, *The Idler*, 81, 3 November 1759.

persona releasing Johnson to criticize his countrymen. The speech is an act of imaginative self-othering that allows Johnson to take the part of the oppressed, translating his own experience of powerful men's injustice and hypocrisy into something more than personal bitterness. It could not, however, have come about if Britons had not heard, and been impressed by, actual Indians' words, in encounters that colonial war made closer and more common than before.

Johnson's Native American was the first of many that British writers would use to criticize the policies and attitudes that drove British imperialism. The Romantic Indian was, more times than not, a figure of honour, courage, liberty and oratorical authority—derived from travellers' or soldiers' accounts—who voiced British writers' opposition to their own government and the commercial colonialism it was spreading, by force of arms and by the power of wealth, around the world.

Take, for example, the hero of Robert Rogers's 1766 verse drama *Ponteach: Or the Savages of America*—a fictional figure derived from the real-life Ottawa leader Pontiac who, in 1763, led an alliance of Great Lakes tribes to war, after the British (flush from their victory over the French) imposed trading terms that the Indians found insulting. Rogers had been in America during the fighting and came to London to make the authorities at home aware of the appalling misrule of their subordinates in the field. In his drama, colonial rapacity is not just casual (the work of 'a few bad apples') but systematic. Remarkably, Rogers shows every aspect of British colonialism in Native America to be entwined: traders cheat the Indians in a cynical way their French predecessors never did; hunters shoot Indians on sight to steal their furs; military officers treat them with contempt; colonial governors lie while embezzling the treaty goods destined by the King's government for the tribes. All these Britons speak of the Indians as beasts and treat them as such: notably, it is the white hunters who scalp the peaceful natives they have just murdered. Savagery, in the drama, is on the white side and stems from greed.

Nobility, on the other hand, is found among the Indians. Ponteach is the first fully-fleshed Native American hero in English literature—for, like the Shakespearean kings he resembles, he is given not just powerful rhetoric but also admirable qualities such as authority, dignity, honesty, wisdom, and a strong sense of political justice:

> Indians a'n't Fools, if White Men think us so;
> We see, we hear, we think as well as you;

> We know there 're Lies, and Mischiefs in the World;
> We don't know whom to trust, nor when to fear;
> Men are uncertain, changing as the Wind,
> Inconstant as the Waters of the Lakes,
> Some smooth and fair, and pleasant as the Sun,
> Some rough and boist'rous, like the Winter Storm;
> Some are Insidious as the subtle Snake,
> Some innocent, and harmless as the Dove;
> Some like the Tyger raging, cruel, fierce,
> Some like the Lamb, humble, submissive, mild,
> And scarcely one is every Day the same;
> But I call no Man bad, till such he's found,
> Then I condemn and cast him from my Sight;
> And no more trust him as a Friend and Brother.
> I hope to find you honest Men and true.[19]

Rogers endows Ponteach with a quality none of the British characters possess—self-conscious interiority. Moreover, although he has the flaws of ambition and highhandedness, these are seen to have emerged from the appalling difficulty of uniting the Indians against the duplicitous and dishonest colonial forces. He is also, of course, despite Rogers's admiration of him, treated with a residual alarm and ambivalence—as if the author was shocked to have created an Indian who so monopolized heroism in the colonial conflict. So Ponteach is, like Macbeth, a man prepared to wade in blood and, as such, frightening, albeit that, unlike Macbeth's, his cause is just. But this bloodiness is not ascribed to Indians' innate savagery, but seen as a terrifying response to British racism and exploitation. Ponteach's final words give him all the awe-inspiring determination, disinterested patriotism, and tragic self-consciousness that the British conspicuously lack:

> 'Tis coming on, Thus Wave succeeds to Wave,
> Till the Storm's spent, then all subsides again—
> The Chiefs revolted:—My Design betray'd:—
> May he that trusts a Christian meet the same!
> They have no Faith, no Honesty, no God,
> And cannot merit Confidence from Men.
> Were I alone the boist'rous Tempest's Sport,
> I'd quickly move my shatter'd trembling Bark,

---

[19] *Ponteach: Or the Savages of America* (London, 1766), Act I, sc. iv, ll. 172–88. On this play, see Marilyn J. Anderson, 'Ponteach, the first American Problem Play', *American Indian Quarterly*, 3 (1977), 225–41.

And follow my departed Sons to Rest.
But my brave Countrymen, my Friends, my Subjects,
Demand my Care: I'll not desert the Helm,
Nor leave a dang'rous Station in Distress:
Yes, I will live, in spite of Fate I'll live;
Was I not Ponteach, was I not a King,
Such Giant Mischiefs would not gather round me.
And since I'm Ponteach, since I am a King,
I'll shew myself Superior to them all;
I'll rise above this Hurricane of Fate,
And shew my Courage to the Gods themselves.

(Act V, sc. V, ll. 52–70)

The Romantic Indian was a new development in his/her complexity, ethnographic detail and oppositional stance, a development arising from colonial contact and imperial war. But the figure also had another major source that became more significant from the 1770s onwards—anxiety about the state of the British ruling classes. The code of chivalry, as it operated to idealize the social hierarchy of eighteenth-century Britain, offered an exchange. The ruling classes gave their protection—ultimately, military protection—to the ruled, in return for being allowed to preserve power among themselves. However, as urbane culture took hold and propriety, refinement and politeness were preferred to valour, vigour, and virility as the appropriate virtues for a gentleman, and as money rather than might gave that gentleman authority, he became further and further removed from the martial virtues that he had once been expected to master. And yet it was still on his ability to protect the interests of the weak—that is to say, both gentlewomen and the common people—that the gentleman justified his monopoly of power and wealth. If he neglected to learn and display courage, honour, and leadership, he would not only be ineffective on the battlefields of Britain's new wars, but also endanger the gentry's justification for keeping power. And by the 1790s many thought that he had neglected to do so: the gentry's weak and unmanly behaviour, critics suggested, destabilized the national compact, provoking the powerless classes to anger and thus opening the door to revolution. It was precisely this process, many thought, that had led to revolution in France. It might lead to revolution in Britain too—and certainly left the nation lacking in military leaders as it faced attacks in its colonies in America and the East Indies and even, after Napoleon's rise, on the mainland itself.

What was needed, in the words of George Canning, was a return
to 'manlier virtues, such as nerved/Our fathers' breasts'.[20] Wordsworth
agreed, calling for the resolute heroes of Milton's day to return and revive
Britain's onanistic, commercialized rulers. And in Native Americans he
and others identified exemplars of the manly virtues that Britons should
be relearning—if only they could adopt them from the Indians without
sacrificing their civilized manners for savage ones. And so Indians became
fascinating and Romantic because they offered a tantalizing glimpse of
the kind of heroic warrior, full of courage, passion, coolness under
fire, and physical power, that Britons might again become. But they
simultaneously became dangerous since it seemed that what naturally
accompanied Indians' martial virtues were cruelty, bloodthirstiness, and
savagery. Britons risked uncovering such characteristics in themselves
(and in their own code of martial behaviour) if they came too close and
if they admitted their fascination for Indians too openly. The Indian
warrior became the British hero whose name Britons could not speak
and so portraits of him characteristically mixed fascinated reverence
with horrified distaste, as we shall see in Charlotte Smith's novel *The
Old Manor House* (in Chapter 6).

While some writers used the figure of the Indian to provide exemplars
to a British gentry that they wanted to reform, others, more radical, used
it to provide an alternative model of a virtuous, heroic common man.
Paine, Spence, Wordsworth, and Coleridge used Indians in this way to
empower the ordinary people—in particular to give the rustic, a rural
dweller uncorrupted by commercial culture or gentlemanly politesse,
both power and charisma. The Romantic Indians of these writers occupy
a large place in this book.

From about 1805 a further development took place, which modified
the British image of Indians once more. As Britain faced the Napoleonic
threat, one-time radical opponents of the government gradually dropped
their opposition. They no longer sought to discredit British rule—at
home or in the empire—through rhetorical figures who voiced their
suffering at British hands. Moreover, these same radicals were horrified
at the bloodletting that had occurred when revolutionary France had
removed its traditional governing hierarchy. They turned, slowly, from

[20] Canning, quoted in Janet Todd, *Sensibility: An Introduction* (London and New
York, 1986), 130–1.

seeking alternatives to commercial culture and gentlemanly manners, to endorsing a reformed version of that culture and those manners as the means by which Britons could and should civilize the rest of the world. Scott, for instance, turned Wordsworth's radical rustics in this direction when he created his heroic, Indianized, martial heroes. Wordsworth himself, in conjunction with Robert Southey, rediscovered his loyalty to a hierarchical Britain ruled by a reformed gentry and defined it as Britain's mission, for the sake of world stability, to export this structure to its empire. Native Americans, in this new definition of empire, were still paragons of courage but would now have to be introduced to 'civilized' virtues—such as subordination to authority, acceptance of Christianity and the work-ethic—and renounce their 'savage' life of hunting and raiding. It was as imaginary willing recipients of this civilizing mission that later Romantic writers portrayed Indians—Felicia Hemans's and Southey's heroes will be examined in Chapter 12.

Such is a history of British-based portraits. I turn now to the third section of the book, that which is devoted to writing from the other side of the situation—and from a new generation of people, who grew up in between Britain and Indians, or mixing both in their heritage and experience. Empire was never simply a matter of the decisions of ministers or the actions of generals, but also of a myriad of local and individual dealings between the indigenous people and the ordinary soldiers, settlers, traders, missionaries, and travellers who found themselves at large in America. As well as fighting and trading with Indians, as well as preaching to them, cheating them of land, Britons married them, and some abandoned white society altogether. As empire played out in countless interactions across the American interior, as London's authority became more and more distant, a new hybrid culture sprouted at the margins of white and Indian worlds—and also within the latter (already changed, as it was, by centuries of trading contact with white men). Britons went native, and sometimes wrote about their experiences, undermining stereotypes and prejudices in the process. These Britons were changed—transculturated to various degrees—and Native Americans were changed too: there arose among the Indians most in contact with whites a new generation of mixed-blood people, who could operate in both cultures. John Ross was one such. Only one-eighth Cherokee by blood, Ross could negotiate effectively with US politicians in English and maintain enough support in the Cherokee towns to be elected Principal Chief time and again. He was the best equipped Cherokee, in the view of his nation, to defend its interests over a forty-year period from 1828. And Ross was only one of the most prominent of a host of Indian/white people who moved between the societies, as traders, trappers, soldiers, missionaries, agents, and warriors.[21] By 1775 there were already over 300 Britons living among the Creeks; the case of Alexander Cameron who had been married into the Overhill Cherokees so long 'he had almost become one of themselves' was increasingly common.[22] This racial and social intermixing, however, was to come under severe pressure as Britain withdrew men and gave up land claims, and as successive US presidents made it a national goal to push Indians to the far West, away from any land coveted by white settlers. As the Indian nations were marched westward in 1830, the always-vulnerable hybrid society began to wither. The ideology of manifest destiny prompted and justified the removals and had no place for an America intermingling white and Indian practices and bloodlines. Likewise, the transformation, from 1812 onwards, of Canada from a mercantile to a settlement colony, as emigrants from Europe poured in, pressurized Indian land, and precipitated the breakdown of the fragile (and themselves not unexploitative) partnerships between traders and Indians that were familial as well as mercantile. Soon, the existence of an intermingled America, even on the fringes, passed from popular consciousness. It is one of my aims to restore it to attention, discussing some of the people who passed their lives in it and wrote about it. That I differ from historians who sought to justify empire by illustrating the essential superiority of white to Indian goes without saying; I differ also, however, from their mirror-images—nativist writers who seek to glorify an essential Indianness, a racial and social purity that the arrival of white colonists polluted. My heroes, instead, are the writers who used the interactions prompted by colonial contact to challenge the ignorance and prejudice that each people (but especially the whites) harboured about the other. They used them, too, to pioneer new ways of living and thinking that were not possible within either one of the cultures alone.

[21] For an overview of Ross's career see Gary E. Moulton, 'John Ross', in R. David Edmunds (ed.) *American Indian Leaders: Studies in Diversity* (Lincoln, NE and London, 1980), 88–106. On McGillivray see Michael D. Green's eponymous article in the same volume.

[22] Cameron, quoted in Colin G. Calloway, *The American Revolution in Indian Country: Crisis and Diversity in Native American Communities* (Cambridge, 1995), 16.

BRITISH AND US ROMANTIC INDIANS

These new ways were, by the third decade of the nineteenth century, under severe threat. Norton is a case in point. Although he embodied the post-war relationship between Britons and Indians at its most complex, self-aware and fully realized (so that even though he was a novelty in the fashionable drawing rooms of society ladies he was well known to a class of men who had been in America), he also embodied the decline of that relationship. The War of Independence split the Iroquois Confederacy; most supported the British and found their lands forfeit to the victorious US (given up without their consent by the British diplomats who negotiated the Treaty of Paris). Some of the Mohawks relocated to land in British Canada: others of their nation did not. The tribe split, his leadership in question, Norton subsequently found himself beholden to the British but his loyalty counting for less and less. The personal admiration that individual Britons (albeit of very high rank) had for him and his people did not translate into the granting of political independence.

Despite such disappointments, not only the Mohawks but most of the tribes of the Ohio valley and the Great Lakes became closer allies of the British than ever before after 1783. They had little choice: after its victory, the US had less and less need for alliances, or even treaties, with Indians. It was commonly assumed that Indians had forfeited their right to their lands by assisting the British (although many had remained neutral, some had helped the rebellious colonists). Between 1787 and the 1840s, nearly five million settlers poured over the Appalachian mountains and the intense competition for land that resulted ensured that the major form of contact with Indians was in vicious frontier raiding, characterized on both sides by theft, murder, and the mutilation of corpses. This warfare refuelled the old fear and hatred of Indians that was evident in the seventeenth-century Puritan captivity narratives and sermons. American writers such as Robert Montgomery Bird, James McHenry, and James Kirke Paulding portrayed Indians as sadistic savages, fuelling a public campaign for the removal of Indians beyond the Mississippi that gathered pace as the 1820s' cotton boom made Cherokee land attractive to southern planters.[23]

---

[23] On Bird's fictions see Richard Drinnon, *Facing West: the Metaphysics of Indian-Hating and Empire-Building* (Minneapolis, 1980), 147–64.

In these circumstances, the British seemed the lesser of two evils to most of the tribes: siding with the Crown appeared to be the only means of gaining some military assistance in opposing the US settlers' encroachments. In the later 1780s and 1790s the tribes of the Ohio valley and Great Lakes area fought US settlement with British support. Despite British betrayals, this alliance was renewed in the War of 1812, because both partners needed the other's military resources to prevent further US invasion of their territory. Thus several generations of Indians, from the Ojibwa of the Great Lakes to the Creeks of the Southern Delta, developed personal ties with British soldiers and agents. Norton was an embodiment of these ties; so was his mentor Joseph Brant, who also visited Britain, meeting aristocrats and literary men, as well as leading warriors into battle in New England. Brant, like many other pro-British Indians, was demonized in the US.

In the war of 1812 Norton provided military assistance to Britain again, but was able to mobilize fewer and fewer warriors for each action. Once more, British diplomats left their Indian allies in the lurch in the treaty they negotiated to end the war (in 1814): all the territory the Indians had gained was handed back to the US. The 1814 peace settlement was the beginning of the end for Indian power on both sides of the white people's border. The British, feeling secure from further attack by the US, no longer needed Indian military force; the US, having preserved the lands it had taken since 1783, accelerated the process of pushing Indians further and further west. Increasingly, the intense relationship born of alliance and battle waned: Indians became problems in the eyes of officials rather than men and women with whom whites lived, loved, fought, and died. Their cultural image changed as a result: many white Americans, for example, supported the plan to remove them beyond the Mississippi not out of hatred but pity.[24] Witnessing the demoralization of the eastern tribes, deprived of almost all their land, bestricken by alcoholism, dying of disease, their children indentured as white settlers' drudges, many US liberals concluded that only their removal to the distant West would save the remaining nations. To argue thus was to ignore the achievements of the 'Civilized Tribes' of the South, who had so successfully adopted white methods that they had become more successful farmers than the settlers.

---

[24] See Bernard W. Sheehan, *Seeds of Extinction: Jeffersonian Philanthropy and the American Indian* (New York, 1974).

In the US, the concept of manifest destiny developed after 1814 in tandem with calls for removal. It was argued that Indians, as nomadic hunters, were at a more primitive stage of cultural development than whites. They would inevitably—and rightly—be eclipsed by the more advanced Anglos, who put the land to improved use in accord with the Biblical injunction 'Be fruitful, and multiply, and replenish the earth, and subdue it' (Genesis 1.28). To this argument racial theorists added the pseudo-scientific 'evidence' that Indians were anatomically inferior to whites—less intelligent and capable of only limited mental improvement. Samuel Morton's *Crania Americana* (1839) implied that Indians were a separate and subordinate species, not humans of the same kind as whites.

Scientific racism and manifest destiny were not entirely absent from the British/Indian relationship. Almost no British authorities, however, argued that Indians were a separate species and few viewed their disappearance from the earth as right or even inevitable. As a result of this difference, Britons remained interested in Indians who crossed cultures—not only chiefs such as Norton but Methodist converts like Peter Jones, the Ojibwa chief who transformed the Credit River Mississauga community, toured Britain collecting funds, and married an English gentlewoman. In the US, the missionary societies opposed President Jackson's 1830 Removal Act unavailingly, though not before their 'Second Great Awakening' had enabled many displaced Indians, born into a tribal and familial culture that had already collapsed, to formulate an identity and a voice for themselves. I shall discuss one of these Indians, the remarkable writer William Apess, in Chapter 14.

In British Canada, the story was one of pernicious paternalism. Only the Crown could buy Indian land and it pressurized Indians into selling for redistribution to immigrants, in return for annually distributed 'presents'. Indians were herded into smaller and more barren reserves without the need for a public campaign for forced relocation. A single government attempt to remove Canadian Indians to barren Manitoulin Island, where they would, the Governor assumed, dwindle picturesquely into extinction, was abandoned. Instead, the Indian Department treated Native Americans, their independence destroyed in white men's wars, as dependent children.

By 1830, Indians were an insignificant minority in Canada, which was itself an insignificant colony by comparison with India. Britain had withdrawn from much of its former territory and role: its engagement with Indians (and theirs with Britain) would never be so close, complex, or significant again. The British literature produced in the wake of late-eighteenth-century engagement, however, was popular and influential on both sides of the Atlantic. The fictional Indians of British writers remained a persistent influence on fledgling US literature. So, for instance, in the novels of Cooper, the tales of Irving, and the narratives of US-based Indians Apess and George Copway it is still possible to observe modes for portraying Indians that developed in the verse of Campbell and Scott and to recognize ways of imagining nature that derived from the poetry of Wordsworth and Byron. Indians were idealized as noble rustics and heroic warriors, only for a new element to be added: they were now located in a vanished past or placed on the verge of death.[25] The dying Indian—a pitiable figure doomed to extinction in the face of the more advanced whites—became the stock figure that US writers developed from their British ancestors, a figure that only reinforced (albeit with expressions of liberal guilt) the self-justifying ideology that whites would inevitably supplant their more primitive neighbours.

TEXTUAL TRANSFER: SOME THOUGHTS ON LITERARY APPROPRIATION OF INDIGENOUS PEOPLE

What was at stake for British writers and readers in the transformation of Indians from real life encounters to the pages of captivity narratives, history books, traders' memoirs, and official reports and into the figures who appeared in fiction and poetry? Not necessarily the same as what was at stake for the Native American writers who shaped the same discourses to their own ends, in the light of their experience and Indian identity.

But to look first at the transformation as it occurred in British literature: usually the native people who fascinated fiction-writers were already seen through British eyes, described in English prose, often for nakedly imperial purposes. Home-based writers had still less unmediated access to 'real' Indians since they were at a double remove. Not only their own preconceptions but also those of the travellers (and often of

---

[25] See Roy Harvey Pearce, *Savagism and Civilization: A Study of the Indian and the American Mind* (Baltimore, 1965), 175–232.

the hack writers who rewrote the travellers' tales for publication) stood between them and the native people they encountered. So it was with textual foreigners, already anglicized, that they worked.

These foreigners were already contradictory, portrayed through the white writer's inherited stereotypes (noble and ignoble savage) as well as conditioned by his other concerns, explicit and implicit. Often, travel writers recorded their own ambivalence about their relationships with the native people they encountered. In remote places travellers were themselves foreigners. They were often vulnerable to indigenous people, and dependent on their superior knowledge and power. Nevertheless they wrote down not only their own vulnerability in strange lands but also their own efforts to assume command and control—to make themselves at home and in charge. And so on one hand the narratives of firsthand encounter—whether by captives, soldiers, travellers or traders—helped crystallize the racialized orthodoxies of nineteenth-century imperialism—that white men and their civilization were superior to Indians—while, on the other, they remained a source of difference, an apprehension of vulnerability that some readers used to question their own society and its colonial ambitions.

This questioning gathered pace from the later 1780s, when a disenchantment with empire-building took hold, in the wake of the loss of the American colonies and of the exploitation of India, that came to a head in the trial of Sir Warren Hastings, the governor-general of the colonies in Bengal. For Whigs and radicals, especially of the younger generation, this disenchantment was also given focus by the French Revolution, which provided an example of a nation throwing off a tyrannical ruling elite. For such men and women, opposition to imperial war and colonial exploitation of native people became a central part of a campaign to change the government and the constitution. Indians whom they read about became inspiration for figures in their own works, figures through which they could dramatize issues that arose from exploration and empire. Romantic Indians, in effect, arose from Britons' encounters with Indians, but were inflected by Britons' reactions to their nation's dealings with other foreign peoples. The rhetoric of anti-colonialism often involved the writing of one indigenous people in terms of another very different one and so Indians, in British accounts, were often shaped by the complexities of imperial politics outside, as well as inside, America.

There was no accurate correspondence between the Indian figures conjured up by poets and fiction-writers and the real indigenous people who lived beyond their texts. The figures, as mixtures of British writer and reader and indigenous people, were projections of Britons' fears, desires and observations, with more to say to Britons than to the indigenous people themselves. They could not make the unmediated words of those people heard. But to recognize this is not to forget their significance: if they put Britons' identities in question, if they undermined the perception that Indians were alien, then they challenged some of the assumptions upon which contemporary colonialism was based. It was harder to accept slavery and the seizing of territory if one no longer felt superior and different to the people who were losing their liberty and land as a result. If Indians enchanted the public—in both senses of that expression—in revealing that it had more in common with 'savages' than it thought it should have, then they achieved a certain power over people's minds. Strangely disturbing and breathtakingly desirable, they were uncanny figures because they suggested that at the heart of the British self was a kinship with the foreign, a kinship that Britons wanted to explore but were frightened to acknowledge. And if there were such a kinship, then personal and national identities, as they were currently constructed, would be breached, for they depended to an extent on Britons' definition of themselves in opposition to the peoples of its empire.

Not all the indigenous people who came back to Britain in textual form gained this enthralling power over the minds of writers and readers. Not all were made to encode Britons' desires as well as fears. Britons did not see themselves—or the parts of themselves they reluctantly recognized—in all of the foreign figures presented to them. Some of those figures (e.g. Burke's Indian 'hellhounds' and Campbell's Mohawk 'monster') did simply configure difference, distance and alienation, serving to strengthen opposition between British selves and colonial others. But others (e.g. Hearne's Dene hero and Wordsworth's Anglo/Indian women) displaced this opposition and challenged Britons' assumption that they and their nation constituted the centre to which foreign places and peoples were the circumference. Romantic Indians, that is to say, were at worst stereotypical—little more than standard renditions of noble or ignoble savagery, derived from Rousseau or Cotton Mather—but at best complex, ambiguous and challenging figures that placed stereotypes in doubt and undermined prejudices.

Romantics may have been united by their fascination with the Indians of America, but they displayed no single view of them that we can simply correlate with ideologies that we would now label imperialist or anti-imperialist. The Romantics were, first and foremost, writers of fiction, writers who explored the implications of their fictions in different ways and discourses, rather than politicians working out an agreed orthodoxy. And so it is not appropriate to find them, en masse, guilty—or innocent—of supporting imperialism, as if imperialism itself was then, as it may seem with two hundred years' hindsight, a defined and coherent force. The imaginative process of creating uncanny figures with power to take Britons beyond their conventional selves and to intuit their kinship with foreigners did not translate into a unique and self-consistent political line. It remained a fictional technique charged with radical potential, but that potential was not always realized—works such as Southey's *Madoc*, for instance, allowed white readers to luxuriate in meeting and melding with uncanny Indian others, only to redraw the lines of difference and opposition still more firmly. Their Romantic Indians thus offered a brief holiday from the Othering process, a holiday that assisted colonialism, by reinforcing that process, helping to make it seem a natural occurrence.

Romantic Indians were not always exotic fantasy-holidays serving to suspend colonial oppositions only to renew them. The genie of uncanny similarity could not, once raised, always be easily put back in the bottle. Nor did all white authors intend to put it back. In what follows, I hope to honour something of Romanticism's fictional excess, to show that, in discovering it to have stepped westwards to an extent we had not previously noticed, we can articulate its figurative power as a historical phenomenon that arose from, and addressed itself to, an encounter with the foreign. It was in transforming Indians into fictional figures, some uncanny, some alien, that Romantics redefined British identity in ways that could not be adequately formulated by the existing social and political discourses. Their poetry sketched out new, half-realized forms of self, in which foreign and familiar met—'strange meetings' which seemed, and still seem, prophetic of the possibility and the difficulty of living at one with what we like to think we are not. But precisely because their writing was so strangely groping towards worlds as yet unrealized, they could not translate it into a single, agreed, set of attitudes. Their Romantic Indians, that is to say, functioned in ways that they could not fully grasp. Exceeding the politically correct readings that they themselves, and others, sometimes made of them, their best fictions remained transforming tales with the power to put the 'real' world (including the national and cultural identities that people believe to be real) into question.

To say this is not to assert that Romantics had special insight into the real nature of indigenous peoples, or to claim that they were able to speak from Indians' own points of view. If they modified and radicalized pernicious stereotypes, they nevertheless often substituted stereotypes of their own, which treated Indians in highly generalized and idealized terms. At their best, they were able to challenge British assumptions of superiority, even if only during the brief and liminal space of fiction and only by depicting idealized Indians. This was a project with potential to make a difference to the treatment of real people in the remote western places that white people were bringing under their command. Here an analogy with the campaign to abolish the slave trade is instructive (a campaign in which many of the Romantics were active). Abolitionists—whether using prose or verse—rarely presented Africans' own words and frequently ignored their cultural individuality but, nevertheless, by representing Africans' fellow humanity, helped persuade Britons to end slavery. Cowper, Coleridge, and Wordsworth, to name but a few, made at least some of their readers ashamed of the not dissimilar exploitation of the other native peoples whom explorers and settlers were bringing under British control. And some of their readers assisted Native Americans in their resistance to colonial injustice—whether perpetrated by individuals or government. Men such as Robert Barclay (who helped John Norton in his land-claim for the Mohawks), and women such as Elizabeth Howell (who assisted George Copway in his arguments for an Indian state), had already imbibed the romanticization of Indians, as their references to Southey, Byron, and Wordsworth reveal.

How did Native Americans themselves transform the image of the Indian they gleaned (in part) from British narratives (both factual histories and fictional texts)? Here, I investigate the words of a number of Indian and mixed-race writers who learnt, in the hybrid culture in which they grew up, to write in English. William Apess was a Pequot campaigner for Indian land rights and Methodist evangelist; George Copway was a Rice Lake Ojibwa and lapsed convert who reinvented himself as a peace campaigner and Romantic autobiographer; Peter Jones was a Credit River Ojibwa and tireless missionary, who wrote a journal of his tour in Britain. All of these writers characterized themselves and other Indians differently from the characterizations of white people, even while they adopted Romantic motifs in some degree. All of them analysed the changing colonial interactions of Britons, colonists and Indians, understanding those interactions to be textual as well as meetings of flesh and blood. Apess, for instance, made a point of attacking the languages of white racism, both casual and scientific. Jones and Copway both married white women of British descent, women powerfully motivated by a desire to help civilize the 'poor Indians' about whom they'd read. Jones's wife even undertook a course of reading histories and travel accounts before leaving London for her new marital home in Canada. Copway's wife helped him lace his writings with quotations from Southey, Byron, and Scott. Thus British Romantic texts shaped these Indians' lives and writings, giving them terms with which to challenge colonial policies and prejudices, even if those terms were neither indigenous to them nor free of limiting assumptions. In responding to these texts some Indians themselves became Romantic writers, finding both leverage and difficulty in appropriating/being appropriated by this white discourse. Romanticism offered some Indians, that is to say, a critical discourse within which lay dangers and tensions as well as means of contesting imperialist preconceptions.

Norton was not alone in exploiting for his own ends Britons' idealized expectations that Indians were natural noblemen—people of courage, honesty, and honour. He was also not alone in writing from an in-between position, treading a difficult path representing his tribe to Britons and vice versa. He was followed to London by John Hunter, a man who, he claimed, was born a white but raised, after capture as a child, among the Osages. Hunter's captivity narrative employed Romantic motifs culled from several travel accounts; it won him sufficient reputation in Britain to launch him on a career as a spokesman for Indians and—back in the US—as a leader of the Cherokees. Romantic writing empowered him, and put him within reach of achieving his goal of an independent homeland for Indians on the Mexican border—although he may never have been raised by the Indians at all.

All the Native American writers examined here used white people's discourses (including the discourse of Romanticism) but wrote back to white people, conforming neither to white stereotypes about Indians nor to Indian nativist thinking (such as the concurrent movement by Tecumseh and his brother the Prophet to return to pre-contact modes of Indian living). This position was difficult and vulnerable, as I shall show. Yet it allowed them considerable rhetorical power. And in some cases it amounted to more than what Homi Bhabha has called 'colonial mimicry' (in which the colonized subject, adopting the colonizer's discourse, is both appropriated by it and at the same time

displaces it—since it is now uttered by one of those it was elaborated
to govern and by one whom, the colonizers presume, is too primitive
to be capable of using it). Some of these hybrid writers adopt a still
more challenging discourse than that, which Bhabha terms the 'affect of
hybridity—at once a mode of appropriation and of resistance' because
they do not simultaneously recognize and mock the colonizers' discourse
from a position of subjugation, but use it, self-consciously mixed with
their own terms and symbols, to remind whites of their actual equality
with them—and, indeed, of whites' dependence on their military
power.[26] Norton, like MacGillivray and Ross, mastered white people's
codes not as a colonized subject but as a leader of a sovereign people,
and he did so as part of a strategic performance in which he also
employed Indian codes. This performance—carried on in speech, dress,
and writing—both served to renew his authority with the Mohawks
he represented and aimed to demonstrate to the British his (and by
extension the Mohawks') sophistication and strength as allies. This kind
of hybridity—at which Hunter also aimed—flourished on a shrinking
'middle ground' (to use Richard White's phrase) in which neither whites
nor Indians dominated each other, but in which neither could ignore the
other.[27] Those who could, by improvising on their knowledge of each
side's traditions, represent each side to the other exerted a (precarious)
power. They can be seen as cultural brokers,[28] people who used their
unusual expertise in both cultures to negotiate, for themselves and
for people they led, advantage, but who also knew enough to achieve
effective compromise and working partnerships. To do so they had to
be able to don masks and costumes—as Norton did in London—like
the tricksters whose cultural power, in many tribes, stemmed from their
ability to transform themselves into animals, spirits, or feared enemies.
By playing roles, such a broker might, for instance, impersonate (and
so interpret) the people of the other side to his own side—or might, as

[26] Bhabha quoted in Beth Fowkes Tobin, *Picturing Imperial Power: Colonial Subjects
in Eighteenth-Century Painting* (Durham and London, 1999), 101. See Homi K.
Bhabha, 'Signs Taken for Wonders', in *Europe and its Others*, ed. Francis Barker *et al.*,
2 vols. (Colchester, 1985), I, 89–106; 'The Other Question ... the Stereotype and
Colonial Discourse', *Screen*, 24/6 (Nov/Dec. 1983), 18–36; 'Of Mimicry and Man: The
Ambivalence of Colonial Discourse', in *Modern Literary Theory*, eds. Philip Rice and
Patricia Waugh (London, 1989), 234–41.
[27] Richard White, *The Middle Ground: Indians, Empires, and Republics in the Great
Lakes Region 1650–1815* (Cambridge, 1991).
[28] See Margaret Connell Szasz, (ed.), *Between Indian and White Worlds: The Cultural
Broker* (Norman, OK and London, 1994).

did Norton, demonstrate to the British that what they, the other side, thought was naturally Indian was itself a performance—and therefore that Indians were sophisticated complex agents rather than unwitting primitives.

When the middle ground lasted long enough and was sufficiently widespread, there were enough such people, and their work was important enough, for a hybrid culture to grow up. It was only, as White remarks (p. xv), when the independent USA grew strong that this middle ground was gradually obliterated, as Indians were reduced to colonized, exiled clients of a victorious white nation. And it was in the period covered by this book that this obliteration began to occur—as Norton personally discovered in 1805 and again in 1814.

For the Indian writers who flourished in the following decades—men such as Copway, Jones, Apess—Indian sovereignty scarcely existed in fact. For them, the situation was much nearer to that formulated in Bhabha's model of mimicry. They wrote in white discourse when whites dominated territory and ruled Indians through an organized apparatus of state. For their words, the concept that Cheryl Walker has (adapting Bhabha) elaborated is useful—'subjugated discourse'. By this term Walker refers to the double-edged quality of much of colonized Indians' writing in English. For example, Apess and Copway employ white liberal stereotypes, referring to themselves by such terms as 'poor Indian' and 'child of the forests'. Walker argues that these terms—though in context they embarrass, disturb or even ironically challenge white readers, bringing their own appropriateness in question—also indicate the Indian writer's internalization of pejorative and infantilizing white definitions. Though the writers do not embrace them as the whole truth about themselves or other Indians, nevertheless they adopt them as an indication of their sense of Indians' humiliating colonized status in a white-dominated world. Such terms, then, are the price that an Indian writer pays when he chooses to write in white people's language and in white people's technology (print): they highlight his awareness that his literary authority, indeed his very literacy, stemmed from affiliation to the non-Indian culture which had successfully deprived most Indians of their independence and many of their pride as well.

Discussing Indians' writings presents many problems. It is sometimes imagined that each writer is the voice of a homogenous group, since frequently there are few other voices from the same tribe, or same period, against which historians can judge it. This, of course, is a fallacy: Indian societies were not univocal or unchanging, even before colonial contact.

Afterwards, they were subject to rapid changes, which generated intense debates and new social and religious organizations. Faced too by disease and death, by white violence and white duplicity, tribes sometimes split or saw the elders lose their authority to warrior youths. Many, including the Mohawks and Cherokees, developed new political structures as they adapted to contact with white neighbours. Indian authors were created by the colonial situation—in that they were writing and publishing in English—and their work diagnosed pressures on and responded to fissures in their nations caused by colonial contact—war, settlement, anglicization, evangelism, disease, alcohol, and so on. Often, their very affiliation to English authorship indicated their marginality in their nation—Copway, as we shall see, being a prime example of this. He did not speak for all of the Ojibwa, or even for all of his natal band, still less for Indianness in general, even though he wrote a history of his nation.

The effects of colonial pressures were, in some cases, to produce factions within nations—and not just pro- and anti-white or just traditional and modern factions, but more complex and shifting realignments. In this context, the Indian writer who published a history of his nation, as did Copway and David Cusick,[29] was often reconstituting a fissured or at least multivoiced group as a unitary one, defined by common traditions and practices rather than by debate or difference. He imagined, rather than simply recorded, a single community[30] as he wrote its history—but did so from a position that attested to difference within it, since writing expressed his difference from many of the tribe and revealed his anglicization. Indeed, it was often a writer's experience of his nation's fragmentation that made it all the more important to imagine its identity anew. If the writer, like Apess, was raised outside a functioning community it became important to piece together a new one from what remained, from his own and other displaced Indians' selves and traditions.

The imagined communities that succeeded best were those that others found to be compelling versions of themselves that they could also subscribe to, capitalizing on existing traditions and practices but adapting them to meet new circumstances—and borrowing skills and

---

[29] On Cusick see Susan Kalter, 'Finding a Place for David Cusick in Native American Literary History', *Melus*, Fall 2002. http://www.findarticles.com/p/articles/mi_m2278/is_3_27/ai_94640668. I am indebted to Kalter's argument in my discussion of Native American historians.

[30] Benedict Anderson, *Imagined Communities* (London, 1991).

resources from other groups. Norton tried to do just this when writing the journal of his tour of the Cherokee country. He aimed to revivify Mohawk identity by crossing Iroquois cultural practices with those of the more populous and rich Cherokees—hence his interest in comparing creation stories, political structures and even sports and games. Later, another cultural broker, John Hunter, attempted a similar crossing of cultures in still less propitious times for hybrid communities, the middle ground having been almost entirely replaced by US dominance. Hunter was a displaced white man supposedly raised, after capture, by Indians. He returned to white society and then joined those Cherokees who had been displaced from their traditional lands to Oklahoma. He then set up the Fredonian Republic, an attempt to realize on the ground a hybrid nation in which white and Indian persons displaced from their own culture could make community together. This was a brave experiment—but its forging of a new community was defeated by those, in both white and Cherokee society, who held power by embodying older and more established versions of community. Conservative leaders joined with ambitious men on the make who manipulated loyalties and exploited rooted notions of identity in their pursuit of land and profit. The new republic was destroyed, its leaders killed—but not before Hunter had attracted many hundreds to try the social experiment.

Copway was the least successful of the Indian writers of the Romantic era in winning support for his imagined community. His route out of the demoralization and destruction of his band involved conversion to a missionary Christianity, and the departure, as a preacher, from his own people to proselytize their traditional enemies whose language he did not speak. The white missionaries allowed him little independence and less pay. Copway was thus uprooted: he was left outside the communal tribal economy and inside, but only just, the white money economy. He proved unable to straddle the two or fuse them to imagine a renewed communal life to which the Ojibwa subscribed. He embezzled money, was rejected by his band, moved east beyond Indian country to New York, and offered himself to white city audiences as the spokesman for all 'children of the forest'. He advocated the creation of a pan-Indian reservation whose language was English, but drew almost no support from other Indians. This scheme was transparently a piece of wish-fulfilment aimed at ending his own position of exile and its terms only reveal how isolated he was.

Jones's writing also reveals difference and polarization rather than a homogenous tribal or racial group. His imagined community conceived the Ojibwa along the lines of white bourgeois respectability. His Christian evangelism gave order and self-respect to some but several times came close to demanding, even of those who subscribed to it, too great a sacrifice of the traditional Ojibwa lifeways they remembered. When he imposed too white a version of identity his converts protested. Some lapsed. Others never converted at all and opposed his community. At the same time, these Christian Indians were being patronized by the whites whose culture they adapted. They were refused the real power that whites awarded themselves—so that Jones's imagined community of Christian Indians mimicking whites came under strain from several sides and was never realized as he hoped.

In face of the kind of historical odds that Jones, Hunter and Copway encountered, their literary visions of community could not help being fragile and vulnerable, prone to internal contradiction as well as external pressure. They are, however, all the more brave and radical for asserting, against such historical difficulties, the possibility of Indians' resurgence in new social formations. Using the white men's terms to set out a future for Indians that was not simply one of extinction or adaptation (the only two options most whites offered them) was a bold, if difficult, task. Romantic terms, as we shall see, helped them set out this future, even as they caused them problems—both empowering them and limiting them. To be a Romantic Indian was, for them, to be a noble figure able to capitalize upon whites' expectations and sympathies. It was also, they aimed, to be an agent of change, able to renew Indians' culture on the land in new forms in an age where Indian nations were coerced by whites. In the following pages, we will see how successful they were in this aim and to what extent a cultural fashion that began back in Britain aided, and to what extent hindered, them.

2

Historians and *Philosophes*

> The *Five Nations* are a poor and, generally called, barbarous People
> bred under the darkest Ignorance; and yet a bright and noble
> Genius shines through these black Clouds. None of the greatest
> *Roman* Heroes have discovered a greater Love to their Country, or
> a greater Contempt of Death.[1]

Cadwallader Colden,[2] the author of these remarks, was a primary source
of one of the central figures of Romanticism—the noble Indian. Colden
passed down to the late eighteenth century a stereotype that colonial war would never entirely displace. Indians figured in the popular
imagination as heroes unsurpassed in courage, as people who respected
courtesy and tradition, as folk full of the wisdom of nature. Interest
focused on their bodies: on their capacity to endure torture without
complaint, on their colour, on their ability to survive with little food.
It also focused on their customs: on their 'magic', on their oratory,
on their song. It was fed by neo-classical ideals: Indians, to British
administrators, resembled the stoical heroes that they had read about
in Tacitus and Cicero—valiant warriors and orators unsoftened by
civilization. By the 1780s, however, after two American wars, matters
had begun to change. Colden's idealistic portrait was in conflict with a
very different one—with a stereotypical image that Britons constructed
out of the shock of colonial conflict. The image drew on elements
of Indian social practices that had long been known to white people,
but gathered them into a new composite in which Indians appeared

---

[1] Cadwallader Colden, *The History of the Five Indian Nations of Canada* (London,
1747), Dedication, v.

[2] Born in Britain, he lived in America for over fifty-five years, negotiating with
Mohawk Indians in his capacity as surveyor-general for the colonial government. His
History became a standard work on Native Americans, cited by later writers on the
Indians and quoted by poets including Southey and Campbell.

as ignoble savages, essentially bestial. It focused obsessively on torture, on scalping, on cannibalism and it was always in tension with the idealistic picture that Colden and others had passed down. Indians, consequently, became fascinating to Britons for their apparent contradictoriness, for their irresolvable mixture of nobility and ignobility, heroism and brutality, dignity and savagery. And this irresolvable mixture of characteristics also made them more human. In this chapter and the one that follows it I shall explore how this ambivalent image came to be constructed, looking first at the neo-classical image of primitive nobility produced by enlightenment gentlemen (colonial officials and European social theorists), then showing how the explosion of narratives after 1756 painted a picture of sub-humanity but also began to sketch out more detailed and open-minded responses to living with Indians.

It was the Scottish enlightenment that turned American Indians into a central focus of historical conjecture by making them living examples of an earlier stage of society. The stadial theory derived from the work of Montesquieu, Adam Smith, and Adam Ferguson. In *De l'esprit des lois* (1748), Montesquieu first popularized a distinction between savages and barbarians on the basis that the former hunted and lived in small scattered nations, while the latter were pastoral and lived in larger settled societies. Having read Montesquieu, Smith and Ferguson adapted the savagery/barbarism distinction into a model that explained historical change by relating social organization to mode of subsistence. Savagery corresponded to hunting and gathering, barbarism to herding, and only on emerging from these stages into those of agriculture and then commerce did a people become a civilized nation. In other words, the causes of the differences between the human societies existing in different parts of the globe could be explained by observable natural features. There was no need to speculate whether Native Americans had been created differently by God or whether they had originally migrated from Asia. Their savagery resulted from their hunter/gatherer existence, which precluded the large settled communities that generated towns, laws and formal government. And their hunter/gatherer existence in turn resulted from the relative ease, for a people few in numbers, of gaining their living from a fertile environment teeming in flora and fauna.

Adam Smith was sure that a commercial, civilized society was preferable to a savage one. Yet he was also certain that some virtues declined as a people progressed from the primitive stage. In his *Theory of Moral Sentiments* (1759), he cited Native Americans as points of contrast with civilized Europeans. Relying on the standard travel narratives of Charlevoix and Lafitau, Smith praised North American Indians' 'self-command': they 'assume upon all occasions the greatest indifference, and would think themselves degraded if they should appear in any respect to be overcome, either by love, or grief, or resentment'.[3] The cause of this stoical behaviour, however, was the lack of social organization characteristic of savagery. Only in more advanced stages of society did people have sufficient freedom from basic needs to afford to be sympathetic. Expecting no sympathy, the savage therefore disdained to appeal for any and kept his feelings under control.

Smith was factually in error—a number of witnesses set out to show that there were many occasions when Native Americans displayed grief and love. Nor were Native Americans exclusively hunter-gatherers: the Iroquois and Cherokees, for instance, had always cultivated land around their towns as well as hunted. They did not fit into the stadial model, and in fact revealed it to be overly schematic. Smith, however, slotted them into the savage category. Native Americans showed, he added, a 'heroic and unconquerable firmness', which 'is not required of those who are brought up to live in civilized societies'.[4] This firmness was exemplified by Indians' courage under torture. They even, Smith showed, sang a song insulting their captors and recounting their exploits while dying at the stake. This death song was to become a central feature in account after account of Indian life—stereotyping all Native Americans as warlike, brave, stoical heroes. Here too, Smith was in error: what he and others saw as essential was, in fact, the learnt social code of a particular group within many Indian tribes—the warriors, young men whose power in their national councils had been greatly strengthened by the almost perpetual fighting that colonialism produced. White people wanted to buy Indians' fur and they wanted to settle their land; the former desire led Indians to fight each other over hunting areas, the latter led them to fight the endlessly encroaching immigrant settlers. And as the colonists pressed upon them, the fighting became more desperate—with torture and scalping common on both sides. What whites witnessed as Indian ferocity, in other words, was, in part, a product of colonial conflict.

Smith's fellow Scot Adam Ferguson also surveyed Native Americans in an effort to explain human progress from savage to civilized. Ferguson's *An Essay on the History of Civil Society* (1767) was a theory built upon the

---

[3] *The Theory of Moral Sentiments*, 6th edn. (London, 1790), Part V, ch. I, para. 19.

[4] Ibid., Part V, ch. I, para. 20.

reports of travellers including the French Jesuits Charlevoix and Lafitau and the British official Colden. Recording Iroquois customs concerning revenge and captivity, and detailing their oratory and their candour, Ferguson generalized from what white men had understood about one Indian nation. He took the particular as evidence for a general analysis that sought to find social causes for Indian culture. This analysis used the stadial model: hunter-gatherers 'have little attention to property, and scarcely any beginnings of subordination or government'. Most North Americans were, in this sense, savages, with personal and family authority the only modes of government.[5] The Native American showed boldness, robustness and agility, though he was unrefined and gross in discrimination. He showed Europeans what they had been: in American tribes we 'behold, as in a mirrour, the features of our progenitors'.[6] Native Americans, it followed, cast a unique light on civilized society, acting as living evidence of the early stages of European civilization that were otherwise recoverable only in the oldest poems and stories. Capable of making and breaking treaties and entering confederacies, Indian nations resembled the small German tribes whom Tacitus had praised in classical times, tribes which, European nationalists claimed, had bequeathed a vigorous love of liberty to northern Europeans up to the present day. Once again, Native Americans were put to rhetorical use in a discourse that was fundamentally concerned not with them but with white Europeans. Both Smith and Ferguson, for all their admiration of Native American qualities, erected a theoretical framework which positioned Indians as morally, socially, and intellectually less advanced than Europeans and which established advancement as a principal social goal that Europeans had best achieved.

Smith and Ferguson were contesting a view of Indians that had gained prominence in France, while relying (in part) on French travel accounts for their information. The French colonies in Canada had, since the early seventeenth century, yielded detailed ethnographical studies of the mainly Algonquin Indian tribes with whom the colonists traded. From 1632 the Jesuit *Relations* provided a mass of detail about tribal society and belief, often written in a spirit of fascinated enquiry rather than dogmatic condemnation. These voluminous accounts were succeeded by the *Lettres édifiantes et curieuses*; neither, however, was translated and

[5] Adam Ferguson, *An Essay on the History of Civil Society*, ed. Fania Oz-Salzberger (Cambridge, 1996), 81, 84.
[6] Ibid., 80.

neither became widely used in Britain. The Scots theorists relied instead on more readily available—and more commercially-minded—portraits by Louis Hennepin and by Lom d'Arce de Lahontan. Hennepin's *A New Discovery of a Vast Country in America* (1698) praised the American landscape as a paradise but saw its native inhabitants as savage and animalistic. He generalized about Indian characteristics on the evidence he gleaned from events that were, in fact, products of colonial contact—focusing on the violence and drunkenness of the Iroquois and Illinois nations—and displayed a monk's outrage for their reluctance to embrace Christianity. Lahontan's *New Voyages to North-America* (1703) took a different view, reflecting Lahontan's own disenchantment with the established order in France, which had failed to give him the advancement he desired. A soldier on the make, Lahontan used what he saw of Indians to attack 'civilization' at home, following a tradition begun by Montaigne's essay 'On Cannibals' (1580), which first expressed the ideal of the noble savage. Lahontan generalized from what he had seen of Iroquois society (including their shamans, their marriage customs, their medicine, their treatment of captives) to create an admiring picture of Indians as happy rustics who contrasted with corrupt Europeans:

The savages are utter strangers to distinctions of property, for what belongs to one is equally another's . . . . They think it unaccountable that one man should have more than another, and that the rich should have more respect than the poor. In short, they say, the name of savages which we bestow among them would fit our selves better, since there is nothing in our actions that bears the appearance of wisdom . . .[7]

Lahontan invented a fictional Indian and had him visit France, incredulous at what he saw. The resultant attack on the perversity of European society helped make Lahontan's one of the most popular travel books in eighteenth-century Europe, preparing the way for Voltaire's and Rousseau's idealization of Indian society at the expense of European.

    Two later, less polemical, French accounts were also influential. Joseph-Francois Lafitau, a Jesuit who had been part of the mission near Montreal, provided (in his *Moeurs des Sauvages Americains* (1724)) much information about the beliefs and practices of the Hurons whom, he

---

[7] *New Voyages to North-America by the Baron de Lahontan*, ed. R.G. Thwaites (Chicago, 1905), 420–21, quoted in P. J. Marshall and Glyndwr Williams, *The Great Map of Mankind: British Perceptions of the World in the Age of Enlightenment* (London, 1982), 200–1.

realized, had a complex social organization that allotted traditional roles, giving women considerable influence in tribal affairs.[8] The Scots—and later the Romantics—also relied extensively on the last Jesuit account to emerge from the French colonies that Britain seized in the Seven Years' War—Charlevoix's *Histoire et Description General de la Nouvelle France* (1744). The personal account of his travels that Charlevoix included in this history detailed his impressions of the Hurons and Iroquois, recounting his puzzled response to their medicine men, for instance. It became one of the principal sources in Britain—as an easily available compendium of information about Indian customs—for literary writers seeking local colour for their works.

Charlevoix was received in Britain in the wake of other French writing that did not take him into account. He was not a major influence on Voltaire, who renewed the ironic revaluation of savagery over 'civilization', or on Rousseau, who depicted Indians as the closest living representatives of people living in a state of nature. Rousseau wrote that the savage state 'is the veritable youth of the World, and that all subsequent progress has been in appearance so many steps toward the perfection of the individual, and in fact toward the decrepitude of the species'.[9] Like Lahontan he idealized noble savagery, but did so as part of a large-scale attack on eighteenth-century assumptions that society improved as civilization advanced. Indians, because they had not embraced agriculture but subsisted by hunting and fishing, were nearer to the virtuous simplicity that European civilization had abandoned.

Rousseau's theories demanded no detailed understanding of Native American society. Indians figured rhetorically to undermine conventional European assumptions that their own manners and mores were superior—Rousseau's call for a return to rural simplicity was addressed to the polite European bourgeoisie. It was as counters in a European argument that Indians functioned in his work. Yet because Rousseau's thought was influential Indians were, as we shall see, idealized in fiction after fiction as innocent, unalienated people living in a harmony

---

[8] Lafitau's contribution to the development of detailed portraits of Indian society is assessed in Sabine MacCormack, 'Limits of Understanding: Perceptions of Graeco-Roman and Amerindian Paganism in Early Modern Europe', in *America in European Consciousness, 1493–1750*, ed. Karen Ordahl Kupperman (Chapel Hill and London, 1995), 79–129 (108–10).

[9] Jean Jacques Rousseau, *Discourse on the Origins of Inequality (Second Discourse): Polemics, and Political Economy*, vol. 3 of the *The Collected Writings of Rousseau*, eds. Roger D. Masters and Christopher Kelly (Hanover and London, 1993), 48–9.

with each other and with nature that Europeans sadly lacked. This perspective was especially influential in France, as in Chateaubriand's *Atala* (1801) and *René* (1802), which offered a Rousseauvian elegy for the Natchez Indians of Mississippi, dispersed by the effects of French colonialism in the 1720s. It was evident too in French travel narratives: Louis Antoine de Bougainville saw the newly-encountered Tahitians as Rousseauvian primitives living at one with a beneficent fertile nature.[10] Later a Rousseauvian element informed the gentle nature-children who featured in Bowles's, Wordsworth's, and Byron's poems about Indians. By this stage, however, a diluted Rousseauvianism had become a widespread fashion.

The Abbé Raynal applied Rousseauvianism to a history of America more systematically than anyone else. In his *A Philosophical and Political History of the Settlements and Trade of the Europeans in the East and West Indies* (1776), he viewed Indian life as a state of nature to contrast with the corruption of the old world:

The respect we show to titles, dignities, and especially to hereditary nobility, they call an insult, an outrage to human nature. Whoever knows how to guide a canoe, to beat an enemy, to build a hut, to live upon little, to go a hundred leagues in the woods, with no other guide than the wind and sun, or any provision but a bow and arrows; he acts the part of a man, and what more can be expected of him? That restless disposition, which prompts us to cross so many seas in quest of fugitive advantages, appears to them rather the effect of poverty than of industry.[11]

Without institutionalized injustice and oppression, without luxury and satiety, the Indian lived in a harmonious state that Europe had lost. Civilization, for Raynal, like Rousseau, was decline rather than progress: the Indian was the kind of foreigner that Europeans would like to be if they could.

Raynal's idealization expressed the 'soft primitivism'[12] of French enlightenment *philosophes*, including Voltaire, Rousseau, and Diderot. It was a powerful discourse, since it used the Indian to overturn the assumptions on which the European social hierarchy depended. But

---

[10] Louis Antoine de Bougainville, *Voyage autour du monde par la frégate du roi La Boudeuse et la flute L'Étoile, en 1766, 1767, 1768 & 1769* (Paris, 1772).

[11] Abbé Raynal, *A Philosophical and Political History of the Settlements and Trade of the Europeans in the East and West Indies*, trs. J. Justamond, 8 vols. (London, 1783), VI, 445.

[12] A term used by Bernard Smith in *European Vision and the South Pacific 1768–1850* (Oxford, 1960).

with regard to the Indians themselves, it was both generalizing and patronizing. Indians, it seemed, were all the same—a species that exhibited one set of characteristics, whether they lived in America or Polynesia, where the newly discovered islanders were also viewed in Raynal's and Rousseau's terms and treated accordingly as happy, innocent, and simple children of nature.

While Raynal idealized, the Scots historian William Robertson gave the explorers' words a different twist. In his enormously popular *History of America*,[13] which became the standard authority in Britain, Robertson developed the environmental determinism that inflected the work of his friends Smith and Ferguson. He observed that not all Indians were the same, and concluded, following Montesquieu, that climate was the reason. Warm climates produced the happiness of which Raynal spoke, because they obviated the need for effort. In such fertile zones, savages enjoyed 'in common the blessings which flowed spontaneously from the bounty of nature'. But this very bounty also cursed the savage because it enervated him: 'the powers of the body are not called forth, nor can they attain their proper strength'. Incapable of toil, the Indian 'resembled beast[s] of prey'. He could not improve his state, could not develop general or abstract reasoning: 'In situations where no extraordinary effort, either of ingenuity or labour is requisite, in order to satisfy the simple demands of nature, the powers of the mind are so seldom roused to any exertions, that the rational faculties continue almost dormant and unexercised.' Only in cold climates 'where subsistence cannot be procured with the same ease, where men must unit more closely, and act with greater concert, necessity calls forth their talents, and sharpens their invention, so that the intelligent powers are more exercised and improved'.[14] Forced by the chilly environment to labour physically and mentally to survive, the northern Indian became resourceful and independent. Northern Indians were the prototypes of Northern Europeans, men capable of creating a hardy civilization. Indians from torrid zones, whether Florida or Tahiti, resembled Orientals, easy prey for despots because they were feeble in body and mind.

[13] William Robertson, *The History of America*, 3 vols. (Dublin, 1777).
[14] Robertson, *The History of America*, vol. II (bk IV), 283, 294, 290, 312–13, 313.

3

War Stories and Tales from the Frontier

Robertson's became the standard reference work about Indians for several generations. But it was far from being the only source of information, and its generalizations did not always chime with the detailed pictures that began to appear in print as British soldiers and settlers arrived in America in unprecedented numbers and met Native Americans at the closest of quarters. In fact, between 1760 and 1776, 55,000 Protestant Irish, 40,000 Scots, and 30,000 English and Welsh emigrated to North America. By 1770 the population of adult colonists was a third of that of England, a fivefold increase since 1700. Not surprisingly, this increase spawned not only intermixing with Indians but also enmity. While some Britons settled to live with Indians, many others encountered them, or feared encountering them, as prisoners taken on the battlefield. After 1750 narratives of captivity achieved a new popularity in Britain, and the public became aware, through their soldier relatives and from press reports, of Indians' custom of torturing some of their captives, while others were adopted into the tribe.[1] In 1763, for example, the *London Magazine* printed a story evidencing the 'Wonderful fortitude of an Onneyoath Captain, burnt by the Hurons; expressive of the savage and brutal Behaviour of the Indians, now destroying our Frontier Settlements in North America'. The story was actually recycled from the French travel narrative of Charlevoix—a sure indicator of the newsworthiness of Indians, and it dwelt on Indians' courage as well as their cruelty. The 'Captain', having been tortured, burned and left for dead, escaped from his pyre and 'armed with the instruments of his punishment, . . . was for some time the terror of a whole village, no body daring to approach a man who was more than

---

[1] On the genre, see Kathryn Zabelle Derounian-Stodola and James Arthur Levernier, *The Indian Captivity Narrative, 1550–1900* (New York, 1993). Also James Axtell, *The European and the Indian: Essays in the Ethnohistory of Colonial North America* (New York and Oxford, 1981), 168–206.

half burnt, and whose blood flowed from all parts of his body'. When the Hurons recaptured him, 'they directly cut off his hands and feet and then rolled him upon some burning coals; and lastly, they threw him under the trunk of a tree that was burning. Then all the village came round him, to enjoy the pleasure of seeing him burn.'[2] Before 1756 few Britons knew of these practices: the lurid and fear-driven captivity narratives that had fuelled New England Protestants' hatred of Indians had made little impression in Britain itself. Neither had the sermons of Cotton Mather's Boston, such as this one advising soldiers in King William's War: 'Once you have but got on the Track of those Ravenous howling Wolves, then pursue them vigorously; *Turn not back till* they *are consumed*. . . . *Beat* them small as the Dust *before the Wind*. . . . *Sacrifice them to the Ghosts of Christians whom they have Murdered*. . . . *Vengeance, Dear Country-man! Vengeance upon our Murderers*.'[3]

London had been deaf to much of this kind of rhetoric: many of the accounts Mather and others dwelt upon, of white (often women) colonists abducted by 'savages', were simply not published in Britain. To the metropolis, the colonists were too few and too far away for such skirmishes to become of pressing concern. As a result, a historical difference arose between British and North American accounts of Indians. Before the Seven Years' War, British accounts were fewer and less detailed, less driven by fear, by the experience of violence, or by the propaganda of the preachers who used that fear and experience for the purpose of cementing a group identity based on alienation. In Britain, safely remote from colonial competition for land, the nation builders' racist polarity of civilized white and savage Indian did not so easily gain ground. Thus a British visitor could write in 1784 that 'the white Americans . . . have the most rancorous antipathy to the whole race of Indians; and nothing is more common than to hear them talk of extirpating them totally from the face of the earth, men, women, and children'.[4] Phrases like 'copper Colour'd Vermine', used of Indians during the War of Independence by Henry William Dwight, bear out

---

[2] *London Magazine*, 33 (1763), 459.

[3] Mather, *Soldiers Counselled and Comforted: A Discourse Delivered unto Some Parts of the Forces Engaged in the Just War of New England against the Northern and Eastern Indians* (Boston, 1689), 28. Quoted in Alden T. Vaughan, 'From White Man to Redskin: Changing Anglo-American Perceptions of the American Indian', *American Historical Review*, 87/4 (1982), 917–53.

[4] J. D. F. Smyth, *A Tour of the United States of America*, 2 vols. (London, 1784), I, 345–6. Quoted in Vaughan, 'From White Man to Redskin', 942.

the visitor's perception.[5] Attitudes such as these made the white settlers who fought on the rebel side in the War of Independence especially cruel: in 1778 General George Rogers Clark had Indian prisoners bound and tomahawked in view of the garrison at Vincennes, declaring 'to excel them in barbarity was and is the only way to make war upon Indians'.[6] South Carolina, meanwhile, placed a bounty of £75 per Indian scalp; in Pennsylvania the price was $1,000. The Kentucky militia began digging up Shawneee graves so as to profit by scalping the corpses.

If America was not, before 1756, a pressing issue in British consciousness, the new circumstances produced by war rapidly made it become one. Nonetheless, it still appeared differently in Britain than in America itself. British soldiers circulated stories of captivity to an eager and alarmed public at home, but these were differently inflected than their American equivalents. To note two obvious differences, the captives were usually the soldiers themselves—arms-bearing males, rather than 'helpless' mothers and wives of homesteaders, as in the American accounts, and they were captured in war, rather than in a raid on what (to whites at least) was a peaceful settlement (though Indians thought differently since such settlements were often on their land).[7] Nevertheless, the British accounts were no longer, as in pre-war days, written at a remove. Soldiers and settlers had direct personal experience of their vulnerability to Indians. The British suffered defeats by combined French/Indian forces at Fort Oswego (1756) and Fort William Henry (1757). After the latter surrendered, Indians killed disarmed and wounded soldiers and camp followers, implanting a deep cultural memory of violence and terror in the British and giving direct experience of the different martial codes by which Indians fought. In 1763, even after the French surrender, Ottawas, reinforced by Wyandots, Potawatomis, and Ojibwas, and led by Pontiac, inflicted a series of defeats on British forts as they campaigned against the unfavourable trading relationship that the British had imposed. Britons, therefore, had as good reason to fear their

---

[5] Dwight to Theodore Sedgwick, 18 February 1779; quoted in Vaughan, 'From White Man to Redskin', 942.

[6] Clark is quoted in Calloway, *The American Revolution in Indian Country: Crisis and Diversity in Native American Communities* (Cambridge, 1995), 48.

[7] 'Whereas permanent settlers feared the native threat to the domestic, metropolitans feared the possibility of acculturation'—hence British stories and novels always showed the captive choosing to return to Britain rather than live with the tribe. Joe Snader, *Caught Between Worlds: British Captivity Narratives in Fact and Fiction* (Lexington, KY, 2000), 183.

Indian enemies as to respect their allies. But it was not just the new possibility of defeat but also its consequences that pushed the soldiers into print. What they, and the British public, wanted to explore was their horrified discovery of their vulnerability, post-battle, to violence. Indians tortured prisoners and the details, as related by those who survived and returned to Britain, were shocking enough to be saleable.

These accounts emerged from horror, fear, and anger; their descriptions helped renew the old cliché that Indians were ignoble, ferocious, bestial. One of the most popular was *French and Indian Cruelty, Exemplified in the Life and Various Vicissitudes of Fortune of Peter Williamson*, an account by a Scots settler on the Pennsylvania frontier—an area attacked by Indians allied to France in 1754. Williamson occupied disputed territory: Indians resented settlers' intrusion, and raids were commonplace. But he gave little analysis of Indian attitudes to white intrusion on their lands or of whites' own violence. Instead he narrated his capture as a traumatic and unheralded exposure to inexplicable ferocity. He had but one way of appealing to the British public who bought edition after edition of his book after his return to Scotland—Indian violence described in such vivid detail as to be pornographic. The reader is supposed to condemn but actually enjoined to dwell on the restaged scenes of torture, after a disingenuous disclaimer designed to justify the scenes on compassionate grounds:

This narrative O reader! May seem dry and tedious to you: My miseries and misfortunes, great as they may have been, may be considered only as what others have daily met with for years past; yet, on reflection, you can't help indulging me in the recital of them: For to the unfortunate and distressed, recounting our miseries, is, in some sort, an alleviation of them.

Permit me therefore to proceed; not by recounting to you the deplorable condition I then was in, for that is more than can be described to you, by one who thought of nothing less than being immediately put to death in the most excruciating manner these devils could invent. The fire being thus made, they for some time danced round me after their manner, with various off motions and antic gestures, whooping, hollowing, and crying, in a frightful manner, as it is their custom. Having satisfied themselves in this sort of their mirth, they proceeded in a more tragical manner; taking the burning coals and sticks, flaming with fire at the ends, holding them near my face, head, hands, and feet, with a deal of monstrous pleasure and satisfaction; and at the same time threatening to burn me intirely, if I made the least noise or cried out: Thus tortured as I was, almost to death I suffered their brutal pleasure without being allowed to vent my inexpressible anguish otherwise than by shedding silent tears; even which, when these inhuman tormentors observed, with a shocking pleasure and alacrity, they would take fresh coals, and apply near my eyes, telling me my face was wet, and that they would dry it for me, which indeed they cruelly did.[8]

Williamson piles story on story, each more gruesome than the last, always terming Indians monsters, devils, beasts. Once free from his Indian captors, he joins a regiment fighting the French and their Indian allies—and records battles in which the victorious British scalped and mangled Indian bodies. He does not, however, dwell on this British violence or conclude on its basis that his countrymen are also bestial. The narrative thus remains a voyeuristic rather than analytical one—readers are brought closer than ever before to the violent rituals of Indian warfare, thrilling to its gory results, only to be reassured of their essential civilized difference from such people.

In *The History of the Life and Sufferings of Henry Grace* British readers encountered yet more Indian cruelty in the context of war. Grace was an Englishman who enlisted in General Lascelles' Regiment and in 1750 sailed for Nova Scotia. There, he was captured while on sentry duty, by a party of Mumack Indians. Remembering events years later, Grace was clearly still shellshocked. He had entered a war economy—the Indians used him as a slave to bring supplies from French forts and were constantly on the move as they attacked English settlements. In these circumstances, the weak were a burden not to be afforded, as Grace experienced directly: 'Sometimes we draw 2 or 3 Cwt. Two of the Prisoners could not draw their Loads, being all Day on the Foot without Food, and the Load so heavy; whereupon they killed them before our Eyes with the Tomahawks, and scalped them, beating the Scalps in our Faces, and added their loads to ours.'[9] Stunned by fear and hardship, Grace was plain and matter of fact in rendition: he indulged in no condemnatory rhetoric, and made no telling insights, although he travelled through the country of the Iroquois and the Cherokees as well as the Ojibwa. Instead, his narrative reveals the demoralizing effect of alienation from one's culture and the dehumanization that results from slavery. Only the women, who hid him from their menfolk's violence during a three-day drunken spree, appeared at all explicable to Grace.

---

[8] *French and Indian Cruelty; Exemplified in the Life and Various Vicissitudes of Fortune of Peter Williamson*, 5th edn. (Edinburgh, 1762 [facs. rpt. Bristol, 1996]), 11–12.
[9] *The History of the Life and Sufferings of Henry Grace*, 2nd edn. (Basingstoke, Reading and London, 1765), 26.

Wartime experience of violence led Britons to complicate an old stereotype, or rather, introduce a new self-contradictory stereotype—the human beast—which largely occluded that of the noble savage in the popular mind, although either could be called upon for a particular occasion. Post Seven Years' War Indians were, in Britons' minds, cruel and fiendish—in Edmund Burke's words 'hell-hounds', in General Jeffrey Amherst's 'brutes'.[10] What was lacking in the popular image was any more complex picture that could comprehend the apparently contradictory aspects of Indian behaviour. Yet some of those who were captured learnt enough about Indians' culture—indeed became closely enough assimilated to it—to create that more detailed understanding. John Rutherford, a Yorkshire trader assisting British officers charting waterways between Detroit and Michilimackinac who was taken in 1763 by Ojibwas fighting in Pontiac's confederation, also appreciated that the treatment of captives was no simple expression of an essential Indian nature—bestial or human—but a ritual with a social purpose, that of removing prisoners who threatened the tribe while testing the suitability of others who might serve it usefully. Rutherford passed an initiation test and was adopted as an Ojibwa warrior.[11] Rutherford was not the only Briton to realize that the Indian violence he abhorred was not a timeless expression of their essential nature but—in part—itself a product of colonial war, of the white powers' cynical encouragement of Indians to fight for their own ends. Henry Timberlake had fought with and against Indians; he would also accompany several Cherokees to Britain in 1762—and he spoke from experience when he declared 'they were pretty hospitable to all white strangers, till the Europeans encouraged them to scalp; but the great reward offered has led them often since to commit as great barbarities on us, as they formerly only treated their most inveterate enemies with'.[12]

The level of cultural understanding and degree of culture crossing achieved by Rutherford was, if rare in captivity narratives and if often ignored in popular reaction to those narratives, reflected in some fictional responses to those narratives (I shall focus on two such—novels by Tobias Smollett and Henry Mackenzie). Such fictions were also

---

[10] Quoted in Linda Colley, *Captives: Britain, Empire and the World* (London, 2003), 185.

[11] Colley, *Captives*, 192–3.

[12] Henry Timberlake, *Memoirs* (London, 1765), pp. 52–53 quoted in P. J. Marshall and Glyndwr Williams, *The Great Map Of Mankind: British Perceptions of the World in the Age of Enlightenment* (London, 1982), 207.

informed by the more nuanced accounts given in traders' narratives of many years' peaceful co-existence with Indians. Thus the war-driven explosion of print about Indians presented many perspectives on them, creating, within fifty years, an awareness of the variety and complexity of Indian societies, and a historical understanding of some of the ways in which colonial politics affected white/Indian relationships at both local and national levels.

From 1776 revolution allied Britons and Indians more closely than before, since most tribes fought with Crown against colony, resentful of the unending pressure on their land by colonist settlers and tied by family to Britons in many cases. British officers knew that the cause of the Crown relied heavily on Indian fighters: Frederick Haldimand, governor of Quebec, reported 'the fidelity of these Indians [the Iroquois confederacy] has alone preserved the Upper Country'.[13] Despite many victories they paid a heavy price: the Iroquois lost their grip on their traditional heartland of upper New York and then found, as Britain made peace in 1783, that their right to their lands was completely ignored in the Treaty of Paris. As the Creek Indian leader Alexander MacGillivray put it, 'after helping the British we have now been betrayed to our enemies'.[14]

Despite the betrayal, it was to the British that the predominantly Algonquinian tribes south of Lake Erie looked for assistance when, in 1783, the victorious US repudiated its former agreement to stop white settlement at the Ohio River. Now it demanded that Indians withdraw beyond the Miami and Maumee rivers. In response the Ojibwa, Delaware, Wyandot, and Shawnee decided to resist. The Shawnee chief Captain Johnny told the Americans 'you are drawing close to us, and so near our bedsides, that we can almost hear the noise of your axes felling our Trees. ... The Boundary is the Ohio River ...'.[15] The 'United Indian Nations', as they termed themselves, raided US settlements in Kentucky and the Ohio in summer 1789. The British, concerned to defend Canada, armed and supplied them and in October 1790 they defeated a US force led by Colonel John Harden; in 1791, advised by British Indian agent Simon Girty, they destroyed another force under Arthur St Clair. At this point, territory as far east

[13] Quoted in Robert S. Allen, *His Majesty's Indian Allies: British Indian Policy in the Defence of Canada, 1774–1815* (Toronto and Oxford, 1992), 54.

[14] Ibid., 247.

[15] Ibid., 64.

as Pittsburgh lay open to the Indians, and the British officers hoped that 'this is the important moment in which the unfortunate terms of the Peace may be alter'd—Perhaps the moment may never return'.[16] The moment was not seized, however, because Britain was reluctant to support an offensive war, and by 1793 divisions split the 'United Indian Nations', leaving the way open for the US army to defeat the warriors at the Battle of Fallen Timbers (August 1794). On this occasion the British closed Fort Miami against the retreating Indians, dramatically demonstrating the limits of their support. By the following year, the Indians had been forced to cede most of the Ohio Valley to the US. Soon it was overwhelmed by white homesteaders.

The last renewal of the British/Indian alliance began without the participation of the Mohawks, who remembered the British betrayal of 1794. But by 1810 the Shawnee, Fox, Sauk, Winnebago, Ottawa, and Potawatomi, frustrated by the westward push of settlement, were ready for war. They were organized by the Shawnee chief Tecumseh and armed by the British who feared that the US intended to carry out the desire of Kentucky senator Richard M. Johnson to see the British 'expulsion from North America and her territories incorporated with the United States'[17]—a desire echoed by Thomas Jefferson. By 1812 the US and Britain were formally at war and it was their thousands of Indian allies that gave Britain the advantage. In August Tecumseh and the British took Detroit and the Michigan territory; in October Norton and the Mohawks helped destroy the US invasion of Canada at Queenstown. Tecumseh won further victories in 1813 only to die at the Battle of Moravian Town, when the British army, isolated from its supply lines, collapsed, surrendering or fleeing.

When the peace treaty of 1814 returned lands to their pre-war status, the Indians knew that the British would no longer assist them to defend themselves. For the British themselves, the treaty led to a lasting peace with the US. Soon it had little need for Indian alliances to defend its colonies. Its borders secure, Canada would become a colony of new immigrants. Its Indians, as Robert S. Allen puts it, no longer required as warriors, came to be seen as wards.[18]

What sort of relationships did the fifty and more years of British/Indian alliance produce? At the outset, fascinated incredulity

---

[16] Quoted in Robert S. Allen, 76: letter from Fort Niagara, November 1791.
[17] Ibid., 117.
[18] Ibid., 183.

characterized the reactions of recently arrived soldiers. British officers in Burgoyne's army of 1777 were intrigued by their Ottawa Indian allies, one writing that they were 'well worth seeing, they being painted in their usual stile and decked out with feathers of a variety of birds, and skins of wild beasts slain by them, as trophys of their courage'. But he also noted that 'their greatest pleasure is in getting beastly intoxicated' and that their war dance was 'curious and shocking, being naked and painted in a most frightful manner'.[19] Indian relations with Burgoyne deteriorated after an officer's fiancée was killed; after the battle of Bennington the Indian warriors, disgusted at their treatment, left the British camp.

By the end of the war Burgoyne's experience was the exception rather than the rule. And common soldiers experienced Indians differently from recently arrived officers. In fact, it had become so common for ordinary ranks to abandon the army for Indian life that treaty after treaty demanded the return of deserters, who were to be court-martialled if they did not prove that they had been detained against their will. The story of Macpherson, told in his own words to John Norton, was typical of many of former soldiers who went to live with the tribes:

During the evening a decent middle-aged man entered, of the name of Macpherson, formerly from Canada. During the war, he had served in a Provincial Regiment, called Sir John Johnson's. After a little conversation, which shewed me that he had been acquainted with several of my friends, I asked him, how he had got into this country, so remote from his old friends and fellow soldiers; where he had served and might have received the reward of his services, at least in a donation of land? He replied, that having received his discharge from the Army, not liking to settle and improve the uncultivated woods, he hired with a Canadian trader from Detroit, who traded in the country to the South west of that Post. With him he proceeded as far as Vincennes, on the Wabache; there having met with the trader's son, returning from the Muscle Shoals, on Tennessee or Cherokee River. This young man gave a florid description of the briskness of trade and the abundance of peltries in that quarter; lamenting his want of hands to assist him in bringing away, that which he had already acquired, and the want of good wherewith to obtain more: he was therefore sent with him in a piroque, with some more goods. They descended the Wabache, and then ascended the Tennessee, as far as the Muscle Shoals. There he found that although trade was brisk, and peltries abundant, yet the trader's son had squandered away all his property with out

---

[19] Ibid., 52: the diaries of St John and Skeensborough (from Lt. William Digby, *The British Invasion from the North: The Campaigns of Gens. Carleton and Burgoyne from Canada, 1776–1777* (Albany, 1887), 120–1, 228–9.)

having obtained any, and had run in debt to all the Canadian traders living at the place: he therefore shewed no inclination to return, and Macpherson could not go alone.

At that time, this place was open to trade from Canada; but the Creeks and Cherokees were generally hostile to the Americans. The former having mistaken him for one of these, and threatening either to make him a prisoner or to take his life, the Cherokees, believing him to be an Englishman, took him under their protection, and conducted him up the river to their settlements. He married a Cherokee woman, with whom he raised a family of eleven children. He concluded by saying that were it not for the love he bore his family, he would yet return to his friends in Canada.[20]

If perceptions altered as Britons and Indians mingled in America, they also changed in the political context of London. Whigs who opposed the increase of Crown influence in government sympathized with the rebellious colonists in 1776 and used horror stories about Indian violence as propaganda in their opposition to the war. Parliamentarians as eminent as the elder Pitt, Prime Minister during the Seven Years' War, and Edmund Burke, the greatest orator in the Commons, recycled the images of ferocious cannibals and savage beasts that had featured when Indians were Britain's enemies between 1756 and 1763. Now, however, these images were designed to make Britons ashamed: the nation lost its honour, Burke insisted, by employing savages to kill civilized white people.

The propaganda was rhetorically colourful, but it insisted on a savage/civilized, red/white opposition that was not apparent to Britons in America such as Macpherson. And so, despite all the wartime recycling of stereotypes to induce guilt, the British/Indian alliance gradually produced more nuanced accounts of Native Americans, written by men who had been on the ground. These contained, in their tensions and contradictions as well as (sometimes) in their surface messages, glimpses of a dawning understanding of the different cultures of different Indian nations—an understanding forged in close and often dangerous personal circumstances. Unlike the grand narratives of enlightenment historians and the rhetoric of parliamentary orators, composed in remote Edinburgh and London, these accounts were full of grainy detail about personal interactions that could not easily be reduced to schematic form. They offer a more varied view of Britain's colonial relationship with Indians than is to be found in the official records of treaties, or the

---

[20] *Norton*, 120–1.

memorandums of generals and governors, especially because many of them were composed by new kinds of men—chancers and improvisers who occupied the margins of white and Indian societies, inventing roles and careers for themselves as go-betweens and manipulators, trading on their knowledge of what each society wanted from the other. I turn now to examine narratives by several such men—narratives that later influenced, in their tendency to exceed the stereotypical image with a plethora of observed details and unresolved attitudes, the literary writers who, never having been to America, nevertheless populated their works with Romantic Indians.

4

Travellers' Tales and Traders' Memoirs

After the Seven Years' War, as Britain expanded its empire across the globe, the narratives of travellers appeared in greater numbers than ever before. Captain Cook's three voyages—the last visiting America's northwest coast and describing the Indians who lived there—caused a sensation. So, when he published his story, did the journey of Mungo Park, who had walked alone into the interior of Africa. In the wake of their narratives, the intrepid explorer became a national hero.

The vogue for narratives relating Britons encountering Native peoples in faraway places extended to America. After 1756 trader after trader and traveller after traveller published his impressions of the Indians he had met. Sometimes these publications were superficial: the result of a few months passing through. More often, however, they were steeped in the detail and close-quarters incident that came from many years' spent living with tribespeople. Whereas Europe-based historians pronounced without ever having been to America, and captured soldiers told of their brief (though intense) experience of Indian life, traders often wrote on the basis of long-term relationships—James Adair, for instance, had married into the Chickasaws and lived among them for over twenty years. His narrative and others like it not only included more detail but also a closer understanding of individual characters. He saw human variety among his Indian hosts and traced the social purposes of the customs and rituals he observed, observing their function in a complex society, rather than treating them as primitive phenomena or natural expressions of the savage state. For this reason, his and others' descriptions of Indians' war- and death-songs, medicine-men, burial customs, dreams, and beliefs carried strange power. They were full of the seamy, gripping detail that stems from immersion in the specific—and this made them a rich source for British fiction writers.

The travel narratives, however close the author's personal relationship with Indians, were products of empire, and as such conformed on one level to the requirements of an official genre. They aimed for a disinterested, detached style, as this helped establish the author as a reliable, truthful witness, making his prose a source of information that officials, historians and men of science could rely upon to guide dealings with Indians. The genre demanded a generalized summary of Indians' manners and customs, under thematized headings, even if the rest of the narrative told of the vagaries of a precarious personal relationship. The result was a tension between the generalized and detached on the one hand, and the individual and involved on the other. The author's peculiar and vulnerable subjectivity often peeped through the cracks of the detached, objective style. When it did so, the narrative became more human, more partial, more unpredictable—and thus more exciting, even as the illusion of objectivity (and the assumption of white superiority that this illusion fostered) collapsed. It was this feature that intrigued literary writers back in Britain.

In what follows, I shall look at a representative sample of the many accounts that engaged the British public—choosing the narratives that most intrigued Romantic writers and examining the aspects of them that proved most influential. I shall show how each of these influential narratives was conditioned by the needs of empire and the demands of the publishing market—in effect deriving the travellers' Indian from an analysis of the means by which he was produced and consumed. In the process, I shall examine the price paid by some of the actual Indians on whom the literary and imperialist work of travel writing was done.

JONATHAN CARVER

By 1802 Carver's *Travels Through the Interior Parts of North America, in the years 1766, 1767, and 1768* had run through three British and seven American editions and had been translated into German, French, Swedish and Dutch (*Carver*). Published for children as well as adults, Carver's words defined the image of the Indian right across the 'civilized' world. His descriptions of Indians healing and mourning, making love and war, fuelled a literary fashion. The Romanticized Indians of poets such as Southey, Coleridge, Bowles, and Campbell owed their being to Carver's apparently authoritative portraits of the Dakota Sioux with whom he spent the winter of 1766/7.

Ironically enough, Carver's popularity stemmed from a narrative for which he was only partly responsible. He was a man of little education who had in fact spent just one winter with the Sioux. A soldier in

Britain's American war with France, a would-be fur trader, and finally, destitute in London, a lottery clerk, he was an unlikely candidate for the role of successful author. And indeed he died before his book became one of the most popular travel narratives of the age.

It was at the behest of his former commander, Major Robert Rogers, the author of *Ponteach*, that Carver had headed up the Mississippi in 1766. Rogers intended to penetrate the West, so as to re-establish a fur-trading presence there that had disappeared when the French were ousted. Indian resentment at this disappearance had led to Pontiac's war of 1763. By 1766 French Canadian merchants were again sending traders into the interior. Rogers wanted to expand British activity in the same way. He also wanted to expand it territorially, to trace the Mississippi to its source and so cross to a navigable Northwest Passage to the Pacific, which would allow quick and easy access to the rich Chinese market for fur. Rogers employed Carver, an experienced frontiersman, as mapmaker to the expedition.

Carver set off from Michilimackinac on 3 Sept 1766 at the end of 1766. Travelling by canoe, he reached his furthest point west, on the St Pierre river (now the Minnesota) a few miles west of its confluence with the Mississippi (now at St Paul). There he met Naudowessie (Dakota) Indians, and spent seven months with them. But Rogers' plan went wrong, bedevilled by his lack of funds, and the attempt on the far West was abandoned. By late 1767 Carver was back at the fort from which he had started. Rogers, it turned out, did not even have the money to pay him, and was soon on trial for treason to boot. By 1769 both men were in the imperial centre, London, Rogers in and out of debtor's prison and Carver seeking to publish to make himself money and to give himself a respectability he did not automatically, as an impoverished former soldier, possess. He sold his field journal to a publisher and his soldier's prose entered a process of transformation aimed at rendering it authoritative and interesting for a sophisticated British—and a largely urban—public, whose interest in Native Americans had been aroused by previous soldiers' stories. Alexander Bicknell, a professional hack writer, re-worked the manuscript journals into a more literary production likely to appeal to readers. Bicknell not only reorganized but also enlarged Carver's manuscript by adding descriptions drawn from the published narratives of Charlevoix, Hennepin and Lahontan. What seemed to be a definitive and empirically observed account was, in part, a borrowed and generalized collage of previous travellers' descriptions of different tribes, different times, and different places. It was, nevertheless, taken as empirical truth[1] and it made Carver's name, partly because it offered graphic simplicity. Having read Carver, Britons who had never travelled West could feel that there was a foreign primitive paradise to which they could escape to live out their desires. His description of American geography (actually reconstructed by his editor) is fantastical rather than factual, fuelling Britons' lust for wealth and love of liberty:

That range of mountains, of which the Shining Mountains are a part, begin at Mexico, and continue northward to the east of California. They are called the Shining Mountains from an infinite number of chrystal stones, of an amazing size with which they are covered and which, when the sun shines full upon them, sparkle so as to be seen at a very great distance.

Probably in future ages, this extraordinary range of mountains may be found to contain more riches in their bowels than those of Indostan and Malabar or that are produced on the Golden Coast of Guinea; nor will I except even the Peruvian Mines. To the west of these mountains, when explored by future Columbuses or Raleighs, may be found other lakes, rivers, and countries, full fraught with all the necessary luxuries of life and where future generations may find an asylum, whether driven from their country by the ravages of lawless tyrants, or by religious persecutions, or reluctantly leaving it to remedy the inconveniences arising from a superabundant increase of inhabitants; whether, I say, impelled by these or allured by hopes of commercial advantages, there is little doubt but their expectations will be fully gratified in these rich and unexhausted climes.

(Carver, 121–2)

Here Carver's text turns the Rockies (still largely unknown to whites) into a temptation rather than a barrier. His words are speculation, but they appear to be fact and the whole passage is an astute advertisement for emigration and colonization. It not only offers wealth and peace, but romance too. The mountains shine with the hidden promise not just of gold, but all that gold symbolizes: beauty, rarity, exclusivity, power. Carver fed the British imagination the romance of exploration, a process without which travellers and colonizers would never have acquired the desire to leave home at all.

Carver's narrative glamorized the American West so effectively that myth became reality. Even the sober and sensible President Jefferson, when he sent Lewis and Clark to cross the continent, expected them to

---

[1] Though it later led to accusations of plagiarism and suspicions that he had never travelled at all. See *The Journals of Jonathan Carver and Related Documents, 1766–1770*, ed. John Parker (St Paul, Minnesota, 1976).

encounter only a 'height of land'—a single range of hills that divided East from West and from which they would navigate with ease down to the Pacific. And he might never have sent them had he realized how complex, daunting and uncommercial the geography actually was. But shining mountains and a 'great river of the West' seemed, to peoples searching for land and prosperity, too good not to be true. So even in the 1830s when trappers and traders had established how hard, unyielding and risky the Western mountains were, the myth still impelled new travellers to the fabled lands of plenty. The story that Carver—or rather his British-based editor—helped to shape fuelled the propaganda of men such as Nathaniel J. Wyeth, who motivated enough New Englanders to travel West for the colonization of Oregon to begin. Travel writing, in America, led enough people to trust their hope over their fear, to prefer their desire to their scepticism, for white empire in the West to be created.

It was not just Carver's description of the land, but his portrait of the Indians who lived there, that excited and empowered fellow whites. Carver's general picture assured his readers that there was an essential Indian character which they could know. It made Indians fascinating but, in the same movement, predictable—important for whites who might have to live with them or pass through their territory[2]—and helped to popularize a menu which traveller after traveller subsequently chose from when commenting on 'Indian customs'. This menu, partial and based on a few tribes, thus influenced what other writers constructed as the significant truth about how Indians were.

SAMUEL HEARNE

One of these writers was Samuel Hearne, a Briton in the employ of the Hudson's Bay Company who, in the year 1771/2, walked to the Arctic shore of Canada, guided by Chippewyan (a group of Dene) Indians. His narrative, not published until 1795, fascinated Wordsworth and Coleridge, because it not only, like Carver's, fixed on the menu of the warrior, the shaman, the tortured, and the stoic but also made these figures disturbingly strange and familiar at the same time (*Hearne*). Like Carver's, Hearne's book as a whole, however, emerged from Britain's

---

[2] See Janet Giltrow, 'Westering Narratives of Jonathan Carver, Alexander Henry, and Daniel Harmon', *Essays on Canadian Writing* (Summer 1981), 27–41.

post-Seven Years' War ability to drive its colonies further inland, into areas formerly under French and Indian control. It served British commercial designs upon the Canadian interior and gave those designs a new direction.

What were those designs in Canada? For Hearne, they were to do with competition with France for the profits of the fur trade. Throughout the eighteenth century, white men from Scotland and France explored Canada to the west and north along its rivers. They did so in pursuit of commodities that could be marketed in Europe and the Far East—chiefly the fur of the beaver and the sea-otter. In the process, they searched for a Northwest Passage that would allow ships to reach the lucrative Asian markets without passing the Capes. Commerce, rather than settlement, was the goal of the imperial authorities in London and their employees in the snowy field. The British had given the Hudson's Bay Company a trading monopoly on all lands draining into the Bay, and it had established forts, to which Indians brought furs to barter for beads, iron, alcohol and cloth. In this system it was the Indians, not the company employees, who trapped and transported fur. Their subsistence culture was changed in the process, with some tribes becoming trading middlemen for those who lived further from the forts and others becoming 'home Indians' who settled around the forts and served the white men's needs for hunters, guards, interpreters, and sexual partners.

Hearne became the first white man to cross the vast tundra of Northern Canada to the Arctic, guided by about six 'Northern Indians'. Equipped with surveying instruments, he set out to increase the geographic and scientific knowledge available to the Company as it planned its future trading strategy. Hearne was led by a Chippewyan (Dene) called Matonabbee, the 'most sociable, kind and sensible Indian I had ever met with' (*Hearne*, 102). In an undeclared reversal of the usual structure of imperial authority, the Native American effectively commanded the white man. Matonabbee chose the route and organized supplies. Paradoxically, it was Hearne's lack of imperial authority that ensured his success. Following rather than leading, he benefited from Indian survival techniques and lived to return from the Coppermine River and the Arctic Ocean.

Hearne had kept field notes during his Coppermine journey and later worked them up into a journal. Shortly before dying he sold this manuscript, which was then 'prepared' for the press—possibly by William Wales (the astronomer who had not only lived with Hearne at Churchill, but circumnavigated the world with Captain Cook and taught Coleridge mathematics at school). Hearne's 25-year-old notes became, in this process, a dramatic narrative carefully shaped to fit the public taste for the picturesque, the romantic, and the sensational. Hearne's *Journey*, in printed form, was not simply his own words, but a composite literary artefact, crafted with an eye to the market for travellers' tales of 'savage' peoples and dangerous adventures.

In several respects Hearne continued a tradition which Carver had recently popularized. Wales made sure that, like Carver's narrative, Hearne's made a set piece description of an Indian 'massacre'. Massacre stories had defined Indians ever since whites' first contact with them on the east coast: Carver had referred to one of the most famous of these before recounting his own experience of Indian violence in the Seven Years' War. Historically, these massacre stories had situated the white man as a victim and positioned the Indian as his savage oppressor. Carver had followed this trend but, in the context of the Seven Years' War, impugned not only the Indians who killed British prisoners but also the French soldiers who deployed them. The massacre tale was now inflected by imperial war and was a tool in anti-French propaganda. Hearne also found himself in a post-war context in which white colonists increasingly used Indians as proxy fighters: it was the Hudson Bay Company's employment of the Dene that involved him in a massacre—not as a victim of 'savages' but as a participant. Anglo-Indian relationships had become close enough, and the market for war stories hot enough, for a white man to publish details of his uneasy complicity with/command of indigenous people's violence. The events occurred on 17 July 1771, during the long Arctic daylight, and Hearne found himself a part of a surprise attack on a small band of sleeping Inuit (the fur trade enemies and competitors of the Dene):

we lay in ambush for some time, watching the motions of the Esquimaux; and here the Indians would have advised me to stay till the fight was over, but to this I could by no means consent; for I considered that when the Esquimaux came to be surprised, they would try every way to escape, and if they found me alone, not knowing me from an enemy, they would probably proceed to violence against me when no person was near to assist. For this reason I determined to accompany them, telling them at the same time, that I would not have any hand in the murder they were about to commit unless I found it necessary for my own safety ... finding all the Esquimaux quiet in their tents, they rushed forth from their ambuscade, and fell on the poor unsuspecting creatures, unperceived till close at the very eves of their tents, when they soon began the bloody massacre, while I stood neuter in the rear.

(*Hearne*, 177–8)

He may have been 'Neuter,' a detached observer, but Hearne, as his revealing use of the pronoun 'we' implies, was too frightened not to join in. He even stripped off his British clothes and tied his hair back, as the Dene warriors did, in preparation. Soon he found himself in the thick of killing:

The shrieks and groans of the poor expiring wretches were truly dreadful; and my horror was much increased at seeing a young girl, seemingly about eighteen years of age, killed so near me, that when the first spear was stuck into her side she fell down at my feet, and twisted round my legs, so that it was with difficulty that I could disengage myself from her dying grasps. As two Indian men pursued this unfortunate victim, I solicited very hard for her life; but the murderers made no reply till they had stuck both their spears through her body and transfixed her to the ground. They then looked me sternly in the face, and began to ridicule me, by asking if I wanted an Esquimaux wife; and paid not the smallest regard to the shrieks and agony of the poor wretch, who was twining round their spears like an eel! Indeed, after receiving much abusive language from them on the occasion, I was at length obliged to desire that they would be more expeditious in dispatching their victim out of her misery, otherwise I should be obliged, out of pity, to assist in the friendly office of putting an end to the existence of a fellow-creature who was so cruelly wounded. On this request being made, one of the Indians hastily drew his spear from the place where it was first lodged, and pierced it through her breast near the heart. The love of life, however, even in this most miserable state, was so predominant, that though this might justly be called the most merciful act that could be done for the poor creature, it seemed to be unwelcome, for though much exhausted by pain and loss of blood, she made several efforts to ward off the friendly blow. My situation and the terror of my mind at beholding this butchery, cannot easily be conceived, much less described; though I summed up all the fortitude I was master of on the occasion, it was with difficulty that I could refrain from tears; and I am confident that my features must feelingly have expressed how sincerely I was affected at the barbarous scene I then witnessed; even at this hour I cannot reflect on the transactions of that horrid day without shedding tears.

(*Hearne*, 179–80)

Hearne's horrific story helped to fix the reputation of Indians for savagery, both in Britain and in Canada itself, where it was still a set text in schools in the twentieth century. It made Indians foreign, the utter opposites of civilized people because they lacked chivalry towards their enemies, even when those enemies were helpless women. As embodiments of savage cruelty, they were enthralling as well as disturbing, but the white colonists could believe themselves clearly justified in ruling and re-educating them.

But there is more than justification driving Hearne's account. Some of its horror stems from his own guilty consciousness of his complicity in the murders. He asserts his difference from the ambush party, only to admit that, out of fear, 'I determined to accompany them'—dressed and painted like them so as not to stand out. To one of the terrified Inuit, there must have seemed to be very little difference between Hearne and the other assailants. To his British readers, it would be apparent that by removing his British clothes he had discarded the symbols of his difference and his authority. In the circumstances, Hearne's argument that he would only participate in the murder if his own safety were threatened seems like specious self-exculpation. The word 'murder', used rather than 'killing', suggests that he is conscious of his guilt. Hearne appears, despite himself, to have adopted what he would like us to believe are Indian habits, though viewing them as cruel. In the primitive lands of the frozen north, so remote from civilization, savagery might, his text implies, be infectious.

Hearne tries to reassure himself and his readers by declaring 'I stood neuter in the rear'. Yet this creates further difficulties: after all, to his fellow white men, he was supposedly in command of the expedition and should, therefore, have been able to prevent the attack, imposing civilized leadership on savage followers. In fact, he had been led by the Dene, so that imperial authority collapsed. 'Neuter in the rear', he was not so much neutral as impotent—his manliness in question not only by the Dene warriors who ridiculed him for pitying the girl they had speared but also by readers who expected him to take control.

Hearne's tears save him. They re-establish his difference from his fellow assailants, re-impose civilized values on the text. They show that the white man feels guilt and pity when Indians do not. If Hearne was complicit with murder, he purges his guilt by compassion of which tears are the bodily proof. Yet those tears are not present in his manuscript journal—they may, as I. S. MacLaren shows, be the editor's invention.[3]

[3] I. S. MacLaren, 'Samuel Hearne's Accounts of the Massacre at Bloody Fall, 17 July 1771', *ARIEL: A Review of International English Literature*, 22/1 (1991), 25–51 and 'Notes on Samuel Hearne's *Journey* from a Bibliographical Perspective', *Papers of the Bibliographical Society of Canada*, 31/2 (1993), 21–45.

Sensibility and compassion, perhaps, were imposed on the narrative to redeem it from the danger of aligning the white man with the Indian. And the true danger of that alignment would be that to suggest that, as colonists sought to spread British power and wealth to more and more uncivilized places, they became as 'savage' as they thought the natives to be. Hearne, that is to say, threatens to reveal the uncanny kinship that Conrad's Kurtz demonstrated 140 years later.

Hearne's massacre story is uneasy in the extreme. It reveals the pitfalls that faced early colonizers in the field and the resultant tensions in the colonial discourse that they produced back at the imperial centre. For although backed by the imperial network of the Hudson's Bay Company and, behind the Company, the British government, Hearne, unlike colonialists in India at this time, was isolated. In the far north, he was far from the bureaucratic and military infrastructure that supported Britons in the subcontinent and effectively put British power onto Indian ground. Isolated and dependent, Hearne not only found that he could not, in fact, assume command as, in theory, he was supposed to do but also discovered, as a consequence, that he could not master the authoritative colonial rhetoric in which Britons' superiority to native peoples was conventionally asserted. There was no stable authorized position for Hearne, no easy access to a discourse in which the relationship of colonizer to colonized, white to native, was already determined.[4] This situation was a result of British involvement of Indians in their own colonial ventures. Expeditions designed to grab territory and resources led to a relationship that confused partnership and exploitation, replacing opposition with complicity. Faced with his own involvement, Hearne was left anxiously exchanging one rhetoric for another in a sometimes desperate attempt to discover a discourse of power in which a distance between himself and the Indians could be formulated. Ironically enough, that attempt resulted in Hearne becoming feminized (i.e. occupying a relatively powerless position). Because he could not assume command, he was unmanned—('neuter')—and re-established his difference from

---

[4] Admirable accounts of the 'tension between the text's motivating ideas and the local contexts and experiences it represents' are provided by Kevin D. Hutchings (whose phrase this is) in his 'Writing Commerce and Cultural Progress in Samuel Hearne's "A Journey . . . to the Northern Ocean"', *Ariel*, 28/2 (April 1997), 49–78 (52). Also by Bruce Greenfield, *Narrating Discovery: The Romantic Explorer in American Literature, 1790–1855* (New York, 1992) and Keith Harrison, 'Samuel Hearne, Matonabbee, and the "Esquimaux Girl": Cultural Subjects, Cultural Objects', *Canadian Review of Comparative Literature* 22/3–4 (1995), 647–57.

Indian 'savagery' by crying as he looked on helplessly. His tears made him compassionate and revealed the civilized values that the Dene supposedly lacked. But they also made him womanly—or a fashionably sentimental man of feeling—a difficult position to occupy as a colonial official and expedition commander. In other words, Hearne resorted to a rhetoric that re-established the white/Indian opposition that 'proved' his 'civilized' difference, but only at the cost of tacitly declaring that this white man, at least, was too womanly to secure either the Indians' obedience or their respect. He could not sustain the role—or rhetoric—of manly command and self-command on which the illusion of colonial authority depended. Unlike his Victorian successors, Hearne could not keep his upper lip stiff so as to demonstrate (to himself and the 'natives') the emotional self-control that supposedly proved his right to authority over them. These Indians are not, as in later years Indians were assumed by whites to be, emotional children properly ruled by a cool and calm white father: quite the reverse, Hearne was the emotionally uncontrolled figure on whom they looked down.

The tensions in Hearne's text are not confined to his difficulties in playing the gender role expected of white colonizers. As an author writing to sell his book on an intensely competitive market, he needed to include sensational events. As a white colonizer seeking to affirm his 'civilized' difference from the 'savage' Indians whom he resembled, he needed to demonstrate his detachment from those very events. Conflicted, he both fed prurient curiosity and claimed to rise above it. So, for instance, he first tells readers that the massacre is 'shocking beyond description' (*Hearne*, 179) and then, having tantalized them, describes it in the passage culminating in the intensely graphic image of the Inuit woman twining round the Dene warriors' spears 'like an *eel*'.

Keen, both physically and rhetorically, to 'disengage myself from [the woman's] dying grasps' (grasps which bring his responsibility and impotence home to him all too tangibly) Hearne backtracks from this most appalling visual detail into a rhetoric of detached observation and generalizing comparison. In Latinate prose and convoluted syntax he tries, linguistically, to create a safe distance between himself and the woman, and therefore between himself and the details that titillate readers but reveal his complicity: 'I was at length obliged . . . otherwise I should be obliged . . . to assist in the friendly office', he writes, simultaneously excusing and detaching himself in a rhetoric of self-exculpation. Obligation, pity, assistance: these abstract notions ride in to remove Hearne and his readers from the gore and to remind them that he differs from the Indians in having access to an ideal ethical code which governs his actions.

But Hearne's rhetorical shift is unconvincing. It is thoroughly compromised by the extremity of the events from which he tries to detach himself. He plays the disinterested detached observer to escape the facts of involvement, but the conjunction of the two is so grotesque as to undermine the ploy altogether—as when he writes with strange impersonality that the spear-thrust intended to finish off the girl who is writhing in agony 'seemed to be unwelcome', as though surprised that she could not recognize that it might indeed 'justly be called the most merciful act that could be done' for her (*Hearne*, 179–80).

The narrative becomes still more bizarre in the next paragraph:

The brutish manner in which these savages used the bodies they had so cruelly bereaved of life was so shocking, that it would be indecent to describe it; particularly their curiosity in examining, and the remarks they made, on the formation of the women; which, they pretended to say, differed materially from that of their own. For my own part I must acknowledge, that however favourable the opportunity for determining that point might have been, yet my thoughts at the time were too much agitated to admit of any such remarks; and I firmly believe, that had there actually been as much difference between them as there is said to be between the Hottentots and those of Europe, it would not have been in my power to have marked the distinction. I have reason to think, however, that there is no ground for the assertion; and really believe that the declaration of the Indians on this occasion, was utterly void of truth, and proceeded only from the implacable hatred they bore to the whole tribe of people of whom I am speaking.

(*Hearne*, 180)

Here Hearne tries to widen the distance between himself and his Indian fellow-killers. They are 'brutish' because they indecently examine the dead women's bodies so as to 'prove' that there is an essential anatomical distinction between Dene and Inuit. Hearne himself, he declares, was too emotionally distressed by the killing to notice. And even after the event, the narrative echoes his disregard in that Hearne remains coy about exactly which part of the women's bodies the Dene investigated. This coyness establishes his civilized propriety and rational detachment by contrast with their prurient and 'savage' curiosity. Hearne, it seems, is now successfully back in command (as a narrator if not as an explorer) because he can again manipulate the discourse of reason. He has 'reason to think', while the Dene are governed by curiosity and hatred.

Once again, however, Hearne's rhetoric of distinction between his rationality and Indians' savagery collapses as he inadvertently declares a likeness between white people's and Indian's activities. His remark about the difference between the Hottentots and 'those of Europe' coyly informs male readers that it is women's labia that the Dene examine. The measurement of the purportedly extra-large labia of Khoikhoi women was, by 1795, the goal of European explorers of Southern Africa. The aim of Captain Cook, John Barrow, and others was to discover empirically whether the labia were naturally large so that natural historians could determine whether there was an essential anatomical difference between the races. On the basis of their enquiries (archly discussed in the pages of their travel books), men of science gained further 'evidence' to justify classifying the races of humankind, on anatomical criteria, into a hierarchy. Whites ('Caucasians') were at the top (the size of white women's labia being one, unmentionable, standard against which others' were judged). 'Hottentots' were at the bottom; Native Americans just above them.

Hearne's remarks remind his readers of this debate—and he even asserts his own expertise on the matter, without detailing the 'examinations' he must have performed to become an expert: 'I have reason to think, however, that there is no ground for the assertion ...'. Britons, it appears, were no less likely to finger women's genitals to prove racial difference than Indians were. But they just knew when to do so and how to represent it: out of view and in the generalizing rhetoric that indicates rationality but names no private parts. Hearne, by the end of the paragraph, has undermined the evidence he had put forward to re-establish the superiority of white man to Indian, civilized to savage. He has also undermined his pose as a tender-hearted, feminized man of feeling since he appears finally not as a figure who is too tearful to 'remark' women's pudendae but as a man of the world, with enough experience to reason on such matters but also with sufficient propriety not to be too explicit. He reasserts masculine—and colonial—authority via the rhetoric of rational observation while the steaming bodies of the violated women lie forgotten beneath his gaze. As we shall see in the next chapter, the language of scientific observation was one of the discourses in which, as the imperial project involved them ever more closely with Indians, white men insisted on their essential superiority to their new allies. It was not a coincidence that the discourses of natural history and racial theory burgeoned in the very period when more and more colonists were participating in Indian culture, as partners in violence, trade, and love.

Hearne's rhetorical struggles reveal several things that will be important in this book: that Native Americans figure in complex and often
conflicting ways in white people's texts, that no single colonial discourse yet predominated as far as late eighteenth-century America was
concerned. There was no solidified orthodoxy, no sole agreed way of
regarding colonizer/Indian relationships. Instead—and literary writers
seized upon this—there was a contest of rhetorics with single narratives
exhibiting often mutually destabilizing ploys in order to negotiate relationships that shifted unpredictably from binary opposition of civilized
to savage, at one extreme, to practical kinship at the other. Because the
texts reveal this struggle, they are rich seams in which to discover the
tensions, the ambivalence, and the sheer precariousness of colonizing
enterprises and narratives in their early years. And because they contain
so much contradiction, Native Americans appear in a way they do not
in the discourses of the later nineteenth century when racist orthodoxies
had crystallized. Something of their authority and their resourcefulness
and something of white man's consciousness of dependence and inferiority registers in the cracks between the rhetorical ploys that Hearne,
and others like him, employ.

It is the authority and resourcefulness of Matonabbee, Hearne's Dene
guide, that registers most powerfully in Hearne's narrative. Matonabbee
appears not as a 'savage' but as a great leader. Matonabbee, Hearne
records, was the son of a match made by the British Governor at Prince
of Wales' Fort. His father was a Northern Indian (Dene); his mother a
slave woman of the Southern Indians; Matonabbee had been brought
up as the adopted son of the Governor. Later, after his marriage,
Matonabbee was employed as a hunter. His life, his very birth, was
shaped by the colonial power. According to Hearne, it was an example
to most people in that colonial power:

It is impossible for any man to have been more punctual in the performance of
a promise than he was; his scrupulous adherence to truth and honesty would
have done honour to the most enlightened and devout Christian, while his
benevolence and universal humanity to all the human race according to his
abilities and manner of life, could not be exceeded by the most illustrious
personage now on record.

(*Hearne*, 329–30)

Indeed, Matonabbee combined the virtues of the civilized nations: 'to
the vivacity of a Frenchman, and the sincerity of an Englishman, he
added the gravity and nobleness of a Turk' (*Hearne*, 330–1). He was

a sagacious leader and a skilled diplomat, who brought peace to warring tribes by his independent efforts. Nowhere does Hearne suggest that his attributes stemmed from his British education; instead, they seem to spring from his natural self-belief and restraint. Hearne is full of admiration and respect rather than the paternalism or condescension often found in white men's portraits of Native Americans. Hearne's deference towards the man who led him to the Arctic and back allows Matonabbee to appear as a complex human being rather than a stereotype of savagery (noble or ignoble).

The portrait impressed Southey, who drew on it for his American epic *Madoc* (1805). And it remains impressive today, one of the most successful attempts by a white man to write about a Native American with neither prejudice nor sentimentality. Matonabbee's end is all the more surprising then. In 1782 the French captured Prince of Wales Fort and carried Hearne and his garrison off to Europe as prisoners. The Indian hunters and servants were left—Matonabbee among them. This is what then happened:

> when he heard that the French had destroyed the Fort, and carried off all the Company's servants, he never afterwards reared his head, but took an opportunity, when no one suspected his intention, to hang himself. This is the more to be wondered at, as he is the only Northern Indian who, that I ever heard, put an end to his own existence. The death of this man was a great loss to the Hudson's bay Company, and was attended with a most melancholy scene; no less than the death of six of his wives, and four children, all of whom were starved to death the same Winter, in one thousand seven hundred and eighty-three.
>
> (*Hearne*, 334)

In its context, this passage is deeply shocking because, up to this point, Matonabbee has been revered as an independent, brave, heroic leader—a man whom Hearne knows is greater than himself. Suicide is completely unexpected and leaves readers struggling to revise the picture they have created. Only then do they realize what was quietly implicit from the start—that Matonabbee was not independent, but utterly dependent, for livelihood, status, and self-respect, on the British whom he served. The man whom Hearne had treated as the unfettered and decisive Native American hero was, from his very birth, living in a fragile in-between zone, neither separate from the British nor one of them. That zone had geographic existence in the Fort and the area around it. It had mental existence in Matonabbee's sense of identity—a fact that Hearne cannot articulate, only wonder at after its destruction. Matonabbee, after the withdrawal of the British, had become foreign to himself, in his native land. He had suffered a colonial alienation that Hearne could only guiltily outline, having himself surrendered the Fort with little resistance and abandoned his 'home Indians'. Back in Britain, Hearne was suspected of cowardice: he had accepted capture by the French too easily, neglecting his duty to defend British territory and the Indians who occupied that territory (thus endangering profits, which depended on Indian loyalty).

Hearne's guilt at his inability to sustain the proper imperial role and protect Fort and Indians is never directly expressed in his narrative. Instead, it appears implicitly in the mixture of sorrow and admiration he feels towards Matonabbee. This mixture helps create the tension in the portrait of the Indian leader: Matonabbee remains one of the most disturbing Indian figures in any English narrative. Complex, menacing, admirable, he is both like and unlike the stereotypical Indians elsewhere in Hearne's text, and both like and unlike Hearne himself. Both 'savage' other and uncanny familiar, he remains unexpected, a contradiction whom Hearne cannot resolve but cannot dismiss either. He remains, too, a textual witness to the new, hybrid people and places being created by Anglo-Indian relationships, and of the fragility and inequality of those places. Matonabbee owes his power, his identity itself, to empire but he is also, ultimately, its victim.

JAMES ADAIR

One of the earliest writers on the Southeast was James Adair, generally agreed to be the most authoritative and detailed source of information on the Indians of what is now North and South Carolina, Georgia, Alabama, Mississippi, and Florida. Adair had the benefit of a lifetime spent in close contact with the tribes of the area—the Chickasaws, the Cherokees, the Creeks (Muskogee), Catawbas, and Shawnees. He was a trader who married an Indian and died among them. His record reveals the complexity of relations between tribes, and the effects on those relations of an equally complex colonial politics (*Adair*).

It was not until 1763 that Britain had gained Florida from France, which, in the same year, ceded its Louisiana territory to Spain. In 1800 the Spanish returned it to France—its western and northern limits still unfixed. Napoleon sold it to Jefferson in 1803. These imperial transfers created instability amongst the Native American tribes, who resented the destruction of their trading relationship with the Spanish, who were replaced by the more exploitative and competitive British. The War of Independence complicated matters further with some tribes fighting with the loyalists, others with the rebels, while others played each side against the other. Inevitably some tribes profited and others fared less well; this and the relentless pressure for land hunger of the whites forced some Indians to migrate North and West to the deserts and plains.

Adair arrived in America at the start of this process. Born about 1709, of Scots-Irish stock, he emigrated to America about 1735, trading with the Catawba and Cherokee until 1744. Then he lived with the Chickasaws for about six years, in their villages on the headwaters of the Yazoo River, Mississippi. In the Seven Years' War he got a Captain's commission and led a band of Chickasaws to war against the Cherokee. In this war Cherokee villages and crops were burnt. The Cherokee were forced to surrender land to the British colonists.

The War of Independence complicated the tense situation further—some tribes allied themselves with the British, others were divided among themselves. Adair's sympathies lay with the rebellious colonists, as his complaints about British injustice make clear. These were probably added to his work in London where he travelled so as to publish his 'Essays'. The book that appeared in 1775 reflected not just Adair's antipathy to the policies of George III's ministers, but his theory that American Indians were descended from the ancient Hebrews (a theory already adumbrated by seventeenth-century colonists such as Roger Williams).

If the book was finished in London, it was begun in Indian country: 'most of the pages' Adair tells his readers, were written among 'our steady old friends' the Chikkasah (*Adair*, 358). It was because he spoke with such detailed knowledge of Indian customs that Adair appealed: in his hands the often-discussed customs of the stereotypical Indian were seen with a more complex understanding of their social, cultural, and political contexts. Many of Adair's British readers were also, as opponents of their own rulers, sympathetic to his conflict of loyalties between the British government and its colonial agents on the one hand, and his 'friendly' Indian in-laws on the other, and again between Britain and the white Americans who rebelled against British rule. These conflicts were legible throughout Adair's text, despite the fact that he included a 'manners and customs' section that generalized about Indian groups whose difference he had explored earlier in his narrative. Adair, in short, was a writer who gained in authority because he revealed his multiple and shifting allegiances, portraying encounters with Indians without obscuring his own conflicting emotions and motives (one of which was to encourage northern whites to form agricultural settlements on Indian land). In love with Indians he had known for a lifetime, and an advocate of their ancient civilization, he was also an apologist for colonization. His discourse was multifaceted and should remind us that some eighteenth-century texts, at least, pushed beyond simple dichotomies between colonizer and colonized and between detached observer and the objectified figures of his observation.

Hearne, Adair and Carver brought a new level of detail, a new closeness to Indian society and a new awareness of complicity to popular accounts of Native Americans. Their Indians were neither noble nor bestial, nor inexplicable composites of the two, but were more fully human. Nevertheless, these writers did not abandon the popular features of previous white portraits of Indians so much as set them in a richly detailed social context, where they resonated differently. The features looked different, too, if one lived with Indians than if they were one's demonized enemies. Adair, for example, painted a comprehending picture of Indian punishment as a social phenomenon:

The Shawano also captivated a warrior of the Anantooèah, and put him to the stake, according to their usual cruel solemnities. Having unconcernedly suffered much sharp torture, he told them with scorn, they did not know how to punish a noted enemy, therefore he was willing to teach them, and would confirm the truth of his assertion, if they allowed him the opportunity. Accordingly he requested of them a pipe and some tobacco, which was given him: as soon as he lighted it, he sat down, naked as he was, on the women's burning torches, that were within his circle, and continued smoking his pipe without the least discomposure—on this a head-warrior leaped up, and said, they had seen plain enough, that he was a warrior, and not afraid of dying; nor should he have died, only that he was both spoiled by the fire, and devoted to it by their laws: however, though he was a very dangerous enemy, and his nation a treacherous people, it should appear they paid a regard to bravery, even in one, who was marked over the body with war streaks, at the cost of many lives of their beloved kindred. And then by way of favour, he, with his friendly tomahawk, instantly put an end to all his pains:—though the merciful but bloody instrument was ready some minutes before it gave the blow, yet I was assured, the spectators could not perceive the sufferer to change, either his posture, or his steady erect countenance, in the least.

(*Adair*, 393)

Adair makes the Anantooèah warrior sublime: he is not so much horrified by the torture as amazed at the warrior's feat of stoicism. The warrior adds willed bravery to fortitude: he defies his captors rather than merely endure their wrath, actively torturing himself. His unmoved indifference, his self-command, gets Adair's admiration and that of British readers who were, at this time, seeking to revive these very martial virtues in their own gentlemen soldiers. General Wolfe and, later, Admiral Nelson became heroes because of the cool and collected manner in which they exposed themselves to probable death. The torture of captives, Adair explained, was not a result of innate savagery but of a code of honour which bore comparison with the codes of classical times (*Adair*, 151). Thus the British gentleman, horrified though he might be at Indians' cruelty, could still safely admire them because, like him, they conformed to a social code which prized courage as the central part of a man's identity and which governed the kinds of violence considered courageous. In the light of their recognition of Indians as classical men of honour, it is not surprising that many British officers were happy to fight alongside Indians and to see them given officer status in the British army.

It was, above all, in the area of spirituality that the post-war narratives complicated the popular stereotypes most fruitfully. Indian religion — in white eyes — was located in the person, since belief was inseparable from the voice and the body of the shaman and from the effect the shaman produced on others. The tribal 'conjurer' was astonishing because he defied the limits of the physical. Fascinated by the causative connection between spirit and flesh, writers focused upon the shaman's ability to make his body seem non-human. Disturbed in the extreme, Jonathan Carver described a 'priest' being 'bound up like an Egyptian mummy' in an elk-skin for the purpose of communing with the 'Great Spirit'. Falling into a trance, the shaman 'worked himself into such an agitation, that he foamed at his mouth'. He then sprang free of his bonds and declared his prediction, which later came true. Carver confessed himself 'greatly astonished' and unable to explain how the shaman broke free or how he correctly predicted the future (*Carver*, 125–7).

No custom was more commented on than shamans' supposed ability to see into the future. Carver recounted how the 'chief priest' of the 'Killistinoes'[5] claimed spiritual power:

'My Brothers,' said he, 'the Great Spirit has deigned to hold a Talk with his servant at my earnest request. He has not, indeed, told me when the persons we

---

[5] Kilistinon — Cree — Indians.

expect will be here, but tomorrow, soon after the sun has reached the highest point in the heavens, a canoe will arrive, and the people in that will inform us when the traders will come.'

[...]

The next day the sun shone bright, and long before noon all the Indians were gathered together on the eminence that overlooked the lake. The old king came to me and asked me whether I had so much confidence in what the priest had foretold as to join his people on the hill and wait for the completion of it. I told him I was at a loss what opinion to form of the prediction, but that I would readily attend him. On this we walked together to the place where the others were assembled. Every eye was again fixed by turns on me and the lake when, just as the sun had reached his zenith, agreeable to what the priest had foretold, a canoe came round a point of land about a league distant. The Indians no sooner beheld it than they sent up an universal shout, and by their looks seemed to triumph in the interest their priest this evidently had with the Great Spirit.

In less than an hour the canoe reached the shore, when I attended the king and chiefs to receive those who were on board. As soon as the men were landed, we walked all together to the king's tent when, according to their invariable custom we began to smoke; and this we did, notwithstanding our impatience to know the tidings they brought, without asking any questions for the Indians are the most deliberate people in the world. However, after some trivial conversation, the king inquired of them whether they had seen anything of the traders. The men replied that they had parted from them a few days before and that they proposed being here the second day from the present. They accordingly arrived at that time greatly to our satisfaction, but more particularly so to that of the Indians who found by this event the importance both of their priest and of their nation greatly augmented in the sight of a stranger.

(*Carver*, 125–9)

Carver found himself unable to explain this foresight. Hearne, however, was less puzzled for he thought he could see reasons for the shaman's power over the minds and bodies of his Indian companions:

Though the ordinary trick of these conjurers may be easily detected, and justly exploded, being no more than the tricks of common jugglers, yet the apparent good effect of their labours on the sick and diseased is not so easily accounted for. Perhaps the implicit confidence placed in them by the sick may, at times, leave the mind so perfectly at rest, as to cause the disorder to take a favourable turn.

(*Hearne*, 232)

The shaman was fascinating—and disturbing—precisely because he eluded the criteria by which white men defined where rationality ended and superstition and imposture began. Hearne diligently searched for empirical evidence that might let him explain shamans' powers as sleights of hand. He succeeded—in part—but could not explain the fact that he still found himself enthralled by them. Rational explanations did not wholly remove the shaman's uncanniness, as his body took on the characteristics of animals and spectres.

Despite himself, Hearne was impressed, and recorded not only the practices of the shamans, but also the spiritual narratives they told. Hearne's discussions piqued British interest in Indian spirituality: the radical intellectuals and poets of the 1790s, as they searched for alternatives to the perverted dogma and corrupt priests of the contemporary Christian church, became fascinated by Indians' understanding of the relationship between natural and supernatural, body and soul—precisely because Indians seemed to have little notion of the rigid divide between the two that had become axiomatic in European thought. Wordsworth was one of those impressed by Indians' different understanding of the mind–body relationship: he developed from Hearne a poem investigating the power of belief and exploring a non-European attitude to the natural world (see Chapter 10). Coleridge, meanwhile, praised the 'speculative Religion' and 'respectable ... cosmogony' of the Indians, as revealed in Hearne's narrative. Their stories about creation, were, Coleridge concluded, not only more 'intelligible' than those of the East Indians (Hindus), but were evidence that all humankind felt a necessity to believe in a supernatural world, a world which more 'primitive' societies described in allegorical and symbolical tales, usually told by 'the old men, and the women'.[6] Coleridge and Wordsworth would go on to tell such tales—sometimes through the voices of Indian figures, in their poems of 1798, inaugurating a new era in British poetry. In so doing, they portrayed Indians neither as noble nor ignoble savages, but made more challenging portraits that the narratives of Hearne, Carver, and Adair made possible. Romantic Indians emerged from a need to elaborate a radical critique of European culture—its traditional beliefs as well as its political practices—but they depended on discovering, in a number of narratives that had been written in support of that culture, information that disturbed the stereotypes by which Europeans framed Indians as their natural inferiors.

While Wordsworth and Coleridge read narratives such as Hearne's against the grain, seizing on the elements that destabilized their explicit

---

[6] *Aids to Reflection*, ed. John Beer (Princeton and London, 1993), 352.

assumptions about Indian inferiority, others sought to reimpose the difference between savage and civilized, in a more apparently reliable, because empirically measurable, way. Hearne himself had recourse to the scientific language of natural history just when his similarity to his Indian companions became most uncomfortable for him. And he was far from alone in this rhetorical move, for in the second half of the eighteenth century, just as colonial expansion brought more white people closer to more native people than ever before, whites began to produce, under the aegis of science, a discourse designed to prove to the last inch the exact gradations of difference between themselves and black and brown people. They turned, in fact, to the language of physical measurement just as increased contact was revealing (as Hearne discovered) that the old stereotypes about savagery did not hold—that whites and Indians often displayed remarkably similar behaviour and character. In America this language of measurement began to replace the older subjective and unsystematic accounts as a source of 'knowledge' about Indians, precisely because the older narratives—like Adair's—could not be relied upon to produce consistent distance between white and 'red'. The new language became part of the baggage of white explorers, shaping how and what they saw and ultimately, after they had published their findings, affecting social relations and political decisions. In the next chapter I tell the story of how it came to prominence—another Romantic-era discourse about Native Americans, and one against which Indians themselves, as well as writers such as Wordsworth, Coleridge, and Blake, had to fight.

5

Indian Bones and What White Men Saw in Them

American. Copper-coloured, choleric, erect. Hair black, straight, thick; nostrils wide; face harsh; beard scanty; obstinate, content, free. Paints himself with fine red lines. Regulated by customs.[1]

With this definition the great Swedish natural historian Carl Linnaeus slotted Native Americans into a system—a general classification of nature—human, animal, vegetable—that, he was sure, he had observed in the world around him. Yet Linnaeus had never been to America, never met any Indians. How could he be so sure of their characteristics? Because he had hard evidence in the form of the observations made by white travellers. And these observations were reliable, he thought, because they were straightforward: to know people's place in nature's scheme it was necessary only to look at their bodies.

In the early eighteenth century natural history was a new study: botanists were not yet fully distinguished from herbalists and gardeners and were looked down upon by the advocates of mathematical science. Linnaeus changed this by introducing a method of classification that allowed plants to be categorized according to simple universally acceptable criteria. He then extended his survey to the animal kingdom and ultimately to humanity. Linnaeus's method divided living things into genera, species, and varieties on the basis of their sexual features. But while he accepted that all humans were of one species, he distinguished *homo sapiens* into seven distinct varieties, categorized primarily by bodily features rather than by social ones. Human difference, according to

---

[1] Linnaeus, quoted in Mary Louise Pratt, *Imperial Eyes: Travel Writing and Transculturation* (London and New York, 1992), 32.

Linnaeus's *Systemae Naturae* (1758), was empirically verifiable in the body.[2] Racial distinctness was written in flesh and blood, rather than in the vicissitudes of history.[3]

Native Americans were grist to the mill of Linnaeus's generalizing scheme. He was not interested in them as individuals but as examples of an organically distinct human variety, the American race. Yet, as Peter J. Kitson has noted, for Linnaeus 'aesthetic and moral qualities appeared to have an affinity with the purely physical'.[4] That is to say, Linnaeus located white people's prejudiced judgements about Indians' customs in Indians' inherent animal nature.

Reliance on others' judgements was a limitation on natural history's authority in the area. When classifying plants, Linnaeus had insisted on careful examination of their organic structure. Inability to perform the same empiricist procedures on Native Americans left natural history's racial categories in doubt. Nowhere was this more apparent than in the work of Linnaeus's French colleague Georges-Louis Leclerc, Comte de Buffon. Using multiple travel accounts as evidence, for he had never been to America, Buffon asserted in his *Histoire Naturelle* (1749–1804) that the nature of the New World was degenerate by comparison with that of the old. Plants were less abundant; animals were weaker; people were feebler. Native Americans were part of a six-fold classification of humanity: their copper skin and supposed lack of stature identified them as a variety (the others being African, Chinese, Tartar, Lapp and European, with the European the most beautiful). According to Cornelius De Pauw, Buffon's Dutch follower, this American variety was, like the continent's flora and fauna, inferior. In his *Recherches Philosophiques sur les Americains, ou Mémoires Intéressants pour Servir à l'Histoire de l'Espèce Humaine* (1768), De Pauw asserted that, under

[2] See Reginald Horsman, 'Scientific Racism and the American Indian in the Mid-Nineteenth Century', *American Quarterly*, 27 (1975), 152–68 and *Race and Manifest Destiny: The Origins of American Racial Anglo-Saxonism* (Cambridge, MA, 1981).

[3] On the rise of race theory and its relationship with anatomical study see David Theo Goldberg, *Racist Culture; Philosophy and the Politics of Meaning* (Oxford, 1993), 23; *Race and the Enlightenment: A Reader*, ed. Emmanuel Chukwudi Eze (Oxford, 1997), 10–14; James L. Larson, *Interpreting Nature: The Science of Living Form from Linnaeus to Kant* (Baltimore, 1994); *Race: the Origins of an Idea, 1760–1850*, ed. Hannah Franziska Augstein (Bristol, 1996), x–xvii; Harriet Ritvo, *The Platypus and the Mermaid and Other Figments of the Classifying Imagination* (Cambridge, 1997), 120–1; David Knight, *Ordering the World: A History of Classifying Man* (London, 1981), 58–81.

[4] Peter J. Kitson, Introduction, p. xv, to vol. VIII of *Slavery, Abolition, and Emancipation : Writings in the British Romantic Period*, ed. Peter J. Kitson and Debbie Lee, 8 vols. (London, 1999).

the influence of America's enervating climate its native peoples had become a degenerate species of the human race, cowardly, and lacking mental capacity. Indians' relative scarcity in the vast continent was attributable to their lack of virility and fertility, as evidenced by their supposed smallness and lack of body hair. Here De Pauw turned what had, in Buffon, been a general contention about American climate and environment into a racist tract aimed specifically against Native Americans. Like Buffon, however, De Pauw was reliant on travel accounts: his evidence about Indians' lack of stature and hair came from the subjective impressions of white visitors many of whom, in fact, were uncertain about what they had observed. Was, for example, the smoothness of Indians' skin proof they were not men enough to grow beards or did they pluck their hair out? De Pauw turned a question on which travellers differed into proof of a naturally occurring racial inferiority.

Buffon's and De Pauw's arguments provoked a passionate response in America in which the bodies of Native Americans came more than ever under scrutiny. This response was made by colonists, who understood that Buffon's climatic determinism implied that whites, under American nature's 'pernicious' influence, would also degenerate, as Native Americans supposedly had, into savagery. Thomas Jefferson, in his 1785 *Notes on the State of Virginia*, showed that Indians were strong in body and mind. As a man on the spot, Jefferson, as even the title of his book advertised, had first-hand empirical knowledge and he cited his experience of Indians' extraordinarily retentive memories, of their sophisticated eloquence and developed sense of justice. He also reported the excavation of burial mounds: Indian bones and artefacts were his court-room exhibits to prove Buffon's and De Pauw's assertions were mere travellers' tales. The indigenous people, animals and plants of America, Jefferson showed in feet and inches, were as large or larger than their European counterparts. There was, therefore, no danger that white colonists would degenerate in the New World.

It is ironic that Jefferson's defence of Native Americans involved disturbing their bodies and turning them into specimens. Jefferson, however, was not a disinterested advocate: it was the colonial project he was defending, seeing that, if Buffon and De Pauw's arguments were accepted, the idea that white people could retain and spread their civilization in America would be threatened. For an infant nation needing new immigrants from Europe, these arguments were politically dangerous. Jefferson's pro-Indian refutation aimed to dispel the danger and went hand-in-hand with his determination, as President of the US, to further white settlement by encouraging Native American nations to move west of the Mississippi. There, he hoped, they would learn to abandon the hunting culture that kept them fixed in the state of savagery and would take up agriculture—the next stage in their belated advance towards civilization.[5]

In 1788 a new, British, voice entered the debate and changed its terms. Henry Home, Lord Kames, a Scottish judge, friend of Adam Smith and David Hume, was well versed in the stadialist theory of history, and accepted their view that American Indians were at the savage hunting stage. But, responding to Buffon, he suggested that the Indians' failure to progress was explicable on the grounds that they, like American nature in general, had had less time to do so than Europeans. In his *Sketches of the History of Man* (1788), Kames speculated that God had created the New World separately and later than the old: Native Americans were not descendants of Adam and Eve. Their lack of hair and 'infecundity' proved their bodily difference and this difference could best be explained on the supposition that 'God created many pairs of the human race, differing from each other both externally and internally; that he fitted these pairs for different climates, and placed each pair in the proper climate; that the peculiarities of the original pairs were preserved entire in their descendants'.[6] It was not only Buffon that Kames cited but also Captain Cook and other recent travellers. Yet Kames simply drew from the latest narratives in order to decide the issues that Buffon had raised: he was neither a systematic nor an innovative interpreter of the new materials generated by Cook's expedition to the Indians of the Northwest coast. He was, however, influential. In sketching out a polygenist theory of humanity, he was one of the earliest natural historians to raise an idea that would later have pernicious consequences for Native Americans—the idea that they were a separate species of humanity, created different and inferior to white people.

Kames's polygenist views were one logical extension of Buffon. The task of refuting them was begun, on behalf of an insulted American

[5] On Jefferson's response to French environmentalism, see Bernard W. Sheehan, *Seeds of Extinction: Jeffersonian Philanthropy and the American Indian* (New York, 1974), 15–44. Also Richard Drinnon, *Facing West: the Metaphysics of Indian-Hating and Empire-Building* (Minneapolis, 1980), 78–116.

[6] Henry Home, Lord Kames, *Sketches of the History of Man*, 4 vols. (Edinburgh, 1788), III, 152; I, 76.

nation, by Samuel Stanhope Smith, of what was to become Princeton University. Like Jefferson before him, Smith deployed a tactic that Kames, stuck in Scotland, could not: he cited first-hand observation against travellers' tales. Smith's example was one of his students:

The college of New Jersey furnishes, at present, a counterpart to this example. A young Indian, now about fifteen years of age, was brought from his nation a number of years ago to receive an education in this institution. And from an accurate observation of him during the greater part of that time, I have received the most perfect conviction that the same state of society, united with the same climate, would make the Anglo-American and the Indian countenance very nearly approximate. He was too far advanced in savage habits to render the observation complete, because all impressions received in the tender and pliant state of the human constitution before the age of seven years, are more deep and permanent, than in any future and equal period of life. There is an obvious difference between him and his fellow students in the largeness of the mouth, and thickness of the lips, in the elevation of the cheek, in the darkness of the complexion, and the contour of the face. But these differences are sensibly diminishing. They seem, the faster to diminish in proportion as he loses that vacancy of eye, and that lugubrious wildness of countenance peculiar to the savage state, and acquires the agreeable *expression* of civil life. The expression of the eye, and the softening of the features to civilized emotions and ideas, seems to have removed more than half the difference between him and us. His colour, though it is much lighter than the complexion of the native savage, as is evident from the stain of blushing, that, on a near inspection, is instantly discernible, still forms the principal distinction. There is less difference between his features and those of his fellow students, than we often see between persons in civilized society. After a careful attention to each particular feature, and comparison of it with the correspondent feature in us, I am now able to discover but little difference. And yet there is an obvious difference in the whole countenance. This circumstance has led me to conclude that the varieties among mankind are much less than they appear to be. Each single trait or limb, when examined apart, has, perhaps, no diversity that may not be easily accounted for from known and obvious causes. Particular differences are small. It is the result of the whole that surprises us, by its magnitude. The combined effect of many minute varieties, like the product arising from the multiplication of many small numbers, appears great and unaccountable. And we have not patience, or skill it may be, to divide this combined result into its least portions, and to see, in that state, how easy it is of comprehension or solution.

The state of society comprehends diet, clothing, lodging, manners, habits, face of the country, objects of science, religion, interests, passions, and ideas of all kinds, infinite in number and variety. If each of these causes be admitted to make, as undoubtedly they do, a small variation on the human countenance, the different combinations and results of the whole must necessarily be very great; and, combined with the effects of the climate, will be adequate to account for all the varieties we find among mankind.[7]

Smith's description is fascinating because it inadvertently deconstructs the racial gaze, for when Smith looks harder and harder into the 'obvious difference between him and his fellow-students' he discovers that difference is not so obvious. Smith himself attributes this discovery not to the reconstruction of his own gaze by the familiarity that had arisen between him and the student, but to physical 'improvement' in the student's features. He sees the acknowledgement of relationship that eye-contact establishes as, instead, a sign that civilization is making the Indian's eye more expressive. Nevertheless, despite his blindness, Smith does, as he inspects ever more closely, realize that there is 'less difference between his features and those of his fellow-students, than we often see between persons in civilized society'. Racial differences, he concludes, are relatively small—not a few essential types but the combined effect of 'many minute varieties' which exist within groups as well as between them and which, in many cases, have social causes. Ironically, he attributes this realization (an enlightened one for its time) not to the effects of a personal relationship on his view, but to changes in the student. Smith will not acknowledge that he himself is a changing, erring, source of views. Nor will he admit to a personal relationship, even a close pedagogical one. The discourse of natural history demands—and is limited by—the illusion of objectivity and neutrality on the writer's part. Hence Smith's insights into the nominality of racial varieties and the dynamics of racial othering emerge only in subterranean tensions that beset his prose.

It is a further irony that Smith's view of an Indian was meant as a defence of Native Americans' full humanity against Kames, since he observes with so prejudiced and Eurocentric an eye and since he reduces the student to a nameless specimen, an embodiment of a whole race. He seizes on an actual person as a rhetorical tactic: Kames could not produce evidence as strong as this. Clearly, the drive to examine Indian bodies in more and more detail took its impetus from disputes within the discourse of natural history that impacted on nationalist and colonialist politics. Smith was a nationalist, his aim being to defend

[7] Samuel Stanhope Smith, *An Essay on the Causes of the Variety of Complexion and Figure in the Human Species to Which Are Added Strictures on Lord Kaim's Discourse on the Original Diversity of Mankind* (London, 1789), 64–7.

America against the inference that the climate was so deleterious to animal life that even civilized humanity would necessarily lapse into savagery. Thus, for Smith, Native Americans were not a separate, later-created species: they were fully human. They were savage; they were inferior; but, as the Princeton student showed, they were capable of improvement, even in their organic features, if removed from tribal into civilized society.

For Smith, civilization could overcome the degenerative effects of a harsh climate: Buffon, in other words, was largely right about the American environment but was too deterministic. The Indians had degenerated into savagery not as an inevitable consequence of the climate but because of the 'uncouth and coarse' customs they had evolved to cope with it (Smith, 52–3). Smith thought these customs arose from ignorance and poverty, and noted that poor white immigrants to 'the lowlands of the Carolinas and of Georgia degenerate to a complexion that is but a few shades lighter than that of the Iroquois' (Smith, 26–7). Nevertheless, such degeneracy would never advance so far among the whites because their bodies had inherited the form that the combination of civilized life and a milder climate had produced in Europe. Inheriting this superior genetic stock, produced by the interaction of social and natural causes, whites were nevertheless in danger, if they did not maintain civilized society, of being 'perfectly marked, in time, with the same colour' as Indians (Smith, 26–7). Racial characteristics, then, were neither essential nor eternally fixed by God, as Kames implied. Rather, whites could darken and Indians lighten according to their mode of living—if they acquired the habit of reflection. 'Knowledge', Smith concluded, is various and would bring about liveliness and variety in the countenance, replacing slackness and vacancy with energy and whiteness.

What happened to his Native American student, his prime exhibit in his battle with Buffon and Kames, Smith did not say. Certainly to meet Smith's expectations he would have had to shed all marks—social as well as physical—of his nation, for Smith's standard of perfection was whiteness. The fate of the Cherokees after 1828 is instructive. Despite becoming a 'civilized tribe', taking up agriculture and business, inventing a syllabary, becoming literate and formalizing their governing council, they were still removed from the land that they had tamed, exiled to an area where the climate was at its most hostile. Many whites did not want Indians to become better at the whites' civilization than they themselves were—and besides, they wanted their land. Smith's strange vision of Indian 'improvement' would remain, for better or worse, a vision.

In Europe, others were responding to Buffon and Linnaeus in ways that made the racial relativism of Smith, prejudiced as it was, seem comparatively benevolent. Immanuel Kant was one. In his *Uber die Verschiedenen Racen de Menschen* (1775), he simplified Linnaeus's scheme, located four racial types in nature and proposed an explanation of how, given the biblical account of creation and accepting humanity had a single genesis, difference had arisen. For Kant, climate and environment were not sufficient to cause the marked differences now observable in the descendants of Adam and Eve. But whereas Smith saw social factors as contributing causes, Kant suggested that the original human stock had been created with specific latent powers that could be triggered by environmental change. Thus migration of the ancestral humans (whom Kant assumed to be white and European in form) into different habitats would bring different latent powers into play. These powers, once activated, altered physical characteristics, which were passed down through generations. Humans were, that is to say, organically predisposed to respond, over time, in particular ways to particular climates. For Kant, it was natural that Native Americans, like African blacks living in hot climates, would respond with darkened skin and indolent temperament. Kant, in effect, naturalized intellectual and moral characteristics seeing them as being produced not just by the external agency of climate but also by the internal one of the *nisus formativus*.[8]

Kant's solution to the phenomenon of difference was philosophically neat but empirically unproven. To others, its categories seemed arbitrary and cumbersome: Native Americans, for instance, were assimilated to the Mongolian category. And so the debate continued, with some writers monogenist, others polygenist, some attributing difference to climate, others to an inner power, others still to a combination of one or other with social influences. Even the number of racial types could not be agreed upon. It is a further irony that, although the men of science disagreed, they all depended on the same group of sources. Charlevoix, Cook, Adair, and Carver were all cited again and again: their impressions of specific Native Americans were used to bolster generalizations about traits that were supposedly inherent to the American type.

[8] See Robert Bernasconi, 'Who Invented the Concept of Race? Kant's Role in the Enlightenment Construction of Race', in *Race*, ed. Robert Bernasconi (Oxford, 2001), 11–36.

It was the new technique of comparative anatomy that gave the natural historians the certainty that they were striving for. Jefferson examined bones; Smith peered into an Indian's face. In Europe another empiricist was inventing a method for scrutinizing human and animal variety still more closely. Pieter Camper, a Dutch anatomist, had made himself a machine for the purpose of calculating the angles formed by facial features. His original intention was to make anatomical drawing more accurate, but he soon saw that he had built a device for fixing racial difference into the firm foundation of the skull. Whereas Smith had found his impressions of racial otherness dissolving as he stared at the student's features more and more closely, Camper would fix that impression into the 'objective' data that empirical science most counted on. By measuring the angle between forehead and jaw line, he would show how a hierarchy existed. At the top was the face portrayed in ancient Greek statuary: its 'facial angle' formed Camper's aesthetic and intellectual ideal. Near the bottom was the 'Negro' only just above the ape. The American Indian lay in between.

Camper emphasized his methodological independence of human bias: his machine did away, he claimed, with the fallible and subjective human observer. It was transparent—not a device to be admired for the ingenuity of its operation, but a frame through which one saw things as they were.[9] Armed with it, the natural historian could escape from the dubious authority of traveller's impressions. What was needed instead was a real head, alive or dead, to yield the measurements that would allow its place on the hierarchy to be fixed.

Camper's invention altered natural history's course and changed its effects on native peoples, since other men of science rapidly grasped its potential to resolve the reliance on travel narratives that limited their authority. The British surgeon John Hunter was soon collecting the skulls of Caribs, Tahitians, Africans and arranging them, in profile, in a rank order based on their facial angles. After Camper, humanity could be exhibited as a gradation, with Europeans above Americans and Africans, who were placed next to apes and the 'lower' animals. Hunter's work

---

[9] *The Works of the Late Professor Camper, On the Connexion between the Science of Anatomy and the Arts of Drawing, Painting, Statuary* (London, 1794). Several historians of science have argued that, in the culture of late eighteenth and early nineteenth-century science, experimentalists had to make their apparatus transparent in order for their demonstrations to be accepted as exhibitions of nature's laws; see, for example, Simon Schaffer, 'Natural Philosophy and Public Spectacle in the Eighteenth Century', *History of Science*, 21 (1983), 1–43.

influenced a generation of students who heard his lectures and worked with his collection.[10] Two among them, Charles White and William Lawrence, were to equate Hunter's gradation of skulls with a racial hierarchy of moral and intellectual worth.

Still more influential than Hunter was J. F. Blumenbach, Professor at Göttingen. A monogenist, Blumenbach rejected the notion that a fixed hierarchy existed in nature and that skin colour could be used to ascertain racial difference. He detached humanity from the apes and affirmed that all humans had degenerated (in his sense, deviated) from an original form. This process meant that no existing humans were pristine descendants of the ancestral stock: all had changed through the generations under social and environmental influences (principally the climate) acting on the formative life fluid (Kant's *nisus formativus*). These changes, Blumenbach asserted, had brought about four human varieties (a number he later increased to five). These varieties, Blumenbach emphasized, were not utterly different for there was a gradual and smooth transition of characteristics among people, making it hard to fix boundaries between groups. Nevertheless, it was possible to identify such groups and one, which he termed Caucasian, was 'the most beautiful race' and the closest to the original stock.[11] Those which had deviated furthest from common ancestors were the Ethiopian and Mongolian. The American, he concluded, was an intermediate group—defined not in its own right but as a transition between Blumenbach's polar extremes.

Blumenbach's intentions were liberal and humane. To disprove the assertions that Indians were not fully human, he combed travel narratives, peered at 'drawings of Americans by the best artists' and, best of all, took 'the testimony of the most trustworthy eye-witnesses'. He also looked at skulls. In the third edition of his *De Generis Humani Varietate* he argued that crania showed 'a constancy of characteristics which cannot be denied, and is indeed remarkable, which has a great deal to do with the racial habit'.[12] Just as important: they could be accessed with ease from Europe once ripped from the tomb by the collectors whom Blumenbach himself sent into Native America. Blumenbach set

[10] For an assessment of Hunter's importance see Stephen J. Cross, 'John Hunter, the Animal Economy, and Late Eighteenth Century Physiological Discourse', *Studies in the History of Biology*, 5 (1981), 1–110.

[11] *De Generis Humani Varietate Nativa*, 3rd edn. (Göttingen, 1795) translated in *The Anthropological Treatises of Johann Friedrich Blumenbach*, trs. Thomas Bendyshe (London, 1865), 269.

[12] *Anthropological Treatises . . . Blumenbach*, 273, 235.

about acquiring the world's largest collection of heads to ensure that his science could be seen to be based on the real objects it represented. His family called it Golgotha. Having collected his bones, Blumenbach strove for better ways to measure them. He replaced the 'facial angle' with description of as many features as possible, chiefly the form of the frontal and superior maxillary bones.[13]

Blumenbach's Golgotha helped to make him the most authoritative natural historian of the period. Seen from a twenty-first century perspective, it appears not as a collection of hard facts—indisputable proof—but as a system of command and control, placing specific items into a literally disembodied order in which the individual is subordinate to the general, the particular to the abstract. In Blumenbach's museum, skulls of different peoples could be compared and contrasted in a way impossible in the places from which the skulls had come (even if the people in those places had thought it worthwhile to do so). The knowledge of indigenous peoples that Blumenbach constructed from their dry bones was, in fact, very limited. Yet as the skulls accumulated in his cabinets, the thin cross-section that they offered became ever longer, allowing natural historians to feel they knew native peoples because they could put them in their proper place. In effect, Blumenbach's Golgotha was a microcosm of colonial power, a demonstration of the workings of empire, as a warehouse of commodities imported for Europe's benefit at the expense of the bodies and nature of the colonized.

Blumenbach's boneyard gave his theories a long life. His racial classification laid the basis of physical anthropology, remaining the most influential model until Charles Darwin altered matters. For men as liberal as Blumenbach himself, the anatomization of race theory was an enlightened and progressive means of confuting apologists for slavery who argued that native peoples were constitutionally animal-like and not fully human. Certainly, the historian J. G. Herder used Blumenbach's anatomical data in this way in his 1784 *Ideen zu einer Philosophie der Geschichte der Menscheit* (Outlines of a Philosophy of the History of Man). Herder vindicated Native Americans against Buffon's accusations of feebleness: skulls and skeletons assured him both that there was a 'family likeness' between Indians who differed in outward appearance

---

[13] These and other measurements were also pioneered by the principal comparative anatomist in France. See Georges Cuvier, *Lectures on Comparative Anatomy*, trs. William Ross, 2 vols. (London, 1802).

and that all were fully human.[14] Herder turned to the latest generation
of explorers to back up these anatomical claims, citing Carver, Adair,
and Cook to prove that the 'one predominant character' of all American
Indians consisted in 'that firm health and permanent strength, that
proud savage love of liberty and war, which their mode of life and
domestic economy, their education and government, their customs
and occupations both in peace and war, equally tend to promote'.[15]
For Herder then, following Adair's and Carver's admiring portraits,
Indians were remarkable people who, in body and mind, were formed
by their and their ancestors' cultural response to their environment.
Even anatomy was partly shaped by culture: Indians' characteristic bone
structure was formed as much by what Indians did as by some god-given
constitution. Racial difference was a product of history working on
bodily potential—as Kant had suggested. In Herder's case, however,
that history was shown to be of people's own making rather than an
inevitable biological response to environment.

Herder did not locate innate moral and intellectual ability in the skull.
Others did, with dangerous consequences for the indigenous peoples
whose skulls supposedly showed them to be naturally inferior. William
Lawrence, a professor of the Royal College of Surgeons, had access
to Hunter's collection of Native American bones. Lawrence was not a
polygenist. Rather, he followed Blumenbach's classification of a single
human species into five varieties and stressed the importance of the
evidence of crania.[16] Lawrence looked with an eye trained by Hunter's
and Blumenbach's craniometry: he saw in individual Native Americans
the bone structure of a whole race (this despite his general caution that
great variety exists between individual members of each group). The
contrast with Smith is instructive: whereas the Princeton principal found
his prejudices confounded the harder he looked his Indian student in
the face, Lawrence found that his view of people simply confirmed
his scrutiny of skulls. A picture of the Mohawk chief Thayendaneega
(Joseph Brant) resembled an engraving of seven Cherokees that in turn
evoked the 'form of a skull' of a 'North American savage executed for
murder at Philadelphia'.[17] Lawrence's individuals are replicas of the

[14] Herder, *Outlines of a Philosophy of the History of Man*, trs. T. Churchill (London,
1800), 161.

[15] Ibid., 155.

[16] William Lawrence, *Lectures on Physiology, Zoology and the Natural History of Man*,
3rd edn. (London, 1823), 285.

[17] Ibid., 313.

type, his living Indians are simulacra of the dead. He begins his *Lectures* with a frontispiece portrait of Thayendaneega as the embodiment of the American variety—an extraordinary man reduced to a specimen of the whole race.[18] American Indians, Lawrence argued, had the lowest flattest foreheads of all, and he assembled casual asides on the subject from the latest travellers to ballast the argument. Thus Cook, Hearne, Lewis, and Clark are recruited as witnesses proving the anatomical point (though that they did so is not surprising since natural historians programmed them to look for it).

Lawrence differed from Blumenbach in the use he made of his anatomical obsession. In Lawrence we can observe the beginnings of Victorian racism, for he uses anatomical difference to posit racialized moral and intellectual characteristics. For Lawrence, bones demonstrated the innate inferiority of native peoples. His argument is especially circular in the case of Native Americans. Their supposed lowness of forehead, Lawrence suggests, may explain the 'singular intellectual defect' in some Indians—they cannot count.[19] To prove their organic innumeracy, all Lawrence cites are three casual remarks taken out of context, by three white travellers. He completely ignores the evidence for the Incas' and Aztecs' sophisticated astronomical computations and fails even to consider whether arithmetic is a learnt system for which tribal peoples had no need. Neither Blumenbach nor Herder had been so blind; unfortunately for Native Americans, however, the skull collecting of which Blumenbach and Herder approved made such blindness much easier. Lawrence had the data drawn from Indian skulls to justify his crude racism.

Lawrence's racism is more and more apparent as he comments on the relationships between races. He declares that it is only in 'the white races we meet, in full perfection, with true bravery, love of liberty, and other passions and virtues of great souls'.[20] Native Americans share with 'the other dark-coloured people of the globe' 'moral and intellectual inferiority' to the 'white races'. To be sure, Lawrence summarizes the best recent writers to show that some Indians have qualities. Nevertheless, their example does not disturb Lawrence's belief that whites are 'more highly-gifted races'.[21] The very fact that the English had, in forty 'short years' built in America a 'mighty empire', whereas 'the copper-coloured

---

[18] On the relationship of race theory to art see David Bindman, *Ape to Apollo: Aesthetics and the Idea of Race in the Eighteenth Century* (London, 2002).

[19] Lawrence, *Lectures*, 487.   [20] Ibid., 415.

[21] Ibid., 414.

natives' 'had not advanced a single step in three hundred' proved Indian inferiority.[22] Sadly, Lawrence does not even recognize the irony that this mighty empire had, in part, been built at Indian expense and from Indians' blood. In Lawrence, natural history becomes more clearly than ever before a discourse glorifying empire and institutionalizing racial hatred. After his work, the way was open for the argument that the manifest destiny of Indians was to die out in face of white colonists: their inferiority was written deep in their bones as well as on their skin. And there was, Lawrence insisted (contra Smith), no evidence that races changed their characteristics in different environments. The 'copper-coloured' men always had been and always would be different and inferior.

Lawrence was no aberration. His views belonged to the mainstream, emerging as they did from the most respected authorities on racial difference and Native Americans. Lawrence was praised by name in the Preface to the most comprehensive—and dangerous—craniometrical study of all. Samuel George Morton's *Crania Americana* (1839) followed the direction in which Lawrence had taken Blumenbach's work. Like the British surgeon, Morton also showed a penchant for generalizing, from the shape of the skull, about what went on inside it.[23] Morton was also adept at interpreting customs to confirm what he thought he saw in his skulls, and then interpreting his skulls to confirm what he thought customs said about Indian character. His self-justifying methodology also included the invention of new racial categories that further biased his picture. He divided the American race into two families—the 'Toltecan' (effectively South American), which showed 'evidence of centuries of demi-civilization', and the 'American' (effectively North American), which 'embraces all the barbarous nations of the New World'.[24] By this means, Morton was able to bracket off the Aztec and Inca civilizations and so fulfil his undeclared purpose of proving North American Indians' innate inferiority and savagery. He set about doing this by associating dubious cranial interpretation with pejorative stereotyping. Thus the Appalachian branch of his American family showed an especial 'truncation of the occiput' and were 'warlike, cruel

[22] Ibid., 414, 419.
[23] Morton, *Crania Americana, or, a Comparative View of the Skulls of Various Aboriginal Nations of North and South America: to Which is Prefixed an Essay on the Varieties of the Human Species* (London, 1839), 6.
[24] Ibid., 63

and unforgiving. They turn with aversion from the restraints of civilized life and have made but trifling progress in mental culture or the useful arts'. Morton's conclusion was that 'the Indian' was naturally subordinate: 'the structure of his mind appears to be different from that of the white man'. On the basis of this supposed organic difference, Morton made a self-fulfilling prophecy of strife: 'nor can the two harmonize in their social relations except on the most limited scale'.[25] And Morton then quoted approvingly Lawrence's conclusion that 'to expect that the American can be raised by any culture to an equal height in moral sentiments and intellectual energy with Europeans, appears to me quite as unreasonable as it would be to hope that the bull-dog may equal the greyhound in speed'.[26] This analogy with dogs suggested the belief to which Morton privately inclined but did not explicitly publish — Indians were a separate, animal-like species. Morton was no more eccentric than Lawrence, for both men worked in the main current of natural history and race theory. Morton derived his skull-assessment technique from Blumenbach and Cuvier and used the observations of Cook, Bartram, and Adair to back up his data. At every stage, in fact, Morton was informed by travel writings which, however, he used to supply his need for traits that were supposedly universal to all Indians and therefore only explicable as racial and organic in origin. Not for Morton Herder's admiring analysis of Indian culture as an intelligent response to environment. Even the complex loyalties and actions of Thayendaneega, the Mohawk chief whom Lawrence had illustrated, are reduced to instinctual drives that education cannot correct: Brant, Morton notes, 'received a Christian education, and even joined in the Christian communion; yet he was readily induced by the British government to resume his savage propensities against the American colonies, and became one of the most bloody and remorseless destroyers in the annals of Indian warfare'.[27]

Morton's *Crania Americana* is a frightening warning of the dangers of empiricist science when coupled to simplistic psychology and to the racism that went hand-in-hand with colonial competition for land. It comes as no surprise to find the notion of manifest destiny quoted approvingly: 'it now seems certain that the North American Indians, like the bears and wolves, are destined to flee at the approach of civilized

[25] Morton, *Crania Americana*, 65, 64, 82.
[26] Ibid., quoting Lawrence, *Lectures*, 501.
[27] Morton, *Crania Americana*, 82.

man, and to fall before his renovating hand, and disappear from the face of the earth along with those ancient forests which alone afford them sustenance and shelter'.[28] In this poetic prose, the impetus of Morton's race science is masked and the work of cheating, uprooting and killing native Americans rendered inevitable—a sublime element of natural law. Blumenbach would never have uttered such a phrase, yet his writing helped to make it possible. It was the confidence gained from craniometry and from the 'facts' reported by trained travellers that enabled deterministic generalizations to be sustained. Morton harvested the words of travellers, as Lawrence, White and Kames had done before him, eliminating in the process nearly everything that made the traveller seem less than an omniscient authority. In natural historians' use of travel sources, none of the traveller's precariousness and vulnerability in a strange land, none of his dependence on the indigenous people, is recorded. His ignorance and partiality do not appear either, nor his wonder and amazed curiosity about people and practices new to him. Nor, needless to say, his understanding of the complexity of Indian lives. The same few features of Indian lives on which previous natural historians had fixed were made to stand for whole complex cultures. This process involved a fixation on accumulating piece after piece of evidence concerning the same traits or customs. Natural historians were fetishists about Indian body parts—their beards, their hair, their skin were pored over, through travel writers' pages and at first hand, in the precious samples retrieved from the Indians themselves.

Morton gathered even more of these samples than Blumenbach. His Native American 'Golgotha' contained 600 crania (later 1,000). And what is most frightening about his book is the sheer scale of the operation by which Morton harvested them. The *Crania Americana* was the result of graverobbing on a mass, systematic scale. US army officers, agents of the Indian department, settlers, businessmen, and amateur historians were all recruited to get skulls for Morton. Men with the authority of government invested in them, men with the lure of money, men with the power of guns all took Indian bodies from graves, both recent and ancient. Distressed, some Indians changed their burial practices to hide graves from whites' view.[29] Others protested in print: the writer

---

[28] *Edinburgh Review*, quoted in Morton, *Crania Americana*, 272.

[29] In his *The European and the Indian: Essays in the Ethnohistory of Colonial North America* (New York and Oxford, 1981), p. 119, James Axtell suggests that white graverobbing actually altered Indian burial practices, in an effort to hide

and campaigner William Apess declared 'The greatest act of hostility toward a nation is to profane the graves of their dead'.[30] But such reactions were already written off, since the collectors already believed Indians morally and intellectually inferior. The harvest of skulls continued so that Morton could subject them to a series of measurements that in turn yielded statistical data. Going a mathematical stage further than Blumenbach, Morton published this data in comparative tables: figures were the Victorian obsession, proving inferiority for all white readers to count on the fingers. But, as Stephen Jay Gould showed,[31] not only were the measurements subjectively chosen and their efficacy in proving mental inferiority nowhere demonstrated, but the figures they yielded were misleading. The data was fiddled, perhaps through inadequate experimental method, perhaps through unconscious bias. Craniometry did not prove what Morton claimed: the conclusions he and others drew from it were bogus.

gravesites from white eyes. On current controversy about anthropology's history of gravedigging and study of remains, see David Hurst Thomas, *Skull Wars: Kennewick Man, Archaeology, and the Battle for Native American Identity* (New York, 2000) and Douglas Cole, *Captured Heritage: The Scramble for Northwest Coast Artifacts* (Norman, OK, 1985); also 'Contested Pasts and the Practice of Anthropology,' special issue of *American Anthropologist*, 94/4 (December 1992).

[30] From Apess's autobiography, published in 1829, *A Son of the Forest*. In *On Our Own Ground: The Complete Writings of William Apess, A Pequot*, ed. Barry O'Connell (Amherst, MA, 1992), 92.

[31] Stephen Jay Gould, *The Mismeasure of Man* (New York and London, 1981).

PART II
BRITISH FICTION

6

Indians and the Politics of Romance

Paradoxically, it was while natural historians were solidifying their racial stereotypes that literary writers, working from the same travel texts, created fictional Indians of complexity and troubling power. Romanticism, however, arose in explicit opposition to the increasing cultural authority being gained by the empiricist discourses, be they political economy, utilitarian philosophy, or natural theology. Indians were a vital part of Romanticism's counter-empiricist discourse, a discourse that promoted the healing power of its own fictionality in opposition to the new science's insistence on its factuality. Romantic Indians, that is to say, did not only differ from the Indians of natural historians but they challenged the claims of natural historians—and empiricists more generally—to speak with truth and authority.

To say this is not to create a simple opposition between Romantic Indians and the new sciences. If, at its extreme, the opposition was stark, there were many cases where fictional Indians reflected the priorities that fiction writers shared with their scientific counterparts. Romantic Indians were not always free from racial stereotyping, some of it derived from travel writers, some of it from natural historians themselves, for it was not simply in the 'facts' found by gentlemen of science that travellers' versions of Indians resounded. Fiction writers also had their own, British, priorities, and it is through these, as well as through the travel texts that the writers adapted, that their Indians are refracted.

Romance writers began to dramatize Britons' relationship with Indians for two reasons. First, the newspaper stories and captivity narratives that told of American war were both exciting and disturbing: they made dramatic material for a story and also focused the moral debate about the propriety of colonial ventures. Second, there was by the 1780s a perception that the British ruling classes were becoming effete and self-indulgent, forgetting the chivalric virtues by which, supposedly, they justified their monopoly of power. As William Cowper put it:

> Ambition, av'rice, penury incurr'd
> By endless riot; vanity, the lust
> Of pleasure and variety, dispatch
> As duely as the swallows disappear,
> The world of wand'ring knights and squires to town.
> London ingulphs them all. The shark is there
> And the shark's prey.[1]

Instead of protecting the weak and powerless by courageously putting the people's interests before their own, they were luxuriating in idleness. They had lost the reputation which their forefathers had learnt in battle: if they were not to be swept away by popular discontent, they had better revive their commanding virtues and thereby earn the populace's obedience. Where better to relearn these virtues than in contact with the courageous warrior Indians?

It was by portraying Indians in these new contexts that the novelists arrived at more detailed, war-based, Indian figures than had before featured in British fictions. They changed stereotypical savages into ambiguous heroes, although they found themselves beset by doubts as they did so. But they also showed Britons themselves altering as a result of their interaction with Indians—acquiring so-called Indian virtues but also changing in unpredictable ways. In this respect, the fictions reflected a new cultural and social influence on the manners and morals of the home country—an Indigenous influence born of empire.

One of the first fictional responses to the American war was Henry Mackenzie's 1773 novel *The Man of the World*,[2] a novel that shows how stereotypical exoticism began to be rewritten under the pressure of the complex encounters produced by colonial battle. Throughout, Mackenzie attacks the way in which money corrupts proper British manliness, a manliness defined in sentimental terms as a capacity to feel for the vulnerable and so act chivalrously towards them. In this scenario, Indians function to reveal how some Britons have become, in their pursuit of money and power, more savage than the savages. So it is that Mackenzie's virtuous hero, exiled from Britain by the injustice of the landowner, escapes from further injustice in the army on its American

---

[1] *The Task*, Book III, ll. 811–17, in *William Cowper: The Task and Selected Other Poems*, ed. James Sambrook (London and New York, 1994), 138.
[2] *The Man of the World* (London, 1773, facs. rpt. New York and London, 1974).

campaign by joining a band of Indians. Their purpose in the novel is to provide a contrast with the institutionalized injustice of British society. In his character's voice, Mackenzie moralizes, seeing on the British side 'fraud, hypocrisy, and sordid baseness, while [the Indian] seemed to provide honesty, truth, and savage nobleness of soul' (II, 190).

Mackenzie's Indians are not quite mere noble savages. Although they are not clearly differentiated and although they conform to stock motifs, they act as rational social beings rather than beast-like others. Mackenzie includes details of the torture of captives and of the death song, clearly drawn from travel accounts. Yet instead of referring these practices to the Indians' inner nature, he explains them sympathetically as initiation tests. When the hero bears them with fortitude, he is released and adopted as the son of a father who has lost his natural son in battle. The father's explanation of affairs is presented as an admirable one: ' "it is thus", said [the Indian], "that the valiant are tried, and thus that they are rewarded; for how should'st thou be as one of us, if thy soul were as the soul of little men; he only is worthy to lift the hatchet with the Cherokees, to whom shame is more intolerable than the stab of the knife, or the burning of the fire" ' (II, 181). The Cherokees teach the paternal lessons that are no longer present in corrupt Britain and they do so quoting Ossian. With the words 'little men' Mackenzie's Cherokee echoes Macpherson's Scots—thus exporting clan values back to the Indians (but Ossian, as we have seen, was itself influenced by depictions of Indians). Thus educated in honour, the 'son' is able, when the Indian 'father' dies, to return to Britain, deeper, stronger, to take up his birthright. A little touch of Cherokee in the night, Mackenzie suggests, is just what the British gentry needs to re-educate itself in the patriarchal virtues for which it once stood. Transatlantic encounters are a means by which a corrupt ruling class can restore itself, rediscovering among 'savages' the martial virtues it had lost.

Mackenzie demonstrates the impact that North American wars, bringing Britons into contact and conflict with Indians on a new scale, had on fiction. Indians were still exotic but were also now within enough Britons' imaginative compass to feature in popular tales that aimed to make romance realistic. They featured in two principal ways: gentle nature-maidens and heroic warriors were contrasting, even opposed figures, yet served the same function of providing the moral and emotional exemplars that were lacking in a capitalist society. Indians were, that is to say, essential (if transient) parts of a sentimental education. They were exotic means by which, for writers of sensibility, the manner and mores that formed the glue of Britain's unequal society could be infused once more with true feeling before they were seen by all to be a hollow hypocritical veneer hiding the brutal self-interest of the classes that monopolized power.

Writing in 1792, Charlotte Smith faced a different situation. In France, the revolution had begun to sweep away the power of monarchy and aristocracy. In Britain, Burke had already made his famous diagnosis that chivalry could no longer keep a (necessarily) unequal society functioning smoothly. The veneer had indeed been stripped away. In this context, Native Americans took on a modified rhetorical function, serving as counters in a political battle waged between Tories and Whig radicals in Britain. Smith was a radical Whig of the middle-class. Like many of this kind, including the dissenters Richard Price and Joseph Priestley, Smith defended the Revolution in its early pre-Terror stages. In her 1793 novel *The Old Manor House*[3] she used Native Americans so as to remind her fellow Britons that the violence of the French people 'struggling for its freedom' (Smith, 360), though 'terrible', was greatly exceeded by the violence of the Indian 'savages' whom the British employed in the American War of Independence. Smith related how ministers had knowingly let loose Indians of 'insatiate' 'rapacity' on the rebellious American population, culminating in the massacre and scalping of white women and children. There are, Smith concluded, 'savages of all countries,—even of our own!' (Smith, 360). The British ministry, however, was more savage than the French, who were an oppressed people struggling for liberty, since it by contrast, was trying to repress the American people's similar struggle. And it was justifying its repression, and the deliberate cruelty of using Indians, on the specious grounds that it was being cruel to be kind. Smith has her virtuous hero Orlando, fighting on the British side, see for himself the cruelty of their Indian allies. But what he 'sees' is the most ignoble and ignorant version of a stereotype, as Smith's adjectives insist: 'the savage thirst of blood which they avowed—that base avidity for plunder, with an heroic contempt of danger, pain, and death, made them altogether objects of abhorrence, mingled with something like veneration: but the former sentiment altogether predominated' (Smith, 360). What Orlando learns in America is that Britain is still more savage than its savage allies because it chooses to ally with them. Native Americans enter the novel to show that the chivalry of Britain's governing class—its ministers and

---

[3] *The Old Manor House*, ed. Anne Henry Ehrenpreis (Oxford, 1989).

army officers—is tainted, and to laud, by implication, the rebellions in America and now France.

How to remove the taint and restore Britons' ruling classes to virtue and liberty is the question Smith poses. Her answer is that a re-education of their feelings is required—a sentimental re-education. It is not a convincing answer precisely because her portrayal of those events shows them to be too deeply rooted in the socio-political structure, a structure which, in turn, shapes people's natures. Smith, that is to say, like many 1790s radicals who increasingly despaired of peaceful social change, was unable to imagine a convincing mechanism by which institutionalized injustice could be overcome without a terrible violence that she was unwilling to endorse. This dilemma left sentiment as the next-best option and, in turn, created a contradiction in her fictional Indians. Having told her readers how savage and base Indians were, Smith asks them to believe that there are exceptions. Orlando meets one younger warrior who differs from the racial stereotype: he has a 'more open countenance'. He acts, as well as looks, more like an English gentleman should act, has 'gentle manners', and has, 'at the risk of his own life, saved a woman from the fury of his relation the Bloody Captain, when he was on the point of killing her with his tomahawk' (Smith, 361). He 'then conducted the woman who had been widowed and driven from her home by *British* troops' to the safety of an American fort, 'hazarding his own life to preserve hers' (Smith, 361).

All this is utterly implausible. Not only does the Wolf-hunter (as Smith calls this chivalrous Indian) differ unbelievably from the other Indians she represents, he also differs from everything travellers and historians related. Indians did not act according to the code of chivalry, which was foreign to them. Nor were younger Indians more natur-ally compassionate, for it was often younger warriors, keen to prove themselves, who were more eager for war. But Smith sacrifices realism for a sentimental, though still racist, lesson, concluding that 'the secret sympathy between generous minds seems to exist throughout the whole human kind; for this young warrior became soon as much attached to Orlando as his nature allowed' (Smith, 361). Wolf-hunter's nature is still limited by his race and it is he who becomes attached to Orlando, rather than vice versa. The 'red warrior' of sensibility naturally admires the young white hero, although Orlando has done nothing to distinguish himself in the warrior's eyes. Wolf-hunter, however, exists to deepen Orlando's heroism, testing his loyalty, courage, and hardiness. Later, when Orlando's scouting party is ambushed by Wolf-hunter's Indian band, Orlando's life is spared when he stoically defies the pain of a headwound and marches with the Indians. Here the novel reflects the increased post-war awareness of Indian practices: it's understood that the tribes adopted or killed captives according to their judgement of their worth. Admiring his fortitude, they adopt him and he becomes a successful hunter, 'distinguished from an Iroquois by nothing but his English complexion' (Smith, 380) and by his ability to write, in his pocket-book, of his beloved lady who is far away in Britain. In other words, Orlando is tested in body and spirit by his encounter, and acquires Indian characteristics in the process. But he does not 'go native', since he retains an inner life that the Indians are not credited with and that is symbolized by literacy. Orlando is able to carry on an inner meditation on 'his Monima, pursued [in his absence] by the cruel Sir John Belgrave' (Smith, 382). And this chivalric consciousness makes him determined to leave the savage life. He does so, strengthened by the test, deepened in the heroic qualities that are missing among the British landowners still at home, and gets the girl and the estate. Smith wraps up her romance and restores the British gentry with a small infusion of Indian life. But the ending is conventional and does not resolve the contradictions that Smith's politicized diagnosis of British society had revealed. Smith's Indians are a rhetorical stopgap for a situation that her genre—the popular romance—has no room to rectify. They are also, of course, a source of exotic colours and Gothic frisson, both dark handsome strangers and savages with hearts.

The limitations of Smith's romance-genre come into clear focus when it is placed alongside an earlier, baggier novel, more capable of admitting into itself the varieties of interaction made possible by colonial war. Tobias Smollett's *The Expedition of Humphry Clinker* (1771) appeared in the aftermath of the French–Indian war and Pontiac's uprising but before the American revolution. This is a picaresque novel, which borrows the form of the picturesque travel tour and is set in a newly-unified Britain—including a trip to Scotland, which had recently been brought back under government control after the 1745 rebellion against Hanoverian rule. Scotland, in the novel, is a country whose colonial bonds to England are still being forged. It is in Scotland that Smollett introduces a character formed by another colonial conflict, the French–Indian war in North America that gave many Britons their first direct experience of Indians. In a brief episode, the Scot Lishmahago describes his capture by Miami warriors (the description is derived from Colden's *History of the Five Nations* and from travel accounts collated by Smollett in the *British Magazine*).[4] It appears to be a standard collection of motifs: torture, death-songs, cannibalism, adoption of the surviving captive. These are now retold, however, as if from direct experience, being war encounters that an ordinary Scot, sitting in 'civilized' Edinburgh, could believably have had. Colonial encounters had come back to Britain, for Lishmahago, it emerges, has been reshaped, in body and mind, by his Indian experiences:

He and ensign Murphy had made their escape from the French hospital at Montreal, and taken to the woods, in hope of reaching some English settlement; but mistaking their route, they fell in with a party of Miamis, who carried them away in captivity. The intention of these Indians was to give one of them as an adopted son to a venerable sachem, who had lost his own in the course of the war, and to sacrifice the other according to the custom of the country. Murphy, as being the younger and handsomer of the two, was designed to fill the place of the deceased, not only as the son of the sachem, but as the spouse of a beautiful squaw, to whom his predecessor had been bethrothed; but in passing through the different whigwhams or villages of the Miamis, poor Murphy was so mangled by the women and the children, who have the privilege of torturing all prisoners in their passage, that, by the time they arrived at the place of the sachem's residence, he was rendered altogether unfit for the purposes of marriage: it was determined therefore, in the assembly of the warriors, that ensign Murphy should be brought to the stake, and that the lady should be given to lieutenant Lismahago, who had likewise received his share of torments, though they had not produced emasculation.—A joint of one finger had been cut, or rather sawed off with a rusty knife; one of his great toes was crushed into a mash betwixt two stones; some of his teeth were drawn, or dug out with a crooked nail; splintered reeds had been thrust up his nostrils and other tender parts; and the calves of his legs had been blown up with mines of gunpowder dug in the flesh with the sharp points of the tomahawk.

The Indians themselves allowed that Murphy died with great heroism, singing, as his death song, the *Drimmendoo*, in concert with Mr Lismahago, who was present at the solemnity. After the warriors and the matrons had made a hearty meal upon the muscular flesh which they pared from the victim, and had applied a great variety of tortures, which he bore without flinching, an old lady, with a sharp knife, scooped out one of his eyes, and put a burning coal in the socket. The pain of this operation was so exquisite that he could not help bellowing, upon which the audience raised a shout of exultation, and one of the warriors stealing behind him, gave him the *coup de grace* with a hatchet.

[4] See Charlotte Sussman, *Consuming Anxieties: Consumer Protest, Gender, and British Slavery, 1713–1833* (Stanford, 2000), 85.

Lishmahago's bride, the squaw Squinkinacoosta, distinguished herself on this occasion.—She shewed a great superiority of genius in the tortures which she contrived and executed with her own hands.—She vied with the stoutest warrior in eating the flesh of the sacrifice; and after all the other females were fuddled with dram-drinking, she was not so intoxicated but that she was able to play the game of the platter with the conjuring sachem, and afterwards go through the ceremony of her own wedding, which was consummated that same evening. The captain had lived very happily with this accomplished squaw for two years, during which she bore him a son, who is now the representative of his mother's tribe; but, at length, to his unspeakable grief, she had died of a fever, occasioned by eating too much raw bear, which they had killed in a hunting excursion.[5]

The motifs are standard but the tone is not. Smollett undercuts Lishmahago's pretentions with mock-heroic vocabulary. Colonial war, Smollett implies, is more grotesque than epic, for manly virtue is literally emasculated in the encounter with Indians. Murphy is castrated; Lishmahago is a (willing) sex slave. Neither is a hero and Lishmahago survives neither through bravery nor authority, but because he is a shrewd and clever adaptor to savage circumstances. He flourishes among cannibal Miamis so well because he has no beliefs to shed. In Lishmahago, in fact, Smollett shows that colonial encounters empower the man of few principles rather than the chivalric hero, he for whom morals as well as manufactures are commodities to trade for advantage. In the colonial culture produced by the meeting of Britons and Indians, survival of the fittest turns out to be survival of the fixer. And this colonial culture impacts on Britain since the culture of the Miamis is comically reflected in Lishmahago and his Edinburgh audience.

The comedy, which centres on carnal appetite, arises from the parallels between what Lishmahago narrates and the reason he's narrating it. He wants to impress Tabitha with his virility as a man of war and, we suspect, a man of love. She is eager to be impressed: 'she seemed to be taken with the same charms that captivated the heart of Desdemona, who loved the Moor for *the dangers he had past*' (Smollett, 229). This mocking aside draws attention to the principal danger that Lishmahago 'past' in the Miamis' hands—castration. He, it turns out, had escaped emasculation (though not scalping) and so was fit for his Indian bride, and now for Tabitha.

---

[5] Tobias Smollett, *The Expedition of Humphry Clinker*, ed. Angus Ross (Harmondsworth, 1967), 228–9.

No sooner has Smollett made a comparison with Othello, than he undermines it. Lishmahago is a half-pay officer looking for a rich widow to end his poverty. Mrs. Tabby's sighs for poor Murphy turn out to be regret that 'he had been rendered unfit for marriage' (Smollett, 229). She is a lusty consumer of pleasures, whose disapproval of the Miamis' cannibalistic consumption immediately gives way to curiosity to 'know the particulars of her marriage-dress'. Smollett, it is clear, gives sentiment short shrift: people in Britain and North America are motivated, and made comic, by their own sensual desires, for fine clothes, rich spouses, drink, food, and sex. Women, in particular, are singled out: in a wholesale destruction of the chivalric code Smollett depicts them not as the fairer and weaker sex but as insatiable consumers of men. It is the women and children of the Miamis who castrate Murphy, who join in a 'hearty meal' on his flesh, who burn out his eyes. Lishmahago's bride is the lustiest of all, able to eat and drink the other women under the table and consummate her marriage the same evening. In a moment of bathos, she is undone by her own excess, dying from 'eating too much raw bear'. In this perverse comic world, human food slips down nicely; it is animal meat that a woman cannot digest.

Smollett's account is singular. Although it derives from the same travel narratives as other representations of the time, it resolutely refuses to position Indians as the others of Britons. They are neither manly alternatives to effete Britons nor ignoble savages against whom white people define their own civilization. Instead, Smollett fixes on Indian women in order to make a misogynist satire on chivalry. The 'squaws' are embodiments of the gross sensual appetites that also motivate British women.

As Charlotte Sussman has shown in an astute critique of the episode,[6] Smollett uses Indians to explore the social effects of colonial involvement. According to Sussman, Smollett's Indians reveal a threefold anxiety produced by Britain's colonial role in America. First, they threaten simply to swallow Britons whole—to kill and consume them. Thus they remind readers of the precariousness of British rule in America's vast land. Second, they raise the spectre that whites will go native, as, in fact, many did, either being adopted after capture or by marrying into native nations. The purity and superiority of the white colony were both threatened if colonists preferred to become Indians. Third, empire produced a mass circulation of commodities, changing social desires and relationships. Hatchets, beads, and alcohol went to the Indians;

---

[6] See Sussman, *Consuming Anxieties*, 85.

furs came to Britain: both peoples became, more than ever before, consumers eager to acquire goods. Tabitha is one such consumer: her lust is as much for Indian dress and decorations as it is for Lishmahago. The colonial world is a world of trade and it creates a new class of transcultural people who flourish in one culture although they come from another. Lishmahago, for example, prospers as an adopted Miami, being elected sachem and 'acknowledged first warrior of the Badger tribe, and dignified with the name ... of Occocanastaogarora, which signifies *nimble as a weasel*' (Smollett, 229). Weasels, of course, are common in Scotland and are more often called cunning. Lishmahago is a clever improvisor, a man who succeeds by adapting himself to each new situation but who is not to be trusted. Back in Scotland, he is trading on his Indian experience, turning his authentic Indian adventure into a source of profit for the marriage market. His wedding present to Tabitha is a 'fur cloak of American sables'—dressing her like his Indian bride and emphasizing his position as a trader (on his American experience). In the consumerist world brought into being by the flow of people and goods into and out of the colonies, Lishmahago is a new figure, a homegrown exotic, a potential trickster with slippery social mobility.

Smollett, Sussman suggests, had adapted travel and captivity narratives in an innovative way, engendering a new comic figure for a colonial age. The comedy is uneasy, for Smollett satirizes commercial society as a compound of cupidity and selfishness, only, at the same time, to recognize a new cultural energy and celebrate a new, if grotesque, colonial identity. In this respect he joins Defoe's celebratory vision of colonial adventure in *Robinson Crusoe* to Swift's satiric attack on capitalist exploration in *Gulliver's Travels*, using an Indian encounter to do so. He was not alone, for one of the most popular stories of the entire eighteenth century focused on a man who was concerned only to trade on his Indian experience.

Inkle and Yarico features an English capitalist, a petty man of accounts who is voyaging to the West Indian colonies to make money. En route, he is shipwrecked and cast ashore in America, where the Indian maid Yarico rescues him. Pledging his love, he takes her to the West Indies, only to try to sell her into slavery. When he discovers she is pregnant by him, he raises her market price. The story was popularized by Richard Steele's rendition of it in the *Spectator* (1711). It was then retold for the rest of the century, in verse and on stage, reaching the height of popularity in the form of George Colman's comic opera of 1787, which received numerous performances in London and toured extensively throughout Britain.[7] *Inkle and Yarico* was a phenomenon that in its beginnings benefited from the publicity gained by the voyage to Britain of Pocahontas. Its enormous popularity undoubtedly led writers to try out Indian fictions, while its sentimental plot was easy to imitate.

The stereotype that *Inkle and Yarico* popularized was that of the Indian woman as an innocent, loving nature-child. Originating in seventeenth-century pastoralism, the figure of Yarico was a shepherdess transplanted to the New World. By the time of Colman's version, she had taken on Rousseauvian shadings too, since she was portrayed as being both more natural and more innocent than Indian men, who were depicted as bloodthirsty hunters. She, to use Rousseau's terms, was in a state of nature; they were one step removed from it. They were not, however, as far removed as Inkle, the young British capitalist, who thinks only of his own interest and puts a monetary value on everything. It is this newly powerful commercial ethos that the tale condemns. Thus a contrast between grasping colonial capitalism on the one hand, and innocent aboriginal subsistence on the other drives the story: the older contrasts of country versus city, Eden versus Babylon are transported onto the imperial system that, in the eighteenth century, was creating dramatic changes in Britons' sphere of thought and action.

The narrative is more interesting and was more popular for what it says about Britons' ideals and sentimental attachments than for anything it says about actual Native Americans. Indeed, so sketchy are its details about American Indians that reviewers, and even one later editor, assumed its aboriginal characters were really black Africans rather than 'red' Indians. In fact, it hardly matters whether they are African or Indian; the tale is simply concerned to show that all native women prefer white men. Inkle's failing is that he takes advantage of this, playing the lovelorn Yarico along and then trying to sell her into slavery. He has failed to act chivalrously: driven as Inkle is by money, Yarico, though she has saved his life, is worth only the price of her flesh. Thus Colman, like Smollett before him, critiqued colonialism by showing that it generates encounters based solely on consumption. Ideals and morals collapse into a kind of cannibalism. The difference is the tone. Writing before the American Revolution, Smollett celebrated, as much as satirized, the excess appetite colonialism released and the figures who turned colonial encounters to their account. Colman, writing as the

---

[7] *English Trader, Indian Maid: Representing Gender, Race, and Slavery in the New World: An Inkle and Yarico Reader*, ed. Frank Felsenstein (Baltimore and London, 1999).

nation lamented the brutality of the war it had fought to preserve its American colonies and as those laments precipitated a campaign to abolish slavery in the remaining colonies, was more simply critical and pathetic. He was abolitionist, anti-capitalist, concerned to warn of the immorality of abandoning the chivalric ethos that had smoothed over gender and class inequalities. Burke was to write in 1790 that, after the French Revolution, the 'age of chivalry is gone'.[8] Colman, writing just five years earlier, showed that, if so, the colonial system and the race relations that this system produced were to blame (as Burke himself implied when attacking Warren Hastings for his treatment of the native population when Governor General of Britain's colonies in India). Even as a pretence, an ideological mask, chivalry had irrevocably slipped, as Yarico's speeches show. Yet her critique is limited because she speaks as a stereotypical nature-child, not as a realized individual. And what she speaks for—the pastoral ideal—is not a liveable alternative to the commercial life. She and the Indian pastoral exist only as ideals against which the sins of actual commercial civilization can be judged. As a fictional Indian she is a purely rhetorical construct.

Colman fudges the ending of the tale for he makes sentiment save the conscience of the capitalist. Inkle is persuaded to relent at the last moment. He does not after all sell Yarico into slavery: love triumphs; Briton and Indian will marry, although they will not go back to the woods to live. Capitalism, after all, has a caring face and the values British people want to identify as national characteristics—decency, chivalry, honour, humour—are reasserted. Thus the opera raises issues about colonialism and race, opens the question of exploitation of Native Americans, only to assuage them in a sentimental ending of tears and laughter. This pattern was to be repeated in the later colonial romances in which the same issues were pressed much harder.

By 1796, when Robert Bage published *Hermsprong*, the English aristocracy seemed more threatened and more openly reactionary than at any time since the Civil War.[9] The revolutionary terror in France had struck fear into British landowners: the result was a government campaign of repression meant to root out threats to the existing social order. Smith's friends—peaceful reformists like Joseph Johnson and Joseph Priestley—were imprisoned and attacked. Bage was a provincial

[8] *Reflections on the Revolution in France* in *The Writings and Speeches of Edmund Burke*, gen. ed. Paul Langford, 17 vols. (Oxford, 1981–), VIII, 128.
[9] *Hermsprong; or Man as he is Not*, ed. Peter Faulkner (Oxford, 1985).

middle-class radical with connections in the same circle, including Erasmus Darwin and Priestley himself. In *Hermsprong* he expressed his contempt for a self-indulgent aristocracy for whom chivalry existed in name only and who abused their unmerited privilege. Also singled out for criticism are churchmen who toady to the landowners, interested only in their own advancement. Together, squire and parson impose a corrupt despotism over their neighbourhood. Into this petty world, Bage sends his hero, a stranger whose origin no one knows. Hermsprong first appears in an act of startling daring, rescuing Miss Campinet from the brink of a cliff when her horse bolts. To this act of athleticism and bravery he adds chivalry, when he aids Miss Campinet after she faints away from fear. A man of action, thrilling to touch, proud of speech, Hermsprong is the Byronic hero in prototype. He disdains the patronage of Campinet's father, the tyrannical and lecherous local squire Lord Grondale. Throughout the novel he speaks and acts against Grondale's abuse of power.

Where does Hermsprong come from? Already fascinated, Miss Campinet asks and he replies 'Amongst the aborigines of America . . . I was born a savage' (Bage, 73). It is his Indian upbringing that gives him his proud independence, makes him, in fact, a hero in the mould of the English liberals who admired the American revolutionaries and still cherished hopes for the French:

I cannot learn to offer incense at the shrines of wealth and power, nor at any shrines but those of probity and virtue. I cannot learn to surrender my opinion from complaisance, or from any principle of adulation. Nor can I learn to suppress the sentiments of a freeborn mind, from any fear, religious or political. Such uncourtly obduracy has my savage education produced. (Bage, 73)

For Hermsprong, and for Bage too, Indians were living embodiments of the fortunate rustics idealized by Horace. They suffer none of the ennui of the 'rich European' (Bage, 88) who is satiated and requires more and more refined (and perverted) pleasures to stimulate him. Indians fight, hunt, and then dance, play, and rest in peace. Yet they are not lacking intellect, for their 'two grand occupations [inventing songs and dances] require much of it' (Bage, 88). And though illiterate, 'what they do know, perhaps they know better' (Bage, 89). Here the novel reflects the latest thinking about tribal cultures: Bage values the Indians' oral culture in similar terms to Herder, Blair, and Ritson, who emphasized the aesthetic achievement of oral poetry.

Hermsprong gains his self-sufficiency, courage and pride from the Indians. He embodies liberal Britons' fantasy of renewing the morals of true gentility by encounter with an other that still lived as Britons themselves once had lived. But Hermsprong, like Ossian, is not, in the end, a Native American. Raised among them, he is by birth half French, half English, the son of Lord Grondale's elder brother. At the end, he gets girl and estate just as in *The Old Manor House*. The only good aristocrat, Bage suggests, is an Indianized one, a hybrid of true civilization and Native American savagery, a man that neither culture could have produced alone.

Given this view, it is not surprising that Hermsprong recommends emigration to America, accepting that only in the new country would honest merit be unfettered, that, in effect, the novel's conclusion was simply wishful thinking. By the late 1790s it was clear that a radical reform of English society would not occur through the renewal of the existing aristocracy. Savage chivalry met civilized privilege only in the fictional field of popular romance. To turn the fantasy into reality it would be necessary to leave Britain's shores for good or to bring about an overturning, rather than a mere reform, of the social order. Bage's friend Priestley left for America in 1794. Other radicals would follow.

It was, however, an earlier emigrant who became the most powerful proponent of a thoroughgoing revolution. Thomas Paine had left Britain for America in 1774. Once in the colony, he played a crucial role in preparing Americans for revolution. His distrust of Britain's governing classes, already acquired in Britain, helped determine the colonists that resistance, rather than compromise, must be their course. In his 1775 article *A Serious Thought*,[10] it is evident that Paine's distrust was deepened in America when he saw the colonial treatment of Indians and Africans:

And when I reflect on the use she hath made of the discovery of this new world—that the little paltry dignity of earthly kings hath been set up in preference to the great cause of the King of kings—That instead of Christian examples to the Indians, she hath basely tampered with their passions, imposed on their ignorance, and made them tools of treachery and murder. . . . When I reflect on these, I hesitate not for a moment to believe that the Almighty will finally separate America from Britain. Call it Independence or what you will, if it is the cause of God and humanity it will go on.

[10] Published in the *Pennsylvania Journal* 18 October 1775. *The Writings of Thomas Paine*, ed. Moncure Daniel Conway, 4 vols. (London, 1996), I, 65–6.

If here Indians play a rhetorical role in Paine's effort to rouse white Americans to a divinely justified rebellion, they soon impressed him in the flesh. In January 1777 he met chiefs of several Iroquois tribes at a council called, at the Indians' request, to discuss the Six Nations' future in an independent America. Acting as secretary of the commission sent by the Pennsylvania Assembly and the Continental Congress, Paine spent four days in discussion and concluded that 'the English government had but half the sense' of his main interlocutor, Chief Last Night.[11]

Paine's respect for Native Americans contrasted with the dismissive attitudes of other revolutionaries—including Washington and John Adams, who were angered by the fact that most remained neutral or aided the British. But Paine's respect, produced by an encounter engendered by American Revolution, became a fundamental part of his effort, in the 1790s, to precipitate a revolution in Britain. In 1795 he published *Agrarian Justice*, a work that went much further than Smith or Bage in its arguments about reform of Britain's landowning class. Paine's pamphlet argued for the redistribution of landowners' wealth. Reform of their feelings and morals was not enough, for it was the 'landed monopoly' itself that 'produced the greatest evil. It has dispossessed more than half the inhabitants of every nation of their natural inheritance... and has thereby created a species of poverty and wretchedness that did not exist before.'[12] To rectify this dispossession, landowners must accept that they owned only their cultivation—their improvement of the land, not the land itself.

Paine's demand derived, in part, from what he had realized about Native Americans. Like Adam Ferguson, Paine saw them as exemplars of life as white people lived it before commercial society. But Paine put Ferguson's comparisons in a new context, arguing not only that Indian life was an enviable stage in human progress but also that it was 'the natural and primitive state of man'.[13] In Paine's analysis, it was more natural because it was more egalitarian and it was more egalitarian because no individual had private property in land. The Indians were living examples of the original and just society in which 'the earth, in its natural ... state was, and ever would have continued to be, the common

---

[11] 'On the Question Will There Be War?', quoted in John Keane, *Tom Paine: A Political Life* (London, 1995), 148.

[12] *Agrarian Justice*, in *The Thomas Paine Reader*, ed. Michael Foot and Isaac Kramnick (Harmondsworth, 1987), 477.

[13] Ibid., 475.

property of the human race. In that state every man would have been born to property. He would have been a joint life proprietor with the rest in the property of soil, and in all its natural productions.' Indian life, Paine concluded, was 'a continual holiday, compared with the poor of Europe' but seemed 'abject when compared to the rich'.[14] The levelling implications of this remark were clear: the poor, now seeing themselves as worse off than people they had been taught to believe savages, were likely to resent their position; which was both unnatural and still more abject than they had thought. And the cause, they could see more clearly, was private ownership of land.

Paine's was a politically powerful manoeuvre: rather than oppose whites to Indians as civilized to savage he compared the two peoples on a scale of wealth and happiness. Indians, in his prose, acted as an example in his explanation of property's causes and as points of social comparison that would prick poor readers' sense of injustice. Indians were living evidence that an equal and just society was no mere chimera and that it was only realizable if the wealth and power that stemmed from landownership was redistributed.

Paine's proposals were political dynamite to Britain's governing classes: after all, political power, social authority and even participation in the political process depended on property ownership. Propertyless men, and all women, could not even vote. But Paine ultimately did not want his countrymen and women to live as communist Indians did. Property division, he accepted, brought the increased productivity needed to sustain a large population: there could be no return to hunting and gathering. Instead, landowners must pay a ground rent to the public purse, from which the propertyless would be supported.

There was another labouring-class campaigner who was still more radical than Paine on the issue of land. Thomas Spence, journalist and bookseller, published Paine's work, but took his views on agrarian justice a stage further. In his journal *Pig's Meat* (1793–96) he attacked the established orders and argued that land should be nationalized. Private landowners would be stripped of their property: all would rent their lands from the public purse. Following Paine, Spence used Native Americans as his rhetorical lever to prize open the existing system. In the frontispiece to the three-volume edition of *Pig's Meat* Spence shows a missionary speaking to three Indians.[15] The missionary

---

[14] *Agrarian Justice*, in *The Thomas Paine Reader*.
[15] *Pig's Meat; or Lessons for the Swinish Multitude*, 2nd edn., 3 vols. (London, 1793–5).

declares, 'God has enjoined you to be Christians, to pay rent and tythes, and become a Civilized People.' One of the Indians replies, 'If rent we once consent to pay, Taxes next you'll on us lay, And then our Freedom's poured away'; all the Indians then declare: 'with the beasts of the Wood we'll ramble for Food, And live in wild deserts and Caves; And live poor as Job, On the Skirts of the Globe, Before we'll consent to be Slaves, My Brave Boys, Before We'll consent to be Slaves!' Here the political allegory is double. Colonial America illustrates Britain and vice versa. Spence suggests that established religion is another of the ideological apparatuses by which the wealthy exploit the poor, being simply a means of persuading the poor that it is right to pay the dues that church and state exact. Spence also links colonial land hunger with domestic domination: each situation is revealed as exploitative by comparison with the other. The British poor are as colonized as American Indians, whose defiant reply, however, positions them as the freeborn proud Englishmen of that imperialist song 'Rule Britannia'.

There was a pressing reason for Spence's Indian allegory: the need to avoid prosecution for sedition and, after 1795, the need to avoid imprisonment without trial. It is for this reason that in his 1796 *Reign of Felicity, Being a Plan for the Civilizing the Indians of North America,* Spence adopts the persona of a farmer who imagines what he might say to an audience of Native Americans. The pretext is General Washington speaking in Congress of the practicability of civilizing Indians—still an unconquered independent people. By this indirect address Spence puts forward his communist programme for the nationalization of land, leading to universal suffrage.

O ye untainted uncorrupted sons of freedom, let me address you on this momentous occasion, with the earnestness and warmth of a friend, though with eloquence far below the importance of the subject. You alone of all the wretched inhabitants of the earth, are yet unwarped by slavish customs, and can profit by advice. Hearken then to the disinterested lessons of a man that pants for the emancipation of all the human race, that has from his infancy endeavoured to discover a system of society, funded on equality, justice, and the individual independence of mankind. But beware of him that aims to establish privileged orders, for he wishes himself principally to profit thereby; whereas the preacher of equal rights and privileges must undoubtedly be honest, as he thereby shuts out himself from any pre-eminence.

Attend then, Indians, now is the most critical moment of your political exist-ence, upon the turn of your opinion depends now the everlasting independence or degradation of your race.—Yes, on the determination to whom you will pay your rents, depends everything valuable in this life.

How then shall we assist you through this critical dilemma?—shall we send a swarm of Clergy among you to receive your rents, and employ you in building churches and monasteries?—Or shall we send a host of armed Israelites, Normans, or Spaniards, to take possession of your country, make you hewers of wood, and drainers of water, and employ you in building them temples, castles, and palaces; nay condemn you to dig your own mines, and in short, to claim you as their eternal tenants and vassals. ... Or shall we advise you to create Lords from among yourselves, who to all intents and purposes would be as pernicious and tyrannical to you as foreigners? Forbid it reason, forbid it justice—No, rather than strengthen the hands of tyrants with your rents, give them to the fishes of the sea—throw them into some bottomless abyss, from whence they will never more rise to enslave you by force, or corrupt you by influence or bribery. Methinks now Indians, I see you wisely determined, and just ready to drop those dreaded rents into the gulp. But hold, my lads, hold! Let us first try if we can hit upon some expedient to save this hard earned wealth from perdition, and yet save your liberties—Now I think I have hit upon it. Is not the public the Lord of the Manor? Does not the country belong to the inhabitants? And is not the land public property?

The public then is Lord of the Manor, and has an indefeasible right to the rents, and will never use them to your hurt.[16]

Spence's rhetoric is as impassioned as his ideas are radical. He calls to the people to awaken and change, petitioning the landless labourers of Britain as landless Native Americans. Indians provide Spence with an ideal of social organization (albeit one that Spence will modify for Britain where money and rent have long been in use) but Indians also provide an ideal gestural audience because they retain the power of decision about their futures (at least rhetorically), thus reminding British readers that they too, despite their history of submission to landlords, have a choice. The allegory works, in effect, to defamiliarize and empower British labourers by making them imagine themselves as Indian others.

By the mid 1790s imagining oneself in a different political and social Britain from the established one was highly dangerous. Paine was in France, having fled Britain with a treason judgement against him. He returned to America in 1802. Priestley was already there. Other radicals who remained in Britain were in retreat, or in jail. To a younger

---

[16] Thomas Spence, *The Reign of Felicity, Being a Plan for the Civilizing the Indians of North America* (London, 1796), 7–8.

generation who were inspired by Paine's and Spence's ideas, emigration to the land where Indians were living, rather than fictional, beings seemed the best solution. That it seemed so owed much, however, to those fictional beings—to the noble and natural primitives who appeared, in novels, plays and political pamphlets, to possess everything that was lacking in repressed and repressive Britain.

7

Native Patriarchs—Pantisocracy and the Americanization of Wales

'Coleridge and I will go together, and either find repose in an Indian wig-wam—or from an Indian tomahawk.'[1]

In the summer of 1794 Robert Southey and Samuel Taylor Coleridge had decided that only by leaving their homeland could they escape political repression and live at liberty. They drew up an emigration scheme and recruited friends and relatives to join them. Together, the emigrants would set up a democratic community without personal property and without servants. Pantisocracy, as Coleridge named it, would be a realization of the just society and natural life about which the philosophers William Godwin and Jean Jacques Rousseau had written.[2] Dedicated to agriculture and literature, the Pantisocrats would live in equality, peace, and harmony, like the Indians among whom they would settle (or, at least, like the Indians as portrayed by Rousseau and Raynal).[3]

By January 1795, the Pantisocracy project was collapsing. Southey was anxious over its costs and worried about his readiness to live, like Indians and frontiersmen, by subsistence farming. He was panicky as well—afraid that local Indians might bear out Carver's stories of tomahawk-wielding savages rather than Raynal's tales of innocent pastoralists. And so he advised a relocation to the less remote and less wild wilds of Wales. There too, he suggested, the Pantisocrats

---

[1] *New Letters of Robert Southey*, ed. Kenneth Curry, 2 vols. (New York and London, 1965), I, 70.

[2] Southey quoted Rousseau on the beauties of unspoilt landscape, and declared that Rousseau's deism 'expresses some of my religious opinions better than I could do it myself' in a letter of 4th August 1793. See *New Letters of Robert Southey*, I, 33.

[3] Southey read Raynal, having borrowed the English edition of 1776 from Bristol Library, in early 1795.

might live out their radical ideals beyond the conventional British social hierarchy and at one with unappropriated nature. In reply, Coleridge, who had firsthand experience of the power of convention and hierarchy in furthest Wales, was emphatic: 'As to the Welsh scheme—pardon me—it is nonsense—We must go to America' (*CL*, I: 132, 150). This response sounded Pantisocracy's death-knell: unable to agree on their destination, the two radicals blamed each other for backsliding, argued, and separated. Neither they nor their recruits ever went to America and found the hoped-for 'repose in an Indian wig-wam'.

The Pantisocracy project foundered fast, but its effects lingered for forty years. Its rapid collapse, that is to say, left Southey and Coleridge to assess why it failed and to develop other discourses in which they could explore its aims and reconsider their commitments. They moved to political journalism and they turned to poetry. In fact, Pantisocracy and its fall-out helped shape the radical writing for which they were first famous. The themes of that writing—opposition to British imperialism, enthusiasm for American liberty, idealization of rural life—have their origin, in part, in the hopes and fears of the Pantisocrats. So does a theme that has been less noticed but is bound up with the others—uneasy fascination with Native Americans. It is this theme that I shall investigate here, showing, in particular, that not only was Pantisocracy modelled, to a greater extent than has been realized, on a representation of Native American society, but that it was by further exploring this representation that, in part, Coleridge and Southey developed the discourse we have come to call Romantic. In the case of the two former Pantisocrats, Indians helped give rise to Romanticism. Both men became writers who brought Indians—and Indian culture—home to Britain when they could no longer be emigrants escaping that home for the backwoods of Native America. In the process they instituted a movement that was to persist in their work and that of their Romantic heirs—a rhetorical movement from Britain to America and back again.

First, Pantisocracy. From the beginning, the scheme was an anti-colonialist colony. It expressed Coleridge's and Southey's discontent with the repression that, as they saw it, Britain exported to its empire. This discontent was expressed in the verse Coleridge was writing at the time. In 'Religious Musings' he condemned Britain's priests and politicians for fomenting violence and slavery in Europe and Africa: 'o'er some plain that steameth to the Sun / Peopled with Death; or where more hideous TRADE / Loud laughing packs his bales of human anguish; / I will raise up a mourning . . .' (*CPW*, I, part i, lines 139–42).

On paper, the Pantisocrats were bellicose sympathizers with revolutionary violence. When they planned their emigrant community,
however, they aimed to find a location so pristine that no wars of
liberation would be necessary. It was because America had already liberated itself from British empire, and because their peaceful revolutionary
hero, Joseph Priestley, had already emigrated there, that they chose
the land of Washington and Franklin. They chose not to settle in an
established town, but near the Susquehannah river in Pennsylvania,
where Priestley was living and where land could be purchased. That
they chose the Susquehannah also stemmed from a fantasy about Indian
life, a fantasy of 'repose in a ... wig-wam' that stemmed from the
idealizing prose of the revolutionary hero Franklin. The Pantisocrats
read Franklin's 1784 *Remarks Concerning the Savages*, a work intended
to encourage emigration to the United States and to portray Indians as
models of the kind of white people Franklin wanted to populate the new
nation—virtuous, self-reliant rural dwellers. Franklin wrote specifically
about the Susquehannah Indians, and Southey quoted him verbatim in
the pantisocratic poem *Madoc* (1805):

There is in every village of the Susquehannah Indians, a vacant dwelling called
the Stranger's House. When a traveller arrives within hearing of a village, he
stops and halloos, for it is deemed uncivil to enter abruptly. Two old men lead
him to the house, and then go round to the inhabitants, telling them a stranger
is arrived fatigued and hungry. They send them all they can spare, bring tobacco
after they are refreshed, and then ask questions whence they come and whither
they go.

In Southey's poem this passage turns into a scene in which Madoc,
fleeing oppression in Britain, is welcomed by Native Americans just as
the Pantisocrats hoped to be welcomed:

> The elders of the land
> Came forth, and led us to an ample hut,
> Which in the center of their dwellings stood,
> The Stranger's House. They eyed us wondering,
> Yet not for wonder ceased they to observe
> Their hospitable rites; from hut to hut
> The tidings ran that strangers were arrived,
> Fatigued and hungry and athirst; anon,
> Each from his means supplying us, came food
> And beverage such as cheers the weary man.[4]

---

[4] Bk V, ll. 199 (note on p. 284) *Madoc*, ed. Lynda Pratt, vol. II of *Southey*.

Coleridge shared Southey's hope of a warm welcome, but sought reassurance that Franklin was right. In late August 1794 Coleridge had a series of meetings with an old schoolfriend who had emigrated to America and had now returned to Britain to sell land in the US. This man recommended the Susquehannah 'from it's excessive Beauty, & it's security from hostile Indians' (*CL*, I, 99). An enthusiastic Coleridge extolled the area's virtues to Southey, and their destination was confirmed.

If the choice of destination reflected white men's notions about Indians, so did the type of society the Pantisocrats wished to set up. The 'generalization of property and the equalization of labour', in Southey's succinct formulation,[5] would, they intended, remove injustice: a programme immediately derived from Godwin, but ultimately patterned after Hebrew and early Christian society, as described by a series of historians of religion by whom Godwin was influenced. By 1795, Coleridge was using these historians as the sources for public lectures on the 'admirable Division of Property' in the Mosaic Commonwealth (*Lects 1795*, 119). The Mosaic insistence that property could not be amassed was, he declared, 'beautiful. ... Property is Power and equal Property equal Power. A Poor Man is necessarily more or less a Slave' (*Lects 1795*, 126). Pantisocracy, it appears, would have been (at least from Coleridge's perspective in 1795) a realization in America of the ancient Hebrew constitution.

Southey and Coleridge knew from what they had read about America that they would not be the only people living there like the ancient Hebrews. According to Paine and Spence, Native Americans' way of life revealed the very equality that Coleridge most valued about the Mosaic commonwealth. Jonathan Carver wrote that the Dakota Sioux 'in their common state are strangers to all distinction of property' and 'Governed by the plain and equitable laws of nature, every one is rewarded solely according to his deserts; and their equality of condition, manner, and privileges ... animates them with a pure and truly patriotic spirit, that tends to the general good of the society to which they belong' (*Carver*, 247). James Adair wrote 'I have observed with much inward satisfaction, the community of goods that prevailed among them, after the patriarchal manner, and that of the primitive Christians' (*Adair*, 17). American Indians, Adair argued, were descended from the ancient Hebrews, from the dispersal of the tribes in the time of Noah.

[5] Southey, *New Letters*, I, 90.

Adair's was only the most detailed presentation of what was an old argument. In 1643 the early colonist Roger Williams[6] had proposed the idea that the Indians had reached America from Tartary, an idea subsequently taken up by Carver. According to Williams, the Indians' life was an echo of the patriarchal community of which the Bible spoke. Rather than being racially inferior to white people, Indians were images of the culture of equality, brotherhood, and commonality described in the Bible and realized by the early Christians. Blake suggested something similar in *The Marriage of Heaven and Hell* (1790), where he not only depicted Welsh bards as prophets of liberty but also made them cousins of both the biblical prophets and Native American shamans. When Ezekiel is asked why he

ate dung, and lay so long on his right and left side. He answered, 'The desire of raising other men into a perception of the infinite. This the North American tribes practise, and is he honest who resists his genius or conscience only for the sake of present ease or gratification.'[7]

Indians, like ancient Hebrews, served as models of people untainted by urban life, as people with untamed imaginations able to perceive what most of the British, cosseted and complicit as they seemed, could not.

As for Blake, so for the radical Southey and Coleridge: the Jewish society that the Pantisocrats were consciously emulating lived on, unselfconsciously, among the Native American tribes. Perhaps, in the light of this alignment, Southey's hope of finding repose in a wig-wam was an expression of his sense that Indians might welcome Pantisocracy as a fellow commonwealth of equality—as a re-creation of an ancient community that, unbeknownst to the Indians, descended from the biblical times.

Settled on the Susquehannah as their destination, expecting Indian hospitality, the Pantisocrats still harboured doubts. Hostile Indians, it seemed, did exist, even if the valley was secure. Travel writers had told them so. In December 1793 Southey had expressed his hopes and fears in a letter: 'Fancy only me in America; imagine my ground uncultivated since the creation, and see me wielding the axe, now to cut down the tree, and now the snakes that nestled in it. ... So this your friend will realize the romance of Cowley, and even outdo the seclusion of

[6] Roger Williams, *A Key Into the Language of America*, ed. John J. Teunissen and Evelyn J. Hinz (Detroit, 1973), 85–7.
[7] *The Marriage of Heaven and Hell*, Plate 13, in David V. Erdman (ed.), *The Complete Poetry and Prose of William Blake*, rev. edn. (New York and London, 1988), 39.

Rousseau; till at last comes an ill-looking Indian with a tomahawk, and scalps me,—a most melancholy proof that society is very bad, and that I shall have done very little to improve it! So vanity, vanity will come from my lips, and poor Southey will either be cooked for a Cherokee, or oysterized by a tiger'.[8]

Southey's fear may well have reflected his reading. Coleridge's similar anxieties undoubtedly had travel narratives and histories as their source. These books told him that, in 1778, the Susquehannah valley had been pillaged by a band of Indians led by British soldiers. Coleridge used the incident to indict his government for employing these 'savages' and human 'tygers' to kill and scalp the white Susquehannah settlers (*Lects 1795*, 56). The Indians, manipulated to serve the interest of the British empire, had despoilt a pastoral and peaceful colony. They were, he said, 'Hell-hounds' violating a pastoral American Eden, armed with tomahawks of British manufacture. Even the America he had longed to live in, the America in which Indian society offered a model of freedom and virtue that white revolutionaries like Franklin could copy, would not, he saw, prove a home untainted by the effects of colonialism.

It was not, finally, fear of Indian attack that stopped the Pantisocrats from sailing. They couldn't raise money to buy the land and they began to disagree about the issue of equality and property. Yet as they tried the idea of Wales as a second-choice location, and as they reconsidered the merits of the scheme in their writings and lectures, the nature of Indian society came to preoccupy them deeply. Southey became a recognized commentator on American Indians, by virtue of works such as the poem that sprang from Pantisocracy—*Madoc*, the massive *History of Brazil*, and the late romance *A Tale of Paraguay*. *Madoc*, especially, explored the relationship between Indians and white colonists, and it is *Madoc* I shall consider in detail here.

Southey began the poem during 1794 and 1795, when Pantisocracy still beckoned. He drafted several versions before finally publishing a far more conservative text in 1805. I look first at the poem's radical origins, before considering its published form. In 1794 *Madoc* was intended as a poem that would supersede the epic as traditionally written. It would be a romance, a semi-mythical treatment of the political and social ideals that had been defined in the Pantisocracy project. Beginning in medieval Wales, it told the story of Prince Madoc who, in a bid to

---

[8] To Grosvenor Charles Bedford, 14 December 1793, *The Life and Correspondence of Robert Southey*, ed. C. C. Southey, 6 vols. (London, 1849–50), I, 196.

escape the political repression that his royal brother, in league with the Saxon king, had spread through his homeland, set sail westwards with a band of willing exiles. Together, they voyaged until, hundreds of years before Columbus, they discovered America, where they settled. Madoc then returned to Wales to collect more emigrants, before sailing across the Atlantic again.

The *Madoc* that Southey wrote in 1794/5 was rewritten several times, reflecting Southey's changing views, before 1805. Revised and extended, the published poem not only told the story of medieval Wales and Madoc's departure, but also featured his encounters with two Native American peoples—the Hoaman tribe and the Aztecas. Thus emigrant Britons were brought into direct contact with Native Americans, although Southey had, of course, neither been to America nor met the members of any tribe. But he had read widely in travel narratives, and his copious notes demonstrate his knowledge of Adair, Charlevoix, Carver and other accounts of Indians. Indeed it was probably in passages from Carver that Southey found the basis of his plot, since Carver cites an ancient Welsh tradition to suggest that Madoc preceded Columbus—a history of Wales written by David Powell:

This historian says, that Madoc, one of the sons of Prince Owen Gwynnith, being disgusted at the civil wars which broke out between his brothers, after the death of their father, fitted out several vessels, and having provided them with every thing necessary for a long voyage, went in quest of new lands to the westward of Ireland; there he discovered very fertile countries, but destitute of inhabitants; when landing part of his people, he returned to Britain, where he raised new Levies, and afterwards transported them to his colony.

(*Carver*, 187)

Southey's plot follows Carver and Powell, save that when Madoc lands in Florida, he does encounter inhabitants—the Hoaman Indian tribe, who pay tribute to the dominant Aztecas. His Welsh emigrants, that is to say, went further south than the Pantisocrats ever intended. James Adair had written lovingly of the Chickasaws of Georgia and Florida, and his portrait influenced the poem. According to Adair, the lands of the deep south were ideal for colonization, and he urged the US administration to 'promote a spirit of emigration among the families of the crowded northern colonies'. Agricultural settlers would be rewarded with a fertile Eden: 'all kinds of vegetables planted, or sowed in their fields, gardens and orchards, either for profit or pleasure, would grow to greater perfection, and with less art and labour, in this tract, than any in Europe, so fruitful is the soil, and favourable the climate' (*Adair*,

458–9). William Bartram's descriptions of Florida as 'an Elysium . . . where the wandering Siminole, the naked red warrior, roams at large, and after the vigorous chase retires from the scorching heat of the meridian sun' also shaped Southey's words (*Bartram*, 105).

In 1794–95 Southey aimed to transform the epic genre by reorienting its traditional subject matter.[9] Instead of celebrating the foundation of the nation in which he wrote (as Virgil and Spenser had done), he sought to show that true heroism lay in escaping from Britain, and the nationalism that dominated Britain, and in adopting an alternative, radical way of life, one which learnt from peoples who were normally considered primitive. Thus he took from his travel narrative sources not only the Edenic location of Florida but also information about Indian customs, information that suggested that British emigrants could rediscover from Native American society the virtues that were under attack in their homeland. He offered, in effect, Indians as exemplars for the British, making his own poem, in the process, an intended hybrid of British radicalism and Indian culture (as seen by white travellers).

It was the combination of emotional openness and adherence to tradition that Southey most admired in Indian culture. He borrowed from Adair a description of burial customs that served to show Indians' 'decent reverence', their natural religion, their ceremonial order, and their respect for elders. Adair suggested that they possessed an untutored natural tenderness—an open sensibility encouraged rather than, as in Britain, suppressed or perverted by the dominant social codes.[10] And he quoted in full a description by Carver, using it to gain the reader's sympathy for the Indian 'queen' Erillyab:

The men, to shew how great their sorrow is, pierce the flesh of their arms, above the elbows, with arrows; the scars of which I could perceive on those of every rank, in a greater or less degree; and the women cut and gash their legs with sharp broken flints, till the blood flows very plentifully.

Whilst I remained among them, a couple whose tent was adjacent to mine, lost a son of about four years of age. The parents were so much affected at the death of their favourite child, that they pursued the usual testimonies of grief with such uncommon rigour, as through the weight of sorrow and loss of blood, to occasion the death of the father. The woman, who had hitherto been inconsolable, no sooner saw her husband expire, than she dried up her tears, and appeared cheerful and resigned.

---

[9] For a detailed discussion of this aim see Lynda Pratt, 'Revising the National Epic: Coleridge, Southey, *Madoc*', *Romanticism*, 2/2 (1996), 149–63.

[10] *Madoc*, Part 1, bk VIII, ll. 84, 101 (*Southey*, II, 84–5, 290–1), *Adair*, 180–1.

As I knew not how to account for so extraordinary a transition, I took an opportunity to ask her the reason of it; telling her at the same time, that I should have imagined the loss of her husband would rather have occasioned an increase of grief, than such a sudden diminution of it.

She informed me, that as the child was so young when it died, and unable to support itself in the country of spirits, both she and her husband had been apprehensive that its situation would be far from happy; but no sooner did she behold its father depart for the same place, who not only loved the child with the tenderest affection, but was a good hunter, and would be able to provide plentifully for its support, than she ceased to mourn. She added, that she now saw no reason to continue her tears, as the child on whom she doated was happy.

[. . .]

Her subsequent conduct confirmed the favourable opinion I had just imbibed; and convinced me, that notwithstanding this apparent suspension of her grief, some particles of that reluctance to be separated from a beloved relation which is implanted either by nature or custom in every human heart, still lurked in hers. I observed that she went almost every evening to the foot of the tree, on a branch of which the bodies of her husband and child were laid, and after cutting off a lock of her hair, and throwing it on the ground, in a plaintive melancholy song bemoaned its fate.[11]

Here radical sensibility turns out to have a prior natural home among American Indians. In pointing his British readers towards Native American virtues, Southey continues the Rousseauvian tactic of criticizing the corruptions of civilization, suggesting that the religious feeling of 'savages' is more natural and honest than the teaching of churches.

In presenting Native Americans as exemplars for his Welsh heroes, Southey was saying something quite specific about a kinship between two rural, radical cultures. He had wanted to relocate Pantisocracy to Wales because he hoped its rural remoteness and social difference would allow an internal emigration from the repressive conditions of Tory England. He also knew that many scholars, keen to revive the neglected culture of the Welsh, had found it to have much in common with that of Native Americans. It was in the figure of the bard that Wales—or rather the romantic Wales invented by antiquarians in the later eighteenth century—came to resemble Native America. Scholars had, since the 1720s, been praising the oral poetry of the Indians. Adair, in 1775, said this about it: 'their style is adorned with images, comparisons, and strong metaphors like the Hebrews; and equal in

[11] *Madoc*, Part 2, bk VI, ll. 102–3 (*Southey*, II, 147, 322–3), Carver, *Travels*, 403–7.

allegories to any of the eastern nations. . . . Their poetry is seldom exact in numbers, rhymes, or measure: it may be compared to prose in music, or a tunable way of speaking. The period is always accompanied with a sounding vehemence, to inforce their musical speech' (*Adair*, 61).

Such views reflected a fashion for the primitive, with American Indians crucial because they seemed to be one of the few remaining *living* examples of an oral culture, in which all men were poets and in which body and words were united. Soon, Britons at home assimilated the Indian into the figure of the ancient bardic poet. Like the dying Scottish bard Ossian who was romanticized by Macpherson, Indians were made to vicariously satisfy a wish for a life that embodied a natural nobility and promised organic wholeness. The literary Indian, like his Celtic counterpart, was created to embody what polite civilization, by definition, excluded. Unlike the ancient Celts, however, he still existed. Thomas Gray's 'The Bard' (1757) made the link obvious for it imagined a Welsh bard, lamenting the victory of the Saxons, but breathing defiance and revenge in poetic strains even as he died.[12] Gray was fascinated by both American Indian and Welsh oral poetry. His bard is a composite of what he had learned from the fashion for both 'primitive' traditions, as his comments to another of his poems, 'The Progress of Poesy' (1757), suggest: 'Extensive influence of poetic Genius over the remotest and most uncivilized nations: its connection with liberty, and the virtues that naturally attend on it [See the Erse, Norwegian, and Welch Fragments, the Lapland and American songs.]'. Gray, that is to say, imagined Native Americans, like the Welsh, as uncivilized people whose poetic genius inspired them to sing of freedom. In 'The Progress of Poesy' he pictured the 'savages' of North and South America as bards:

> In climes beyond the solar road,
> Where shaggy forms o'er ice-built mountains roam,
> The Muse has broke the twilight-gloom
> To chear the shiv'ring Native's dull abode.
> And oft, beneath the od'rous shade
> Of Chili's boundless forests laid,
> She deigns to hear the savage Youth repeat
> In loose numbers wildy sweet
> Their feather-cinctured Chiefs, and dusky Loves.
> Her track, wher'er the Goddess roves,

---

[12] *Thomas Gray and William Collins: Poetical Works*, ed. Roger Lonsdale (Oxford, 1977), 52–8.

> Glory pursue, and generous Shame,
> Th'unconquerable Mind, and Freedom's holy flame.
>
> (ll. 54–65)[13]

So too Southey's Wales. Like Gray's, it was a place of bards and warriors, of eloquence and defiance of colonizers—a place shaped by his
prior idealization of noble savages in America. Thus his representation of the British rural landscape and its people—a representation
that helped to constitute what we have learnt to call Romanticism—was, in part pre-formed by his idealization of America and
its native Indians. In what he had read in Carver, Adair and other
travellers, in the Indian songs he had admired and imitated, Southey
found a home in which his political and social ideals could take
root, a remote home that he proceeded to bring back to the nearer shores of Wales when American emigration proved too risky and
impractical.

By the end of the eighteenth century, many Welsh intellectuals
accepted that Welsh was derived from Hebrew and that the nation
originated in the line of Gomer, or of Samothes (both Noah's grand-
sons).[14] Just like Native Americans, the Welsh were direct descendants
of the ancient Hebrews—via the Druids who had come from the East
before settling in Wales and inspiring later generations of poet-singers.
In 1784 Edward Jones published his *Musical and Poetical Relicks of the
Welsh Bards*, with a frontispiece engraving quoting Gray's 'Bard'. Bardic
poetry, Jones said, proved the 'very high degree of cultivation' of the
Welsh in ancient times. That poetry, Jones continued, suffered under
'the tyranny exercised by the English over the conquered nation.'[15]
Southey was to quote Jones's translations in *Madoc*. Jones made an
explicit connection between the Welsh and Native Americans, for he
declared that, before Columbus, Welsh bards had referred to Madoc's
discovery of a land to the west. And Edward Williams, the self-styled

---

[13] *Gray and Collins*, ed. Lonsdale, 46–51. I am grateful to Adam Rounce for drawing
my attention to this poem.

[14] On the Welsh belief that they descended from the Hebrews, and that Welsh and
Hebrew were related languages, see E. Wyn James, ' "The New Birth of a People":
Welsh Language and Identity and the Welsh Methodists, c. 1740–1820', in *Religion and
National Identity: Wales and Scotland, c. 1700–2000*, ed. Robert Pope (Cardiff, 2001),
14–42 (20–23).

[15] Jones, *Musical and Poetical Relicks of the Welsh Bards: Preserved by Tradition, and
Authentic Manuscripts, from Remote Antiquity; Never Before Published* (London, 1784),
1–2, 10.

Iolo Morganwg, of whom Southey wrote 'he had more knowledge of the traditions and antiquities of his own country than ... will ever be possessed by any one after him' then took up Madoc's 'discovery', radicalizing it in the process.[16] By 1792 Morganwg regarded the bardic lore as 'the patriarchal religion and theology', and argued that Madoc had exported it to America.[17] Now, he suggested, more Welsh people should follow suit, emigrating to create a Welsh colony that would live out the ideals of the French revolutionaries—'the purest principles of Justice, Peace and Liberty'.[18] The colonists, he hoped, would be welcomed by Madoc's descendants, a tribe of Indians who still spoke Welsh.

The Madoc story was to provide Southey with the genesis of his poem, designed to contribute to the Welsh national revival and to establish Southey's own reputation. It was also to lead to several efforts to locate Madoc's descendants, a tribe of Welsh Indians who had gradually moved north from the Florida landfall. These were unsuccessful, and Southey accepted in the published *Madoc* that the tribe could not exist. Yet this did not stop him predicating his whole poem on similarities between the medieval Welsh and the American people. He rewrote the Welsh past in terms of what travel accounts told him of the Native American present: the noble bards and orators of the American plains and valleys were converted into his medieval Welsh heroes. This, of course, was only to take one stage further the Americanization of the Celts that, in Scotland, Ferguson, Blair and Macpherson had already begun. Thus Southey gave the Welsh pride in their priority as the culture in which liberty and patriarchal virtue was preserved. But he did so by a sort of reverse colonization, depicting the Welsh past with an ideal derived from travellers in America, who were themselves steeped in the fashion for the primitive. Ultimately this was a circular process of import/export in which Wales and America shaped each other, but what drove the representation of both was an English radical's need to find a home for a successful alternative to his own repressive national culture. First, the far west is idealized as the opposite—or other—of England, then its supposed character is relocated in the near west, closer to home. America, that is to say, is transplanted into Wales, part of Britain but opposite to England and its civilization. Wales becomes a colonial/local hybrid, conceived *by the English*, on the model of

[16] Letter of 24 January 1827, in *Life and Correspondence*, V, 285.
[17] Quoted in Gwyn A. Williams, *Madoc: The Making of a Myth* (London, 1979), 104.
[18] Quoted in Williams, *Madoc*, 134.

America, as so near-but-yet-so-far from the dominant culture from which they write.

In the mid-1790s Southey and Coleridge hero-worshipped the American revolutionaries and idealized Native Americans, because they welcomed their revolutionary freedom from British colonialism. Southey brought this idealized view of the land of Franklin and Washington, of heroic and noble savages, back to Wales, hoping to find in Welsh culture a similarly vigorous natural liberty that would serve as a ground for resistance to the English. By 'the English' Southey not only meant the English government of Pitt, but the common people who were complicit with that repression. The Welsh, he imagined, might, like Indians, be resistant to the mind-forged manacles that fettered the English.

In the 1805 *Madoc*, Southey stresses the Welsh admiration for the Indians as soon as the Welshmen land in America. The Welsh bard Iolo finds his unwritten lore is exceeded by that of the Indians: he is 'a child in knowledge' compared with them. Madoc, the hero, himself sings a bardic song to the harp, and Southey quotes the recently translated bardic triads as the epigraph to the whole poem. This aligns what he intended to be his major work with a bardic culture that will flourish again in America when extinct in Wales—if not because of the actual presence of a tribe of Welsh Indians in America then by virtue of Southey's own Welsh/American poem which he identifies as a new/old bardic song. *Madoc*, that is to say, is a would-be hybrid, an English version of a Welsh bardic poem as reconstructed, centuries later, by a scholar as steeped in Native American song as in medieval Welsh. Coleridge was to attempt something similar when he added the marginal glosses to 'The Rime of the Ancient Mariner': it became a Romantic enterprise to construct poems that commented upon their own historical narratives by incorporating a multilayered apparatus of texts, narrators and notes from different periods. *Madoc*, as the reviewers pointed out, was a sort of archive of historians' commentaries on the Welsh and Indian peoples it described.

If Wales had been a seat of liberty, why not settle there or endorse its present-day radical culture? Because by 1805 Southey knew he was colonizing the past when he idealized Welsh bardism and heroism. Indeed, *Madoc* is also a political allegory of the defeat of radicalism in 1790s Britain—revolutionaries did not find welcome in Wales when fleeing from English persecution, as John Thelwall found when hounded out of his refuge near Brecon, as Coleridge discovered when abused as a democrat in Bala, and as Southey realized in the vale of Neath, when a landlord refused to let him, as a radical, rent the house in which he hoped to find rural peace. The published *Madoc* replaces Pantisocracy's Welsh location with another—with an emigration in time rather than one through space. Southey returns to medieval Wales, and to its transplantation into America, when he cannot find a refuge for liberty in contemporary Wales and cannot cross the Atlantic to America either. As such, it is Southey's equivalent to *The Prelude*—not an emigration within the poet's own mind, but one to an ideal past where the defeat of radical hopes can be repaired.

Comparisons with *The Prelude* are a reminder that Southey's Romanticism is social and political where Wordsworth's is personal and introspective. But while this wider scope reveals that Southey was more determined than his Grasmere neighbour to dramatize public issues, it also left plenty of room for his own hesitancies, prejudices, and blindspots to be displayed. And indeed the Welsh/American ideal past of *Madoc* often proved, despite his attempts at hybridization, unresolved or self-contradictory. Southey responded to the ambivalence he felt with regard to Native Americans by attempting to subject the relationships between white emigrants and Indian inhabitants to a static fixed order. And so, as he revised the poem he began in 1794, he undercut his own initial attempt to imagine a hybrid culture arising from the union of the emigrants and the locals. Even at the levels of plot and location, Southey retreated from the uncanny possibility that he had at first entertained—that his Welsh emigrant had metamorphosed into a Native American founder of an Indian civilization in America. Moreover, Southey's portrait of social interactions in the contact zone was simplistic, undermining the cross-cultural similarities that it ostensibly existed to reveal. Unsure whether Indians would welcome exiles from Britain in their wig-wams or with their tomahawks, Southey grouped Native Americans into two contrasting and stereotypical peoples. In *Madoc* the Hoamen are noble savages—rural, oral, natural, but vulnerable to the corrupting influence of others because they are innocent. The Aztecas, on the other hand, are civilized, urban, sophisticated, barbarous and hierarchical. The Hoamen accept the Welsh; the Aztecas reject them.

It is the relationship of the Hoamen and the Welsh that best preserves Southey's original enthusiasm over the idea that indigenous cultures were organic alternatives to repressive and hierarchical societies such as England's. Nevertheless, Southey's Welsh are never tempted to abandon their beliefs or customs in favour of Indian practices, however much they recognize a kinship with certain, localized, aspects of Hoaman society. The kinship lies in the open expression of feeling and in the ability to express that feeling movingly in an oral form that is both traditional and spontaneous. For example, the Hoaman 'queen', Erillyab, is sublime in her calm dignity as she narrates her grief over her father's death:

> My father fell
> In battle for his people, and his sons
> Fell by his side; they perish'd, but their names
> Are with the names we love, . . . their happy souls
> Pursue in fields of bliss the shadowy deer
>
> (Part 2, Bk VI, ll. 99–103)

Erillyab's words here, derived from the travel narrative of Carver, with their vision of the spiritual presence of the dead in nature, are some of the most moving in the poem. Southey gives her sublimity and dignity so as to make his readers see her as the heroine.

Yet though Erillyab is admirable, she ultimately defers to the emigrants. Madoc proposes they should 'hold united reign, / O'er our united people; by one faith, / One interest bound' (Part 2, Bk XXIV, ll. 30–2). But this is a briefly indulged fantasy, for Southey prefers one in which a grateful people ask for a subordinate position under Madoc's governorship. Erillyab replies 'Dear Friend, and brother dear! enough for me / Beneath the shadow of thy shield to dwell, / And see my people, by thy fostering care, / Made worthy of their fortune' (Part 2, Bk XXIV, ll. 39–42). Here the image of the shield is important since it represents in chivalric terms the technological superiority in arms that will allow the iron-clad Welsh to triumph over the Aztecs (who used copper but not iron). It asks us to see Madoc's military power as a form of knightly duty to protect a damsel in distress. Traditional British gender relations, in effect, naturalize the colonists' assumption of control. The Welsh will be the rulers, rather than the equals, of the Indians they admire. After all, the Indians' queen asks them to be so.

Erillyab is not the only Hoaman whom Southey put in a position of feminine weakness. His paternalist re-working of the Pantisocratic scheme came to depend on imagining Indians as willing supplicants, as childlike figures who request the support of the masculine, knightly Welsh. The crucial character here is Lincoya, a Hoaman youth who becomes the squire to Madoc's knight. Southey enjoys Madoc's sense of his own personal and linguistic superiority as Lincoya mimics his speech:

> Nor light the joy I felt at hearing first
> The pleasant accents of my native tongue,
> Albeit in broken words and tones uncouth
> Come from these foreign lips.

(Part 1, Bk V, ll. 162–5)

As the native boy mumbles in Welsh, Southey reproduces one of the primal scenes of colonialism. From this moment it is accepted that the inhabitants of America will learn Welsh — although Madoc's men are the foreigners in this land. Madoc is delighted by Lincoya's attitude of filial submission and feminine weakness. Clearly, by 1805, deference from a servant class, either native or imported, was a fundamental aspect of Southey's colonial desire. Lincoya's words sanction a colonialist fantasy in which the Indians ask for white men's protection: colonial war is presented (and justified) in the guise of a nationalist liberation struggle.

Colonial war? In 1794–95 Southey had been a vehement opponent of Britain's wars with France and America, and their colonies in the West Indies and the Pacific. Pantisocracy was a rejection of such war. Why, in 1805, was he presenting it as a necessity for his emigrant hero? The answer, I think, has much to do with his interpretation of events in the later 1790s. Both he and Coleridge had, since their first meeting, attributed much of the power of repressive government to priestcraft. They had attacked the clergy of the Church of England for blessing state violence at home and abroad. Bellicose clerics, they argued, not only betrayed Christ's message of peace and equality but also infected the minds of ordinary people. Like pagan priests, they dazzled them with mystery and blinded them with superstition, so that they stayed loyal to the very authorities that kept them in subjugation. America, Southey and Coleridge hoped, would be a haven from the loyalist 'church and king' people who drove radicals such as their hero Joseph Priestley and their friend John Thelwall from their homes.

By the late 1790s, the French people seemed to have followed a similar bloody path as the Revolution turned from a peaceful, constitutional movement into a government of calculated terror. In Coleridge's analysis, the movement from which he had hoped so much had gone wrong because priestcraft had returned in new apparel. The French people were mirror-images of Britons since, blinded by loyalty not to priests but to revolutionary leaders who replaced priests, they also

hounded democrats to death. Liberty, he wrote in 'France: An Ode',
fled 'Alike from Priestcraft's harpy minions, / And factious Blasphemy's
obscener slaves' (*CPW*, I, part i, ll. 95–6). Southey, likewise, saw
Robespierre as a leader who resembled a pagan priest: his 'wild eloquence'
enthralled the French into feeding the revolution with human sacrifice:
'murder'd by thy rage / How many an innocent victim's blood has
stain'd / Fair freedom's altar' (*The Fall of Robespierre*, Act III, l. 201;
Act II, ll. 249–51. *CPW*, III, part i). Revolutionary enthusiasm was,
it followed, a modern equivalent of religious fanaticism. The French
Jacobins and the English clergy who vilified them were kith and kin:
both were contemporary versions of the high priests of former ages.

Armed with historical narratives about Aztec religion, confronted by
the religions of Catholicism and Jacobinism, Southey wrote ancient
America in the image of his fear of the fanaticism that seemed to be
spreading over modern Europe. It was to explore the fatal attraction
of that fanaticism, as well as to reveal its dreadful consequences,
that Southey had Madoc confronting an Azteca empire whose priests
commanded loyalty from the very people they oppressed. Madoc's
America, that is to say, is a country in which Southey's love and loathing
of fanaticism, and the analysis to which that love and loathing gave
rise, are overlaid upon his earlier pantisocratic translation of Godwin
and Rousseau. The result is a confused and fractured work that fits
his ambivalent attitudes towards Native Americans into Europe-driven
(and often contradictory) scenarios.

The confusion extends to Madoc's Christianity, which resembles
nineteenth-century muscular Protestantism more than it does the medieval Welsh Catholicism that, historically, he was supposed to believe
in. But Madoc's faith is marked by Southey's Protestant-dissenter's
fear of fanaticism—both Mexican and Roman. He is an iconoclast
determined to break idols and the priesthood who manipulated them.
And he insists on destroying 'superstitious' practices: it is the human
sacrifice of the Hoamen to the Azteca gods that causes Madoc to fight
on their behalf. The Aztecas seal their doom because they will not detach
themselves from their superstitious reverence. They cannot overcome
their sensual thralldom to a religion that exploits miracle and mystery,
ritual and rite. Those of the Aztecas who are not killed and who will
not abandon their beliefs are permitted to leave Florida (only, if we
extrapolate the poem's logic, to build an empire in Mexico which Cortes
would later destroy). This leaves the area free for a paternalist colony
to be envisaged, for the Hoamen now convert to Madoc's religion (in

fact the religion of Madoc): 'aknee they fell before the Prince, / And in adoring admiration raised / Their hands with one accord' (Part 2, Book VII, ll. 230–2). Seen as a more primitive people than the Aztecs who had conquered them, the Hoamen are also portrayed as being more easily redeemable because less controlled by entrenched institutions and systematized beliefs. Madoc converts them to a authoritarian Protestantism, sure in his 'authority / From Heaven, to give the law, and to enforce / Obedience. Ye shall worship God alone, / The One Eternal' (Part 2, Bk VIII, ll. 52–5). In effect, Southey contrives the triumph of a paternalist anti-jacobinism. He dedicates his poem to rooting out attraction to superstition (including his own attraction). Thus *Madoc*, in 1805, overwhelms though it does not entirely banish, the work of the 1790s radical who had hoped to live in a Pantisocratic community in harmony with, rather than authority over, the native peoples of America.

Such is Southey's gendered colonialist fantasy: the Welsh and the Hoamen live happily ever after under Madoc's patriarchal government. Yet the poem often, as Marilyn Butler has noted, unintentionally calls into question that superiority of British character and beliefs which it seeks to endorse.[19] Indeed, it comes close to undermining the justification of colonialism it sets out, and was seen to do so by contemporary reviewers who were disturbed by its comparison of Christianity with heathen religions.[20] As in his Orientalist epics, Southey's avowed intention of demonstrating the dangers of superstitious colonial religions backfired because of his deist and dissenting past. His suspicion of ritual and dogma made him seem not simply to be attacking (as a good Protestant) Catholicism, but rather to be undermining Christianity in toto. Southey's comparative religion got him into trouble because it effectively aligned Christian and heathen ritual, as when he portrayed Aztec cannibalism in words normally used to describe the communion cup:

> He said, and gave
> Ocellopan the vase … Chiefs, ye have pour'd
> Your strength and courage to the Terrible God,
> Devoted to his service; take ye now
> The beverage he hath hallow'd. In your youth
> Ye have quaff'd manly blood, that manly thoughts

[19] See Marilyn Butler, 'Orientalism' in *The Penguin History of Literature. Vol 5: The Romantic Period*, ed. David B. Pirie (Harmondsworth, 1994), 395–447.

[20] See *The Eclectic Review*, 1 (December 1805), 899–908 in *Robert Southey: The Critical Heritage*, ed. Lionel Madden (London and Boston, 1972). See also *The Monthly Review*, 48 (October, 1805), 113–22.

Might ripen in your hearts; so now with this,
Which mingling from such noble veins hath flowed,
Increase of valour drink, and added force.
Ocellopan received the bloody vase,
And drank, and gave in silence to his friend
The consecrated draught.

(Part 2, Bk X, ll. 188–99)

Here Southey sounds a note learnt from his Unitarian heroes, mentors and friends (radical religionists and politicians such as Joseph Priestley, John Prior Estlin, George Dyer, and Coleridge himself): he implies that the grail, and the Eucharist itself, is a heathen superstition. His dislike of Church ritual and Trinitarian doctrine persists alongside his apparent endorsement of orthodox Christianity over Azteca religion. The central ritual of the Christian worship is echoed in the Azteca drinking the human sacrifice's blood. To conventional Britons—Trinitarians by virtue of their allegiance to the Church of England—Southey's counter-productive poem had collapsed the distinctions it had been attempting to make, infecting the colonizer with the barbarity it found in the natives and tainting both with the heretical radicalism of British Unitarianism.

This criticism was perceptive, for Southey was indeed more interested in the moral and social improvements which Protestant missionaries might bring to superstitious colonies than he was in Christianity's truth. He supported his arguments about missionary work by quoting *Madoc*.

It is absurd to go to savages with tales of mysteries, the true method of converting them is by showing them, like the old blind man in Madoc, how little difference there is in the basis of our faith.

'Know ye not him who laid
The deep foundations of the earth . . .?
                    '. . . We also know,
And fear, and worship the Beloved One.'
'*Our God*', replied Cynetha, '*is the same,
The Universal Father.*'

(Part 1, Bk VIII, ll. 138–53)

Such language the Quakers may hold with perfect truth: in fact, it is the language which they have held to the Indians, and which the Indians understand. Let them go on in doing good to them, and time and example, and the Universal Father, will bring about the rest.[21]

---

[21] *Annual Review for 1806*, 593. Quoted in Geoffrey Carnall, *Robert Southey and his Age: The Development of a Conservative Mind* (Oxford, 1960), 78.

Ironically enough, the poem that had begun, in 1794, as a vehicle for Southey's anti-imperialist, anti-British politics, had become, by 1807, the source of an imperialist ideology that Southey was all too eager to inculcate. In fact Southey's explicit interpretations of what *Madoc* implied suggest that it had become a colonialist fantasy centred on a Protestant and paternalist mission to civilize—if necessary by military force. Native Americans were crucial to this fantasy because it was on their deference, on their willingness to be 'liberated' from the empires that held them in thrall, that the viability of benevolent colonialism depended. And this willingness was apparently proved by travel writers, such as Las Casas and Adair, who wrote of Indians' acceptance of Christianity and their admiration of white people. Southey's fictional Hoamen, then, embodied his hopes for other peoples, whom his countrymen ruled in fact. Britain, Southey argued, had more chance of converting unsophisticated rural peoples than it had of ancient religious civilizations like the Aztecas. Such entrenched civilizations, his poem suggests, always threatened to convert the colonizers, for their fanaticism was not only horrifying but also fascinating in its excessiveness. Hindus and Irish Catholics, Southey concluded, resembled the Aztecas: their priests would have to be extirpated by force—or the people sent into exile. Nothing, he argued in 1807, would redeem Ireland 'but a system of Roman conquest and colonization—and shipping off the refractory savages to the colonies'.[22] Like the Aztecas whom Madoc forced out of Florida into Mexico, the Irish would be sent to the wilds of America, where their fanaticism would be too remote to do damage. Having begun *Madoc* as a would-be Pantisocrat emigrating to set up a colony of liberty and peace, Southey was now advocating the forced and violent removal of others. The social revolutionary of 1794 had become a reactionary bigot, without even perceiving the irony of his volte-face.

But perhaps it was not such a volte-face as it seemed to Southey's critics. After all, it was to escape becoming complicit with repressive societies, in which popular credulity was manipulated by priests and politicians, that the Pantisocrats wished to sail to America. And it was to achieve the same ends that Southey now wanted the Irish shipped there by force. In effect, he still saw fanaticism as the chief political danger and still idealized the backwoods life, the life lived by the Indians

---

[22] Quoted in Carnall, *Southey and his Age*, 80.

of the plains and forests, as its cure. Occupied with breaking the land, free from absentee landlords, the 'refractory' Irish would escape the clutches of their priests, throw off superstition, and become hardy, Native Americans. Such was the fantasy, and it was an authoritarian variant of the original Pantisocracy scheme.

8

The Indian Song

Blair, Ritson, Gray, Scott, Morganwg, Southey: by the 1790s several generations of British writers had recorded their admiration for the songs that Indians sang. Indian songs had become fashionable, moving from the narratives of traders, travellers, and soldiers such as Henry Timberlake where they first appeared in the 1760s, into magazines and newspapers. Many Britons then penned their own approximations of the originals, turning Native Americans into primitive bards, in whose spontaneous overflow of feeling a sublime unity with nature was immediately accessible. Indian songs fascinated Britons, not least because, being oral and immediate, they were seen as unpremeditated effusions of a culture that embodied all that urban, polite, civilization lacked. Whether they sang of peace or violence, of the spirit or the flesh, Native Americans seemed autochthonous, organic, free.

The British 'Indian songs' turned a supposedly oral spontaneous form into literary printed verse. They were, in effect, at a greater remove from Indians' words than they pretended, since they were penned in response to the English prose of travellers rather than to the Native Americans themselves. This prose already framed Indians according to the desires of white people (travellers, editors, publishers, the public) to gather evidence of an authentically primitive spirituality like that which Europeans had possessed in the past but which in North America still existed in the flesh. Turning these accounts into verse, the songs were at a double distance and doubly literary, though they pretended to orality as Macpherson's Ossian poems did. They were also more or less stereotypical: many song-writers represented Native Americans as noble savages blessed with a natural spirituality and a harmony with their environment, or as warriors of extreme ferocity. Some, however, achieved more original portraits, giving their fictional Indians the ability to disturb these conventional categories.

According to the antiquarian and scholar Joseph Ritson, Indians were horrifyingly different from modern Europeans. Yet it was precisely because they were so different and so horrifying that he included them in the introduction to his attempt to revive the oral poetry of England's past. Indians, he argued in his *Historical Essay on the Origin and Progress of National Song* (1783), demonstrated what modern Europe had lost, as was nowhere more apparent than in the song that was uniquely theirs—the death song. The death song was fascinating because it rang out loud and clear while the man who sang it was destroyed. The singer was not a minstrel commemorating warriors' deeds but a warrior himself, and he sang as his captors slowly killed him by a series of 'excruciating tortures, of which a European can scarcely form the idea'. 'These,' Ritson declared, 'it is the height of heroism for the victim to bear with apparent insensibility.' The death song, then, was proof of heroic fortitude—a poetry born of violence and the mortification of the flesh. Nevertheless, for all its connotations of Christian martyrdom and classical stoicism, the death song was different, since Indians neither spoke of heaven and forgiveness nor acted with restrained dignity but breathed defiance at their executioners. To illustrate his point, Ritson quoted a Cherokee death song, in which the warrior uses images of weapons to fight his torturers. Arrow-shots and hatchet blows bespeak his defiance as his words seek to turn themselves into deeds:

> Remember the arrows he shot from his bow;
> Remember your chiefs by his hatchet laid low:
> Why so slow? Do you think I will shrink from the pain?
> No:—the son of Alknomook will never complain.

> I go to the land where my father is gone;
> His ghost shall rejoice in the fame of his son.
> Death comes like a friend, he relieves me from pain:
> And thy son, O Alknomook, has scorn'd to complain.[1]

For all Ritson's declarations about Indian otherness, this Cherokee is a very European Indian. The decorous couplets, the stoic contempt for self-pity, the filial reverence, are all expressions that gentlemen in Europe would recognize and approve. Yet, because they emerge from the tortured body of a 'savage' who is taunting his equally 'savage' captors,

---

[1] *A Historical Essay on the Origin and Progress of National Song* in *A Select Collection of English Songs*, 3 vols. (London, 1783), I, ii.

they become extraordinary—a composed formulation wrenched from extreme violence. Although the song's poetic form and moral precepts are familiar enough, its cruel occasion is what makes Ritson include it. The Indian song is enthralling because it suggests how many of the values that Europeans admire are not dependent on a gentlemanly education or an ancient civilization but are found in the most primitive and fierce of peoples—found also in circumstances so painful that all coherent utterance seems impossible.

Ritson's Cherokee is a Britons' version of a savage, created by Ritson's need to find new, folk, roots for the martial values of European gentlemen, roots which would demonstrate the openly heroic, physical and emotional origin of what, in civilized Europe, had shrunk into a polite and proper code of manners. He is also a fiction drawn from other Britons' texts, from the travel narratives that described how white men viewed the Indians they encountered. After 1763 the vogue for travel writing ensured that death songs became set-piece elements on the menu of Indian customs that the public expected to find when it read of North American tribes. Henry Timberlake included an example in his 1765 narrative of his wartime mission to the Cherokee council. In decorous English translation it spoke of warriors preparing for battle:

> We'll leave our clubs, dew'd with their country's show'rs
> And, if they dare to bring them back to ours,
> Their painted scalps shall be a step to fame,
> And grace our own and glorious country's name.

Timberlake commented that 'both the ideas and verse are very loose in the original and they are set to as loose a music, many composing both tunes and song off hand, according to the occasion; though some tunes, especially those taken from the northern Indian, are extremely pretty, and very like the Scotch!'[2] Here too, then, was evidence of the similarity of Indian and Scottish clan that Ossian, Norton and Scott exploited.

For James Adair, the death song rendered Indians awe-inspiring as well as savage, as he attempted to show by including a dramatic vignette:

The death-signal being given, preparations are made for acting a more tragical part. The victim's arms are fast pinioned, and a strong grape-vine is tied round his neck, to the top of the war-pole, allowing him to track around, about fifteen

[2] *The Memoirs of Lieut. Henry Timberlake (Who Accompanied the Three Cherokee Indians to England in the Year 1762)* (London, 1765), 57 (the verse) & 59 (the commentary).

yards. They fix some tough clay on his head, to secure the scalp from the blazing torches. Unspeakable pleasure now fills the exulting crowd of spectators, and the circle fills with the Amazon and merciless executioners—The suffering warrior however is not dismayed; with an insulting manly voice he sings the war-song! . . . The women make a furious on-set with their burning torches: his pain is soon so excruciating, that he rushes out from the pole, with the fury of the most savage beast of prey. . . . Now they scalp him . . . dismember, and carry off all the exterior branches of the body, (pudendis non exceptis) in shameful, and savage triumph. . . .

[. . .]

Not a soul, of whatever age or sex, manifests the least pity during the prisoner's tortures: the women sing with religious joy, all the while they are torturing the devoted victim, and peals of laughter resound through the crowded theatre—especially if he fears to die. But a warrior puts on a bold austere countenance, and carries it through all his pains:—as long as he can, he whoops and out-braves the enemy, describing his own martial deeds against them, and those of his nation, who he threatens will force many of them to eat fire in revenge of his fate, as he himself had often done to some of their relations at their cost.

(*Adair*, 390–1)

Adair places readers in a 'crowded theatre' so as to turn the events into a sublime spectacle. The effect of this is to make readers voyeurs: we are asked to look on at the vividly described torments, to thrill to the cruelty of 'savages', to stand as onlookers somewhere near the torturers. But then Adair distances us before we question our motives for reading. Having placed us in proximity to savage bodies—a proximity that is charged with a sadistic homoeroticism, he lets us withdraw to make general inferences about the origins of cruelty in education and custom. This withdrawal redraws the line between civilized reader and savage Indian that the theatre of torture had blurred: readers ponder the reasons for the Indians' actions in a way the Indians themselves do not. Simultaneously, however, the general inferences suggest that Indians' terrible violence is not the product of innate savagery or bestiality, but of a cultural conditioning which Europe has itself not always escaped. Indians, Adair shows, are taught by their society to be cruel just as in Lisbon 'tender-hearted ladies are transformed by their bloody priests' into gloating voyeurs of burnings at the stake. Civilized nations too, Adair implies, can succumb to the allure of spectacular violence if they abandon rational detachment and enter the theatre of cruelty for longer than the brief vicarious moments that he allows. Indians, it follows, represent a tantalizing embodiment of cruel pleasures that Europeans must resist precisely because they find them so desirable. Looking on from safety at the pains of others—the dynamic of the sublime as Burke defines it—reaches its apogee, and its limit case, as we watch the Indians watching other Indians die. Adair's Indian torturers, in effect, represent the part of us he would have us resist by reason and detachment, but only after he has indulged it enough to draw us in.

If Adair's Indians reveal the corrupt pleasure that the powerful take in dramatizing their power, they demonstrate the dangers of the sublime. While bringing that late eighteenth-century aesthetic into question, they also suggest an alternative to its circuit of voyeurism and violence. The warrior who does not fear to die effectively refuses to become the target of his torturers' laughter. He rejects their derision, singing his death song so as to contest power to the end. Voicing his defiance, he refuses to accept victimhood, declines to admit the vulnerability of his body even as it is literally taken to pieces. He does his best to frustrate his enemies' pleasure, and may ultimately, if he is courageous enough, win their respect instead. Thus the death song becomes his last resource, a final self-assertion in which his humanity is demonstrated, even as his life ends. As such, it is both noble in itself and a form of terrible enquiry—a means that Indians use to test each other's resolution, to probe the determination with which they maintain their identity. The theatre of cruelty is also, Adair hints, a theatre of discovery, a philosophical experiment in which what is revealed is the warrior's sense of centredness in his own being. It is not for nothing that he compares the Indians' tortures to the 'Romish inquisition': the Native Americans are philosophers of nature using the most direct means to reveal their subject's true belief about what he is.

As a poetry that was closer to the body than any other kind, the death song seemed to be an overflow of being into language—an articulation of essential self without the intervention of self-consciousness or pre-meditation. As such, it appeared to occupy the opposite pole to polite, urbane and urban writing—the decorous, schooled literature of gentlemen. And, as such, it established Indians as ideal representatives of the unity and authenticity that gentlemen, weary of the sophisticated culture they had learnt, imagined they wanted but could not admit to wanting in their own persons, lest they appear savage. The Indian of the death song, it follows, was not simply the other but the secret twin of the British male reader—the embodiment of his taboo desire.

The genre continued to encode British fantasies and fears as the eighteenth century ended in violent war. Adair, Carver, and Ritson were tapping into a cultural need that was also serviced by the increasingly popular discourse of sublimity, a need born of a growing tension in polite culture. On the one hand gentlemen were supposed to be more refined, more urbane, at a greater remove from the bodily. They needed polished manners suitable for drawing rooms and salons—the domestic places where much of social importance now occurred. On the other hand, Britain's imperial involvements caused many new wars, in which gentlemen were expected to fight, hence there arose a perceived need for them to rediscover the manly, physical prowess that supposedly underlaid the code of chivalry and honour. This perception bred an anxiety as to whether the British governing classes *could* rediscover martial virtues or whether they had been emasculated by polite culture. Paine called the House of Commons a 'seraglio of males', the more moderate Canning called desperately for a return to heroic masculinity 'such as nerved our fathers' breasts'.[3] Indians possessed heroic masculinity in abundance—or so the death song suggested. Perhaps translating the death song into English would perform a similar function—transfusing heroic physicality into British culture without forgoing the supposedly more polished forms of 'civilization'.

And yet the death song was not easily borrowed, for the very extremity of its utterance made its incorporation within polite culture problematic. It also made it fascinating. The death song was an inherently unstable model, for it opened up the twin paradoxes that the body is most vital when being destroyed and that being is declared most immediately as it is overwhelmed by death. Britons' interest in the genre thus revealed both homoerotic and macabre fixations, as if the cultural repression of gentlemen drove their desire to extremes: their desire for powerful sensual experience could only be acknowledged when confined to safely remote and ungentlemanly foreigners. Taking aesthetic pleasure in Indians' pain, readers could vicariously satisfy a wish for a knowledge of the flesh that gentlemen could not be seen to enjoy in their own persons. And so the dying Indian became a dangerously attractive hero who took familiar ideals to unfamiliar extremes, an uncanny figure for a strange part of the British gentleman that could not be acknowledged in itself.

By the mid-1790s two distinct strains of Indian song were current in British poetry. The death songs presented by Ritson, Carver and others

---

[3] Paine, *The Rights of Man*, ed. Henry Collins (Harmondsworth, 1969), 249; Canning quoted in Janet Todd, *Sensibility: An Introduction* (London and New York, 1986), 130–1.

depicted the Indian as pitiless and ferocious, uncannily fascinating and horrifying. Pastoral songs, meanwhile, showed Indians as innocent and carefree, as Rousseauvian nature-children. Both strains, however, focused on Indians' organic unity with themselves and with nature. Both made them autochthonous beings for whom word and deed, and mind and body, are one. Both, that is to say, turned them into symbols of the natural wholeness that European civilization seemed to have lost. And both, by doing so, made them deeply attractive to the young poets who admired Gray and Ritson and who, after the failure of the French Revolution to precipitate a transformation of Britain, were searching for new models of liberty and equality. By 1798, Indian songs were central to the new writing that Southey, Coleridge, and Wordsworth were together pioneering and that issued in Southey's 'Songs of the American Indians' (1799) and most famously in *Lyrical Ballads* (1798). The three poets understood that song was the best genre in which to represent Indians precisely because the tribal society they so admired depended on oral, not written, memory. And their songs and tales were forms whose orality betokened their affiliation not just to rural, but also to unlettered indigenous culture. The lyrical ballads of the late 1790s, those new/old poems that became the epitome of the new poetry called Romantic, aspired, generically, to an authenticity of which Native Americans were the best living example.

Southey, for instance, made the Hurons' reverence for the dead into a lyrical lesson for his own hierarchical and corrupt civilization:

> The Iroquois will hear
> That thou hast ceased from war;
> 'Twill be a joy like victory,
> For thou wert the scourge of their race. . . .
>
> And where is That, which, in thy voice
> The language of friendship spake?
> That gave the strength of thine arm?
> That fill'd thy limbs with life?
> It was not Thou, for Thou art here,
> Thou art amongst us still,
> But the Life and the Feeling are gone![4]

Well-informed about Huron customs, Southey described the preparation of a funeral canoe, in which the dead man is placed for his voyage to

---

[4] He published the poem in the *Morning Post*, 24 October 1799, as 'The Huron's Address to the Dead'. See *Southey*, V, 387–9.

the country of the dead. Speaking with one voice, the Hurons achieve a communal dignity as they address their dead 'brother'. They are united by their shared respect for him and by their common belief in the presence of the dead in nature. Like Wordsworth's Lucy, rolled round in rocks and stones and trees, the dead Huron will still figure in the life of the living, who intimate his presence in the nature they occupy with him. The Hurons, that is to say, offer Southey and his readers a shared version of what Wordsworth's nature-religion gives him alone—an intimation of immortality:

> Brother, we sing thee the song of death—
> In thy coffin of bark we lay thee to rest;
>   The bow shall be plac'd by thy side;
> And the shafts that are pointed and feather'd for flight.
>   To the country of the dead
>   Long and painful is thy way;
>   O'er rivers deep and wide
>   Lies the way that must be pass'd,
>   By bridges narrow-wall'd,
>   Where scarce the soul can force its way,
> While the loose fabric totters under it.
>   Safely may our Brother pass!
>   Safely may he reach the fields,
> Where the sound of the drum and the shell
> Shall be heard from the regions of bliss.
>   The Spirits of thy Sires
>   Shall come to welcome thee:
>   The God of the Dead in his bow'r
> Shall receive thee, and bid thee join
> The dance of eternal joy.
>
> Brother, we pay thee the rites of death—
> Rest in the bower of delight!
>
>   (ll. 42–63)

The voice of a community that is truly Romantic because it embodies harmony between body, spirit and nature, Southey's death song is a validation of Native American culture in stark opposition to the use that natural historians and race theorists were making of dead Indians at the same time. It is dignified not ferocious, ceremonial not a cry of revenge. It reflects his reading, since the communal role that formal songs played in Indian life is stressed by the travel narratives that Southey was using in preparing *Madoc*. William Bartram, for example, cited a song that moved a young Chactaw slave girl to tears, since it reminded her of her dead father and brother:

The meaning of the chorus was

> All men must surely die,
> Tho' no one knows how soon,
> Yet when the time shall come,
> The event may be joyful.

These doleful moral songs or elegies, have a quick and sensible effect on their passions, and discover a lively affection and sensibility: their countenance now dejected, again, by an easy transition, becomes gently elevated, as if in solemn address or supplication, accompanied with a tremulous, sweet, lamentable voice: a stranger is for a moment lost to himself as it were, or his mind, associated with the person immediately affected, is in danger of revealing his own distress unawares.

(Bartram, 506)

Like Bartram, Southey—and his readers—are 'strangers' who are drawn in to sympathize with Indians' emotions because they respond to Indian oral poetry. By Englishing the Indians' songs, Southey Indianizes his readers, aligning their emotional response with those of supposedly uncultured 'savages'. The effect is to reverse assumptions about the superiority of British civilization to Indian savagery, and of writing to song. Southey's Indians are models for Britons not just of what they imagine they have lost (Edenic innocence and unity) but also of the virtues normally associated with Christian civilization—compassion, dignity, the organization of reverence into ceremony and form. If they are idealized to satisfy Britons' needs, then they are idealized afresh—Southey gives his imagined Indians more complexity and more cultural status than pastoral portraits had hitherto allowed them. This is not to say that Southey somehow discovers 'real' Indians whereas previous Britons had dealt only in fantasies. Southey's Indians are as much a blend of travellers' narratives and personal desires as were his predecessors'. It is to say, rather, that the blend that Southey makes is more complex and challenging since it gives Indian cultural practices (or his approximation thereof) power to teach Britons a lesson in the areas in which Britons thought themselves superior.

Southey's valorization of Indian song extended beyond a single, searching example. His 'Songs of the American Indians' (1799) are his parallel to the songs Coleridge and Wordsworth collected in *Lyrical Ballads*—part of a joint project to revitalize British verse and British society on the artistic and social models provided by other 'primitive' cultures. Southey also wrote supposedly African and Australian songs at this time; Coleridge imitated the chants of Native American girls[5] and the spells of Africans. But Southey's Native American song-cycle is the most thoroughgoing rendering of an indigenous people's poetry that any of the Romantics achieved. The five poems that he composed in 1798 and 1799 represent an attempt to give authority to Native American voices, an attempt characterized not just by Southey's own radical politics and aesthetic desires but also by a genuine effort to present an accurate rendition of Indian customs and beliefs. They speak collectively for American Indians, yet do not simply generalize as if all Native Americans are the same. Each poem identifies voices and customs of a particular tribe or area, from the Hurons in the Northeast to the Peruvians in South America. And though many are death songs, each speaks from a different context. The last poem in the cycle, for example, reverses the procedure of the others since it is spoken by a grandfather extolling the virtues of his dead son. 'The Old Chikkasah to his Grandson' is, nevertheless, a death song that, like the other poems in the cycle, links words with warlike deeds. Songs, it seems, existed to commemorate valour and celebrate the body of the valiant. Words pass deeds down to the next generation, binding it to the memory of the forefather's actions, which thus live in tribal tradition in the form of standards to which the young must aspire. It is a patriarchal vision, a society modelled on the male warrior, as the Chikkasaw patriarch makes clear:

> The Heroes were met to receive their reward;
> But distinguish'd among the young Heroes that day,
> The pride of his nation thy Father was seen:
>> The swan-feathers hung from his neck,
>> His face like the rainbow was ting'd,
>> And his eye,—how it sparkled in pride!
> The Elders approach'd, and they placed on his brow
>> The crown that his valour had won,
>> And they gave him the old honour'd name.
> They reported the deeds he had done in the war,
>> And the youth of the nation were told
>> To respect him and tread in his steps.

---

[5] His song, 'Lewti' was originally supposed to be voiced by an Indian woman—the singer became Circassian at a later stage. See *CPW*, I, part i, 457.

As we sate in our hut on his grave,
Thou hast heard me full often repeat
How bravely he fought, and how nobly he died.
His war-pole now is grey with moss,
His tomahawk red with rust,
His bowstring, whose twang was death,
Now sings as it cuts the wind.
But his mem'ry is fresh to the land,
And his name with the names that we love.

Go now and revenge him, my boy!
That his Spirit no longer may hover by day
O'er the hut where his bones are at rest,
Nor trouble our dreams in the night.
My boy, I shall watch for the warriors' return,
And my soul will be sad
Till the steps of thy coming I see.

(ll. 16–48)[6]

Southey's interest in the Chikkasaw stemmed from his reading of Adair: Adair had fought alongside the Chikkasaw against the Cherokee and the French, and emphasized the importance they attached to inculcating the principle of revenge in even the youngest children:

There never was any set of people, who pursued the Mosaic law of *retaliation* with such a fixt eagerness as these Americans. They are so determined in this point, that formerly a little boy shooting birds in the high and thick corn-fields, unfortunately chanced slightly to wound another with his childish arrow; the young vindictive fox, was excited by custom to watch his ways with the utmost earnestness, till the wound was returned in as equal a manner as could be expected. Then 'all was straight,' according to their phrase. . . .

(*Adair*, 150)

The test of a young warrior was his ability to accomplish a daring raid to revenge a dead elder. Southey, versifying his travel narrative source, gets the ceremonial details right and builds from them an idealization of a rural, organic, patriarchal society in which the young conform to the example of the old, the past governs the present, and morality descends through the male lines. As in *Madoc* (which Southey was rewriting when he wrote the Songs), the father's word and deed are the medium of

---

[6] From the *Morning Post*, 21 September 1799.

government and the tribe—an extended family—is the organic society
in which that word and deed have living power. Southey's Chikkasaws,
in fact, reveal something fundamental about his Romanticism (and, to a
degree, about Wordsworth's also). Native Americans were appealing to
both poets because they gave an example of a rural community that was
patriarchal in structure and familial in size, so that the male's authority
could be disseminated by example when he was alive and orally after his
death. In the tribe, Southey found a model of an unchanging, traditional
community centred on the word of the father (a finding that ignored
the considerable matriarchal influence upon the question of bloodline
and identity in many Indian nations). It was precisely its lack of this
centre that Wordsworth disliked about contemporary urban society.
Too large, too dispersed, too fragmented: city-culture had broken the
bond between father and offspring (as *Michael*, for instance, reveals).
The father's example could not be witnessed, nor his word be heard,
beyond his immediate circle leaving each generation to ignore the lessons
of the previous one and search endlessly for novelty instead. Opposing
this urban culture with the oral community of Indians and of the rural
Welsh and Cumbrians (their nearest British equivalents) was at once
radical and conservative. By 1799, Southey's and Wordsworth's Indians
were, in effect, the first progeny of the Burkeanism that the poets were
increasingly to develop. They were the radical, indigenous cousins of the
great English aristocrats on whose transmission of land from father to
son Burke founded the English constitution. Or, to put it another way,
the Romantics sang Indian songs in order to *give* as much sublimity
to 'natural' patriarchs as Burke had *found* in the titled noblemen who,
since time immemorial, had inherited power in Britain.

It was not only in *Lyrical Ballads* that Wordsworth and Coleridge
adapted Native American lives and voices to form their own new poetic.
In the winter of 1798/9 Wordsworth read about idyllic Indians in
William Bartram's *Travels* while beginning the revaluation of rural life
in the English Lake District that was to become *The Prelude*. Some of
the first lines he wrote turn his own Lakeland childhood into an Indian
idyll of the kind Bartram had placed in Florida:

> Oh, many a time have I, a five year's child,
> A naked boy, in one delightful rill,
> A little mill-race severed from his stream,
> Made one long bathing of a summer's day;
> Basked in the sun, and plunged and basked again
> Alternate, all a summer's day, or coursed

Over the sandy fields, leaping through groves
Of yellow groundsel; or when crag and hill,
The woods, and distant Skiddaw's lofty height,
Were bronzed with a deep radiance, stood alone
Beneath the sky, as if I had been born
On Indian plains, and from my mother's hut
Had run abroad in wantonness, to sport
A naked savage, in the thunder shower.[7]

(*Prelude* (1805), Bk I, ll. 291–304)

For Wordsworth in 1798 to live at one with nature was to feel it mark the flesh. It was to acquire the unfettered body and liberated soul of a savage, and that savage was depicted as an American Indian, his nakedness revealing his unafraid communion with his own—and nature's—physical power. And in return the landscape became Indian in its colouring, 'bronzed' like the naked savage who is at one with it. The Lake District, in effect, became a rural home, within Britain, for the uncommercial authenticity that, for Wordsworth, the Indian warrior embodied in America. Wordsworth's Lake District, that is to say, was shaped in part as a home for Britons who resembled the 'red men' he had read about. His Lakeland 'freemen' were heroic and natural indigenes on the model of imaginary Indians.

Real Indians feature in *The Prelude* too—not in the Lake District but in London. Wordsworth encounters them there only to discover that the great metropolis, symbol of the commercialized and capitalistic society he dislikes, renders them pale shadows, their organic unity turned into a cheap trick. The 'Hunter-Indian' 'from remote / America' is, Wordsworth discovers, merely one of many 'specimens of man' visible in the capital's streets (VII, 240–1, 236). The Indian is reduced to one of the spectacles of a city that makes trivial exhibitions out of the most deep-rooted cultures. Like the 'English ballad-singer' and 'Ossian ... / Summoned from streamy Morven' (VII, 196, 561–2) he is uprooted, at best a face in the London crowd, at worst a 'raree show' demeaning the authenticity which he embodies in his rural home.

In making the 'Hunter-Indian' an example of the authenticity that he thought was perverted in London, Wordsworth was attacking the commodification of foreign bodies by imperial London's culture of fashion, display, and consumerism. He summed his feelings up in the

---

[7] For the lines as they appeared in the two-part *Prelude* manuscript see *The Prelude 1798–99*, ed. Stephen Parrish (Ithaca, NY, and Hassocks, Sussex, 1977), 43.

phrase 'getting and spending we lay waste our powers'. What London did to the Indian was turn him into a skin show to titillate the city's endless lust to experience something new. Consumerism, for Wordsworth, was an ultimately self-destructive sexual addiction to look at the foreign, an addiction to which the bodies of rural Indians and Scots alike were prostituted. The Indian became just another new imperial commodity, a new product sent from the colonies to be consumed by men and women at the imperial centre, until, 'craving for extraordinary incident',[8] they turned to something still newer.

In *The Prelude*, the rural Indian, and the 'Indian' boy that Wordsworth had been in the Lake District, were the polar opposites of another symbolic London figure, the deracinated blind beggar:

> ... a blind Beggar, who, with upright face,
> Stood, propped against a wall, upon his chest
> Wearing a written paper, to explain
> The story of the man, and who he was.
> My mind did at this spectacle turn round
> As with the might of waters, and it seemed
> To me that in this label was a type,
> Or emblem, of the utmost that we know,
> Both of ourselves and of the universe.

> (Bk VII, ll. 611–19)

The beggar reveals that the culture of London turns people into zombies: it empties inner identity onto the demeaning paper that is merely pinned to his body to represent his alienation from himself and his dependence on others.

Wordsworth could imagine no greater contrast than that between the hunter Indian and the London beggar, for the Indian hunter was the very epitome of organic man, man with no split between the body and the signs that signified its being. As Jonathan Carver, for one, revealed, the warrior's deeds were not only immediately celebrated in his own speech (as in the death song) but cut into his flesh with fish-teeth and sharpened stones:

Their success in war is readily known by the blue marks upon their breasts and arms, which are as legible to the Indians as letters are to the Europeans.

The manner in which these hieroglyphicks are made, is by breaking the skin with the teeth of fish, or sharpened flints, dipped in a kind of ink made of the

---

[8] Preface to *Lyrical Ballads* (1800) in Duncan Wu (ed.), *Romanticism: An Anthology*, 2nd edn. (Oxford, 1988), 359.

soot of pitch pine. Like those of the ancient Picts of Britain these are esteemed ornamental; and at the same time they serve as registers of the heroic actions of the warrior, who thus bears about him indelible marks of his valour.

(*Carver*, 337)

In the warrior writing and self are reconciled: to Carver his being and its meaning are one as was the case with ancient Britons, when bodily deeds were written on the body. Nature and the self are reconciled too, since the skin is carved with the teeth of fish dipped in pitch-pine soot. The Indian is here a fantasy of unity and authenticity, having no split between soul, body, and the letters that represent him—the flesh made word. The flesh of Indians was fascinating because of what and how it signified. And it was fascinating even after death. For Wordsworth and other Romantics, the bones of the Indian dead, and the beliefs of the survivors about those bones, revealed a more natural spirituality at work than that taught by the Anglican Church. James Adair described the practice of burying the dead beneath dwellings so that contact could be maintained between the living and their deceased relatives. Wordsworth idealized a similar uncivilized belief in 'We Are Seven'. The seemingly natural religion of the Indians provided a pattern for the natural religion that early Romanticism preferred to book-learning and church-teaching.

By early 1799 Wordsworth, Southey, and Coleridge[9] had, together, put Indians and Indian songs to the fore of the new poetic movement that was to dominate early nineteenth-century literature. The Lake poets, as reviewers called them, wrote of American lakes and Indian rustics as well as English ones and would not have been able to express their visions of rural community without having absorbed Native American culture as pictured by travellers. Native Americans, in short, were vital figures in the formation of early Romanticism: their bodies, their customs, their society, and, above all, their oral poetry influenced Romanticism's content and form. So, as we shall see in the next chapter, did their gender: the Romantic balladeers were most fascinated of all by Indian women, and by the relationship they imagined themselves having with those women.

---

[9] On Coleridge's response, in notebooks, to Bartram's portraits of Seminole Indians, see John Livingston Lowes, *The Road to Xanadu: A Study in the Ways of the Imagination* (London, 1978), 411, 468–9. See also *CN*, I, 218, 220, 221, 222.

9

Shamans and Superstitions: 'The Rime of the Ancyent Marinere'

The most profound literary response to what Britons wrote about Native Americans was also the most oblique—a poem that was not set in America at all and whose hero was not a Romantic Indian but a British sailor. Yet Coleridge's 'The Rime of the Ancyent Marinere' (1798) was thoroughly imbued with what he had read about the Dene and Cree of Hudson's Bay, and it brought that reading home to his own countrymen. In this chapter, I shall investigate how he came to develop his reading about Indians into one of the strangest poems in the language.

Reminiscing about the temperate climes in which he and Wordsworth had lived in 1797, Coleridge wrote that his friend was not sufficiently interested in the superstitions of the place. By 'the place' he meant the rural west of England, and by 'superstitions' he meant the folk beliefs of villagers. It was amongst these that he found material for his 'psychological' poetry: both 'Frost at Midnight' and 'The Three Graves' hinge on such superstitions, continuing the emphasis on rustic belief that is central to the poems included in *Lyrical Ballads*. It was in the preface to 'The Three Graves', too, that Coleridge revealed that his interest in the psychology of superstition stemmed as much from his reading about Native Americans and Africans as from his encounters with English West Country folk. In this respect he shared an interest with his friends Wordsworth and Southey and indeed it was his reading of travel narratives that lay behind poems such as 'The Complaint of the Forsaken Indian Woman' and 'The Sailor who Served in the Slave Trade'.

In the Preface to 'The Three Graves' Coleridge remembered how he had

been reading Bryan Edwards's account of the effects of the *Oby* witchcraft on the Negroes in the West Indies, and Hearne's deeply interesting anecdotes of similar workings on the imagination of the Copper Indians ... and I conceived the design of showing that instances of this kind are not peculiar to savage or barbarous tribes, and of illustrating the mode in which the mind is affected in these cases.

(*CPW*, I, part i, 338)

What Coleridge found compelling in Hearne was his discussion of the 'conjurers' amongst his Indian companions. Hearne noted their 'very extraordinary piece of superstition; which is no less than that of pretending to swallow hatchets, ice-chisels, broad bayonets, knives ... out of a superstitious notion that undertaking such desperate feats will have some influence in appeasing death and procure a respite for their patient'. One 'dangerously ill' man 'soon recovered' after the conjurer, in Hearne's presence, swallowed a bayonet, following it up with twenty-four hours of incantations (*Hearne*, 210, 211, 213). The believing mind, apparently, could control the body. The bayonet, like a fetish, convinced the patient because it was a visible and tangible token of the shaman's power to break boundaries of the internal and external and surpass limits of the body. Thus it put the body's relationship to the outside world in question.

Hearne's narrative suggested a more sinister side to Indian medicine. The conjurers could, he discovered, literally think people to death:

When these jugglers take a dislike to, and threaten a secret revenge on any person, it often proves fatal to that person; as from a firm belief that the conjurer has power over his life, he permits the very thoughts of it to prey on his spirits, till by degrees it brings on a disorder which puts an end to his existence: and sometimes a threat of this kind causes the death of a whole family; and that without any blood being shed, or the least apparent molestation being offered.

(*Hearne*, 233)

As for Hearne's 'Copper Indians,' so, Bryan Edwards suggested, for black Africans. Edwards was considered something of an expert on Africans, having written about them in his *History Civil and Commercial of the British Colonies in the West Indies*. In this work Edwards described the manners and customs of the slaves. He focused in detail on a custom that stemmed from Africa but flourished in the West Indian colonies. The plantation slave, Edwards shows, believed in the spells and curses of obeah-men:

his terrified imagination begins to work, no recourse is left ... he presently falls into a decline, under the incessant horror of impending calamities. The slightest painful sensation in the head, the bowels, or any other part ... confirms his apprehensions, and he believes himself the devoted victim of an invisible and irresistible agency. Sleep, appetite, and cheerfulness, forsake him, his strength decays, his disturbed imagination is haunted without respite, his features wear the settled gloom of despondency: dirt, or any other unwholesome substance, become his only food, he contracts a morbid habit of body, and gradually sinks into the grave.[1]

Coleridge's interest in Hearne and in Edwards was both psychological and political. He wanted to examine his own countrymen's complicity with repressive leaders in terms of what explorers told him about Indians and Africans. It wasn't only these explorers either: Coleridge read in Carver's *Travels* of the power of a Sioux medicine-man: 'one of the *Indians* being worked upon, became insensible, and had all the symptoms of a crisis; when he came to himself, he assured the sailors, he had *seen* their companions, that they were safe, and would ere long arrive at the same place: which came to pass'.[2] For Dr John Ferriar, meanwhile, the beliefs of 'the Indian tribes of North America' illustrated 'the credulous tendency of the mind' in present-day Britain:

All the marches of the Indians are regulated by the dreams of the old warriors, who, under this pretence, often convey information gained by spies to the young men: but it must be observed that they only pay attention to dreamers of established character. They have their regular diviners, or conjurers also, who are at the same time physicians.[3]

It was because he too linked Indians and modern Britons that Coleridge declared that 'It would be singularly desirable, ... to try the effect of animal magnetism [Mesmerism/hypnotism] on a sick Indian'.[4] Although he never managed to fulfil it, Coleridge's desire stemmed from a deep interest in the power, in rural and oral cultures, of imagination and belief.

It was just this power that he dramatized in narrative form in his rural ballad 'The Three Graves'—and the 'Ancient Mariner'. Both poems depend on belief in a curse. In 'The Three Graves' the scenario goes

[1] Bryan Edwards, *The History, Civil and Commercial of the British Colonies in the West Indies*, 2 vols. (London, 1793), II, 91–2.

[2] John Martin, *Animal Magnetism Examined in a Letter to a Country Gentleman* (London, 1790), 22.

[3] John Ferriar, MD, 'Of Popular Illusions, and particularly of Medical Demonology', *Memoirs of the Literary and Philosophical Society of Manchester*, 3 (1790), 23–116 (28).

[4] British Library Egerton MS 2800 f.88; quoted in John Livingstone Lowes, *The Road to Xanadu, A Study in the Ways of the Imagination*, rev edn. (London, 1978), 501.

as follows: Edward, the hero, marries Mary, after seeking her widowed mother's approval. Initially, the mother gives her approval but then tells Edward to switch his affections to her. Edward rejects her advances; she then curses him and his bride. It is Edward's guilt that he has provoked these advances that makes him susceptible to the curse. But he is guilty for another reason too: his dreams tell him that he desires his mother-in-law as well as his wife and it is their discovery of incestuous desire, a discovery that the rational mind cannot control, that lets the curse work. Spellbound by his interpretation of dreams, Edward becomes a guilty victim of unspeakable knowledge. He is a subscriber to his mother-in-law's curse because it articulates what he now knows he had repressed.

That Coleridge understood curses as a matter of repressed guilt and violated taboos is apparent in a later discussion of obeah and shamanism: 'The supposed exercise of magical power', he wrote, 'always involved some moral guilt, directly or indirectly, as in ... touching humours with the hand of an executed person &c. Rites of this sort and other practices of sorcery have always been regarded with trembling abhorrence by all nations, even the most ignorant, as by the Africans, the Hudson's Bay people and others.'[5] Edwards's African obeah-men and Hearne's Hudson's Bay shamans gained their 'supernatural' power from their culture's shared guilt, from its complicity with their violation of taboos.

It was not simply guilt that produced superstition. It also stemmed, Coleridge wrote, from powerlessness—a powerlessness of which the slave was the extreme case—from 'having placed our summum bonum (what we think so, I mean,) in an absolute Dependence on Powers and Events over which we have no Controll' (*CN*, II, 2060). Ignorance was a form of this powerlessness: superstition sprang from 'the consciousness of the vast disproportion of our knowledge to the *terra incognita* yet to be known'.[6] And in Coleridge's analysis, Britain was as full of ignorance and (mental) slavery as its colonies. It was on these conditions that tyrannical government thrived. In Pitt's Britain, willing slavery and political witchcraft perpetuated each other, ensuring that tyranny remained in power. Coleridge recalled (in 'France: An Ode') how Britons had been bewitched. 'A slavish band', they did the bidding of a cruel monarch who bound them with 'a wizard's wand' (*CPW*, I, part i,

---

[5] *Coleridge's Miscellaneous Criticism*, ed. T. M. Raysor (London, 1936), 202.

[6] Ibid., 321.

ll. 27, 29). 'A willing slave', Coleridge wrote in a letter, 'is the worst of slaves. His *soul* is a slave' (*CL*, I, 122). The people, he decided, were complicit with their oppressors. Brought up for generations to believe in their own inferiority, they were mental slaves who were incapable of independence because they craved a master. In proportion to their own powerlessness, he concluded, subjugated peoples granted others powers that *seemed* supernatural. Unscrupulous tyrants took advantage of this tendency to cement their authority: using 'wizard spell[s]', they ensured those they oppressed would stay spellbound by their power ('Sonnet: to Burke', l. 8, *CPW*, I, part i). The superstitious rural characters of 'The Three Graves' illustrated a mental process that, Coleridge thought, underpinned the social and political order, since the people of Britain and France, 'slaves by their own compulsion', were mentally as manacled as the West Indian slaves were physically ('France: An Ode', l. 86, *CPW*, I part i). The government had a talismanic hold on their minds. Belief in the rightful power of Church and State was Britain's shamanism.

Coleridge's view of shamans was, it appears, largely a negative one (unlike Blake's). For Coleridge, shamans illustrated the ways in which superstition worked rather than revealed the power of creative vision. He made no endorsement of their imagination as such, for he understood it to depend on the manipulation of complicity and guilt. Nevertheless, though this was a highly critical view of Native American belief, it was not a dismissive one, since Coleridge's poems develop considerable dramatic sympathy with minds that believe in spells, prophecies and curses. In 'The Three Graves' and 'Christabel', Coleridge re-creates the psychology of a culture that believes in a magical universe where the object-world is affected by the morality of human words and deeds. And he shows that psychology to be as much British as foreign: the poems are shaped by Coleridge's reading about shamans and obeah-men yet feature British protagonists, heroes with whom British readers suffer and *see visions*—through whose eyes they experience a magical view of nature. Thus Coleridge brings Indian and African minds (as he imagines them at least) home to his own culture: through his 'supernatural' ballads we're drawn to participate in (partly) Indian and African ways of seeing and being. To an extent then, Coleridge validates these ways even while he treats them as the superstitions of more 'primitive' periods and peoples.

Coleridge's treatment of mental slavery reached its apogee in 'The Rime of the Ancyent Marinere' (written in 1797 when collaboration with Wordsworth on 'The Three Graves' petered out). 'The Rime' is a poem

about the political, social, and personal consequences of superstition
and about the way superstition proceeds from 'the consciousness of the
vast disproportion of our knowledge to the terra incognita yet to be
known'.[7] It is a poem that could not have been written if Coleridge had
not read Hearne's account of Native American shamanism and found
there an insight into the psychology of belief. It may, too, have sprung
from Coleridge's meeting Hearne at school in 1791, in the company of
Hearne's friend William Wales. Wales, Coleridge's teacher, had lived
with Hearne on Hudson's Bay and also sailed, with Captain Cook,
further south into Antarctic waters than ever before. 'The Rime', full of
polar scenery as well as curses and spells, seems to combine the mental
and physical discoveries the two men made and, perhaps, told the young
Coleridge about.[8]

The mariner's mental voyage into a living death of superstition begins,
as in 'The Three Graves', with a casting-out ritual. His shipmates,
ignorantly superstitious, strive to give his shooting of the albatross
supernatural significance. First they blame him, then praise him, then,
on no empirical evidence, blame him again. They try to influence the
weather that threatens the ship by making him bear and purge the blame
for it. By this means they hope to overcome their own powerlessness to
control the events on which their lives depend. And so they ostracize
and curse him:

> And I had done an hellish thing
> And it would work 'em woe;
> For all averr'd, I had kill'd the Bird,
> That made the Breeze to blow.
>
> (1798 text, ll. 91–4, *CPW*, I, part i)

The mariner internalizes the blame and accepts the role of scapegoat
because he knows he has violated the crew's taboo, and because he too is
superstitious enough to believe in the reality of such taboos. Violating it
brings him anguish and isolation, but also a terrible authority. The bird
is hung around his neck—a sign of his guilt but also a fetish embodying
his uncanny power.

---

[7] *Coleridge's Miscellaneous Criticism*, 321.

[8] On Hearne's visit to Coleridge's school in 1791 see Ken McGoogan, *Ancient Mariner: The Arctic Adventures of Samuel Hearne, the Sailor who Inspired Coleridge's Masterpiece* (New York, 2004), 271–3; on Wales's influence on the poem see Bernard Smith, *Imagining the Pacific: In the Wake of Cook's Voyages* (New Haven and London, 1992).

> Ah wel-a-day! What evil looks
>   Had I from old and young;
> Instead of the Cross the Albatross
>   About my neck was hung
>
> (ll. 139–42)

Having accepted his social sin and become a pariah, the mariner believes himself to be suffering from a still worse form of alienation—a form that is a grim parody of companionship. He works with the living dead, so near but yet so far from those dearest to him:

> The body of my brother's son
>   Stood by me knee to knee:
> The body and I pull'd at one rope,
>   But he said nought to me—
> And I quak'd to think of my own voice
>   How frightful it would be!
>
> (ll. 341–6)

Here, in this ghastly scenario, Coleridge had found a dramatic language capable of universalizing the diagnosis of the age he had made in his political writings: alienation is brought home to the family and slavish obedience is written on the body. Like shaman-cursed Indians, the crew manifest the effects of their belief in their own bodies. Their gaze becomes spellbinding:

> All fix'd on me their stony eyes
>   That in the moon did glitter.
>
> The pang, the curse, with which they died,
>   Had never pass'd away:
> I could not draw my een from theirs
>   Ne turn them up to pray
>
> (ll. 436–41)

The gaze and touch of the dead was vital to the shaman, as Coleridge knew from travel narratives. According to Charlevoix, for instance, the 'jugglers' of the Miami Indians 'placed . . . on a Kind of Altar, some Pagods made with Bear Skins, the Heads of which were painted green. All the Savages passed this Altar bowing their Knees, and the Jugglers lead the Van, holding in their Hands a Sack which contained all the Things which they use in their Conjurations. . . . During this time the Jugglers made a Shew of bewitching some of the savages, who seemed ready to expire.' The shaman, Charlevoix continued, assumed the power to reanimate animals' corpses: he 'takes a dead Animal, [and] gives the Company Time enough to be well assured that he is dead, then by means of a pipe which he has thrust under the Tail, he causes it to move'.[9]

Wielding animals' bodies, the shamans became, apparently, possessed with their spirits. They also became uncanny—their power concentrated in their strangely transformed bodies and in the fetishes that betokened that transformation. James Adair recorded that 'when the Indian physicians visit their supposed irreligious patients, they approach them in a bending posture, with their rattling calabash ... and in that bent posture of body, they run two or three times round the sick person, contrary to the course of the sun. ... Then they invoke the raven, and mimic his croaking voice' (*Adair*, 173–4). This kind of animalistic performance was sufficient to terrify the missionary David Brainerd, who described a fetish-wielding Delaware 'conjurer' in his journal:

As he came forward, he beat his tune with the *rattle*, and danced with all his might, but did not suffer any part of his body, not so much as his fingers, to be seen: and no man would have guessed by his appearance and actions that he could have been a human creature, if they had not had some intimation of it otherwise. When he came near me, I could not but shrink away from him, although it was then noon-day, and I knew who it was, his appearance and gestures were so prodigiously frightful.[10]

The mariner, the dead animal hung round his neck, resembles the shamans Coleridge had read about. Like the shaman and the obeah-man who, Coleridge suggested, are treated with 'trembling abhorrence' because they touch people with the hand of an 'executed person', the mariner becomes uncanny, a fetish-wielder who enthrals the fetish-worshipping crew. Coleridge made the connection explicitly in a notebook entry that linked his poem to superstitions about the fetishized dead body: 'Eldridge and his Warts cured by rubbing them with the hand of his Sister's dead infant/knew a man who cured one on his Eye by rubbing it with the dead Hand of his Brother's—Comments on Ancient Mariner' (*CN*, II, 2048). The 'conjurer' (here an Englishman) worked by complicity. If one accepted his cure or curse, one also became tainted

---

[9] Charlevoix, *Letters to the Duchess of Lesdigueres, Giving an Account of a Voyage to Canada, and Travels through that vast Country, and Louisiana, to the Gulf of Mexico* (London, 1763), 141.

[10] From Brainerd's journal (1745) incorporated in Jonathan Edwards, *An Account of the Life of the Late Reverend David Brainerd* (Edinburgh, 1765), 356.

by the 'moral guilt' of touching the dead. The mariner works in this way too: he acquires power over his fellows by making them touch his body, a body that embodies his guilty violation of the boundary between life and death. He is a cursed victim who passes on guilt by the curse inscribed in his flesh:

> I mov'd my lips: the Pilot shriek'd
> And fell down in a fit.
> The Holy Hermit rais'd his eyes
> And pray'd where he did sit.
>
> (ll. 560–3)

He spellbinds those who come into contact with him. To stay and listen, as the wedding-guest discovers, is to replace the loving union of the wedding party with the guilty community of the living dead. It is to become a 'savage' or a 'slave' by our own compulsion—obedient, in fear and desire, to a tribal magician.

It is only at the very end of the poem that the reader hears again the narrator's voice that began it. Everything in between, in the 1798 version, is relayed to us by the mariner himself or by the fascinated guest. There is no neutral objective viewpoint. According to De Quincey, Coleridge had planned 'a poem on delirium, confounding its own dream imagery with external things, and connected with the imagery of high latitudes'.[11] And the mariner may, for all the reader can tell, be delirious. He may be imagining everything, his guilt making him superstitiously project a supernatural drama onto the natural world. Lacking a neutral perspective, we cannot tell, with the result that if we keep reading on we come to experience the world as the mariner sees and tells it. We plunge deeper and deeper into his mental journey whether or not he is as mad as his glittering eye suggests. Hallucinations and superstition his visions may be, but they seem as real to us as they do to the mariner, as real as do the shaman's spells to the Indian. Like the wedding guest, who stands for the reader within the poem, we are haunted by a story that is transmitted through and into the body.

If the mariner was mistaking their reverie-worlds for reality, then his curses, spells, and tales made his listeners share those worlds. Coleridge set out to make his poem affect the reader in the same way. Poetry of this kind becomes like obeah, like a wizard's spell or shamanistic rite, making an imaginary world seem real enough to affect readers physically—their

---

[11] Quoted in *Samuel Taylor Coleridge: Poems*, ed. John Beer (London, 1993), 209.

spines tingling and hair standing on end. It is, that is to say, aligned with the imagination of 'primitive' cultures, is a power that places the 'civilized' man among the 'savage' people he would like to feel superior to. 'The Rime' makes the reader experience the mental enslavement to another that, for Coleridge, is the superstitious imagination. By drawing readers into the superstitious imagination he makes them, for a while, experience the terrors and dangers (personal and social) that stem from ignorance, guilt and complicity. The reader, like the wedding guest, is left 'sadder and wiser' about his own tendency to believe the spells of those who have—or seem to have—power.

Coleridge had generated a poetry which collapsed the assumed superiority of Briton to slave, European to Indian, using the ethnographical information provided by travellers to lay bare the mechanisms by which fear and desire are produced and internalized, the mechanisms by which, in response to the culture they lived in, people shaped themselves in subservience to and/or in power over others. This poetry was, in effect, the most profound outcome of his ability to learn from accounts of native peoples an analysis of his countrymen. It was the strange, uncanny, and incisive hybrid of the English rural ballad with the American and African peoples as British travellers represented them.

But there remained a task for Coleridge—one for which the travellers' tales gave him no help. If poetry could give readers a taste of their own capacity to be complicit with power, offer them a share in imagining the world superstitiously, then it could show them that knowledge of the world was not a given, but an imaginative process in which they played an active part. This demonstration, bringing self-reflection about, might commence the reformation of the slavish self that Coleridge considered essential if political liberty was to be achieved. But it could only do so if imaginative transformation could be controlled by the will. But this transformation would not come by learning from Native Americans, because Coleridge's interpretation of their beliefs led him to view Indians as mentally enslaved by their ignorance.

The year 1798, then, and that greatest poem-collection of the era, *Lyrical Ballads*, saw the apogee of Wordsworth's and Coleridge's enthusiastic and inquiring encounter with Native Americans. The encounter had profound effects, helping to generate a new kind of poetry and a more profoundly engaged representation of Indians than any British writers had hitherto achieved. It would be left to other Romantic poets, however, to continue and deepen it in the Lake poets' wake.

10

White Men and Indian Women

It was nearly always white men who met Indian women firsthand and then wrote about the experience. What they wrote depended heavily on what kind of author they considered themselves to be. Those writing travel narratives tended to turn a few brief encounters to a generalized picture, pronouncing on the women en masse, as a phenomenon to contrast to European women. Those narrating their stories of captivity or of living as traders spoke of adoption by mothers and of relationships with partners. Their understanding was specific, and nuanced, although not free of the contradictions that arose from conflict between their experience, their desires, and their expectations about gender roles.[1]

For Samuel Hearne, Indian women were both sublime and pathetic so long as they could be portrayed as victims of their menfolk—female work-slaves used as beasts of burden:

It has ever been the custom among those people for the men to wrestle for any women to whom they are attached; and, of course, the strongest party always carries off the prize. A weak man, unless he be a good hunter and well-beloved, is seldom permitted to keep a wife that a stronger man thinks worth his notice: for at any time when the wives of those strong wrestlers are heavy-laden either with furs or provisions, they make no scruple of tearing any other man's wife from his bosom, and making her bear a part of his luggage.

(*Hearne*, 141)

Hearne considers himself more compassionate and understanding of the women's needs and virtues than their own husbands, fathers and

---

[1] On these contradictions see Sylvia Van Kirk, *'Many Tender Ties': Women in Fur-Trade Society in Western Canada, 1670–1870* (Winnipeg, 1980) and Jennifer S. H. Brown, *Strangers in Blood: Fur Trade Company Families in Indian Country* (Vancouver, 1980). Brown shows that white traders had a long tradition of marrying Indian women, finding them useful as interpreters, informants and intermediaries, and that some women acquired greater power than was normal in white or Indian society by fulfilling this inter-cultural role. She also shows that North West Company officials were not above seizing Ojibwa women by force as 'payment' for Indian debts in trade—and then selling these women to their own voyageurs (pp. 83–6).

brothers are. Ignoring, for the moment, the women's own loyalty to those men, he makes them pitiable victims, fitting them into a popular sentimental category and demonstrating his own civilized sensibility by contrast to Indian men's savage callousness.

But the picture painted by other travellers was more complicated than Hearne's. Carver did not simply position Indian women as victims and men as their bestial overlords. Instead, he argued that Indian polygamy was governed by custom and social rank rather than brute strength. He showed it to be compatible with chastity and praised the numerous instances he found of monogamy: 'there are many of the Indians who have but one wife, and enjoy with her a state of connubial happiness not to be exceeded in more refined societies' (*Carver*, 372). Indian women were regarded on the whole as chaste, modest, and virtuous in their sexual conduct because they were governed by their husbands and by the customs of their tribe. Here white men found themselves in sympathy with what they perceived (incorrectly) to be a patriarchal society.

Overall, the narratives display the white authors' confusion, a confusion that makes them strive all the harder to fit Indian women into one or another aesthetic category and gender role so that they and their readers might know how to judge them. Viewed as ferocious and vengeful, Indian women seemed both threatening and unlike most European women. Yet they were not written off as masculine heroines or savage beasts since, stoical and resigned to pain, they were also potentially pitiable victims or sublimely passive endurers—like Shakespeare's Marina, yet lacking her appealing innocence. Hearne, for example, repeatedly tried to assimilate Indian women to the natural sublime, ignoring the other characteristics that did not fit this bill. Among those characteristics were loyalty and domestic work: in Canada Indian women became the 'country wives' of many fur traders, and often proved to be astute at running the business of the trading post as well as skilful in negotiating between whites, Indian, and métis. Practical and resourceful companions, they often forged lifelong partnerships with traders, some even retiring to Montreal or to Scotland with their husbands. Hearne also declared his own Indian 'wife' to be beautiful, compassionate, and loving. He idealized her and experienced bitter remorse when she starved to death after he was taken captive by a raiding French warship.

In Canada the practice of intermarriage between traders and Indian women was long enough established to be governed by deep-rooted, though informal, custom. So too in Cherokee and Creek country, where Scots and Indians had been living together since the 1720s and 1730s. To a traveller, these social arrangements were novel. When William Bartram visited from 1773 to 1777, for instance, the harmonious rural co-habitations that he witnessed seemed charming and enviable. Like an urbanite on a pastoral excursion, Bartram brought his own preconceptions with him, viewing Indian women as seductively innocent maidens who invited dalliance and rape like so many Greek nymphs. If Hearne tried to assimilate them to the natural sublime, Bartram made them conform to the topos of pastoral and neo-classical beauty. Occluding many of the facts he had himself observed, Bartram aestheticized the Seminole women to make them sexually appealing precisely because they seemed too innocent to be fully conscious of their sex appeal.

What Hearne and Bartram had in common was a strategy for dealing with their own confusion at Indian women's cultural difference. They sought to tame the women's elusiveness, and simultaneously resolve their own uncertainty, by imagining themselves having a privileged relationship with them (and, through them, with nature itself), a relationship that their menfolk did not have. Hearne used the natural sublime, Bartram the beautiful—two opposed, though established, aesthetic categories that suggested predictable emotional responses and effaced the women's cultural complexity, turning them into embodiments of a natural wilderness that could never be fully possessed, only tasted in part. It was these very strategies that appealed to the Romantic poets, searching for images of organic society as they were. On reading Bartram and Hearne, however, they found not only that Indian women were, contradictorily, both sublime and beautiful, but also that neither of these aesthetic categories fully explained the other characteristics that the Indian women displayed. The texts contained a residue, arising from their authors' unresolved confusion and ambivalence, which was not resolved by their explicit conclusions. Their Indian women *seemed* conventionally sublime and/or beautiful, but the portraits were strongly enough haunted by a sense of the women's elusive otherness for the categories to be significantly destabilized. It was this disturbing elusiveness that intrigued the Romantic poets and that they tried to re-create in the poems that they were inspired to write. Southey's 'Dirge of the American Widow' is a case in point. Informed by Adair's description of Chikkasah women torturing captives, it offers a picture of a young woman grieving after her husband's death in battle. Haunted by his voice, she is a lovelorn figure who potentially possesses the appealing

qualities of the beautiful (as defined in Burke's influential treatise). She
is weak, feminine, in need of masculine strength to guide and protect
her—a strength the white reader might imagine himself supplying, in
the absence of her warrior-husband:

> 'Twas the voice of my husband that came on the gale,
> The unappeased spirit in anger complains,
>> Rest, rest AMALAHTA! be still!
>> The day of revenge is at hand.
>
> The stake is made ready, the captives shall die,
> To-morrow the song of their death shalt thou hear;
>> To-morrow thy widow shall wield
>> The knife and the fire; be at rest!
>
> The vengeance of anguish shall soon have its course,
> The fountains of grief and of fury shall flow;
>> I will think, AMALAHTA, of thee,
>> Will remember the days of our love.
>
> AMALAHTA, all day by thy war-pole I sat,
> Where idly thy hatchet of battle is hung,
>> I gaz'd on the bow of thy strength
>> As it wav'd on the stream of the wind.[2]
>>
>>>> (ll. 1–16)

The white reader might also be impressed by the sublimity of the Indian
physique, as she describes it—might thrill with awe at the fearsome
physical nature that the now safely dead warrior embodies:

> When the black and blood-banner was spread to the gale,
> When thrice the deep voice of the war-drum was heard,
>> I remember thy terrible eyes
>> How they flash'd the dark glance of thy joy.
>
> I remember the hope that shone over thy cheek
> As thy hand from the pole reach'd its doers of death,
>> Like the ominous gleam of the cloud
>> Ere the thunder and lightning are born.
>>
>>>> (ll. 21–8)

---

[2] Published in the *Morning Post*, 11 September 1799, see *Southey*, V, 385–6.

The sublime and beautiful are both invoked by Southey: both, however, are destabilized by the widow's cultural difference from European moral and aesthetic codes. She is not finally categorizable as beautiful—or conventionally feminine—because she dedicates herself to a cruel revenge that makes her as fierce as her dead husband. Her lovelorn lament prepares for a terrible vengeance, and she displays no consciousness of there being a discrepancy between passive lament and active violence, or female delicacy and masculine activity. In short, she takes what in Britain would be a masculine role, without any suggestion that she thereby loses her femininity. She steps beyond the feminine beautiful (the category in which the poet at first seemed to confine her), into the masculine sublime, straddling the two aesthetic categories that, according to Burke, were as much opposites as were men and women. And so it became apparent that neither the aesthetic categories nor the gender roles that Britons believed to be natural were adequate to comprehend her. Consequentially, they seemed limited and partial; readers were left unsure how to judge her and were left to acknowledge that she, as an Indian, possessed a tribal identity that was not reducible to the categories into which white culture was organized. Ultimately Wordsworth was troubled enough by this identity to reject Indian life and Indian nature altogether: he came to see Indian 'wildness' as being dangerously destructive of the emotional and moral structures that he defined as being naturally British. When he was writing *Lyrical Ballads*, however, his interest in Indians led him to make some of the most uncanny poems he ever wrote—strange meetings between conventional aesthetic categories and figures who elude those categories.

HEARNE AND THE SUBLIME

Samuel Hearne was the traveller who troubled Wordsworth most productively. If travel writing's variety allowed multiple and contradictory readings, few travel texts were as arrestingly ambivalent as Hearne's. In one and the same passage, he was capable of giving admiring and nuanced accounts of Indians' harmony with their hostile environment and of condemning their cruelty to each other, as in this discussion of a lone woman his party encountered in the wilderness:

On the eleventh of January (1772), as some of my companions were hunting, they saw the track of a strange snow-shoe, which they followed; and at a considerable distance came to a little hut, where they discovered a young woman sitting alone. As they found that she understood their language, they brought her with them to the tents. On examination, she proved to be one of the Western Dog-ribbed Indians, who had been taken prisoner by the Athapuscow Indians in the Summer of one thousand seven hundred and seventy; and in the following Summer, when the Indians that took her prisoner were near this part, she had eloped from them, with an intent to return to her own country; but the distance being so great, and having, after she was taken prisoner, been carried in a canoe the whole way, the turnings and windings of the rivers and lakes were so numerous, that she forgot the track; so she built the hut in which we found her, to protect her from the weather during the Winter, and here she had resided from the first setting in of the fall.

From her account of the moons passed since her elopement, it appeared that she had been near seven months without seeing a human face; during all which time she had supported herself very well by snaring partridges, rabbits, and squirrels; she had also killed two or three beaver, and some porcupines. That she did not seem to have been in want is evident, as she had a small stock of provisions by her when she was discovered; and was in good health and condition, and I think one of the finest women, of a real Indian, that I have seen in any part of North America.

The methods practised by this poor creature to procure a livelihood were truly admirable, and are great proofs that necessity is the real mother of invention. When the few deer sinews that she had an opportunity of taking with her were all expended in making snares, and sewing her clothing, she had nothing to supply their place but the sinews of rabbits' legs and feet; these she twisted together for that purpose with great dexterity and success. The rabbits &c. which she caught in these snares, not only furnished her with a comfortable subsistence, but of the skins she made a suit of neat and warm clothing for the Winter. ... The materials, though rude, were very curiously wrought, and so judiciously placed, as to make the whole of her garb have a very pleasing, though rather romantic appearance.

[...]

The singularity of the circumstance, the comeliness of her person, and her approved accomplishments, occasioned a strong contest between several of the Indians of my party, who should have her for a wife; and the poor girl was actually won and lost at wrestling by near half a score different men the same evening. My guide, Matonabbee, who at that time had no less than seven wives, all women grown, besides a young girl of eleven or twelve years old, would have put in for the prize also, had not one of his wives made him ashamed of it, by telling him that he had already more wives than he could properly attend. This piece of satire, however true, proved fatal to the poor girl who dared to make so open a declaration; for the great man, Matonabbee, who would willingly have been thought equal to eight or ten men in every respect, took it as such an affront, that he fell on her with both hands and feet, and bruised her to such a degree, that after lingering some time she died.

When the Athapuscow Indians took the above Dog-ribbed Indian women prisoner, they, according to the universal custom of those savages, surprised her and her party in the night, and killed every soul in the tent, except herself and three other young women. Among those whom they killed, were her father, mother and husband. Her young child, four or five months old, she concealed in a bundle of clothing, and took with her undiscovered in the night; but when she arrived at the place where the Athapuscow Indians had left their wives (which was not far distant), they began to examine her bundle, and finding the child, one of the women took it from her, and killed it on the spot.

This last piece of barbarity gave her such a disgust to those Indians, that notwithstanding the man who took care of her treated her in every respect as his wife, and was, she said, remarkably kind to, and even fond of her; so far was she from being able to reconcile herself to any of the tribe, that she rather chose to expose herself to misery and want, than live at ease and affluence among persons who had so cruelly murdered her infant. The poor woman's relation of this shocking story, which she delivered in a very affecting manner, only excited laughter among the savages of my party.

(*Hearne*, 263–7)

Hearne asks readers to admire the Indian woman's lone resourcefulness: she is a paragon of fortitude, 'romantic' in her ability to dwell at one with nature, surviving in what seems the harshest of environments. A nature-woman, she is both housewifely and sublime—a woman of awesome 'singularity', who exceeds what Hearne thought possible and what the other Indians achieve. Alone, but turning the snowy wilderness into a home, she satisfies Hearne's desire for an encounter with nature in its essence. He idealizes her, only to show that his awestruck reaction is not shared by the Indian men. His admiration is disinterested: he views her as he would a natural object, solely for a vicarious emotional experience. Theirs is brutally self-interested: they compete to take her as their chattel. The fate of Matonabbee's wife suggests, in this context, that women are used as objects, won and kept by the strongest male. Indian society seems close to that of brutes; apparently only the white man can appreciate the woman's sublimity in any other terms than the desire to possess and to subject. The white explorer's aesthetic sensibility (and those of his readers) demonstrates his moral superiority: he is more chivalrous and paternalistic than the woman's own menfolk. The text, in effect, creates a special, singular relationship between the lone woman and the observing explorer. Eventually, this relationship was used to identify British colonialism as a benevolent paternalism. White readers would be assured that British government was better for Indian women than rule by Indian men.

The encounter with the Dog-ribbed Indian woman is not the only example of Hearne using the natural sublime to construct a special relationship between white traveller and Indian women. He also described how his Indian guides abandoned one of the women who, having fallen ill, could no longer keep up with the party:

> it is the common, and indeed the constant practice of those Indians; for when a grown person is so ill, especially in the Summer, as not to be able to walk, and too heavy to be carried, they say it is better to leave one who is past recovery, than for the whole family to sit down by them and starve to death; well knowing that they cannot be of any service to the afflicted. On those occasions, therefore, the friends or relations of the sick generally leave them some victuals and water; and, if the situation of the place will afford it, a little firing.
>
> *(Hearne, 219)*

The abandoned woman recovered sufficiently to rejoin the party, but could not keep pace and was finally left behind. Hearne concludes:

> A custom apparently so unnatural is perhaps not to be found among any other of the human race: if properly considered, however, it may with justice be ascribed to necessity and self-preservation, rather than to the want of humanity and social feeling, which ought to be the characteristic of men, as the noblest part of the creation. Necessity, added to custom, contributes principally to make scenes of this kind less shocking to those people, than they must appear to the more civilized part of mankind.
>
> *(Hearne, 219)*

Hearne seeks to overcome his desire to condemn by explaining the practice in terms of Indian customs, which he understands as a rational response to the harsh climate. Here his ambivalence about his Indian companions is especially strong as he inclines towards blame then exculpation. He is shocked by his encounter with a custom that is so alien to his own culture's values and so apparently callous, while he is also haunted by the idea of the woman starving and freezing to death, alone.

If Hearne was haunted, Wordsworth was even more troubled. After reading Hearne, he chose not just to imagine the woman's lonely death from the traveller's viewpoint, but also to narrate it from her own. 'The Complaint of the Forsaken Indian Woman' (1798) personalizes Hearne's third person narrative, shifting the focus from the white man's to the Indian woman's emotions. But in making this shift, Wordsworth develops what is implied in Hearne's account of the other lone Indian woman—the Dog-ribbed Indian whose isolation in the wilderness makes her both 'romantic' and sublime. Wordsworth, that is to say, makes the Forsaken Indian Woman both a pitiable victim of male-governed Indian society and a sublime other: she is awe-inspiring in her stoical embrace of oncoming death, an embrace that makes her fascinatingly but also admirably alien:

> My journey will be shortly run,
> I shall not see another sun,
> I cannot lift my limbs to know
> If they have any life or no,
> My poor forsaken child! if I
> For once could have thee close to me,
> With happy heart I then would die,
> And my last thoughts would happy be.
> I feel my body die away,
> I shall not see another day.
>
> (*LB*, ll. 61–70)

The Indian woman is allowed her cultural difference—and admired for it—because she looks calmly at death without fear even though she has no Christian anticipation of an afterlife. She is, then, sublime—a human who speaks from as close to nature as it is possible to get.

Yet she is also a doubting, fearful, regretful person, a person with a character, rather than just a voice of nature. As a mother, she grieves for the child who has been taken from her. As a member of the tribe, she laments her separation:

> Too soon despair o'er me prevailed;
> Too soon my heartless spirit failed;
> When you were gone my limbs were stronger,
> And Oh how grievously I rue,
> That, afterwards a little longer,
> My friends, I did not follow you!
> For strong and without pain I lay,
> My friends when you were gone away.
>
> (ll. 23–30)

Wordsworth gives his Indian woman a psychological complexity that is absent from Hearne's portraits. Although he assimilates her to the natural sublime, he does so without occluding her cultural difference. She may invite admiration, may entreat pity, may seem a victim of

Indian men, (and the poem's very title alludes to the cry Jesus made on the cross when he suspected God, like man, had abandoned him), yet readers cannot simply assume that they can comfort her when her own people do not. We may desire to do so, but her repeated insistence on the sheer fact of her coming demise ultimately resists our vicarious emotional succor. Pitiable and awesome in turn, she is finally neither but rather a self-enclosed, self-fulfilling prophet of her own death, a person whose acceptance of what her tribe has left her to face is neither praised nor condemned, neither wholly inexplicable nor exclusively understood. Wordsworth leaves her an enigma, and us in an emotional quandary as to our relationship with her (and with other people of markedly different cultures). In doing so, he unsettles the languages of sentiment and sublimity that he inherited from Hearne but also (since his song is a feminized death song) from Ritson. Both are invoked; neither language is sufficient to comprehend her actions or explain her song fully.

'The Complaint' is not the only Lyrical Ballad to feature an Indian woman. 'The Mad Mother' is also about a woman who is—or may be—a Native American. As Wordsworth stated in a letter of 1836, she is 'either of these islands, or a North American. On the latter supposition, while the distance removes her from us, the fact of her speaking our language brings us at once into close sympathy with her.'[3] The poem itself leaves her identity uncertain: the mother is brown of cheek, with 'coal black hair' and knows how to 'build an Indian bower', yet is in Britain, speaking English. She is, in fact, both different from and familiar to other Britons, an alien within, or foreign native, who escapes known categories of identity. Wordsworth, in fact, makes judging her nationality impossible: his narrator is not only not omniscient, he is unsure of the basic facts:

> Her eyes are wild, her head is bare,
> The sun has burnt her coal-black hair,
> Her eyebrows have a rusty stain,
> And she came far from over the main.
> She has a baby on her arm,
> Or else she were alone;
> And underneath the haystack warm,
> And on the greenwood stone,

[3] *The Letters of William and Dorothy Wordsworth, The Later Years*, ed. Ernest De Selincourt, rev. Alan G. Hill (Oxford, 1982–8), part iii, 293.

> She talked and sung the woods among—
> And it was in the English tongue.
>
> 　　　　　　　　　　　　(*LB*, ll. 1–10)

The bundle on her arm, possibly a dead baby, suggests that she is derived from Hearne's account of the Dog-ribbed Indian woman concealing her baby 'in a bundle of clothing', only for the Athapuscow women to discover it and kill it (*Hearne*, 266). Charlevoix, also observing the Indians of Canada, stated that 'some Mothers have been known to have kept the dead Bodies of their Children whole Years, and could never go from them; others draw milk from their Breasts, and pour it upon the Tombs of these little Creatures'.[4] Throughout the poem, the mother speaks about the sensation of drawing milk from her breasts: 'Suck, little babe, oh suck again! / It cools my blood, it cools my brain; / Thy lips I feel them, baby, they / Draw from my heart the pain away. / Oh, press me with thy little hand, / It loosens something at my chest' (ll. 31–6). Breastfeeding creates an intense intimacy into which much of her identity is concentrated. But what she says is as disturbing as it is loving, for it suggests that the relationship with the beloved baby excludes—indeed perverts—all others: 'A fire was once within my brain, / And in my head a dull, dull pain; / And fiendish faces—one, two, three, / Hung at my breasts, and pulled at me' (ll. 21–24). After this statement, the mother seems mad. Yet it is hard to be sure. It is never established beyond doubt whether she has a live baby, a dead one, or only a bundle of rags on her arms. How then can readers know whether she is distracted or, if she is, whether she is benevolent or malevolent? What seems like insanity may be a maternal love so intense that it prefers an 'Indian' life beyond society, sheltered by nature. Certainly her vision of such a life is full of maternal protectiveness and is, confusingly, both pathetic and unsettling:

> Then do not fear, my boy! for thee
> Bold as a lion I will be;
> And I will always be thy guide,
> Through hollow snows and rivers wide.
> I'll build an Indian bower; I know
> The leaves that make the softest bed:
> And if from me thou wilt not go,

---

[4] Charlevoix, *Letters to the Duchess of Lesdigueres, Giving an Account of a Voyage to Canada, and Travels through that vast Country, and Louisiana, to the Gulf of Mexico* (London, 1763), 274.

> But still be true 'till I am dead,
> My pretty thing! then thou shalt sing,
> As merry as the birds in spring.
>
> (ll. 51–60)

The woman has all the characteristics of Indian women: not only will she build an Indian bower, but will teach the boy 'how the owlet sings' (mimicking birds was an essential part not only of the tricksters' role but of the Indian hunter's). Yet we are left unsure whether to admire her as a loving 'Indian' at one with nature, or to pity (and fear) her as an unhinged obsessive, likely to do (or have done) her baby harm. And because we are unsure, we cannot either dismiss her as a lunatic or idealize her as a noble savage. The last stanza, for example, seems to offer the beautiful dream, expressed so powerfully in Rousseau, Raynal and Bartram, of finding in Indian life a prelapsarian unity with nature:

> Oh smile on me, my little lamb,
> For I thy own dear mother am.
> My love for thee has well been tried;
> I've sought thy father far and wide.
> I know the poisons of the shade,
> I know the earth-nuts fit for food;
> Then, pretty dear, be not afraid—
> We'll find thy father in the wood.
> Now laugh and be gay, to the woods away,
> And there, my babe, we'll live for aye.
>
> (ll. 91–100)

Yet the reference to 'poisons of the shade', in context, raises the possibility that she will kill the child rather than part with it or see it grow up. And so the poem refuses conventional emotional resolution: should we purge pity or fear? Not knowing, we are forced instead to experience our own attitudes fluctuating. And what results from this experience is a sense of the woman's power and of the inadequacy of social structures and aesthetic schemes to understand it. The familiar/distant, British/Indian woman is uncanny and her uncanniness reveals the stark profundity with which a way of being is lived out, a way for which there is no name, and that is other and close-to-home at once. The Mad Mother, that is to say, is marked by Indianness for the same reason as the Forsaken Indian Woman: for Wordsworth, in *Lyrical Ballads*, Indian women reveal the irreducible individuality with which people experience the rural life that seems, from a distance, familiar and undifferentiated. The Forsaken Indian Woman is not the exception but the defining case amongst all the rural women in Wordsworth's collection: his mad mothers, female vagrants are all forsaken Indian women—or at least aspire to her indigenous state. Like the Indian, all Wordsworth's women gain a certain power as they sing out their own interpretation of their bodily distress. By voicing their state orally and immediately, they come to define their being by it and even to embrace it. What seems 'madness' may, Wordsworth suggests, be the 'Indian' voice of a woman who has come to accept and even to will her isolation and death. Freedom in nature reaches its apogee in an individual difference from civilization experienced as an embrace of otherness. The language of rural life, it seems, is at its most authentically experienced when spoken by a woman who is embracing alienation or oblivion.

It was in its apprehension of this kind of Indianness that Wordsworth's poetry was new and original (or, in the opinion of early reviewers, powerfully peculiar). Wordsworth's songs differ from other songs of the 1790s in their gendered uncanniness: in his hands the ballad is exalted to the status of lyric when it acquires the autochthonous self-identity of the Indian woman's song of death or madness. In these poetic circumstances the male poet and his readers threaten to become vampiric: if death and madness are the ultimate Indian/indigenous states, then more forsaken women and mad mothers will be required in whom men can locate unique, uncommodified identity. The risk here is that as the poet searches for uncanny indigenes to challenge 'civilized' assumptions he threatens to turn them into commodities of his own—commodities destined to die.

BARTRAM AND THE BEAUTIFUL

It was the uncommodified uniqueness of Florida that excited Wordsworth when he read William Bartram but it was the danger involved in commodifying that uniqueness that led him to turn away from his enthusiasm for Indian life. This may seem surprising, for Bartram's text is far less disturbing than Hearne's, employing as it does pastoral beauty rather than the sublime.

Bartram is not just a recorder and idealizer. He is the engagingly modest and inoffensive hero of his own story, a prime example of what

Mary Louise Pratt has called the myth of anti-conquest—a colonist who appears so vulnerable, peaceful, and inoffensive that he scarcely seems a representative of a culture that wished to appropriate the lands of indigenous people.[5] Bartram's playfulness offers to displace any real colonial violence into an arch Ovidian neo-classicism. But Bartram also fantasizes, turning Indian women into fruits of an Arcadian garden. They are as natural and simple as the strawberries they pluck:

> a vast expanse of green meadows and strawberry fields; ... companies of young, innocent Cherokee virgins, some busily gathering the rich fragrant fruit, others having already filled their baskets, lay reclined under the shade of floriferous and fragrant bowers of Magnolia, Azalea, Philadelphus, perfumed Calycanthus, sweet Yellow Jessamine and cerulian Glycine frutescens, disclosing their beauties to the fluttering breeze, and bathing their limbs in the cool fleeting streams; whilst other parties, more gay and libertine, were yet collecting strawberries or wantonly chasing their companions, tantalizing them, staining their lips and cheeks with the rich fruit.

> This sylvan scene of primitive innocence was enchanting, and perhaps too enticing for hearty young men long to continue idle spectators.

> In fine, nature prevailing over reason, we wished at least to have a more active part in their delicious sports. Thus precipitately resolving, we cautiously made our approaches, yet undiscovered, almost to the joyous scene of action. Now, although we meant no other than an innocent frolic with this gay assembly of hamadryades, we shall leave it to the person of feeling and sensibility to form an idea to what lengths our passions might have hurried us, thus warmed and excited, had it not been for the vigilance and care of some envious matrons who lay in ambush, and espying us gave the alarm.[6]

In fact, Bartram and his companions respect the maidens' modesty and taste only the strawberries, enjoying a pastoral meal on the green meadow. Bartram consummates his colonial desire not by raping the Cherokee virgins, but by gathering the flora to which he likens them. Nevertheless, the hints of colonial violence are present, the savage idyll provoking the sophisticated traveller to want to possess its innocence. Wordsworth picked up both the idyll and the dangerous desire it provoked when he put Bartram into verse in 'Ruth'. In this poem, added to the second edition of *Lyrical Ballads* (1800), Wordsworth is at first intoxicated, as Coleridge had been, by Bartram's description of

[5] Mary Louise Pratt, *Imperial Eyes: Travel Writing and Transculturation* (London and New York, 1992), 7.

[6] William Bartram, *Travels through North and South Carolina, Georgia, East and West Florida* (1792: facs. rpt. Savannah, GA, 1973), 355.

the verdant landscape of Florida and the contented life lived there by the Seminoles. The poem tells the story of a 'White Indian', a youth so intoxicated by the life of noble savagery that he emigrates, and persuades his love Ruth to emigrate, to the southern states of the US:

> The Youth of green savannahs spake,
> And many an endless, endless lake,
> With all its fairy crowds
> Of islands, that together lie
> As quietly as spots of sky
> Among the evening clouds.
>
> 'How pleasant,' then he said, 'it were
> A fisher or a hunter there,
> In sunshine or in shade
> To wander with an easy mind:
> And build a household fire, and find
> A home in every glade!
>
> (ll. 67–78)[7]

This is conventional noble savagery: Wordsworth plays on an established topos and calls on the stock aesthetics of the beautiful.

Yet when Ruth and her youthful lover arrive in America the idyll turns out to be dangerous because the beautiful innocence of Indian women and the delights of the nature that they inhabit (and symbolize) cannot be accessed by the visitor without encountering Indian men. And Indian men turn out to be seductive for the wrong reasons: their wildness does not invigorate but corrupts the morals and emotions of unsuspecting Britons. When Ruth's beloved 'youth' comes under the influence of its nature and its natives, he abandons her for a life of 'lawless' liberty:

> But ill he lived, much evil saw,
> With men to whom no better law
> Nor better life was known;
> Deliberately, and undeceived,
> Those wild men's vices he received,
> And gave them back his own.
>
> (ll. 145–50)

Here Wordsworth betrays doubts about wildness and liberty that reflect his growing distance, by 1800, from revolutionary politics. But he

---

[7] *Lyrical Ballads*, 2nd edn. (1800).

ponders these doubts by setting them on a foreign stage: his Indian men pervert themselves in an American landscape whose free growth then symbolizes their wildness. The idyll becomes a dystopia, the noble savage an ignoble 'slave of low desires'. Emigration to live among Indians produces a vicious circle of immoral exchange—'civilized' white men who idealize savage life are corrupted by and in turn corrupt the Indians they emigrated to join. This bleak vision is, in part, a Wordsworthian rebuke to his pantisocratic fellow poets. It is also a retreat from the poetic vision Wordsworth had himself expressed in the *Lyrical Ballads* and *Prelude* of 1798.

Why did Wordsworth retreat? The cause, I think, was to do with the different dynamics that arose between male writer and male Indians. In the ballads of 1798 he had ignored Indian men. The Forsaken Indian Woman and the Mad Mother are alone signifying to the traveller/poet in isolation. What he learns from them is difficult and elusive—a lesson in their individual irreducibility. But nobody else interferes to claim possession of them or define their meaning. Wordsworth's uncanny Indian women, strange destabilizations of the sublime and beautiful, depend on the effacement of Indian men. In 1800, however, his source material led him not to expiring Indian women but to forceful Indian men. Bartram idealized Indian women, but found his Ovidian fantasies colliding with the grimmer reality presented by their menfolk. He saw shocking scenes of dissipation in which white traders and native Americans encouraged each other in debauchery—Indian 'wildness' reacting to the white men's poisoned gift of alcohol:

White and red men and women without distinction, passed the day merrily with these jovial, amorous topers, and the nights in convivial songs, dances, and sacrifices to Venus, as long as they could stand or move; for in these frolicks both sexes take such liberties with each other, and act, without constraint or shame, such scenes as they would abhor when sober or in their senses; and would endanger their ears and even their lives: but at last their liquor running low, and being most of them sick through intoxication, they became more sober; and now the dejected lifeless sots would pawn every thing they were in possession of, for a mouthful of spirits to settle their stomachs, as they termed it.[8]

This scene stands behind Wordsworth's comment 'Those wild men's vices he received / And gave them back his own'. Unable to ignore such

[8] Bartram, *Travels*, 253–4.

disgusting descriptions, unable either to efface Indian men from the scene Bartram had opened to his eyes or to treat them as uncorrupted noble savages, Wordsworth rejected them altogether. Ruth returns, and represents Wordsworth's own return, from the drunken forests to more temperate climes.

11

Political Indians

It was another young poet, Thomas Campbell, who dramatized in depth the white/Indian violence that made Wordsworth turn away from romanticizing Indians after 1800. Like Coleridge, Campbell was a man of radical Whig sympathies who admired the American Revolution and regarded its leaders not as rebels against rightful British rule but as heroes of liberty. In the poem that made his name, *The Pleasures of Hope* (1799), he praised Benjamin Franklin and damned British imperialism in Africa, the West Indies and India. In his next major work, *Gertrude of Wyoming* (1809),[1] he turned his attention to the effects of British colonialism in America, basing his narrative on notorious events that occurred during the War of Independence.

These events were, by the time Campbell turned his attention to them, already thirty years old and already the subject of intense discussion on both sides of the Atlantic. Speeches had been made in Parliament, sensational stories published in the papers, eyewitness accounts incorporated in popular histories. In all these often violently opposed representations, the 'nature' of Indians was at stake and their involvement in colonial politics in question. And since the events involved the killing of white people by Indians led by other white men, the discussion they provoked opened issues of complicity, guilt, honour and loyalty split on racial lines.

The events began in 1778, in the war for dominance of America that pitted Britain against its own colonists, a war involving regular British troops, loyalist or 'Tory' white Americans, 'rebels' or pro-independence white Americans, and, on both sides, Indian tribes. By 1778 the British were harassing the rebels by sending troops of rangers, allied with Indians loyal to British government, to attack garrisons and burn homesteads and crops. This unorthodox warfare, however, intensified opposition in

---

[1] *Gertrude of Wyoming: a Pennsylvanian Tale and Other Poems* (London, 1809).

Britain because it constituted a departure from European conventions.
By attacking homesteads and by employing Indians to do so, the British
army seemed to be abandoning the code of honour and chivalry, which
dictated that mercy be shown to the unarmed and that women and
children should not become victims. Worse still, to opponents of the
alliance, employing Indians was to encourage 'savages' to be still more
savage, to subject white women and children—still subjects of the
Crown—to the murderous violence of 'braves' who knew no mercy.

Whether or not he was genuinely horrified, the former first minister
Pitt the Elder seized on the association to focus opposition to a war in
which he did not believe. Speaking in Parliament, he painted Indians
as grim as he could with the intention of winning a debate about
white people's colonial politics. War with the American colonists was
wrong, and the use of Indian fighters revealed that the government
had abandoned its civilized standards: the Indians were 'these horrible
hell-hounds of savage war!' (*Lects 1795*, 56n.). In February, Edmund
Burke added his voice to the debate. In what was considered his greatest
speech, he spoke for three and a half hours against Britain's use of
Indians. He inveighed against their 'native cruelty' which 'consisted
in human scalps, in human flesh, and the gratifications arising from
torturing, mangling, roasting alive by slow fires, and frequently even
devouring their captives'.[2] Burke presented the Indian warriors in terms
specified in his own aesthetic theory as belonging to the sublime of
horror. Here the imagined Indians served the Whig parliamentarian's
articulation of colonial guilt. He exaggerated Indian violence in order
to prick the consciences and disturb the imaginations of a House of
Commons that regarded itself as the guardian of civilized values.

In July 1778 an incident occurred which seemed to be the realization of the horrors conjured up by Burke's sublime rhetoric. Mohawks
commanded by Major John Butler, a loyalist colonist, attacked the colonial garrison at Wyoming, Pennsylvania. According to rebel accounts,
Butler's white troops 'were so disguised and painted, as not to be
distinguished from the Indians', and proceeded to act in a 'savage'
manner. They defeated the small garrison and then pillaged the valley.
The now defenceless women and children were forced to flee over the
mountains, many dying en route. But the survivors brought tales of
seeing the garrison (mostly comprised of their aged or infirm menfolk)
scalped, tortured, and burnt to death after being outflanked by the

---

[2] Burke, in *Annual Register* (1778), 'History of Europe', 111.

Indians—Butler reported taking 227 scalps. Contemporary historians portrayed the affair as shameful to Britain: one wrote that the 'expediency of employing monsters in human shape will be tried by unalterable laws' of posterity.[3]

In Britain, the Wyoming massacre acquired legendary status, helping to shape the image of Indian warriors for generations to come. Southey and Coleridge were too young to remember the war with America, yet they knew all about the Wyoming affair and worried about it when they planned their own colony in the area. The Pantisocrats had planned to establish their colony by the Susquehannah river, having read about the Edenic nature of the area in Franklin, Cooper, and in the reports of the Wyoming 'massacre' which had so outraged Burke and other anti-war Whigs. By 1795 Coleridge was writing publicly of Indian hostility as he imagined the 'massacre' at Wyoming as the destruction of a virtuous community reminiscent of Pantisocracy:

What the wisdom of Agur wished, the inhabitants of Wyoming enjoyed—they had neither Riches or Poverty: their climate was soft and salubrious, and their fertile soil asked of these blissful Settlers as much labor only for their sustenance, as would have been otherwise convenient for their health. The Fiend, whose crime was Ambition, leapt over into this Paradise—Hell-hounds laid it waste. *English* Generals invited the Indians 'banquet on blood': the savage Indians headed by an Englishman attacked it. Universal massacre ensued.

(*Lects 1795*, 56)

Borrowing the Whig rhetoric of Pitt and Burke, Coleridge makes the Indians savage and bestial in order to make their use seem more shameful to the British government he opposes: they become 'Drinkers of human Blood' and 'Feasters on human Flesh . . . seen in horrid circles, counting their scalps'. They are 'human Tygers . . . called from their woods, their attack regulated by Discipline' (*Lects 1795*, 57). Britain, in other words, had made the Indians worse than they already were. British discipline and Indian savagery made a vicious circle of violent influence.

Coleridge's stereotypical rhetoric was less than disinterested. Like Burke and Pitt he pictured Indians as savage *by nature* because it suited

[3] *Annual Register* (1778), 'History of Europe', 111, 113. The events were debated in Robert Macfarlane, *The History of the Second Ten Years of the Reign of George the Third* (London, 1782), 379, *Account of the Dreadful Devastation of Wyoming Settlements, in July 1778. From Gordon's History of the American War in Archibald Loudon, A Selection of the most Interesting Narratives of Outrages Committed by the Indians in Their Wars with the White People*, 2 vols. (Carlisle, 1808, rpt. 1888, facs. rpt. New York, 1971), I, 103.

his political campaign at home in Britain. The image of the Indian became intertwined with British and colonial American politics—as the tribes themselves did if they allied with one or the other of the white people's sides. Reviving the Wyoming affair of 1778, Coleridge was influenced not only by elder Whig parliamentarians, however, but also by the new force given to Indian violence by the publication of Carver's *Travels Through the Interior Parts of North America* in 1788. Carver had been present when Indians allied to the French killed prisoners at Fort William Henry in 1757; his graphic description of defenceless women and children, as well as wounded men, hunted as they fled and tomahawked, and of Indians drinking their blood as it flowed warm from their wounds, made the alliance of white men with Indian warriors a burning issue again (*Carver*, 320–7). Fired by images of horrific violence, Coleridge used the by now common view that employment of Indians tainted Britain as he indicted the counter-revolutionary war and exploitative colonialism of 1795:

In Europe the smoking Villages of Flanders, and the putrified Fields of La Vendee—from Africa the unnumbered Victims of a detestable Slave-trade—in Asia the desolated plains of Indostan and the Million whom a rice-contracting Governor caused to perish—in America the recent enormities of their Scalp-Merchants—the four Quarters of the Globe groan beneath the intolerable iniquity of this nation!

(*Lects 1795*, 58)

It was this kind of rhetoric that Campbell invoked when he decided to write a poem on the Wyoming events. The Indians of his Wyoming are overdetermined, inhabiting a poetic place in which their roles are prescribed by the needs of a poet writing in terms of domestic and imported traditions—traditions that did not necessarily dovetail. Campbell's Wyoming can be seen as the uneasy confrontation of a poetic tradition (itself based on travel accounts) with the political rhetoric of the Whig party.

Like Coleridge, Campbell depicted the Wyoming settler community in pastoral terms—virtuous, innocent, peaceful. It had in fact been wracked by strife between Pennsylvania and Connecticut colonists competing for the same land since it was first sold by the Indians in 1755. In 1770 several were killed, as bitter skirmishing led to sieges and to the burning of crops and homesteads. By 1775, when Britain and its American colonies went to war, old feuds between the settlers were entrenched. The War of Independence allowed their renewal, with

the aid of the British and of Indians who resented settlers' attempts
to expand into their own territory. Campbell recounts nothing of this
history, but neither does he follow Coleridge in simply portraying
the Indians as beasts. He suggests that the Wyoming Indians are also
capable of virtue and loyalty and that their harmony with nature makes
them naturally noble. These suggestions are based less on a detailed
knowledge of local circumstances than on Campbell's reading of the
standard accounts of Indians. His notes cite the sources from which
the 'figurative language' of the Indian characters is drawn: Cadwallader
Colden and Thomas Jefferson.[4] On the authority of these accounts
Campbell shows tribal society to be as internally peaceful as he claimed
the settler community to be: 'As these people live in a state of equality,
and without fear of internal violence or theft in their own tribes, they
leave their doors open by night as well as by day.'[5]

Campbell's principal source, Isaac Weld (Wild), asserted that 'no
people on earth are more alive to the calls of friendship' and this view
is reflected in Campbell's principal Indian—Outalissi.[6] This Oneida
Indian chief rescues the boy Henry Waldegrave, who has been orphaned
by a Huron Indian attack on a settlement. On the dying wish of Henry's
mother and at great risk to himself, he delivers Henry into the care of
Albert, Gertrude's widowed father. Outalissi is a noble savage, 'A stoic
of the wood', who is nevertheless full of paternal feeling for 'another's
woe' (canto I, stanza 24), as his song of blessing reveals:

> Sleep, wearied one! and in the dreaming land
> Shouldst thou the spirit of thy mother greet,
> Oh! say, to-morrow, that the white man's hand
> Hath pluck'd the thorns of sorrow from thy feet;
> While I in lonely wilderness shall meet
> Thy little foot prints—or by traces know
> The fountain, where at noon I thought it sweet
> To feed thee with the quarry of my bow,
> And pour'd the lotus-horn, or slew the mountain roe.

> Adieu! sweet scion of the rising sun!
> But should affliction's storms thy blossom mock,
> Then come again—my own adopted one!

[4] Campbell, *Gertrude*, 81, 94–7.   [5] Campbell, *Gertrude*, 82.
[6] Isaac Weld, Jr., *Travels Through the States of North America and the Provinces of Upper and Lower Canada During the Years 1795, 1796, and 1797* (London, 1799), 398.

> And I will graft thee on a noble stock:
> The crocodile, the condor of the rock—
> Shall be the pastime of thy sylvan wars;
> And I will teach thee, in the battle's-shock,
> To pay with Huron blood thy father's scars,
> And gratulate his soul rejoicing in the stars!—
>
> (canto I, stanzas 25–6)

Outalissi's paternal affection is expressed in his desire to teach Henry the physical skills of hunting and fighting. He is himself defined by his physical embodiment of nature.

> But dauntless he, nor chart, nor journey's plan
> In woods required, whose trained eye was keen
> As eagle of the wilderness, to scan
> His path, by mountain, swamp, or deep ravine,
> Or ken far friendly huts on good savannas green.
>
> (canto I, stanza 27)

Not only is his song a spontaneous overflow of natural feelings but he is eagle-like in his reading of the landscape. He is a primitive man as much at home in the wilds as is a beast. The details of his direction-finding ability were taken from Weld, who argued 'the North American Indians are extremely sagacious and observant, and by dint of minute attention, acquire many qualifications to which we are wholly strangers. They will traverse a trackless forest'.[7] Such abilities allowed Campbell to continue the Romantic tradition of portraying Indian men as unalienated possessors of nature's secrets. He could not, however, reconcile this portrait with his fascinated depiction of Indian bodies as excessive and fierce. His image of Indian men remained complex and self-conflicting, with the result that he divided his characters into good Indians (noble, courteous, full of nature's lore) and bad ones (cruel, warlike, untrustworthy, savage).

Outalissi is a good Indian, composed of stereotypical images of the noble savage. But it is his loyalty to white men and his paternalism that are most emphasized, to make him appealing to readers sitting at home in domestic comfort. After his departure, the poem moves forward fifteen years, to picture romantic love. Henry, it transpires, had been sent away to England. He now returns, disguised; Gertrude recognizes him and the two declare their love. But this love is destroyed as the hostile

---

[7] Campbell, *Gertrude*, 83.

forces of Butler's Indians, loyal to the British, attack Wyoming. Fleeing
to the fort, Gertrude and her father are killed, leaving Henry bereft.

The poem does not end with Gertrude's death and Henry's grief, but
with Outalissi's death song. And this is consistent, for it is the Indian's
paternalism in which Campbell has been most interested throughout.
Outalissi stands in the position of father to Henry, and this relationship,
in Campbell's vision of colonialism, offers the possibility of peace and
love between settlers and Indians. And whereas it was conventional to
portray colonists in the father's position, with the colonized natives their
children, here Campbell makes the Indian the patriarch. He tempers
the fierceness of the warrior with a father's love as Outalissi recognizes
the now adult Henry:

> 'It is my own,' he cried, and clasp'd him to his soul
>
> Yes! thou recall'st my pride of years, for then
> The bowstring of my spirit was not slack,
> When, spite of woods, and floods, and ambush'd men,
> I bore thee like the quiver on my back,
> Fleet as the whirlwind hurries on the rack;
> Nor foeman then, nor cougar's crouch I fear'd,
> For I was strong as mountain cataract:
> And dost thou not remember how we cheer'd
> Upon the last hill-top, when white men's huts appear'd?
>
> (canto III, stanzas 13–14)

After Gertrude's and Albert's death, it is Outalissi's death song that
speaks to and for Henry, who is prostrate with grief. Outalissi sets
him and the reader a fatherly example, grieving but retaining a heroic
manfulness:

> To-morrow let us do or die!
> But when the bolt of death is hurl'd,
> Ah! whither then with thee to fly,
> Shall Outalissi roam the world?
> Seek we thy once-lov'd home?—
> The hand is gone that cropt its flowers!
> Unheard their clock repeats its hours!—
> Cold is the hearth within their bow'rs!—
> And should we thither roam,
> Its echoes, and its empty tread,
> Would sound like voices from the dead!

> Or shall we cross yon mountains blue,
> Whose streams my kindred nation quaff'd;
> And by my side, in battle true,
> A thousand warriors drew the shaft?
> Ah! there in desolation cold,
> The desert serpent dwells alone,
> Where grass o'ergrows each mould'ring bone,
> And stones themselves to ruin grown,
> Like me, are death-like old.
> Then seek we not their camp—for there—
> The silence dwells of my despair!
>
> But hark, the trump!—tomorrow thou
> In glory's fires shalt dry thy tears:
> Ev'n from the land of shadows now
> My father's awful ghost appears;
> Amidst the clouds that round us roll,
> He bids my soul [f]or battle thirst—
> He bids me dry the last—the first—
> The only tears that ever burst—
> From Outalissi's soul;—
> Because I may not stain with grief
> The death-song of an Indian chief.

(canto III, stanzas 37–9)

Thus it is on the father/son relationship that Campbell focuses, with the white youth absorbed into the patriarchal tradition of the Indian invoking his fathers, whilst the Indian is moved enough by the settlers' plight to cry, despite his stoicism.

The poem ends, then, with the nobility of the Indian endorsed through the stereotypical motif in which Indian courage was idealized for white readers—the death song. But this lofty and noble conclusion can only be sustained by relegating the slaughter that readers knew to have occurred at Wyoming to the background—as several reviewers of the time complained. The price which Campbell pays for this displacement is obscurity. His plot is hard to follow without the details of what occurred. But the guilt-provoking details of British-organized Indian violence persisted in readers' minds anyway. Ultimately, Campbell tried to cope with anxiety about these details by blaming the violence on the inner nature of an Indian—a stereotypical bad Indian to contrast with Outalissi. In this way he could lament the fact that Britain had chosen to employ Indians in its war without tracing the brutality of Wyoming directly to the character of white men. The Indian became monstrous so that the whites who used him to further their political ends would not themselves seem savage.

The bad Indian of the poem is the Mohawk 'Monster Brandt' (canto III, stanza 16)—a fictionalization of John Norton's mentor Thayendanagea who, we saw in Chapter 5, featured in Lawrence's race theory as the epitome of the 'American race'. In the poem, Brandt is condemned by Outalissi—good Indian accusing bad. This, in fact, is a travesty of history, for both the Oneidas and Mohawks were Iroquois and as such had been allied for many years in the Six Nations federation, playing one white colony against another in their own favour. It was only when the American rebels pressed hard upon the Oneidas, and the Crown upon the Mohawks, at the outbreak of the War of Independence, that the Federation split. The Oneidas sided with the revolutionaries, the Mohawks with the British—both tribes too weak to remain united and neutral in face of white pressure. Brandt's and Outalissi's opposition, then, is no innate binary, no longstanding tribal enmity, but the recent result of white men's interference in Indian councils. Yet in Campbell's racist version of colonial war Indians are betrayed by each other, not by whites.

Campbell glosses over inconvenient political details and has Outalissi accusing Brandt of blood-drinking and describing his merciless cruelty:

> Scorning to wield the hatchet for his bribe,
> With Brandt himself I went to battle forth:
> Accursed Brandt! he left of all my tribe
> Nor man, nor child, nor thing of living birth:
> No! not the dog, that watch'd my household hearth,
> Escap'd, that night of blood, upon our plains!
> All perish'd—I alone am left on earth!
> To whom nor relative nor blood remains,
> No!—not a kindred drop that runs in human veins!
>
> (canto III, stanza 17)

Campbell then describes the attack on Wyoming in terms of the inhuman appearance of Brandt's Indians: 'Whoop after whoop with rack the ear assail'd / As if unearthly fiends had burst their bar' (canto III, stanza 19). In fact the assault on Wyoming was commanded by Butler; the Indians in British pay played a subordinate role. But Campbell does not focus on the British. Instead, he contrasts Brandt's hired ferocity with the 'virtue' of the colonist defenders, whom 'liberty' not money combines. Thus Brandt loses the moral argument though he is victorious in battle.

Campbell stereotypes Indians in order to play down the guilt of the British and of the American settlers (many of Butler's troops pillaging Wyoming were settlers who had been turned off their land by those they were now attacking). He divides Indians into good and bad because he will not explore white 'savagery' and because he cannot reconcile what he perceives to be contradictory Indian characteristics. His simplistic division later came undone, when he was unexpectedly visited by Thayendanagea/Brant's son,[8] who had read, and resented, Campbell's portrait of his father. Campbell had relied on accounts of Brant which showed him as an ill-disciplined savage who, though a Captain in the British army, 'could not help revenging himself on the only chief of the party that he saw taken'.[9] Campbell was amazed that his poem had been read by Brant's son. But he should not have been: Brant was a cultured man who had translated St Mark's gospel into Mohawk. Representing his people, he visited London in 1785 where he was introduced to the King and Queen and met Boswell. He became a companion of the Prince of Wales, whose dissolute behaviour was reputed to have lessened his enthusiasm for the British monarchy. After his return to America he became a landowner and a slaveholder of consequence, who was reported to have killed one of his sons in a quarrel. He was a complex man, who resented Britain for reneging on its promises to grant Indians land in return for help in its war, but who benefited personally from his ability to move between cultures.[10]

Brant's son was able to show to Campbell's satisfaction that his father had not been at the Wyoming battle. Campbell then published an apology for showing him as a 'bloody and bad man (even among savages)',[11] although he did not alter his name in the poem, which therefore retained the marks of its poet's inability to resolve the tensions that beset his stereotypes when the complexities of colonial war became unexpectedly visible. As the phrase 'among savages' suggests, Campbell had not jettisoned his stereotypical view of most Indian men as uncultured fierce warriors. Neither Brant's complex biography nor Outalissi's loyalty to whites sufficed to rescue Indians from definition by images of the 'unearthly' horror of their bodies and their deeds. Campbell had

---

[8] Brant, rather than Brandt, was the family's preferred spelling.

[9] Weld, *Travels*, 406.

[10] On Brant, see William L. Stone, *Life of Joseph Brant (Thayendanagea)*, 2 vols. (Albany, NY, 1864).

[11] Quoted in Mary Ruth Miller, *Thomas Campbell* (Boston, MA, 1978), 61.

not learnt the lessons of his own poem, which shows the paternal and patriarchal values it inculcates to be most powerfully exemplified in Indian tradition. Perhaps the idea that the most authoritative, beloved, and loving father was an Indian proved too strange to take up—even if that Indian was friendly to whites and their values. Certainly Sir Walter Scott's reaction suggests so, for he compared the final scene to the 'savage witnessing the death of Wolfe', in Benjamin West's famous painting, as if Outalissi were mourning a hero to whom he looks up rather than lamenting on behalf of a prostrate adopted son.[12]

Scott's review of *Gertrude* was characteristic of many in which the tensions between Campbell's 'Arcadian' idealizations and the political implications of the Wyoming affair were noted. He declared, 'We do not condemn this choice of a subject in itself eminently fitted for poetry', but hoped that Campbell would in future choose one 'more honourable to our national character, than one in which Britain was disgraced by the atrocities of her pretended adherents'.[13] *The Anti-Jacobin*, opposed to Campbell's Whiggism, decided that 'the beauty of poetry will not make amends for the perversion of facts'.[14] Romanticizing Indians, Campbell discovered, raised political hackles on both British and Native American sides even when the events concerned were thirty years' old. Many in Britain were not ready for a fiction that exposed their own side in war to criticism nor for one that made British ladies dependent on the protection of 'savages'. Campbell found that the poem's hostile reception impeded his career; that reception also signalled the beginning of the end, in Britain, for fictions that espoused the Indian cause against that of the empire. There would be few further radical Indians expressing British authors' dissent from their own government and its colonial policies.

[12] Scott, review of *Gertrude*, *Quarterly Review*, 1 (May 1809), 241–58 (242).
[13] Ibid., 243.
[14] *The Anti-Jacobin Review and Magazine*, 34 (September 1809), 1–9 (6).

12

The Mission to Civilize and the Colonial Romance

Gertrude of Wyoming was far more popular in America than Britain. Exculpated of any blame for events at Wyoming, portrayed as innocent victims of Indian and British acts, white Americans welcomed Campbell's portrait. Campbell was agreed to have drawn 'the ideals of the Indian character ... in Outalissi' and to have instilled a 'love of country' by making the landscape a source of 'those local associations produced by history and moral fiction'.[1] Oliver Wendell Holmes wrote that Campbell had made Wyoming 'lovely to the imagination as well as the eye'.[2]

As Holmes's words suggest, Campbell's poem, for all its limitations and idealizations, indeed because of them, achieved a certain currency in a young nation wishing to make itself feel sentimentally rooted in its recently settled soil. The division of Indians into good (who help menaced white women) and bad (addicted to violence), the assumption that even good Indians will make way, by dying, for the white settlers (epitomized by a virtuous and beautiful damsel), proved influential on Fenimore Cooper, for it showed how chivalric roles might be redistributed across the racial divide, how a love-plot might palliate, if not resolve, colonial conflict, and how guilt over treatment of Indians might be assuaged (without conceding any land or power).

Cooper quoted *Gertrude* in *The Pioneers* (1823)—using as the epigraph to the climax of his novel the noble Outalissi's death song ' "And I could weep"—th'Oneida chief / His descant wildly thus begun— / "But that I may not stain with grief / The death-song of my father's son." '[3] As Robert Clark has shown, the citation suggests that Cooper

---

[1] Quoted in Mary Ruth Miller, *Thomas Campbell* (Boston, MA, 1978), 67.
[2] Quoted in Miller, *Campbell*, 67.
[3] *The Pioneers* (New York and London, 1988), 396.

seized on Campbell's simplistic opposition between two once-allied Iroquois tribes—'bad' Mohawk and 'good' Oneida—as a model for his own duo Hawk-eye and Chingachgook, the Mohegan.[4] For centuries Mohegans, displaced by colonial settlement, had been pushed into border conflict with their neighbours the Mohawks and with the Iroquois alliance of which the Mohawks were part. Few in number and surrounded by settlers, they had, of necessity, to make peace with whites. The War of Independence found them, at the colonists' desire, persuading the Oneida to take the American side (thus splitting the Iroquois alliance and ending the biggest Indian power block on the continent). When Cooper encountered the Oneida after the War, surviving Mohegans were living among them. To a white American, they and their hosts were 'friendly' Indians. Cooper, who grew up on land recently ceded by the Mohawks, idealized the Mohegans because the length of their loyalty to the settlers made the much more recent loyalty of the Oneidas (their hosts) appear also to have longevity. Obscuring the divisive role of white settlers and distorting recent colonial politics, Cooper used the Mohegans, as it were, to naturalize Indian loyalty and to render the Mohawks, in contrast, not only disloyal but also alien—because allied to, first, the imperialist French and, later, the imperialist British. Thus by subjecting Campbell's schematic opposition of Indian hero and villain to a symbolic displacement Cooper mystified still further Campbell's mystification of colonial conflict. The effect was to assuage guilt over seizing Indians' lands and to calm anxiety about Indians' resentment: if the Mohawks and other Indians remained implacably independent and hostile, Cooper implied, this was simply in their nature. The loyalty of the Mohegan, whatever he'd suffered, assured readers that he, and hopefully also the other, more uncertainly loyal Indians he subsumed, both recognized the white settlers' virtues and pitied their vulnerability. In this respect he was a version of Campbell's Outalissi who reassuringly suggested that Indians' acceptance of white incomers was natural (because long-established) and that it resulted from their (sad) recognition that the colonists' superior civilization must supplant their own.

What Cooper learnt from Campbell in the US, he also learnt from Scott (as Campbell himself had). Scott was critical of Campbell's politics, but he produced his own verse—and then prose—romances featuring

---

[4] Robert Clark, 'The Last of the Iroquois: History and Myth in James Fenimore Cooper's *The Last of the Mohicans*', *Poetics Today*, 3/4 (1982), 115–34 (127).

heroic warriors and endangered damsels. *The Lay of the Last Minstrel* (1805) was followed by *The Lady of the Lake* and *Rokeby*. Although these were not set in America but Scotland, Scott made the link between clan culture and Native Americans in his notes—citing the travel texts that Campbell had also cited.[5] From Scott, Cooper learnt that romantic love allowed colonial violence to be portrayed without a political solution being proposed: a happy ending could be achieved by uniting a boy and girl who symbolized the union of the warring cultures. Or the destruction of one culture by another could be naturalized, even as it was lamented, by the dying words of an indigenous clansman who accepted the inevitability of its passing and dedicated his last strength to helping the vulnerable girl who was the representative of the new. This was a lesson that Byron also eagerly acquired, for although the youthful Lord criticized Campbell's inaccuracy as to background detail, he was impressed enough by the example of *Gertrude* to model his own colonial romances upon its plot—as well as on Scott's.[6] In this way, Campbell's Native Americans sponsored the creation of Byron's Turks, Albanians, and Pacific islanders, as well as Scott's Highlanders. And Campbell, Byron, and Scott, together, were to be the most influential writers on white American portraits of Indians. *The Last of the Mohicans* (1826) echoes Scott's title as well as citing Gray's 'The Bard'. Fenimore Cooper's Indians owed much to the Celtic heroes that British antiquarians had invented out of the Scottish and Welsh past and out of the Native American present. Like them, Cooper also used travel writers as source books: Carver's account of the massacre at Fort William Henry shaped his picture of Indian warfare just as it had shaped Scott's of Scottish battles. Thus white American authors' Indians were the end result of a cumulative cycle of literary import/export in which ancient Celts and contemporary Native Americans were imaged in terms of each other over and over again.

That process was to take another turn in the writing of Felicia Hemans, which responded to Scott, Campbell, and Wordsworth in portraying love between Indian man and white woman. In Campbell, this love is not sexual, but paternal (thus avoiding scandalizing British racial prejudices by imagining miscegenation). Hemans adapted this

[5] In *Rokeby* he cited Adair. See note 25 to the poem (on p. 391 of *The Poetical Works of Sir Walter Scott*, ed. J. Logie Robertson (London, 1926)).

[6] See *Byron's Letters and Journals*, ed. Leslie Marchand, 12 vols. (London, 1973–82), VIII, 21–2.

genteel displacement of romantic and sexual love, as similarities between Campbell's vocabulary and her own reveal.[7] In her poems, however, the narratorial perspective places males as the endangered, passive victims, saved by women's intervention, thus reversing the topos as Campbell expressed it. Hemans effectively updates the Pocahontas story for the era in which the role of gentlewomen was circumscribed, with the maternal being one of the few approved areas in which they could openly claim authority.

In the 'Indian Woman's Death Song' (1828) Hemans draws on recent travel narratives, on Fenimore Cooper's novel *The Prairie* (1827), which, in a chapter naturalizing white men's prejudices, depicts an Indian wife's grief that her husband, a chief, prefers a white captive woman. Hemans makes the wife into her narrator, thus producing an Indian figure derived from a white American man's text that was itself influenced, like Hemans herself, by Byron, Shelley, and travel narratives.[8] Her heroine, that is to say, is thoroughly transatlantic and fictional—stemming from white men's condescension towards Indian women, who they presume to be racially inferior to white women. If Hemans's pre-text is Cooper, her poem itself is immediately reminiscent of Wordsworth's 'Mad Mother':

> Proudly, and dauntlessly, and all alone,
> Save that a babe lay sleeping at her breast,
>
> A woman stood: upon her Indian brow
> Sat a strange gladness, and her dark hair waved
> As if triumphantly.
>
> (ll. 7–11)[9]

Hemans attempts to capture a Wordsworthian uncanniness so as to make her heroine confound British expectations. The attempt does not go very far: Hemans's poem is far more conventional than death songs of *Lyrical Ballads*. Her heroine is far less rooted in a detailed presentation of Indian customs: she is a generic Indian who, if violent, is violent only towards herself and child and only because she has been disappointed

---

[7] For instance, the 'green savannas' (l. 26) of Hemans's 'Song of Emigration' (*The Works of Mrs. Hemans with a Memoir by Her Sister*, 7 vols. (Edinburgh, 1839), VI, 29–31) echo the 'savannas green' of *Gertrude* (part I, l. 249).

[8] See the editors' apparatus to the poem in *Felicia Hemans: Selected Poems, Letters, Reception Materials*, ed. Susan J. Wolfson (Princeton, NJ, and Oxford, 2000), 379.

[9] Published in Hemans, *Records of Woman with Other Poems*, 2nd edn. (Edinburgh and London, 1828 [facs. rpt. Oxford and New York, 1991]), 104–8.

in love. There is no question of her troubling British notions, like the women in Southey's Indian songs, by participating in torture. Instead, she turns out to be an only slightly foreign allegory of a contemporary British literary figure—the beautiful maiden who, betrayed by a man, despairs and takes her life. Hemans uses the Indian woman to give this well-worn figure renewed novelty, to make the lovelorn maiden sublime as well as patriotic.

> Roll on!—my warrior's eye hath look'd upon another's face,
> And mine hath faded from his soul, as fades a moonbeam's trace;
> My shadow comes not o'er his path, my whisper to his dream,
> He flings away the broken reed—roll swifter yet, thou stream!
>
> The voice that spoke of other days is hush'd within *his* breast,
> But *mine* its lonely music haunts, and will not let me rest;
> It sings a low and mournful song of gladness that is gone,
> I cannot live without that light—father of waves! roll on!
>
> Will he not miss the bounding step that met him from the chase?
> The heart of love that made his home an ever-sunny place?
> The hand that spread the hunter's board, and deck'd his couch of yore?—
> He will not!—roll, dark foaming stream, on to the better shore!
>
> (ll. 20–31)

Hemans's view is gendered differently from Wordsworth's; she blames the woman's fate directly on men. This is only mildly feminist, however, since it implies that women, Indian and British, have no independent sense of identity and therefore cannot survive romantic disappointment. And the Indian woman's reproaches position her as a would-be angel of the hearth, almost transparently a proper nineteenth-century English lady whose innermost desire is to keep home for her man. She will uphold the domestic sphere as a place of gentle feminine retreat for her 'warrior', who conducts public affairs outside it. In the absence of such a cosy marital home, Hemans's heroine seeks a substitute in nature:

> Some blessed fount amidst the woods of that bright land must flow,
> Whose waters from my soul may lave the memory of this woe;
> Some gentle wind must whisper there, whose breath may waft away
> The burden of the heavy night, the sadness of the day.
>
> (ll. 32–5)

The landscape is a beautiful, feminine space that soothes troubles away; it is a comfort station that reveals far more about Hemans's unwillingness to escape the restrictive definitions of femininity favoured by conservative gentlemen and women in nineteenth-century Britain than it does about Indians' understanding of the land in which they live.

Hemans's feminization of the Indian song reaches its climax in 'The American Forest Girl' (1828). In this poem the warrior who is about to be tortured is not Indian at all, but British. Substituting a Briton for an Indian in this way allows Hemans to establish a colour contrast between 'red' and 'white' men that is meant to configure a moral difference:

> 'Sing us a death-song, for thine hour is come' —
> So the red warriors to their captive spoke.
> Still, and amidst those dusky forms alone,
> A youth, a fair-hair'd youth of England stood,
> Like a king's son; though from his cheek had flown
> The mantling crimson of the island blood,
> And his press'd lips look'd marble.
>
> (ll. 3–9)[10]

The fair and pale youth among the dusky warriors is an image of delicacy amid darkness. He is also, it emerges, the embodiment of docility amid savagery—a mother's boy among vengeful men. Hemans portrays him tied to the stake but thinking of his hearth and home, which turns out to be a place of pastoral content and feminine comfort:

> he might *see* the band
> Of his young sisters wandering hand in hand,
> Where the laburnums droop'd; or haply binding
> The jasmine, up the door's low pillars winding;
> Or, as day clos'd upon their gentle mirth,
> Gathering, with braided hair, around the hearth,
> Where sat their mother;—and that mother's face
> Its grave sweet smile yet wearing in the place
> Where so it ever smiled!—Perchance the prayer
> Learn'd at her knee came back on his despair;
> The blessing from her voice, the very tone
> Of her '*Good-night!*' might breathe from boyhood gone!—
> He started and look'd up:—thick cypress boughs,
> Full of strange sound, waved o'er him, darkly red
> In the broad stormy firelight;—savage brows,
> With tall plumes crested and wild hues o'erspread,
> Girt him like feverish phantoms; and pale stars

[10] In *Records of Woman*, 132–5.

> Look'd thro' the branches as thro' dungeon bars,
> Shedding no hope.—He knew, he felt his doom—

(ll. 19–37)

While his delicate body and his longing for maternal security feminize the boy, they also eroticize him. They make him attractive to Indian women because they make him different from the fierce and coarse Indian men. An Indian maid, termed 'a young slight girl—a fawn-like child / Of green savannas and the leafy wild', after 'gazing on the victim long' takes pity on him (ll. 53–4, 59). Her own pastoral delicacy, Hemans implies, attracts her to the boy who is so visibly 'the fondly rear'd—the fair / Gladdening all eyes to see' (ll. 45–6). The gentle white youth moves the gentle nature-girl to a desire that takes the sublimated form of compassion:

> the pity of her soul grew strong;
> And, by its passion's deep'ning fervour sway'd,
> Even to the stake she rush'd, and gently laid
> His bright head on her bosom, and around
> His form her slender arms to shield it wound
> Like close liannes; then rais'd her glittering eye,
> And clear-toned voice, that said, 'He shall not die!'

(ll. 60–6)

The maid becomes his surrogate mother, expressing her love in the decorous and proper form of maternal protectiveness. And this sudden action, Hemans tells us, moves even the savage warriors to compassion: 'their dark souls bow'd before the maid' as they felt 'something of heaven' appear in her tender expression and beautiful body (ll. 71, 75). They let the captive go free:

> 'He shall not die!'—the gloomy forest thrill'd
> To that sweet sound. A sudden wonder fell
> On the fierce throng; and heart and hand were still'd,
> Struck down, as by the whisper of a spell.
> They gazed—their dark souls bow'd before the maid,
> She of the dancing step in wood and glade!
> And, as her cheek flush'd through its olive hue,
> As her black tresses to the night-wind flew,
> Something o'ermaster'd them from that young mien—
> Something of heaven, in silence felt and seen;
> And seeming, to their childlike faith, a token
> That the Great Spirit by her voice had spoken.

They loosed the bonds that held their captive's breath;
From his pale lips they took the cup of death;
They quench'd the brand beneath the cypress-tree;
'Away,' they cried, 'young stranger, thou art free!'

(ll. 67–83)

In effect, they see the light—setting aside their native 'darkness' of skin and soul because they are moved by the girl who pities the white man. But she herself is moved by his fairness: whiteness, Hemans suggests, equals gentle delicacy; redness equals a masculine ferocity that only a woman's tenderness can dilute. This tenderness takes the form of the 'dusky' woman's desire to mother the 'pale' white man—a desire that, although Hemans does not admit as much, is a displaced form of sexuality. Significantly, it is only after 'gazing on the victim' that the Indian maid rushes to him. She is a voyeur of helpless, menaced white beauty before she is its saviour.

Hemans's poem imposes a fantasy on Indian/white relations that is both coyly racist and conventionally feminized. It's a sentimental and proper Romanticism in which pity overcomes cultural difference and women save men from their masculine violence by appealing to their feminine better natures. The boy is suitable for saving because he is already within the sphere of proper femininity (the idealized cottage home in which a flowery family of sisters and mothers flourishes). And so the poem is a piece of wish-fulfilment that emerges from gender conventions in Britain. Without denying her gentility or declaring her sexual desire, the domesticated English gentlewoman mothers her way to power in the world of men, turning war to peace. Or, at least, her substitute the Indian maid does. So confined are the roles allowed the English gentlewoman that it is only on an Indian stage and with an Indian surrogate that Hemans can picture her being able to turn her feelings into effective action in the public world. The epigraph tells readers that 'woman' has the 'power to suffer and to love' but the poem shows that only in foreign societies does this power effect change.

But the fantasy remains fantastical. If the scenario of gentle maids moving violent men to eschew violence is unlikely in a British context, in an Indian one it is absurd, for Native American women were acculturated in neither of the nineteenth-century British ideals for ladies: genteel delicacy and chivalric mercy. Hemans imposes a thoroughly British version of femininity on her Indian maid, treating her simply as a cipher in which to encode the anxieties and hopes of the proper British lady.

Her poem is a sign of its times, a tale for a post-Waterloo conservative Britain looking for a way to make colonial interactions seem moral and amicable. It is ultimately a particularly reductive imposition of British ideals on Native Americans, one that modifies, by re-gendering the chivalric love-plot pioneered by Campbell, the uncanny and radical figures that British men created in the 1790s. As such, Hemans's work does emotional work on behalf of the new, evangelical, justification of empire as a civilizing mission. However, whereas the missionaries preached, Hemans feels: she offers compassion as the emotion that will reform savages, making them give up their savage customs and become like Britons.

Both Campbell and Hemans addressed colonial America in dramatic narratives that appeared, but only appeared, to resolve conflict. In fact, the resolution was an illusion: the love-plot produces an ending that substitutes for, rather than enacts, any social or political resolution. It thus helped to palliate guilt and fear over the injustice being committed upon Native Americans, reassuring readers that the only Indians who would continue to resent white people were irredeemably savage and cruel, and therefore justifiably subject to punishment or death. 'Good' Indians would pity and assist good whites, then die or withdraw to allow them to live in peace and security unmolested by their fellow Native Americans.

These narratives were seminal, for the image of the dying Indian, doomed to extinction but allowing whites to inherit his nobility and his knowledge of nature, was taken up by American Romantic writers. Hemans had cited Fenimore Cooper in 1828; in 1841 he returned the compliment, including this epigraph in *The Deerslayer* (1841): 'Thou'rt passing from the lake's green side, / And the hunter's hearth away; / For the time of flowers, for the summer's pride, / Daughter! thou canst not stay.'[11] Indians were now cycled and recycled as text from New York to London and back by white writers looking to romanticize their disappearance. They blossomed as literary figures even as they withered in their original territories. On this occasion, Cooper's epigraph from Hemans legitimizes his narrative drive to occlude the mendacity, exploitation and violence involved in dispossessing Indians of their land. It assists Cooper in suggesting that white frontiersmen are *the* authentic Americans because they have acquired Native Americans' knowledge

[11] Hemans, 'Edith. A Tale of the Woods', II, 191–4 in James Fenimore Cooper, *The Deerslayer* (New York and London, 1987), 32.

of the country without acquiring Native American savagery—and have acquired it from a people who were always already destined for destruction. Thus Cooper's frontiersmen heroes, having learnt to follow a forest trail from the Delawares, lament the Indians' current state as though it is an inevitable result of a moral lapse—a biblical 'fall'—rather than the product of their own landhunger. They admire the Indians' nobility only when it is clear that they are an inferior and doomed people who will not be able to compete with the whites, who have inherited their at-home-ness in American nature.[12] Thus they praise Chingachgook, as

the best of loping redskins. … If he had his rights, he would be a great chief; but, as it is, he is only a brave and just-minded Delaware; respected, and even obeyed in some things, 'tis true, but of a fallen race, and belonging to a fallen people. Ah! Harry March, 'twould warm the heart within you to sit in their lodges of a winter's night, and listen to the traditions of the ancient greatness and power of the Mohicans![13]

Cooper's indebtedness to Hemans is merely one case of many in which white Americans adapted British Romantic fiction: Washington Irving, for instance, learnt much about Romantic rustics from British poets before he conferred Indian qualities upon Rocky Mountain fur trappers, thus depicting these white pioneers as the true heirs of the American West.[14] And so the British Romantic Indians of Hemans and Campbell helped shape the rather different figures conjured up by white American writers. They also assisted in the development of new kinds of literary Indian at home: British Indians. Hemans imagined Canada as a virgin land in which Britain's rural poor might make a new start, real Indians having already died out and left their forests to immigrants from the glens. In her 'Song of Emigration' (1827) she has her Scottish speakers say

> All, all our own shall the forests be,
> As to the bound of the roebuck free!

[12] On this motif see Fiona Stafford, *The Last of the Race: The Growth of a Myth from Milton to Darwin* (Oxford, 1994), 242–3.

[13] Cooper, *Deerslayer*, 33.

[14] According to critics Bruce Greenfield and Frederick Turner, writers gradually effaced Indians' presence from the country—the 'frontier' became a border between whites and a yet-to-be settled wilderness rather than a line separating American and Indian nations. See Bruce Greenfield, *Narrating Discovery: The Romantic Explorer in American Literature, 1790–1855* (New York, 1992), Frederick Turner, *The Frontier in American History* (New York, 1962).

None shall say, 'Hither, no further pass!'
We will track each step through the wavy grass;
We will chase the elk in his speed and might,
And bring proud spoils to the hearth at night.

But, oh! the grey church-tower,
And the sound of Sabbath-bell,
And the shelter'd garden-bower,
We have bid them all farewell!

We will give the names of our fearless race
To each bright river whose course we trace;
We will leave our memory with mounts and floods,
And the path of our daring in boundless woods!
And our works unto many a lake's green shore,
Where the Indian's graves lay, alone, before.

(ll. 31–46)[15]

Hemans, as we have seen, was hardly the first poet to romanticize emigration. Her heroes Wordsworth, Coleridge, and Southey had all considered it in the 1790s. Twenty years later they had, however, arrived at a position closer to Hemans's than to their own earlier Pantisocratic one. They had turned away from the radical Indians that featured in their 1790s writing. Such Indians were too oppositional, too violent, and too revolutionary for an era of Napoleonic war when Britons turned to an anti-revolutionary and pro-empire loyalism in face of the threat from France to both homeland and colonies. By 1814 Southey was advocating, as a prophylactic against the spread of revolutionary fervour, the use of missionary colonies to export Britain's Protestant ethics around the world. In his 'Ode, Written During the War with America, 1814' he effectively redefined Pantisocracy for the new age, turning it into a national and official imperial mission. Addressing England, he proclaimed

Queen of the Seas! Enlarge thyself;
Send thou thy swarms abroad!
For in the years to come,
Though centuries or millenniums intervene,
Wher'er thy progeny,
Thy language, and thy spirit shall be found, . . .

[15] In *The Works of Mrs. Hemans*, VI, 29–31.

If on Ontario's shores,
Or late-explored Missouri's pastures wide,
Or in that Austral world long sought,
The many-isled Pacific, . . . yea where waves,
Now breaking over coral reefs, affright
The venturous mariner,
When islands shall have grown, and cities risen
In cocoa groves embower'd . . .
Where'er thy language lives,
By whatsoever name the land be call'd,
That land is English still, and there
Thy influential spirit still lives and reigns.

(stanza 13)[16]

This 'influential spirit' would be Anglican Christianity, spread by missionaries. Let, he continued, 'thy Gospel light! / Illume the dark idolater, / Reclaim the savage' (stanza 14).

The pious hopes and imperialistic politics of Southey's laureate ode constitute one, conservative, reading of the *Madoc* poem that he had begun as a radical project. By 1814, Southey was, in effect, presenting Native Americans according to the stereotypes that, in 1794, he had conjured up only to supplant. Idolatrous barbarians and/or benighted savages, Indians now fell into one of two narrow categories that Southey drew tighter still, as if the prospects of equality, intermarriage, and hybridization that he once entertained had never existed. Native Americans were now defined from an official British viewpoint, as a problem and a task for Britain to solve, an inferior people whose existence offered Britain a mission. Here Southey succinctly formulated the Victorian justification of empire, at the expense of Indians. Their differences, cultural and historical, from Britons and from each other, were no longer of interest and nor were their knowledge-traditions and social formations. What mattered was that they appeared as a convertible mass, an uncivilized group that challenged Britain to prove that the successful transmission of Protestant culture across the world was its destiny.

Wordsworth also sacrificed his former radical, uncanny Indians, in favour of settlement colonialism. This amounted to the acceptance, with regret, of the inevitable passing of his own ideal rustic hero, for he now

---

[16] *The Poetical Works of Robert Southey, Collected by Himself*, 10 vols. (London, 1837–8), III.

imagined contemplative solitaries as Indians who were to be respected, but also to be doomed to extinction:

> True, the intelligence of social art
> Hath overpowered his forefathers, and soon
> Will sweep the remnant of his line away;
> But contemplations, worthier, nobler far
> Than her destructive energies, attend
> His independence, when along the side
> Of Mississippi, or that northern stream
> That spreads into successive seas, he walks;
> Pleased to perceive his own unshackled life,
> And his innate capacities of soul,
> There imaged. . . .
>
> (*Excursion* (1814), bk III, ll. 925–35; *WPW*, V)

Here Wordsworth identifies the Indian as the epitome of the sublime, introspective rustic that he had upheld (and aspired to be) contra the commercial, capitalistic urbanite. Now, however, he accepts the Indian's extinction under the pressure of market forces' 'dire rapacity'. The Indian will be replaced, even in the Canadian forests, by the mass population that endangered such rustics in Britain. Indeed, he will be replaced (although Wordsworth does not admit it) so that rustics in Britain can remain intact. He will die to serve Wordsworth's need to preserve British contemplatives in peace—for the poet declares it Britain's destiny to export its excess population to the empire. If they stayed, the 'masses' threatened social stability because, discontented with their lot, they were vulnerable to radical politicians. And they threatened to bring a cheap gimcrack culture to all Britain's unspoilt places. Transported to America, however, they were miraculously transformed into emissaries of British liberty:

> So the wide waters, open to the power,
> The will, the instincts, and appointed needs
> Of Britain, do invite her to cast off
> Her swarms, and in succession send them forth;
> Bound to establish new communities
> On every shore whose aspect favours hope
> Or bold adventure; promising to skill
> And perseverance their deserved reward.
>
> (*Excursion*, IX, 375–82)

By 1825, then, Romantic poets seemed to have turned full circle. Having begun by idealizing Indians as figures who embodied their rejection of the dominant social values of eighteenth-century Britain, they had ended by urging a reformed church and state to colonize them. Britain, they, hoped, would purge itself by embracing the mission to spread what was best about itself to the ignorant natives of America. For Anna Laetitia Barbauld, what was best included Britain's writers: Native Americans, she conceived, would be educated in utilitarian theology and georgic poetry. Rooted in their own country, they would, as a consequence, dream the pastoral dreams of England's green and pleasant land:

> ... Thy stores of knowledge the new states shall know,
> And think thy thoughts, and with thy fancy glow;
> Thy Lockes, thy Paley shall instruct their youth,
> Thy leading star direct their search for truth;
> Beneath the spreading Plantain's tent-like shade,
> Or by Missouri's rushing waters laid,
> 'Old father Thames' shall be the poet's theme,
> Of Hagley's woods the enamoured virgin dream,
> And Milton's tones the raptured ear enthral,
> Mixt with the roar of Niagara's fall.
>
> (*Eighteen Hundred and Eleven, a Poem* (1812), ll. 81–96)[17]

After years of war with revolutionary France, and years facing the repressive backlash which that war precipitated, Romantic poets no longer idealized Indian wildness and communistic social structure. Indians were to be converted to Englishness or, if they remained indifferent to this process, displaced by emigrant British colonists.

It was in response to both conversion and displacement that Indians began to turn Romanticism's figures back upon their authors. Native Americans, once educated in English by missionaries, proved neither to be compliant nor quiescent—still less on the verge of inevitable extinction. They challenged and interrogated the whites who wrote them down or wrote them off, using the whites' own Romantic figurations to do so. Let us now see how.

---

[17]   *The Poems of Anna Letitia Barbauld*, eds. William McCarthy and Elizabeth Kraft (Athens, GA, and London, 1994), 157.

PART III
NATIVE AMERICAN WRITING

13

John Norton/Teyoninhokarawen

Eighteenth-century Britons took their portraits of Indians from soldiers' stories; the writers that grew up reading them increasingly got the chance to meet Indians in person. Southey, for example, encountered an 'Indian' in a British fairground, recording the experience in his 1807 publication *Letters from England*:

Passing through St. George's-fields I saw a sort of tent pitched, at the entrance of which a fellow stood holding a board in his hand, on which was painted in large letters 'The Wild Indian Woman'.—'What,' said I to my companion, 'do you catch the savages and show them like wild beasts? This is worse than even the slave trade!' 'We will go in and see,' said he. Accordingly we paid our sixpence each, and, to our no small amusement, found one of the lowest order of the worst kind of women, her face bedaubed with red and yellow, her hair stuck with feathers, drest in cat skins, and singing some unintelligible gibberish in the true cracked voice of vulgar depravity. A few passers-by, as idle and more ignorant than ourselves, who had in like manner been taken in, were gazing at her in astonishment, and listening open-mouthed to the rogue who told a long story how she came from the wilds of America, where the people are heathen folk and eat one another.[1]

For Southey, the encounter was disgusting: he'd seen a white woman faking the manner of an Indian, reducing a native culture to the cheapest of tricks. The encounter does, however, suggest that there was commercial currency in Indians and a staple menu of Indian characteristics that even hucksters knew. These characteristics were the staples of travel and captivity narratives and common Britons were prepared to pay to be taken in by counterfeit versions of them.

An altogether classier encounter took place at Trinity College Cambridge in 1805. On 12 March a huddle of students watched their Indian guest—John Norton—perform a war-dance. The neo-classical halls of

[1] Letter 55 of Robert Southey, *Letters from England*, ed. Jack Simmons (London, 1951), 337–8.

Britain's most prestigious university could not have been further away from the tawdry booth of St George's Fields. So too the young gentlemen who watched differed from the ignorant passers-by who gawped at the 'Wild Indian Woman'. Nevertheless this Indian also dressed in skins, feathers, and paint to impress his audience and he also performed a stereotypically Indian custom for the entertainment of white people who saw themselves as civilized and Indians as savage. Was he then, despite the august venue, an abject spectacle, dancing out the role of untamed primitive for his white masters?

One of the lookers-on was Charles Allanson Winn, Lord Headley. Headley had seen the dance before in America. He recorded his impressions of it in terms that show that it provoked thought rather than confirmed stereotypes:

> The war-dance—I have seen Mr Norton go through it—several times in his country when properly performed three or four stand near & sing a particular tune which is accompanied by the drums; then they get up in pairs and represent a battle; they first advance leaping from side to side with astonishing rapidity: this kind of zigzag motion is to prevent the adversary from taking a settled aim with his rifle; Mr Norton says that this manoeuvre puzzles even the best shot; sometimes however they are hit when the combatants are come near to one another they draw their swords and make a desperate cut or two, one falls the other takes out his knife scalps his fallen adversary hangs the scalp upon his girdle & retires exulting—I observed when Mr. Norton danced that his whole appearance was instantly changed; instead of being mild & humane, his countenance assumed a most savage & terrific look; he sprang forward to seize his enemy with amazing ferocity; the action was both manly & graceful.[2]

In the introduction I showed Norton confounding Britons' expectations in Bath and, later, in Upper Canada. Here in Cambridge too his performance was educative. Headley perceived that it was neither an exotic but meaningless spectacle nor an overflowing of innate savagery. It was a military exercise, a practice drill designed to make the warrior a difficult target. It was a training manoeuvre, but also a performance intended to confuse and terrify an enemy: Norton assumed a 'savage and terrific' look for the role, but this look was not seen as being natural to him. And though he sprang forward with ferocity, he was no human tiger—his dance had aesthetic qualities: it was judged as a sophisticated expression of skill and art, a thing of manliness and grace, two of the qualities that British gentlemen prided themselves upon.

[2] The Headley Manuscript, ff. 37–8. MS 13350, New York State Library.

No fool, Norton was aware that by appearing in public as an Indian he always risked being viewed as a curiosity. If not regarded as an exotic primitive like the 'Wild Indian Woman', he faced being seen as an imposter, too cultured to be a real 'savage'. Why then, given this danger, did Norton whoop, sing, and dance for his British hosts? He did not, after all, need to satisfy the demands of a white entrepreneur who had ferried him from America to be exhibited for money, as did the Cherokees brought to Britain by Henry Timberlake in 1762. Unlike them, Norton had arrived under his own steam with fluent English and a network of influential acquaintances. He had also arrived with a political goal, aiming to win title to the lands on the Grand River that the Crown had 'granted' to the Mohawks after they had lost their New York territories in the War of Independence. It was in pursuit of his political goal that Norton performed: his dance was part of a conscious strategy aimed at winning Britons to his cause. Like the trickster-figure admired in many Indian cultures, Norton improvised different roles, mimicking Britain's prejudiced versions of Indians then appearing, almost in the same moment, in white people's guises—officer, gentleman, agricultural improver. At Trinity College, for example, Norton followed his dance with another performance that hybridized British and Indian manners and costume. Again, Headley recorded the eye-opening effect:

His manners are perfectly surprising; he has a native politeness, which makes him act with the greatest propriety in all companies. I do not know any one who receives or gives any thing at table with so pretty and pleasing a grace. . . . a chintz handkerchief was bound about the head under which was a piece of red silk of the same texture as our officers' sashes, on one side was put an ostrich feather on the other hung his tail in such a manner that the end of it reached to the middle of the forehead. I must mention that the tail consists of the hair which grows at the top of the head only . . .[3]

As Headley testified, Norton's performance commanded attention and he used that attention to speak to effect about his nation and his mission: 'He was listened to with the utmost silence, no other voice but his could be heard in a room containing above 40 people. The surprise of different persons was very astonishing almost all came with the idea of seeing an uncivilized savage; but after they had been for a short time in his company, the story was materially changed and this is the man we call a savage said one; these are the people we think absolute cannibals.'[4]

---

[3] Ibid., ff. 46–7.   [4] Ibid., ff. 57–8.

Norton set about deflating popular myths: 'women,' he remarked, 'are treated in a much more respectful manner than in England & . . . they possess very superior power.' Britons' typical view, that Indian women were 'the slaves of their husbands, doing the hard labor & resigning their property to him', was 'a strong instance of the erroneous opinions entertained concerning the Mohawks [which] must have originated in total ignorance of the nation'.[5] So also was the impression fostered by captivity narratives that Indians tortured their prisoners to death. The great majority of captives, Norton insisted, were adopted into the tribe. The Mohawks, it followed, were not barbaric or bestial but a nation with a civilized social structure, perhaps more civilized in some respects than Britain's. Promises made to them should therefore be kept.

Norton had been adopted into the Mohawk tribe and chosen as a chief because of the very talents he was now deploying in Britain. The Mohawks needed leaders who were skilled enough in the manners and customs of the British not just to interpret what the British said and did, but also to change their hearts and minds. Norton was such a leader, because he used his upbringing, education, and adult career cleverly to become a superb manipulator of both the cultures that shaped his identity. That identity was unusual. By the 1760s many Cherokees were of mixed blood, their fathers white (often Scottish) traders, their mothers Indian. Over the next decades of war, other Indians would be born to white women captured in raids and adopted into the tribe.[6] Norton, however, claimed to be the son of a Cherokee taken captive, as a boy, by the British when they raided the Cherokee town Kuwoki in 1760. The Cherokees accepted this claim when Norton visited them in 1809, remembering the abduction, though they had never again seen the boy whom Norton claimed to have become his father. The boy was in effect adopted into the British tribe, for the officer who plucked him from the burning village took him home to Scotland. There, Norton was born, his mother Scottish. He was schooled in Dunfermline and Edinburgh and then followed his father into the British army. By 1785 he was in Canada with his regiment; in 1787 he deserted; in 1788 he received his discharge; and in 1790 he became master of the school at the Six Nation village on the Bay of Quinte, Ontario. It was this

[5] The Headley Manuscript, ff. 12–13.

[6] On this see James Axtell, 'The White Indians of Colonial America', in his *The European and the Indian: Essays in the Ethnohistory of Colonial North America* (New York and Oxford, 1981), 168–206.

position that brought him into contact with the Mohawks who had relocated to the British colony after the loss of their territory in the Revolutionary War. According to the *Missouri Gazette* he 'became at once as perfect an Indian as ran in the woods, having his ears cut and his nose bored'.[7] If he was indeed half Indian by blood it was clearly at this time that he became half Indian in his social identity. If he was, as some Canadian officials who wished to discredit him argued, wholly white, he nevertheless began, at this time, to become sufficiently Indian eventually to be adopted by the tribe.[8] Leaving schoolmastering, Norton became by 1793 a trader on the Miami River, selling articles to the Indians for the American Mr Askin of Detroit. Here it became harder and harder to live along the margins of British, Indian, and Anglo-American society since from 1790 to 1794 the Miami Indians, with covert aid from the British, were fighting US armies as they tried to stop white settlement on their lands. Norton avoided the conflict and after the Indians' defeat chose to return to a life in which there were fewer conflicting claims on his loyalty. He took the post of interpreter in the British Indian Department, at the request of the Mohawk chief Joseph Brant.

Brant was the leader of the Mohawks who had moved to the Grand River. As such, he was a chief (though not a paramount chief) of the Iroquois (Six Nations) alliance. With his approval, Norton acquired importance as an interpreter and diplomat for the Indians as well as for the British. In 1799 he was elected a chief. 'Shortly after,' this, he remembered, 'I resigned my place in the Indian Department.'[9] He was now socially an Indian, whatever blood ran in his veins, for the Iroquois had a long tradition of adopting people, whether white or Indian, and accepting them as full members of the tribe. Henceforth he would exploit his dual identity as a cultural broker[10] solely on the Mohawks' side. Donning different masks, playing different roles for

---

[7] *Missouri Gazette*, 16 June 1816, quoted in Carl F. Klinck's 'Biographical Introduction' to *Norton*, xxxiii.

[8] Given that the adoption of whites, blacks and other Indians was common practice in many Indian tribes, it would be inappropriate to regard Norton as no Indian if both his parents were white. He was accepted as Indian by the Mohawks and Cherokees; to disqualify him now on the ground of blood quotient would come dangerously close to the behaviour of the nineteenth-century race theorists.

[9] Speech of 12 February 1807, Ayer MS 654, ff. 119–20, Newberry Library, Chicago.

[10] See Margaret Connell Szasz (ed.), *Between Indian and White Worlds: The Cultural Broker* (Norman, OK, and London, 1994).

different audiences, Norton was the best Mohawk politician available to deal with the powerful Britons—and the Mohawks knew it. Like McGillivray of the Creeks, and Ross of the Cherokees,[11] he would exploit his knowledge of Anglo culture to negotiate on his tribe's behalf, simultaneously using the authority that this expertise gave him within the tribe to adapt its traditional political structure to serve it in the new colonial situation. In the process, he increased his own power, status, and wealth, as Ross and McGillivray also did. But he was also playing roles within Mohawk culture, using his knowledge of Iroquois customs, expectations, and power-structures to win authority and respect within his tribe, even as he took it in directions that not everyone approved of. Some of the Mohawks, at least, opposed Norton, for the issue of the land they lived on split the Grand River community.

The issue originated in colonial war but worsened during colonial peace. When Britain's American colonists rebelled in 1776 the Mohawks sided with the British government. The rebels, after all, were the same colonists who had been illegally settling on Indian land. The Mohawks had especial reason to fight on the British side, for they had longstanding familial ties to the leading Indian agent William Johnson. Joseph Brant, in fact, had acquired influence in Six Nation councils at the behest of his influential sister, Molly Brant, Johnson's wife. These ties bound Mohawk policy to British: during the war Brant travelled to London with Johnson's successor to clarify lines of command.

When the Treaty of Paris concluded the peace in 1783, the Mohawks experienced a double loss. The war had already split the Iroquois alliance; now the peace simply handed land to the US, as if the Indians had never possessed it. The Crown's poor compensation for this betrayal was the purchase, in 1784, of Ojibwa land in Canada, which it permitted the Six Nations to occupy. In practice, it was mostly Brant's Mohawks who moved there. But the British did not grant the Six Nations individual rights to own, sell, or buy the land, nor collectively were they allowed to dispose of it to anyone other than the Crown. In effect, it was subject to the same paternalist policy that, since 1763, the British had operated with regard to all Indian land. This policy was intended to prevent

---

[11] On Ross, see Gary E. Moulton, 'John Ross', in R. David Edmunds (ed.), *American Indian Leaders: Studies in Diversity* (Lincoln, NE, and London, 1980), 88–106. On McGillivray see Michael D. Green's eponymous article in the same volume and John W. Caughey, *McGillivray of the Creeks* (Norman, OK, 1938).

individual Indians being cheated by landhungry whites into selling their nations' territories, often for a few kegs of rum and some paltry presents.

Brant was not content with these terms, which only reminded the Mohawks of their new diminished status as clients dependent on the British remembering the services they had rendered in the days of their independent power. And Brant had a scheme for the Mohawks' future. Since the Grand River was hunted out, it would not support the traditional Iroquois economy, yet was too large for the remaining Mohawks to farm. They would sell land to white settlers and invest the proceeds to provide, in perpetuity, an annuity for the tribe. Although the Crown sold some land on the Mohawks' behalf in 1802, it would not allow them to make sales or issue leases under their own authority. Brant, who had profited personally by arranging the land sales, declared the refusal 'astonishing'.[12]

It was to gain full title to the land and so throw off the paternalist restriction that Norton travelled to Britain as Brant's diplomat. The Indian Department in Canada was not informed: the Mohawks were trying to go over the heads of the colonial authorities. By June 1804 Norton was in London. He had Brant's powerful friends the Duke of Northumberland, the Earl of Moira, and Sir Evan Nepean on his side, but it was with Quakers that he lived. It was a Quaker, Robert Barclay, who introduced him to the Bath and West of England Agricultural Society, where he spoke of the Mohawks' need for tools. Norton had decided that his nation, reduced in numbers and hemmed in by whites, could survive neither by hunting nor by 'presents' from government. 'Improvement', that is, learning white people's social and technological systems, was the only possible future for a tribe becoming a smaller and smaller minority in a land in which immigrants were constantly arriving. To this end, Norton cultivated the Clapham Sect evangelicals who advocated missionary enterprise in the colonies. These men were well connected: eventually their influence would help get Norton's proposals the backing of ministers.

The plan fell foul of the Indian Department. In 1805 Norton found the London government kept him waiting outside ministers' offices while it sought advice from Canada. It claimed to have lost the paperwork giving the land and refused his offer to recite the treaty verbatim from memory. This refusal indeed reveals the difference between the cultures—a difference even Norton's dual identity could not bridge.

---

[12] Quoted in James J. Talman, 'Historical Introduction', *Norton*, cii.

The Britons demanded written evidence; Native Americans, coming from an oral culture, were quite used to relying on memory and trusting each other's oral word as to the fact. As Teyoninhokarawen, Norton was insulted that the government would not trust his oral speech; as Norton too he was insulted they would not accept the word of a gentleman as to his own veracity.

When word came from Canada, it was not advice but a devastating counterpunch. William Claus, Indian agent, opposed to the land grant and reluctant to be bypassed, had exploited tensions within the Six Nations, inducing a few of the Grand River Mohawks to join Seneca chiefs in council on the US side of the border. Envious of Brant's influence, wealth, and power, these Indians signed what Claus dictated, a despatch declaring that Norton had no authority to negotiate on the Nations' behalf. The signatories were given 'presents' from the Indian Department stores. Some were encouraged to call themselves chiefs. It was a classic example of British colonialism's modus operandi of divide and rule. On receipt of the document in London, Norton's mission was hopeless. He returned to Canada a few months later.

In Canada, Norton's authority was renewed when the Grand River Mohawks confirmed him as leader. After Brant's death in 1807 he continued to lobby his British contacts over the grant, and this effort bore fruit in a proposal put by the Foreign Secretary to the Lieutenant Governor. The Governor's reply, however, scotched the scheme:

How far these people are capable of receiving a Grant from the Crown, rests with higher Authority. Your Lordship however must be aware, that if they are eligible to hold lands by that Tenure, they become subject to His Majesty and entitled to all the privileges of Natural Born Subjects, they will then become Electors, and qualified to be chosen Members of the House of Assembly. Are we prepared My Lord for such a change? We have already seen Brant, in virtue of a Grant of Land, made to him some years ago for his Military Services, at the head of an Electioneering party to place one of the most worthless and dangerous men (Mr. Thorpe) perhaps in the King Dominions, in the House of Assembly.

What may not be expected when every Savage in the Country become possess'd of the same privilege?[13]

This was paternalism at its most condescending. As long as the Indians remained landless, they would be dependent on presents that could be reduced if the governor saw fit.

[13] Quoted in 'Historical Introduction', *Norton*, civ.

By the time the governor composed his reply, Norton was far from the Grand River. Tired of political disputes and private jealousies, he had gone on a long journey to the Cherokee country in (what is now) Tennessee. He travelled by canoe and on foot, arriving on 21 June 1809 and staying until April 1810, meeting all the principal chiefs and attending their councils. He had several aims on this visit. He wanted to meet his relatives and discover more about his father's capture. He also wanted to investigate how the most populous and prosperous Indian nation had adopted white agriculture and how it was faring under pressure from the US. Norton had another aim too—to record his journey in an English narrative. He succeeded, composing nearly a thousand manuscript pages for his British friends to prepare for the press. It was a remarkable achievement, one of the greatest travel narratives of an era in which such narratives abounded and were the most authoritative sources of information about unfamiliar people and places. It was also one of the most notable literary works by a Native American, a comprehensive account of Cherokee society and politics, of the history, customs, and beliefs of the Six Nations, and of the Iroquois part in the War of 1812, all written in an elegant prose that establishes the author as a gentleman of judgement and feeling.

Although Norton wrote the journal as a public document rather than a private diary, it was not published, probably because its sheer scale made the costs too large for his British contacts easily to bear. It lay in the Duke of Northumberland's library until 1970 when it appeared in a meticulously prepared edition by Carl F. Klinck and James J. Talman (*Norton*). The failure to publish was a great loss, for the journal was intended throughout to enlighten the British about Indian culture and dispel the crude assumptions about savagery that, even after fifty years of interaction, persisted in works such as Campbell's *Gertrude of Wyoming*. It represented the Six Nations not as clients dependent on handouts but as a people of independent agency who had fought alongside the British because, after public debate, they had judged it right to do so.

Although Norton was never polemical this implication was clear by virtue both of what he said and of how he said it. A master of the detached prose that established the observer as a reliable witness, he articulated on paper the political maturity and shrewdness of judgement that he showed the Iroquois policymakers to possess. The Six Nations were, the journal suggested, the moral and intellectual equals of the Britons, even if inferior in material wealth. They were conscious, as well, that Britain was under a moral obligation to them.

Norton's writing thus re-orientated the travel narrative genre to which it ostensibly conformed. Typically, white men's narratives about Indians, however sympathetic, had been published in the context of opening 'primitive' people to civilized eyes, a knowledge-producing operation that assisted later travellers—soldiers, land agents, government officials, for instance—to deal with them. Norton replicated the narratorial position that white travellers typically took, but as an Indian, an Indian exploring his family relationships to the Cherokees whom he discussed, he destabilized the equation of detached narrator with a rational, truthful white man observing a superstitious, fanciful native. Norton the Indian-Scot collapsed the opposition, hybridizing British literary style and Indian knowledge, becoming a more reliable source on Indian languages, history, and spirituality than the white experts. In so doing Norton exposed the partiality of the rules of the ethnographic game or, in Foucault's terms, the racial bias of the truth regime on which travel writing depended.

Throughout the narrative, Norton was able to report Indian customs from the inside and thereby refute the opinion that white traveller after white traveller had repeated until it seemed like fact. Rousseau and Raynal had argued that Indian men were indolent: they hunted when they had immediate need but neither tilled the ground nor stored provisions for the future. The savage lived in a perpetual careless present. Later, Buffon had developed an environmental explanation that accounted for this indolence: American nature was too feeble to produce vigorous beings. Norton was able to demolish these notions, showing not only that hunting was a demanding skill but that hours of idle amusement also had the purpose of exciting 'utmost exertions of strength and activity'; sports made the hunter 'acute in circumventing the enemy, unerring in his aim ... cool in extremities of danger' (*Norton*, 126). Norton was making a political point here, since the supposed fact of Indian laziness was seized upon by advocates of Indian removal, who argued that whites deserved Indian land because they would improve it, whereas Indians could not, being too indolent. In this context Norton's detailed descriptions of flourishing Cherokee plantations also had a political purpose, since the state of Tennessee had already begun to demand the Cherokees cede land to whites and move to Arkansas.

Norton rendered the Cherokee replies to these demands in the journal, giving chief Selukuki Wohhellengh (Turtle at Home) a speech of great force, combining argumentative logic with a secure invocation of the words of past leaders, embarrassing the Americans by reminding them of their inability to live up to their own heroes' promises:

After the Tree of Peace was planted, and we had reposed from the toils and injuries of war, under its expanding shade, the advice of your Great Beloved Man (General Washington) sunk deep in our minds. He advised us not to make hunting our principal occupation; but to direct our attention to the extension and cultivation of our corn fields, the increase of our cattle, the learning the useful arts; and that our females should acquire skill in spinning, and in the manufacturing of cloth. We have followed his advice, and already feel ourselves benefited thereby. We are now clothed in the manufacture of our women, we possess numerous herds of cattle, and cultivate extensive fields of corn. This has opened our eyes, and taught us the use and value of land; for without it, we could neither raise cattle, corn, nor cotton, whereof to manufacture cloth. You must know this, and had we not been assured, that it was the case, we could never have supposed that you would think of asking us for more land; as thereby you render inconsistent, the advice of your late Beloved Man, which ought not to be; for though he is no more, yet his word should remain.

(*Norton*, 123–4)

The Americans are allowed no reply to this in the journal: Norton constructs the episode to give to the Cherokees his readers' admiration and sense of justice.

On another occasion Norton celebrates the witty and mock-pitiful retort of another Cherokee chief, Bloody Fellow:

Brothers, We thought we had already let you have a sufficient extent of our lands to have accommodated all your people, both rich and poor; and if we should continue to comply with your requests, we would soon be left without any ourselves: but as it is lamentable to see our fellow creatures suffering for want of land whereon to raise the means of subsistence, while we enjoy abundance, I shall engage to provide land for them, if you will permit me to make the first allotments within your own territory, and when I can find no more unoccupied land therein, I shall grant them in ours.

(*Norton*, 161)

After thus establishing the Cherokees as masters of public speaking, Norton includes a hymn to nature that transplants the conventional language of the British picturesque to a deeply politicized America.

It was now past the middle of April and the Sun's cheering rays seemed to give additional lustre to every surrounding object;—the foliage of the stately trees that crowned the summits of the surrounding hills, moved by the pleasant western gale; the clear refreshing streams glistening through the glassy meads.

Alternately the eye was attracted by these delightful prospects and the mind
by the contemplation of the situation of these kind friends and companions
from whom I was on the eve of separating. Long may they possess thee fertile
vallies and airy hills (did I inwardly pray) and may they increase in virtue and
in number to fill them with inhabitants, who may gratefully acknowledge the
bounties they enjoy from the beneficent hands of that Great and Benevolent
Being from whom all good proceeds!

(*Norton*, 161)

Here, as elsewhere, the reader is invited to share Norton's swell of
aesthetic appreciation. Attachment to Nature, Norton shows, depends
on a feeling-at-home that itself relies on a sharing of friendship. He is
able to appreciate the beauty of the scene because he feels suddenly at
home in the country his once-distant relatives have welcomed him to.
It is, Norton suggests, on a revelation of acceptance in a community
that landscape aesthetics depend, but that community must be rooted
in a place, so that people and country reflect each other. Like Coleridge
in Somerset, Norton comes to the realization that patriotism begins at
home in a love of country that is a love of a local community in which
he feels in place. Also like Coleridge, Norton feels (and asks readers
to feel) that love all the more deeply because he is acutely aware that
the country is menaced by foreign invaders. But whereas for Coleridge
and his British readers the invaders are the old enemy France, for
Norton and his audience they are American whites, people who until
relatively recently had been British subjects. To put it simply, Norton's
romanticization of the Cherokee country enlists aesthetics to displace
conventional racial loyalties, inviting readers to feel emotionally at home
with him in Indian culture. No longer are they detached observers of
Indian others: they now take their place alongside an Indian narrator
who has discovered in the generosity and intelligence of his Indian hosts
a far more deeply interfused sense of where he belongs and who he
is. The Tennessee settlers do not possess this sense and so the reader
concurs with Norton's hope that the Cherokees will never lose their
land. Norton has deconstructed the civilized/savage rational/primitive
opposition on which travel writing so often rested, for this is emphatically
not a question of white reader feeling pity for dispossessed Indian. The
Cherokees embody what Norton discovers in their presence about
himself as well, the Wordsworthian insight that to be able to experience
and articulate love one must be, and know oneself to be, at home.

There is pathos in Norton's discovery, stemming from his awareness of
how fragile the Cherokees' deeper humanity now was as their collective

rootedness came under attack from the ever-insecure US immigrants. It also stemmed from his own status as a Mohawk, a tribe already uprooted from its territory and now themselves insecure immigrants in a British colony. Nowhere does he feel at home as the Cherokees do and he himself does in their country. But he must leave.

Norton arrived back at the Grand River in June 1810. There, he worked on his journal, lobbied the Indian Department for title to the land, and planned a move to the West. The War of 1812 interrupted Norton's plan; he led Iroquois warriors in the defence of Canada and was rewarded with the rank of Captain and permission from General Provost to represent the Grand River people without interference from the Indian Department. His courage had won what diplomacy had not. In 1815 he returned to Britain and put his young wife and son in school in Scotland. On this trip he met Walter Scott, whose brother had enthused about him in 1814, and the author of *The Lady of the Lake* became a 'staunch friend'.[14] Promoted to Major, Norton was in Canada again in 1816, farming his own land. It seemed that he had been able to turn his dual identity to personal advantage for proving his worth to British officers and cultivating British philanthropists had brought him money and authority, even if they had not won the Mohawks the land and instruction they desired. In 1823, however, discovering that his wife was encouraging the romantic attentions of a young Mohawk, he killed the lover in a duel. Found guilty of manslaughter and fined £25, Norton left his wife and the Grand River, never to return. Again he went south to the Cherokees, this time to their new lands in Arkansas. After 1824, no one in Canada heard from him again. Perhaps he died in Arkansas, among his relatives, living out the rooted identity he had made so romantic a possibility in his writing. It is tempting to imagine so, for this great man and remarkable writer deserved to meet such an end. Yet if he did so, it was against the odds—for he was now isolated from his Mohawk family and his British friends, in a place to which the Cherokees had only recently been exiled. For Norton, like all Indians post-1783 and 1814, a community organically rooted in a natal country was more and more a community that existed only in memory and imagination.

---

[14] 'Biographical Introduction', *Norton*, lxxxix.

14

A Son of the Forest: William Apess

Nearly all the Indians who published books in the Romantic period had been converted to Christianity and then tutored in English. To some evangelicals, such Indians proved the value of a missionary empire: they showed that indigenous people could be civilized and would benefit from the cultural as well as technological superiority of the white lifeways they acquired. Not all the Indians so educated, however, simply reflected whites' hopes back to them. William Apess certainly did not.

Apess was a Pequot of mixed white/Indian descent and a radical author who campaigned against racial stereotyping and white hypocrisy. He had reason to: the Pequot nation had been almost extermin-ated by the colonists in 1637. Male survivors had been sold into slavery; those few who remained were not allowed to use the tribal name. By the time of Apess's birth in 1798, they were confined to small reservations in Connecticut, which probably, according to the estimate of Barry O'Connell, contained no more than two hundred people.[1] Apess himself grew up as an indentured servant in white fam-ilies, ran away and joined the US army, fighting against the British in 1814. He left the military in 1815 as he 'could not think why I should risk my life and limbs in fighting the white man',[2] drif-ted in and out of drunkenness and menial jobs and, in December 1815, became a Methodist. Thereafter, Apess, like many other Pequots who blended traditional shamanism and revivalist evangelism, found spiritual fervour and a purposeful identity. In 1827 he became an exhorter (effectively an itinerant preacher). This role gave him repu-tation: 'crowds flocked out,' he remembered, 'some to *hear* the truth

---

[1] See O'Connell's excellent introduction to his collection of Apess's writings, *On Our Own Ground: The Complete Writings of William Apess, A Pequot*, ed. Barry O'Connell (Amherst, MA, 1992). All further references to this text are cited in parenthesis as *Apess*.
[2] Quoted in Bernd C. Peyer, *The Tutor'd Mind: Indian Writers in Antebellum America* (Amherst, MA, 1997), 134.

and others to *see* the "Indian"'.[3] It helped make him a writer—his texts take the form of Protestant spiritual histories and conversion narratives.[4]

But Apess was never wholly content with the language of orthodox Methodism: he transformed evangelist discourse to articulate specifically Indian issues, campaigned for the rights of the Mashpee Indians over their land, and authored five books, narrating his life, explaining his conversion, challenging white people. Apess's publications include one of the earliest full-length autobiographies by a Native American, *A Son of the Forest* (1829), an account of notable Christians in his nation, *The Experiences of Five Christian Indians of the Pequot Tribe* (1833) (which included the polemical *An Indian's Looking-Glass for the White Man*), and the revisionist history of early colonialism, the *Eulogy on King Philip, as Pronounced at the Odeon, in Federal Street, Boston* (1836). In this chapter I shall examine each of these texts, focusing on two aspects in particular—Apess's use of Romantic motifs and his multifaceted attack on the languages of 'scientific' racism.[5]

Apess was a remarkable writer who deployed the motifs that white culture made available to him to make white readers reconsider their assumptions: rejecting the term 'Indian' and calling himself a 'son of the forest', for example, he revalued a cliché with which white authors had portrayed Native Americans as simple children of nature who needed paternal guidance by their Anglo-American superiors. Such language, Apess showed, was nearly always a self-serving sham by which colonists palliated their racism and greed.

---

[3] Ibid., 137. Quoted in Peyer, *The Tutor'd Mind.*

[4] As David Murray reminds us, Apess was producing artefacts—books—that existed in and for the white people's world. David Murray, *Forked Tongues: Speech, Writing and Representation in North American Indian Texts* (Bloomington, IN, 1991), 57.

[5] On Apess and racial stereotyping see Anne Marie Dannenberg, '"Where, then, shall we place the hero of the wilderness?" William Apess's *Eulogy on King Philip* and Doctrines of Racial Destiny', in *Early Native American Writing: New Critical Essays*, ed. Helen Jaskoski (Cambridge, 1996), 66–82. Other useful investigations of Apess's rhetorical devices include Hilary E. Wyss, 'Captivity and Conversion: William Apess, Mary Jemison, and Narratives of Racial Identity', *AIQ*, 23/3-4 (1999), 63–82, Randall Moon, 'William Apess and Writing White', *Studies in American Indian Literatures*, 5/4 (1993), 45–54, Karim Trio, 'Denominated "SAVAGE": Methodism, Writing and Identity in the Works of William Apess, A Pequot', *American Quarterly*, 48/4 (1996), 653–79, Sandra Gustafson, 'Nations of Israelites: Prophecy and Cultural Authority in the Writings of William Apess', *Religion and Literature*, 26/1 (1994), 31–53, Laura Murray, 'The Aesthetic of Dispossession: Washington Irving and Ideologies of (DE)Colonization in the Early Republic', *American Literary History*, 8/2 (1996), 205–31.

Apess's writing always has his own life as its foundation. His own experiences act as a counterpoint for even his most general arguments. In *The Experiences of Five Christian Indians*, he begins by recalling the discrimination that afflicted his childhood, as one white family after another expected him to act as their servant:

> Had my skin been white, with the same abilities and the same parentage, there could not have been found a place good enough for me. But such is the case with depraved nature, that their judgment for fancy only sets upon the eye, skin, nose, lips, cheeks, chin or teeth and sometimes, the forehead and hair; without any further examination, the mind is made up and the price set.
>
> (*Apess*, 123)

Here Apess writes, as few of the natural historians did, in terms whose generality is rooted in personal experience. He knows how it is to be subject to what he identifies as the racial gaze, which turns a person into a collection of generic racial features. Adding 'sometimes, the forehead and hair' to the list, he alludes to the very features on which natural historians had focused. The Indian, he implies, is subject not just to widespread racism, but also to a racism guided by the science of comparative anatomy. This gaze has moral consequences, leading the whites to pre-judge ('the mind is made up') and to see the Indian only in terms of economic worth ('the price is set'). 'This', Apess continues, 'is something like buying chaff for wheat, or twigs of wood for solid substance'—that is, the white buyer gets only the fragments he has reduced the Indian to and so misses the whole man, while the Indian finds himself turned into detritus. Both the whites and the Indians lose out, but especially the Indian: 'I was alone in the world', Apess declares, 'and none to speak for the poor little Indian boy' (*Apess*, 123).

Reviewing his youth, Apess writes with passionate force, using the white people's medium to put his own specific words in place of the generic features that constituted him in most white people's unseeing eyes. His literary style is all the more subversive for its complexity: Apess mixes lament with accusation, direct questions with subtle inversions. It is with one of these inversions that he challenges the language of current science most effectively, for when he refers to 'depraved nature' in the above extract, he only *seems* to be echoing white writers' verdict on Indians. He is, in fact, turning the term back onto white people: their 'judgment for fancy' reveals their own depraved nature. The organic inferiority lies not in Indians but in the people who have been so corrupted by racist discourse that they can only see in parts. Writing for himself, he allows no glossing over of Indian anger at anatomical procedures that treated them as fragmented bodies to be valued at white people's (low) price. It was, he argued, the white racists who had depraved natures, and the literary wit he argued it with should itself have been sufficient to show men such as Lawrence and Morton that Native Americans were just as sophisticated and intelligent as Anglos. Yet, as Apess knew from experience, the minds of these masters of objectivity had always been already made up.

Apess tried to disturb his white readers' complacency by rhetorically putting them in the place they put Indians. He asked them how they would feel to be hissed at on the grounds of colour and how they would act if their ancestors' tombs had been desecrated. And he gave a voice in English to Chicakaubut, a Massachusett Indian who found, in 1632, that the colonists had robbed his mother's grave:

When last the glorious light of the sky was underneath this globe, and birds grew silent, I began to settle as is my custom, to take repose. Before my eyes were fast closed, methought I saw a vision, at which my spirit was much troubled. A spirit cried aloud, 'Behold, my son, whom I have cherished, see the paps that gave thee suck, the hands that clasped thee warm, and fed thee oft. Can thou forget to take revenge of those wild people that have my monument defaced in a despiteful manner, disdaining our ancient antiquities and honorable customs? See, now, the sachem's grave lies, like unto the common people of ignoble race, defaced. Thy mother doth complain and implores thy aid against these thievish people, now come hither. If this be suffered, I shall not rest quiet within my everlasting habitation'

(*Apess*, 282)

Apess used many voices to narrate his and other Indians' experience. This one is Romantic: the diction is archaic, the scene sublime, the sentiments honourable. It is a literary construct that Macpherson might have given Ossian or Gray put in the mouth of his Bard. In this context, however, it shows the Pilgrim Fathers as 'wild' people and the Indians as dignified. And it reminds nineteenth-century Americans that their heritage—and the still continuing practice of grave-robbing—forced Indians to experience desecration, generation after generation.

Apess deliberately attacks the racial categories of the day as the fetishes of insecure white people. He himself, he narrates in *A Son of the Forest*, is descended from a white grandfather while his grandmother was 'a female attached to the royal family of Philip, king of the Pequot tribe of Indians' (*Apess*, 3). Apess uses this ancestry to make himself rhetorically the embodiment of a revised, anti-colonialist history of America that contests the history usually written by white men. His white grandfather is a commoner and his Indian grandmother royal, rather than a savage. Moreover, she descends from a king, the Philip of King Philip's war (of 1675 in which Philip/Metacom led an alliance of Wampanoags with Mohawks and Mohegans against the colonists, burning the town of Providence and killing thousands, before the colonists, victorious, killed him and his supporters, reducing the tribes to ruin and selling survivors into slavery). Philip was not, for Apess, the cruel and bloody savage of Anglo-American lore, but a man 'overcome by [the] treachery' of the whites. Elsewhere, Apess calls Philip the greatest American as a leader of superior prowess even to Washington. He is a hero because he resisted the white colonists only after they had betrayed Indian trust, a process Apess consistently shows to be continuing unabated. Claiming descent from Philip, then, allows Apess to position himself as one in whose blood past injustice (and resistance to injustice) flows into the present (and the present into the past). For Apess, history is now as well as then.

Descended from a white/Indian union in which the white was inferior in social status to the Indian, Apess grew up to learn that American society insisted on the opposite. His Indian parents split and left him to his grandparents, but they had been degraded (his word) by the introduction to Pequot life of hard liquor:

Shortly after my father left us, my grandmother, who had been out among the whites, returned in a state of intoxication and, without any provocation whatever on my part, began to belabor me most unmercifully with a club; she asked me if I hated her, and I very innocently answered in the affirmative as I did not then know what the word meant and thought all the while that I was answering aright; and so she continued asking me the same question, and I as often answered her in the same way, whereupon she continued beating me, by which means one of my arms was broken in three different places. I was then only four years of age and consequently could not take care of or defend myself.

(*Apess*, 5–6)

Apess is always a political analyst: even so horrific experience as this prompts a warning to white readers that Indian abuse is a consequence, in part, of a colonialist process in which alcohol is a means of destroying native people's social bonds and loosening their grip on the land.[6]

---

[6] On alcoholism as a response to colonial domination and ensuing demoralization, see Gary B. Nash, *Red, White, and Black: the Peoples of Early America* (Englewood Cliffs. NJ, 1974), 255.

But this cruel and unnatural conduct was the effect of some cause. I attribute it in a great measure to the whites, inasmuch as they introduced among my countrymen that bane of comfort and happiness, ardent spirits—seduced them into a love of it and, when under its unhappy influence, wronged them out of their lawful possessions—that land, where reposed the ashes of their sires; and not only so, but they committed violence of the most revolting kind upon the persons of the female portion of the tribe who, previous to the introduction among them of the arts, and vices, and debaucheries of the whites, were as unoffending and happy as they roamed over their goodly possessions as any people on whom the sun of heaven ever shone. The consequence was that they were scattered abroad. Now many of them were seen reeling about intoxicated with liquor, neglecting to provide for themselves and families, who before were assiduously engaged in supplying the necessities of those depending on them for support.

(*Apess*, 7)

Here the Romantic stereotypes about the tribal Indian were access-ible only in elegiac mode: happy natives roaming over their goodly possessions were people of the past. The hour of splendour in the grass was gone—this age of innocence, however, was not located in a Wordsworthian childhood but a pre-colonialist Eden. Apess, in other words, showed the influence of Romantic and Rousseauvian treatments of tribal life as a rural idyll but, in placing the idyll in the past, created a pathetic contrast to the present reality. He adapted a Romantic motif so as to evoke his own regret and provoke a similar sadness in his readers, destroying in the process the other Romantic assumption that Indian life displayed now how Europeans had lived thousands of years before.

It is a testament to his brilliance as a writer that Apess managed not just to elegize a lost idyll but to lay out a method for its renewal. He did so by adapting to his own ends the forms of consciousness articulated in English literary discourse, as when he described an epiphanic 'spot of time' experienced during a hunting trip to the Bay of Quinte:

On the very top of a high mountain in the neighbourhood there was a large pond of water, to which there was no visible outlet;—this pond was unfathomable. It was very surprising to me that so great a body of water should be found so far above the common level of the earth. There was also in the neighbourhood a rock, that had the appearance of being hollowed out by the hand of a skilful artificer; through this rock wound a narrow stream of water: it had a most beautiful and romantic appearance, and I could not but admire the wisdom of God in the order, regularity, and beauty of creation.

(*Apess*, 32–3)

Here Apess's language is that of a Christianized Romanticism, a momentary intimation of the extraordinariness of nature is registered explicitly as an aesthetic intuition but is then, as in Paley's *Natural Theology*, used as evidence of a designer God. The intimation does not, as in Wordsworth, prompt a self-analysis of the creative spirit. And yet the moment is not, after all, wholly contained by conventional piety, for Apess derives from it a new revelation of belonging *as an Indian* to a place and a community. He writes, 'I then turned my eyes to the forest, and it seemed alive with its sons and daughters. There appeared to be the utmost order and regularity in their encampment.' Indians, Apess can now see and say, are the true inheritors of a nature whose beautiful order has just been revealed to him. He can affirm, and thereby take his place among, a people who embody the wisdom of God in his creation. This not only reasserts communal pride as an Indian, but also suggests that Indians, unlike whites, remain unalienated from Eden. In other words, Apess adapts two British discourses—Romantic nature-worship and Christian natural theology—to change his and his readers' consciousness of what it is to be an Indian. It is to be but also to know oneself to be closer to nature and therefore to the Great Spirit who made nature than anyone else. This, of course, is not noble savagery but a highly self-conscious act of literary self- and group-creation. It is a passage in which white people's discourses foster a reconstruction of Indian identity. For Apess, and for many East Coast Indians born into a tribal culture that had survived colonialism only in tattered and scattered fragments, such self-conscious acts were a seminal means of recreating self and nation.

Apess had much need to recreate an Indian self and nation. He had been alienated from Indian life and Indianness early. After escaping his grandparents, the boy Apess was 'bound out' to a succession of white families who, in return for his indentured labour, provided board, lodging, and education. It was thus that Apess acquired literacy in English, thus too that he found himself doubly displaced as a marginal subordinate moving from white family to white family just as he had previously been passed from parents to grandparents as his nation fragmented. Looking back, the adult Apess turned his childhood into an education in racism's self-alienating consequences. He learnt that even the name used for him designated him not as an individual person but as a racial category:

I thought it disgraceful to be called an Indian; it was considered as a slur upon an oppressed and scattered nation, and I have often been led to inquire where the whites received this word, which they so often threw as an opprobrious epithet at the sons of the forest. I could not find it in the Bible and therefore concluded that it was a word imported for the special purpose of degrading us. At other times I thought it was derived from the term *in-gen-uity*.

Apess's derivation of the word may originally have been the naïve idea of a child; printed in his autobiography, however, it becomes a witty retort to the casual yet cruel racism of whites. Nevertheless, this retort could have little power against the almost universal colonial assumption that Indian spelt inferior, an assumption that craniometry such as Morton's tended to reinforce. Apess countered this assumption by choosing a different term—'native'—and claiming uniqueness: 'I humbly conceive that the natives of this country are the only people under heaven who have a just title to the name, inasmuch as we are the only people who retain the original complexion of our father Adam' (*Apess*, 10). Here, Apess combated white racism with a race argument of his own, reviving the ideas of Christian allies of Indians such as Roger Williams and James Adair, who had already affirmed that Native Americans were descendants of one of the lost tribes of Israel. Apess adds an element to the argument, colouring it, so as to overturn white people's hierarchy of skin colour by showing copper skin to be nearer to the shade of Adam and of Jesus (whom Apess reminds readers was a brown Jew). Blumenbach, as I showed in chapter 4, had seen all humans as descendants of Adam and Eve but had assumed the original colour to be white. For most natural historians after him, Europeans (Caucasians) had degenerated least from the Adamic original, Indians more, and Africans most. Apess's arguments not only counter these assumptions but also expose their colour prejudice. Moreover, Apess shows he can extrapolate history from the Bible just as well as Europe's men of science. Not surprisingly, the more racist and materialist natural historians, including Lawrence and Morton, dismissed the argument that Indians originated in the lost tribe of Israelites. Biblical history, they realized, could be used many ways, unlike the hard data that they milked from their skulls and bones.

Apess's nativist arguments were all the more effective because he knew white people well enough to beat them at their own rhetorical games. He knew them so well because he had been brought up to share their prejudices even while he was the victim of these prejudices. He recorded the degree of alienation that he experienced when, as a boy, he became desperate to escape the stigma of being Indian. Placed by the white people outside their tribe, although reared in it, Apess was also left outside Indian society, which he was taught to fear:

I cannot perhaps give a better idea of the dread which pervaded my mind on seeing any of my brethren of the forest than by relating the following occurrence. One day several of my family went into the woods to gather berries, taking me with them. We had not been out long before we fell in with a company of white females, on the same errand—their complexion was, to say the least, as *dark* as that of the natives. This circumstance filled my mind with terror, and I broke from the party with my utmost speed, and I could not muster courage enough to look behind until I had reached home. By this time my imagination had pictured out a tale of blood, and as soon as I regained breath sufficient to answer the questions which my master asked, I informed him that we had met a body of the natives in the woods, but what had become of the party I could not tell.

(*Apess*, 10–11)

There are multiple grim ironies in this anecdote. That the boy should have wished so strongly not to seem Indian that he ran from his 'brethren of the forest' is one. That the white women seem dark enough to be natives is another, revealing the absurdity of the Anglo-American obsession with colour as a sign of racial difference. That the Indian boy had been so fed on tales of terror that he genuinely saw all Indians as threatening others is perhaps the saddest. The adult Apess learns from the incident that racism begins early, that white children are afraid because they are deceived at their mothers' knees.

As well as recollecting his own boyhood emotion, Apess presented an alternative history of Indians, built on the same travel writers and historians whom the race theorists cited. Here again Apess challenged white writers on their own ground, using their own method. He quoted old and new authorities (Las Casas and Clavijero on South America, Robertson and the Cherokee historian Boudinot on the north) but collected instances of colonists' cruelty to Indians, rather than examples of Indian savagery. Travellers' testimony proved to be fertile territory for the confutation of the racial stereotypes that Europeans often drew from it. Apess turned the tables, arguing from the same sources his readers trusted as impeccable (because they were white and gentlemanly). At the same time, Apess concentrated on deeds rather than on the traits that were supposedly organic to the whole race. He accused white colonists for their immoral actions but never descended to their level by suggesting these actions stemmed from some flaw that is inherent in their race. Rather, he impugned their greed, using the Christian moral code to show how the sin of covetousness led to depravity.

Apess's Christianity was not merely rhetorical. Yet he was never comfortably absorbed into the religion of the colonists and was no acquiescent white man's Indian, his native culture replaced by a tame Christianity.[7] On the contrary, Apess found a model for his radical critique in the discourses that Methodism made available to him. Thus, for example, Apess rewrites the trials that, in conversion narratives, beset the Christian on his way to faith, as acts of racial abuse by white people. Thus too he writes his own hymns, as Methodists commonly did, using them to insist that the Indian converts he describes are better than any of the colonists whose natal religion Christianity was. He identifies the words of the Bible not with the colonists who had brought it to America, but with a Jewish culture that he, as a descendant of a lost tribe of Israel, inherited. This gives him authority to lambast the colonists with their failure to live out their own religious principles. He links past and present, moving from the early colonists to his own experience at white Christian's hands and arrives at a remarkable conclusion: 'I do not hesitate to say that through the prayers, preaching, and examples of those pretended pious has been the foundation of all the slavery and depredation in the American colonies toward colored people' (*Apess*, 304). In other words, colonial religion had been an essential cause, rather than an opponent, of colonialism's worst results. Apess had come to understand the ideological function of colonial Protestantism in aiding and abetting genocide.

The acuteness of Apess's analysis is matched by the incisiveness of his imagination. His writing succeeds because it deploys so many means of disturbing readers' assumptions. One example is the fictional scenario he created in *The Experiences of Five Christian Indians*. Addressing the reader directly and explicitly as a white person, Apess asks him/her to act as a judge, but then leaves the judge squirming as he plays with biting irony on the language of colour prejudice:

I would ask you if you would like to be disenfranchised from all your rights, merely because your skin is white, and for no other crime. I'll venture to say,

---

[7] Here I take a different view from Arnold Krupat, *The Voice In The Margin: Native American Literature and the Canon* (Berkeley, 1989), 148–9, who stresses the constraints placed on Apess by his authorial and religious position. More recent historians of Christian Indians in the late eighteenth century have emphasized the vigorous independence that lies just below the deferential surface of many texts. See Margaret Connell Szasz, 'Samuel Occom: Mohegan as Spiritual Intermediary', in Szasz (ed.) *Between Indian and White Worlds: The Cultural Broker* (Norman and London, 1994), 61–78 and Cheryl Walker, *Indian Nation: Native American Literature and Nineteenth-Century Nationalisms* (Durham and London, 1997), 51.

these very characters who hold the skin to be such a barrier in the way would be the first to cry out, 'Injustice! Awful injustice!'

But reader, I acknowledge that this is a confused world, and I am not seeking for office, but merely placing before you the black inconsistency that you place before me—which is ten times blacker than any skin that you will find in the universe. And now let me exhort you to do away that principle, as it appears ten times worse in the sight of God and candid men than skins of color—more disgraceful than all the skins that Jehovah ever made. If black or red skins or any other skin of color is disgraceful to God, it appears that he has disgraced himself a great deal—for he has made fifteen colored people to one white and placed them here upon this earth.

(Apess, 156–57)

Apess follows this with a fable to counter natural history and race theory, a fable about skins and what is legible in them:

Now let me ask you, white man, if it is a disgrace for to eat, drink, and sleep with the image of God, or sit, or walk or talk with them. Or have you the folly to think that the white man, being one in fifteen or sixteen, are the only beloved images of God? Assemble all nations together in your imagination, and then let the whites be seated among them, and then let us look for the whites, and I doubt not it would be hard finding them; for to the rest of the nations, they are still but a handful. Now suppose these skins were put together, and each skin had its national crimes written upon it—which skin do you think would have the greatest? I will ask one question more. Can you charge the Indians with robbing a nation almost of their whole continent, and murdering their women and children, and then depriving them the remainder of their lawful rights, that nature and God require them to have? And to cap the climax, rob another nation to till their grounds and welter out their days under the lash with hunger and fatigue under the scorching rays of a burning sun? I should look at all the skins, and I know that when I cast my eye upon that white skin, and if I saw those crimes written upon it, I should enter my protest against it immediately and cleave to that which is more honorable.

(Apess, 157)

If this scenario seems bizarre, it is deliberately incongruous so as to reveal the absurdity of reading people by their appearance. What Apess writes on the skin, instead of racial traits, are actions, so that his imaginary meeting makes the facts of white oppression legible in the body. In doing so, he pits his discourse, parodic, grotesque, fabulous, shrewd, against the dead prose of the high priests of empiricism and objectivity—the race theorists who saw only native inferiority in the dead skin and bones over which they pored.

Apess's writing is unique: his dual experience as a white-raised, displaced Indian gave him a viewpoint and a language that no other writer possessed. This language was shaped by the genres of Protestantism (the sermon as well as conversion narrative), by the motifs of Romanticism (the rural idyll and the Ossianic sublime) but also by a satirical wordplay that other Christian Indians, including Samson Occom, had earlier used to unsettle the beliefs of Christian whites. Apess is far more public and more aggressive in his sarcasm and parody than Occom ever was, yet the fact that both missionary Indians used English in this way suggests that it is a defining feature of Native American writing in this period, a feature that emerges from the need to turn the language of whites back against them, to possess it rather than be possessed by it. It turns the linguistic colonization that writing in English constituted into an act of destabilization: Apess takes control, for his own ends, of the language that might assimilate him. This is a strategic literary act, artful, active, knowledgeable, and is thus different from and more incisive than the mimicry of which Homi K. Bhabha has written, in which an indigenous person unsettles the colonists' discourse by reproducing it in a different context and from a different position. Such mimicry was largely an effect of the material conditions in which colonial discourse is disseminated—the native culture gives the imperialist's words new, disturbing, significance without necessarily intending to disrupt it. What this Marxist account ignores is the artistic achievement of the controlled linguistic act in which a native person, such as Apess, appropriates the colonist's language, imaginatively creating a new radical discourse that contests colonial assumptions in the colonists' medium. Such a discourse must speak with the tools of subversion—comedy, parody, and irony—as well as argument. It is by these means that it gains its leverage and maintains its independence. Yet that independence is fragile, built upon a bitter hybridity. Apess was at home in neither white nor Indian society: in white because he was not fully accepted, in Indian because tribal life was breaking down under pressure from colonization. His was a precarious position and Apess faded from historical record after 1838 and died in obscurity, his work forgotten.

15

Captive, Campaigner, Conman: John Hunter

During the winter of 1823/4, a short, swarthy, and plain young man, of no known parentage, was the biggest star in London. John Dunn Hunter—as he called himself—had arrived from the USA only a few months earlier, yet was soon 'pressed with multitudes of invitations to routs and balls, and parties, from ladies of the highest rank and fashion'.[1] This was social success on a Byronic scale, yet Hunter had few of Byron's advantages: he was neither a poet nor a lord, neither darkly handsome nor daringly witty. In most respects he seemed distinctly ordinary. He was, however, like the author of *Childe Harold*, a writer who had seen dangerous places and strange peoples. And he had one quality that made him more Byronic even than Byron himself: he had not just visited wild regions, and not simply been marked by what he saw in those regions, but had actually been raised by the tribes that lived there. Hunter was, so he said, a white man who had been brought up by Indians from the age of three, when a party of Kickapoos had killed his family and taken him captive. He had grown into manhood with the Pawnees, the Kansas, and finally the Osages, losing all memory of his natural parents and of the English language. It was only in 1816, when the Osages proposed to murder a white fur-trader, that Hunter abandoned his tribal identity, betraying the Osages' plan to the trader and then, haunted by conscience, plunging alone into the wilderness, where he lived an 'outcast' until he encountered a group of French traders. Brought to New Orleans, he then worked in the fur trade and as a boatman, learning English for a few months in school and in the books that he carried with him on camp. Discovering that educated

---

[1] 'Viator', *Natchitoches Courier*, 20 March 1827, quoted in Richard Drinnon, *White Savage: The Case of John Dunn Hunter* (New York, 1972), xx. My account of Hunter's life is indebted to Drinnon's study throughout.

people were interested in his story, he wrote it down, with the aid of an 'editor', and published it in Philadelphia as *Manners and Customs of Several Indian Tribes Located West of the Mississippi.*[2]

It was a sensational story and when the London firm of Longman, Hurst, Rees, Orme and Brown re-published it in April 1823, it seemed still more so, for it was retitled *Memoirs of a Captivity among the Indians of North America, from Childhood to the Age of Nineteen.*[3] Widely reviewed, the publication made Hunter a fascinating figure and the first edition sold 1,500 copies within three months. A second edition appeared in 1823 and a third the following year. Hunter then followed his narrative across the Atlantic and was received in its wake. The London hostesses who adored him had already consumed him in print: however plain his appearance he was pre-glamorized by his tale of suffering, survival, and savagery. He embodied, in safe form, the allure of the exotic: in Hunter, High Society ladies could see—and touch—a respectable white man shaped by a 'savage' life that they themselves would never be allowed to access in its native habitat. They pitied him as the child wrenched from its parents, they admired him as the Indian warrior: he was, remembered one acquaintance, 'surrounded with beautiful women, whose eyes yielded a tribute'.[4] Ladies flirted and frolicked with him in a way that was not granted to purely British gentlemen: according to American witness John Neal, Hunter would 'look very savage at the women, flatter them to their faces, threaten to jump down their throats before a room full of company ... romp with them as they had never been romped with before'.[5]

Hunter's social success was not solely based on the romantic aura that ladies saw in 'savages'. If he had simply seemed a sexual adventurer he would not have been received, as he was, into respectable salons or invited to the great houses of the country gentry. In fact, the thrilling virility of the white 'redman' was but one element of his Indianness: Hunter astutely used to his own advantage the stereotypes that already made the Indian a Romantic figure in the heated imaginations of the British. For instance, when not frolicking with the ladies, he appeared as a man whose Indian manners flattered the values of his British hosts: Sir

[2] See Drinnon, *White Savage*, 4, 260–1 (Bibliographical Essay).

[3] Ibid.

[4] *Natchitoches Courier*, 20 March 1827. Quoted in Drinnon, *White Savage*, 28.

[5] John Neal, ' "Mr. John Dunn Hunter;" the Hero of Hunter's Captivity Among the Indians, &c.', *London Magazine*, V (May–August 1826), 317–43 (322–30).

William Knighton noted of him that, 'being taught by the Indians that it was presumptuous in a young man to speak before his superiors in age, he is silent unless particularly addressed'.[6] Such deference not only authenticated his Indianness but also ensured that the British gentry would experience no social embarrassment in his company. Within months he had been taken up by men of rank, including the wealthy botanist Sir James Edward Smith, the famous improving agriculturalist Thomas Coke, and, most prestigious of all, the King's youngest son the Duke of Sussex.

Hunter impressed such men by mastering British social occasions without being coached, as if his education as an Indian had given him a natural gentility—a dignity that was adaptable to new, 'civilized' circumstances because it came from within. Thus Hunter let Britons play out the fantasy of the Indian who was a model for the gentleman, because, despite his lack of civilization, he showed a sense of honour, a respect for authority, and an understanding of social propriety. Hunter's was an astute act of self-presentation by which he succeeded in jettisoning the hallmarks of primitiveness and distinguished himself from other native visitors who were assumed to be ignorant and uncouth. John Neal sarcastically recalled: 'Did he wear white kid gloves, neither wrong side out nor on the wrong hands, or go to court with a bag and sword, a chapeau under his arm, his hair powdered. ... Then, how apt he was! How truly a North American savage! How altogether above the parade of savages, who go to court in their own hide and feathers!'[7] Hunter, in short, allowed Britons to think as well of North American Indians as they wanted to—and to rate them above the other indigenous people of the empire.

What most recommended Hunter was his project to save Indians. The plan was to turn Indians from hunters to farmers, on the best new British principles. By adopting Coke's methods and machinery they would be able to prosper on far less land than they needed as hunters. They would thus suffer far less from the depredations of the settlers who took their territory and the traders who addicted them to alcohol. Like Norton before him, Hunter wanted agricultural advice, but refused gifts of equipment, declaring that he would pay for what he took. Thus he convinced his hosts of his disinterestedness while appealing to the aspects of Britishness in which they took most pride—their love of

[6] Lady Knighton, *Memoirs of Sir William Knighton,* 2 vols. (London, 1838), II, 56–7.
[7] Neal, 'Mr. John Dunn Hunter', 322–3.

improvement and their belief that it was their duty to 'civilize' other nations. Smith's reasoning reveals this process at work: he introduced Hunter into polite society, he said, because Hunter was 'going back with the noble design of improving [the Indians] on the wisest and best principles'.[8] Walter Scott was another who interested himself in the project, just as he had in Norton's Mohawk translation of the gospel. Their vanity flattered and their paternalist assumptions tickled, the British welcomed Hunter and supported his scheme.

At times the British were so fascinated by Hunter's Indian viewpoint they had to remind themselves that he was a white man. They competed for his attention because they wanted to see themselves through the eyes of one who was both like and unlike them, a white who was red, a seemingly civilized man who had emerged from savagery. Selfhood and otherness merged in Hunter and gave him a unique position that carried authority—he could tell the whites both what they did and did not want to know about themselves, as in this exchange recorded by Knighton:

I asked what were his first impressions upon seeing civilized life? He replied, 'amazement'. He could not have imagined seven years ago, which was the first time he saw New York, that anything he now sees could exist. He also added, 'I can never be surprised again: but what made me unhappy was to see the distress of the poorer inhabitants, for among the Indians none are suffered to want.'[9]

If Hunter seemed a man of compassion—lamenting the inequality and hardship produced by urban capitalism, he also appeared as a man of sensibility, whose feelings of chivalry towards women led him to criticize the hypocrisies of polite society. The following remarks were calculated to make tribal culture, and Hunter himself, appeal to the ladies, emphasizing as they did love, rather than status, as the determining factor in marriage:

Mr Hunter spoke with great warmth of his horror of the usual motives for marrying in England. 'Here,' he said, 'you marry for money, for rank, for beauty, for anything but love: therefore you must be bound to each other for life, to prevent greater confusion. But with the Indians it is otherwise; and I think the bond of marriage would take away all their love. The warriors love the Squaws with their whole heart; but they would not be their slaves.'

[8] *Memoir and Correspondence of the Late Sir James Edward Smith, M.D., Fellow of the Royal Society of London etc.*, ed. Lady Smith (London, 1832), I, 513–14.
[9] *Memoirs of Sir William Knighton*, II, 59.

Upon my asking him whether the Squaws were not considered inferior beings, he said, 'You mistake the term: Squaw means woman. But we cannot despise them. They are our mothers; they form us: we leave our young warriors to their care, and they are held in estimation just in proportion as our children are brave and virtuous, or the contrary, for we think education all-powerful in the formation of character.'[10]

As a man who had been expected to be savage, but who seemed so tender-hearted in person, Hunter resembled nothing more than one of the heroes of Byron's Eastern tales or Mackenzie's novels of sensibility. He turned these romantic fictions, so popular with women readers, into a living, breathing reality, there in their drawing rooms.

When Norton had visited Britain, he had come with a commission from his tribe and with the approval of its chief, already well-known to the British. Hunter, by contrast, came out of nowhere—without recommendation from any Indians or Indian agents. He was all the more enticing for the suddenness of his appearance—a phenomenon miraculously translated from Indian country. It was his book that was his herald, predisposing people to see authenticity and extraordinariness in this ordinary man—for not only did it appear as authoritative about Indians as Carver, Hearne, and Mackenzie but also seemed the most remarkable adventure story 'since De Foe made Alexander Selkirk his own under the fiction of Robinson Crusoe'.[11]

Hunter's story showed respect for Indian culture but scarcely any culture shock or vulnerability. It discussed the moment of capture, and the separation from his parents, only briefly, since they occurred when he was so young he could hardly remember them. If the text resembled any previous narratives at all, it was only in the manner in which it turned acculturation to Indian life into a romantic adventure—a process that made it resemble the fictional captivities romanticized in the novels of Smith, Smollett, and Mackenzie more strongly than it resembled other captivity narratives themselves. The principal readers of such fictions were women, and Hunter appealed to them by recounting how, as a boy, he had endured taunts from the Indian children, how he had lost family after family as he was taken from one tribe by its enemies, and how he had come to love his adoptive mother:

The treatment I received from Hunk-hah and her daughter chimed in harmonious concordance with the vibrations of my bosom: I gave loose to their

---

[10] *Memoirs of Sir William Knighton*, II, 60–1.
[11] In *The Literary Gazette*, 19 April 1823, 242.

indulgence, and sincerely loved and respected them, as much, it appears to me, as if they had really been allied to me by the strongest ties of consanguinity.[12]

Hunter's prose, pompous and Latinate, is nevertheless fashionable: here he uses the jargon of sensibility, explaining his emotional reactions in terms of physical sensations, and thus aligning himself with the trembling heroes of sentimental fiction.

It is, however, the content more than the style that gives the narrative its affective power. Hunter describes himself growing from a little boy lost into a revered hunter and intrepid explorer, but makes a point of reassuring his white readers that he was no bloodthirsty warrior. A man of feeling not a warlike savage, Hunter includes several tableaux of the kind familiar to admirers of travel writing, highlighting his aesthetic sensitivity to landscape (a sensitivity normally taken to be a sign of a gentleman). In the following passage he describes a discovery that he made when on a hunting expedition along the La Platte River—a mysterious cave:

The entrance to this cave was rather above the ground; and though narrow, of easy access. The floor was generally rocky, and much broken; though in some places, particularly in the ante-parts, strips of soil appeared, covered with animal ordure. Parts of the roof were at very unequal distances from the floor: in some places it appeared supported by large, singularly variegated, and beautiful columns; and at others it supported formations resembling huge isicles, which I now suppose to be stalactites.

Lighted up by our birch-bark flambeaux, the cave exhibited an astonishing and wonderful appearance; while the loud and distant rumbling or roar of waters through their subterranean channels, filled our minds with apprehension and awe. We discovered two human bodies partly denuded, probably by the casual movements of the animals which frequent this abode of darkness; we inhumed and placed large stones over them, and then made good our retreat, half inclined to believe the tradition which prevails among some of the tribes, and which represents this cavern as the aperture through which the first Indian ascended from the bowels of the earth, and settled on its surface.[13]

Besides displaying the Indians' reverence for the dead body, this passage employs the cant phrases of the Romantic sublime, ensuring that

---

[12] Hunter's *Memoirs of a Captivity among the Indians of North America, from Childhood to the Age of Nineteen: With Anecdotes Descriptive of their Manners and Customs. To Which Is Added, Some Account of the Soil, Climate, and Vegetable Productions of the Territory Westward of the Mississippi*, 3rd edn. (London, 1824), 35–6. All quotations from Hunter are from this third, expanded, edition.

[13] *Memoirs*, 29.

Hunter presents events in terms likely to be both reassuringly familiar and emotionally powerful to his white readers. As a narrator, Hunter never seems to be presenting beliefs or attitudes that are unassimilable to those of white people—or even to be beset by tensions arising from the difference between his Indianized upbringing and his more recent immersion in the expectations of 'civilized' society. There is little strangeness or otherness in his prose, little that his readers might find alien or uncomfortable: it fits the conventional bill.

The narrative owed much of its success to this lack of cultural strangeness, to its ability to depict Indian life in accordance with British cultural and aesthetic discourses. It also succeeded by surprise. For instance, Hunter revealed that, only a few years after Lewis and Clark completed their epic journey over the Rocky Mountains, he and a few other Osages had also reached the Pacific. Although he was sketchy on the details of their route and the Indians they encountered, he described the view they finally gained of the Pacific in glowing terms:

The unbounded view of the waters, the incessant and tremendous dashing of the waves along the shore, accompanied with a noise resembling the roar of loud and distant thunder, filled our minds with the most sublime and awful sensations, and fixed on them as immutable truths, the tradition we had received from our old men, that the great waters divide the residence of the Great Spirit, from the temporary abodes of his red children. We here contemplated in silent dread, the immense difficulties over which we should be obliged to triumph after death, before we could arrive at those delightful hunting grounds, which are unalterably destined for such only as do good, and love the Great Spirit. We looked in vain for the stranded and shattered canoes of those who had done wickedly. We could see none, and we were led to hope that they were few in number. We offered up our devotions, or I might rather say, our minds were serious, and our devotions continued, all the time we were in this country, for we had ever been taught to believe, that the Great Spirit resided on the western side of the Rocky Mountains, and this idea continued throughout the journey, notwithstanding the more specific water boundary assigned to him by our traditionary dogmas.[14]

Again Hunter manipulates the rhetoric of the sublime, combined this time with pious affirmations. The contemplation of nature's vastness leads to thoughts of God—and Indians turn out to be good Burkeans.

To explore North America to the western sea had been the goal of white people for centuries. Hunter, by showing Indians had achieved this goal, was pointedly placing them (and himself) on the same level

---

[14] *Memoirs*, 69.

as white America's greatest heroes. Yet he had a still greater—and more Romantic—hero to offer British readers, the Shawnee leader of the pan-Indian alliance that, in conjunction with British troops, defeated the US in many battles in the War of 1812. Tecumseh was already revered in Britain as a great statesman and as a noble ally. Hunter gave readers a vivid picture of him on tour, rallying support among the western Indians:

I wish it was in my power to do justice to the eloquence of this distinguished man: but it is utterly impossible. The richest colours, shaded with a master's pencil, would fall infinitely short of the glowing finish of the original. The occasion and subject were peculiarly adapted to call into action all the powers of genuine patriotism; and such language, such gestures, and such feelings and fulness of soul contending for utterance, were exhibited by this untutored native of the forest in the central wilds of America, as no audience, I am persuaded, either in ancient or modern times ever before witnessed.

My readers may think some qualification due to this opinion; but none is necessary. The unlettered Te-cum-seh gave extemporaneous utterance only to what he felt; it was a simple, but vehement narration of the wrongs imposed by the white people on the Indians, and an exhortation for the latter to resist them. The whole addressed to an audience composed of individuals who had been educated to prefer almost any sacrifice to that of personal liberty, and even death to the degradation of their nation; and who, on this occasion, felt the portraiture of Te-cum-seh but too strikingly identified with their own condition, wrongs, and sufferings.

This discourse made an impression on my mind, which, I think, will last as long as I live.[15]

Here Tecumseh is romanticized in the sense that his political speech is represented as a spontaneous overflow of (patriotic and noble) feelings. It is important that, like a Wordsworthian solitary, he is 'untutored': his performance is overwhelming because it is organic, emerging from an inner conviction that is felt in the soul rather than learnt from books. Hunter is left a changed man, awed by Tecumseh's overwhelming voicing of his inmost self. And so he declares Tecumseh the greatest orator of all time, an estimation that, Hunter explicitly tells his readers, is not an exaggeration. Clearly, patriotic fervour, when it comes naturally, makes the deepest impression of all. It carries conviction by a communication of emotion, rather than logical argument, and vindicates the Indians' nobility; the US, by contrast, is implicitly engaged on the immoral task of degrading the tribes.[16]

[15] *Memoirs*, 43–4.   [16] *Memoirs*, 44.

Hunter gave British readers heroes; he also gave them a cause to feel morally superior to the US, with whom they had been at war only ten years' previously. Hunter declared 'that the American community in particular, which has become great and powerful as it were on the destruction of Indians, owes the accomplishment of this measure [of assisting them and preventing their extinction] . . . to its own character, to justice, and to moral right'.[17] And he impugned the scientific authorities as well as the poor white settlers, rejecting as a self-serving myth the doctrine that Indians were organically subordinate to whites: he had only scorn for 'the philosophers of the day [who] would rank them in their moral and physical endowments and capacities to improve, as intermediates to their own proudly cultivated race, and baboons or apes'.[18] By depicting US hostility to Tecumseh, by highlighting the landgrabbing of white settlers and by attacking the beliefs of racial theorists, Hunter allowed Britons to contrast their own admiration and concern with Anglo-Americans' hypocrisy and greed. The *Monthly Review*, for instance, concluded: 'The Whites civilize the Indians as settlers clear a forest—by felling all before them!'[19] In The *Quarterly*, meanwhile, George Procter played the US determination to clear the forests off against a picturesque description of Indians being fostered in their woodland habitat by admiring British soldiers:

From the shores of Lakes Superior, and Huron, and Michigan; from the heads of the Mississippi and its tributary streams; from the immense forests and prairies spread over that part of the continent, and bordering on those waters, Indian nations descended to the country about Detroit, to join their hands in the same cause, and to take up the hatchet with their British Father, against the Long Knives, as they termed the Americans. . . . The encampment of this large body of warriors, with their women and children presented a singularly wild and imposing spectacle. The effect was strongest by night, when the blazing watch-fire threw its red glare upon the swarthy figures which danced or grouped in indolence around it; and the sound of the war-song, the shout, the yell, were strangely varied at intervals by the plaintive cadence of the Indian drum; while the dark foliage of the forest slumbering in the calm brilliance of a Canadian night, was half hidden, half revealed, as the light of the fires shot up to heaven, or sunk into gloomy embers.[20]

---

[17] From Hunter's 'Reflections on the Different States and Conditions of Society', 453–62 of the *Memoirs*, quoted in Drinnon, *White Savage*, 40.

[18] Ibid., 40.

[19] *Monthly Review*, cii (Nov.–Dec. 1823), 243–56, 368–81 (370).

[20] Procter, *Quarterly Review*, 78.

With this description, Procter responded to Hunter's scenic romanticism with an idealized tableau of his own experiences in Canada during the War of 1812, when Britons and Indians had fought as allies against the US. Clearly, Hunter liberated Procter's need to define Indians as noble warriors and men of nature. Hunter had written in terms that Britons steeped in Romantic aesthetics appreciated, inspiring his reviewers to imagine idealized scenarios in which British colonies worked by cooperation between white officials and native inhabitants who valued Britain's principled rule and mission to civilize, whereas the US exploited and destroyed. In other words, Hunter's narrative suited Britons' desire to romanticize their own past dealings with Indians, a desire that emerged from their resentment of the independent USA and from their guilty awareness that their government had betrayed its Indian allies not once but three times, when, in 1783, 1794, and 1814, it made peace treaties ignoring Indians' territorial rights.

For all his condemnation of American whites, Hunter left the Osages and went to live as one of them. According to the *Memoirs*, he made this decision suddenly, although traders had for a considerable time been seducing him with stories of the great achievements of the Anglos. He made his choice in traumatic circumstances: the Osages, drunk on the brandy supplied by fur-traders, resolved to kill them. They murdered and scalped one; but Hunter, revolted by their drunken frenzy, warned a second, a Colonel George Watkins, in time, thus betraying tribal solidarity. He was then horrified to find that Watkins wanted to involve him in retaliatory violence, expecting Hunter to demonstrate his loyalty to his white identity by helping the traders find and kill the Osages. This was too quick and too Judas-like; Hunter refused to participate and insisted on departing by himself: 'I determined on abandoning his party,' he wrote, 'in search of consolation and quiet to my half-distracted mind.'[21] Hunter was now no longer the pitiable boy or proud explorer, but the Romantic hero of his own tale, a man with a compelling inner drama, an introspective, bitter, solitary figure, who nevertheless felt sure he had acted aright.

I looked back with the most painful reflections on what I had been, and on the irreparable sacrifice I had made, merely to become an outcast, to be hated and despised by those I sincerely loved and esteemed. But however much I was disposed to be dissatisfied and quarrel with myself, the consolation of the

[21] *Memoirs*, 107–8.

most entire conviction that I had acted rightly always followed, and silenced my self-upbraidings.[22]

With these words Hunter aligned himself with the alienated tragic hero that British readers had fallen in love with when Byron made it central to poem after poem. Like the Giaour, Cain, and Fletcher Christian, Hunter has a complex self-awareness, knowing he has sacrificed his own peace for the peace of two communities who were not worthy of the sacrifice.

Reviewers were enamoured of this Byronic prophet in the wilderness. The *Literary Gazette* quoted at length from this part of the narrative, calling it 'this strange solitary life, than the picture of which we do not remember anything more striking in any poet'.[23] The *Monthly Review* enthused about the 'romantic ... air' of the 'striking' tale: Hunter's Byronism, with its fall from autochthonous innocence into alienated experience, had found its target.[24]

Hunter took care to show that, despite his separation from his Indian self and despite his disgust at white Americans' treatment of the tribes, he was not irrevocably bitter and twisted, because he had learnt to recognize the benefits of civilization: 'I must confess', he declared, 'the struggle in my bosom was for a considerable time doubtful, and even now my mind often reverts to the innocent scenes of my childhood, with a mixture of pleasurable and painful emotions that is altogether indescribable. But my intercourse with refined society, acquaintance with books, and a glimpse at the wonderful structure into which the mind is capable of being moulded, have, I am convinced, unalterably attached me to a social intercourse with civilized man, composed as he is of crudities and contradictions.'[25] This ambivalent endorsement further recommended Hunter to his hosts, for it showed that he was sure he had made the right decision in opting for life in white society, but was neither naïve about its faults nor forgetful of his Indian self. Nevertheless, his love of Indian life is here associated with infancy: the implication is that one progresses, rightly, from childlike Indianness into adult civilization. This, Hunter concludes, is the position at which he has now arrived—a clear-sighted embrace of the white people's world, an embrace by an outsider better able to see its faults than one who has been entirely raised within it.

---

[22] *Memoirs*, 110. [23] *Literary Gazette*, 3 May 1823, 278–9 (279).
[24] *Monthly Review*, 243. [25] *Memoirs*, 14.

Hunter did not stay in Britain so long that the novelty of his viewpoint wore off. By the summer of 1824 he had departed for the US, intending to bring agriculture to the western Indians, although exactly where or how was not clear. In this respect he differed from Norton and from later Indian visitors such as Peter Jones: Hunter could not claim to represent any particular group of Indians; he was not a cultural broker employed by a Native American group because of his expertise in Anglo culture as well as their own. He was no tribe's leader or emissary, but was a speculative loner using his putative Indian past, in Britain, to gain leverage for himself and his own ideas. A visitor in Britain, rather than a native, he would return to Indian country as visitor too—a man without ties of kinship in either community. In their absence, Hunter exploited his brief British acquaintances: among other new-found patrons for his idealistic scheme Thomas Coke and the Duke of Sussex wished him well and contributed to his expenses.

Hunter was gone but he was not forgotten, because in 1826 General Lewis Cass, Governor of the Michigan Territory and Superintendent of Indian Affairs, having read Procter's *Quarterly* review and then the *Memoirs* themselves, published an article asserting that Hunter was an impostor. Cass, who knew the Arkansas country personally, had checked Hunter's names and dates. He had found no evidence that Tecumseh ever visited the western tribes, or that Colonel Watkins ever existed, and produced a statement from John Dunn, whose name Hunter claimed to have taken in gratitude for his kind assistance, denying all knowledge of the ex-captive. Other white men who dealt with the Osages also swore there never had been a white captive among them. Still others claimed Hunter had only a rudimentary knowledge of the languages of the Indians who had supposedly brought him up. No witnesses could be found of the capture of Hunter's family; no surviving relatives or neighbours came forward either. Hunter, it seemed, was a liar—probably a former soldier and trader who had some frontier experience but certainly not an Indian by education. To Cass, the whole affair was evidence of Britons' credulity, a credulity that stemmed from their eagerness to believe themselves fairer in their treatment of Indians than their US counterparts. He implied that it suited British political self-regard to accept a romanticized view of Indians. Equally, discrediting Hunter, and undermining notions of Indian nobility, vindicated US Indian policy, for which Cass was responsible. The authenticity of the *Memoirs* was now an issue in a propaganda battle between two old enemies in which their colonial treatment of Indians was an indicator of their relative virtue.

It was apparent that Cass's attack was politically motivated. Nevertheless, the evidence he assembled was—and remains—hard to refute. Cass renewed the concerns which even the first reviewers had experienced about the authorship of the narrative—could a man who spoke no English and neither read nor wrote until age twenty, a man whose education was so perfunctory, write in the way the *Memoirs* were written? Was the narrative actually composed by its 'editor'—in which case, how much of it was true? According to a friend who lived in the same London lodging house, Hunter had himself composed several sections added for the British edition—in which case, given their stylistic consistency with the rest, he was the author of his narrative. But then could he really have been as inexperienced in English as he claimed? And there is also the disturbing lack of detail as to people, incidents, and places: much of what Hunter reveals about the Kickapoos, Kansas, and Osages was little different from the generalized discussions of Indian customs to be found in many travel books and histories. Then again, this may have been a result of an effort to emulate the conventional literary style of such successful and authoritative books—a genuine captive narrating his life within orthodox literary constraints. It is impossible to be certain.

The strongest evidence suggesting that Hunter was an impostor came from John Neal, an American writer who had also shared Hunter's London lodging house. Neal admitted he had been taken in by Hunter until he had read Cass's charges, but also distanced himself from Cass's political bias. Reviewing his daily contact with Hunter, however, Neal felt that he had been taken for a ride. What, he asked, were Hunter's motives for posing in the way he did? He answered, damagingly, that they included moneymaking. Hunter, he claimed, had taken money under false pretences from many, once he had first won their confidence by pretending to be above pecuniary considerations.[26] Yet Neal did not think the desire for money was Hunter's main impetus. Nor did he attribute it to a desire for fame, or even to the ego-satisfaction gained from successfully deceiving notable people. On the contrary, Neal thought, Hunter was a prisoner of a ruse that had probably been suggested to him by others, in an attempt to overcome poverty on the US frontier. Once his experiences had been worked up and published, and met such unexpected success, he had had to live out the role that had begun as a literary fiction: 'I believe in my heart, [that Hunter] was obliged to persevere in the course of deception long and long after he

[26] Neal, 'Mr. John Dunn Hunter', 319, 325.

would have given it up, if he could.'[27] But he could not, for he had no
community to return to, having become, to everyone he encountered on
both sides of the Atlantic, the figure, genuine or false, he claimed to be.

It's unlikely that we will ever know for sure whether Hunter was what
he claimed to be or, if he wasn't, how much experience of Indian life
he really had. But the most interesting question about him is not why
he did what he did, but why and how he attracted so many eminent
Britons to him. Again, Neal has some insight into Hunter's secret,
suggesting that Hunter turned himself into a blank canvas, on which
Britons painted their fantasies about the Indians who already fascinated
them by reputation. 'He was', Neal argued, 'overrated here, prodigiously
overrated—but where is the wonder? The people of this country had
never seen, what we see every day in America, savages bursting from the
solitude—savages when they first appear ... growing beautiful as they
approach the light. Here he passed for a prodigy—while, at home, he
made no sort of stir, till he had been here.'[28] In other words, had Britons
seen more of the genuinely romantic real Indians, they would have
found Hunter much less romantic than they did. His success depended
on ignorance.

Neal's verdict was only half right. Britons did project their fantasies
about Indians on to Hunter, and he did allow them to do so. But they
admired him not because he was an authentic 'savage bursting from the
solitude', but because he was both white and Indian, one of us and one
of them. It was the loss and subsequent reclaiming of white identity, the
blend of savage and civilized, that made Hunter fascinating—just as
it had Norton/Teyoninhokarawen before him. And Hunter was more
Romantic still than Norton, because he was now without a nation of his
own, having suffered the double trauma of captivity and return—and
the latter for idealistic, self-sacrificial reasons. That Felicia Hemans
wrote a poem about him is a sign of how Romantic he seemed; what the
poem says reveals that it was his duality and difference that made him
appealing (especially to women):

The Child of the Forests
Written After Reading the Memoirs of John Hunter

Is not thy heart far off amidst the woods,
    Where the Red Indian lays his father's dust?

---

[27] Ibid., 322.   [28] Ibid., 330–1.

And, by the rushing of the torrent-floods
    To the Great Spirit bows in silent trust?
Doth not thy soul o'ersweep the foaming main,
To pour itself upon the wilds again?

They are gone forth, the Desert's warrior-race,
    By stormy lakes to track the elk and roe;
But where art thou, the swift one in the chase,
    With thy free footstep and unfailing bow?
Their singing shafts have reach'd the panther's lair,
And where art thou?—thine arrows are not there!

They rest beside their streams—the spoil is won—
    They hang their spears upon the cypress-bough,
The night-fires blaze, the hunter's work is done—
    They hear the tales of old—and where art thou?
The night-fires blaze beneath the giant-pine,
And there a place is fill'd, that once was thine.

For thou art mingling with the city's throng,
    And thou hast thrown thine Indian bow aside;
Child of the forests! Thou art borne along,
    E'en as ourselves, by life's tempestuous tide!
But will this be? And canst thou *here* find rest?—
    Thou hadst thy nurture on the Desert's breast.

Comes not the sound of torrents to thine ear,
    From the Savannah-land, the land of streams?
Hear'st thou not murmurs which none else may hear?
    Is not the forest's shadow on thy dreams?
They call—wild voices call thee o'er the main,
Back to thy free and boundless woods again.

Hear them not! Hear them not!—thou canst not find
    In the far wilderness what once was thine!
Thou hast quaff'd knowledge from the founts of mind,
    And gather'd loftier aims and hopes divine.
Thou knowest the soaring thought, the immortal strain—
Seek not the deserts and woods again![29]

---

[29] Hemans's poem appeared in the *New Monthly Magazine*, 10 (March 1824), 282.

Hemans's Hunter is a forlorn figure, for although he retains a secret bond with a nature that represents childhood, innocence and liberty, a bond that the urbanites of Britain have lost, he nonetheless knows too much of the white world to be able to return to savage innocence. While this does respond to Hunter's own description of himself as an outcast, and to his ambivalence about the white civilization he has chosen to embrace, it is not profound—Hemans uses an entirely standard equation of Indians with childhood and innocence and of civilization with adulthood and knowledge. Her verse is a conventional exercise in Romantic savagery—incorporating standard scenic features (the bow and arrow, the spears, the cypresses) that did not actually feature in Hunter's account or in contemporary Osage society. Behind it is an Indianized pastoralism, adapted from Ossian (to whose 'tales of old' Hemans alludes) and from Wordsworth, in which the American wild is romantic to the degree that it acts as an unfallen opposite to the careworn city. It suggests that Hunter was popular because he fitted himself so neatly into Romantic categories, making himself available for pity as well as wonder. That he was so successful demonstrates their currency of these categories, and the continuing British hunger to see them lived out in the flesh. Both the currency and the hunger had to do with Britons' need to clear their consciences about their colonial treatment of native peoples and to feel superior to the US. They could congratulate themselves for recognizing the nobility of Indians and acting to assist them when their former colony did not—just as they did, after abolishing the slave trade in the British colonies, when slave-holding America claimed to be a land of liberty.

When Hunter reached America, it was as if he heeded Hemans's advice. He did not return to tribal life, but carved out a role for himself assisting Britons to turn their Romantic images of Indians into social reality. In November 1824 he accompanied Robert Owen, the industrialist and social reformer, on his journey to the town of Harmonie, Indiana. Owen was a veteran paternalist, who had used his wealth to build the model town of New Lanark for his workers, where their lives were supervised in the interests of (Owen's vision of) social justice. Now he wanted to set up a similar planned community in America, where, he told a delegation of Choctaw and Chickasaw Indians visiting Washington, whites and Indians could live together as one:

He said Indians taken when young amongst white, would become like whites, and vice versa and he concluded that it would be possible to unite the good in the Indian and in the civilized lives, so as to make them a being superior to both. He further said it would be possible to bring all knowledge of the world together to one place so that each might enjoy the benefit of it. The Indian replied that he agreed with him.[30]

This was a utopian vision, based as it was on a top-down plan in which political history and cultural difference were not considered. But it was a plan inspired by Owen's admiration for Hunter, who after all personified a harmony between whites and Indians that, hitherto, had flourished only when Indians adopted whites into their tribes. Hunter's *Memoirs* had mentioned several white captives living happily as Indians, and concluded that captives almost never wished to return to white society once assimilated to Indian life. On this occasion, Hunter told Owen he had not felt so at home as he did with the Indian delegation since he had 'left his own people'.[31] He now longed to return to the West.

Hunter and Owen travelled west together but parted ways on the Ohio River. Hunter proceeded south to his old fur trading base of New Orleans while Owen continued on to Harmonie, which he went on to buy for £30,000 and rename New Harmony. There he established a communist community run entirely on cooperative principles decided by the settlers themselves. No Indians were in fact included, and the scheme had broken down in dissension by 1828. Owen tried briefly to create another similar community in Mexico, but was stymied by a change of government there. He returned to Britain and dedicated himself to promoting the cooperative movement there.

It was in Mexico that Hunter began the last and most extraordinary phase of his career as a white Indian, a phase dedicated to turning his plan to save the Indians into a reality. Whether an impostor or not, he now began to use the authority he had acquired to get for the Western Indians a territory that would not be vulnerable to the endless desire of the US—both settlers and government—for land. In 1825 and 1826, with the support of Henry George Ward, the British emissary, and the Cherokee leader Richard Fields, Hunter went to newly independent Mexico, claiming to represent no less than twenty-three Indian tribes, to seek a grant of land which the tribes might hold communally and govern themselves. Here Hunter, himself a displaced person, was acting, or claiming to act, for other displaced people—the Cherokees

[30] *Diary of William Owen From November 10, 1824, to April 20, 1825*, ed. Joel W. Hiatt (Indianapolis, 1906 [rpt. Clifton, NJ, 1973]), 43–4.
[31] Hunter quoted in Drinnon, *White Savage*, 162.

in Arkansas were those who, under severe pressure from US settlement, had abandoned their native lands in the East and moved west of the Mississippi. They had no traditional bond with the country they now occupied. Hunter offered them a vision of a new country, on which new bonds could be formed—nothing less than a new home that was indisputably their own. Perhaps this imagined community stemmed from his own desire to cease standing between communities without one of his own; perhaps, too, it stemmed from a hunger for power. Certainly, it did not stem from his own deep immersion in Cherokee (or other Indian) society: he was not a trusted chief but a newcomer with a scheme who appealed because it spoke to their needs and because he seemed to have useful leverage in white counsels.

Both the appeal and the leverage proved shortlived. US minister Joel R. Poinsett, coveting these Texas lands for his own country and opposed to the creation of a strong Indian state between America and Mexico, used all the influence he could muster to remove from the Mexican government all those in favour of the plan. Poinsett succeeded; Hunter was promised that Indians could apply for individual land grants, but the bid for a tribal territory was turned down. Hunter then showed the depth of his attachment to the idea of guaranteeing Indians land immune from US encroachment. He cut a deal with Benjamin Edwards, Herman Mayo and other leaders of Anglo settlers in Texas, and on 21 December 1826 they jointly declared a republic—called Fredonia.

Texas was to be divided into two areas—one of Indians, the other of white settlers—the new republic beginning at Sand Springs in southern Rusk County and running west to the Rio Grande. Hunter prepared to possess the land by moving Cherokees across the border; meanwhile Peter Ellis Bean arrived in East Texas as an agent of the Mexican government. He proceeded to divide and rule the Cherokees by promising land and money on an individual basis to those who opposed Hunter and Field. The Cherokee council repudiated the agreement and those who had not been bought off felt themselves too weak to send men to assist the new republic. Bean then had two Cherokee chiefs, rivals of Fields, paid to murder its architects. Hunter, in the words of an early historian of Texas, 'left them, saying he would go alone and share the fate of his American friends in Nacogdoches. ... He proceeded to join the Americans accompanied by two Indians [Big Mush and the Bowl, civil and military Cherokee chiefs]. He stopped at a creek near the Anadagua village, to let his horse drink, and while thus unguarded in his security, one of his savage companions shot him with a rifle in the shoulder.' While Hunter solicited for his life, saying 'it was hard . . . to die by the hands of his friends', the Cherokee raised his gun again and shot him to death. The Fredonian Republic perished, to the relief of both Mexican and US governments, and Texas was free of an Indian country that might stand in the way of Poinsett's ultimate aim—that it should become part of the USA.

Hunter had at least died for a cause he believed in, though, ironically enough, shot in cold blood by one of the Indians he claimed to represent. His death, though, was not a case of Indians' racist rejection of a white man—after all, his fellow leader, the Cherokee Fields, was also killed. Rather it was a case of a desperate pan-Indian idealism, newly introduced by a white outsider and always vulnerable to its lack of roots within Cherokee society, being undermined by Anglo-Americans in the service of the US and Mexico, who exploited political tensions within Indian nations that were under severe pressure. This was to tell again an old story—a story that white people had been telling since they set one eastern tribe against another in the Pequot War of 1636–7. It was a story that distressed Hunter's British friends—but it was not unfamiliar to them: Britain was acting in the same way in its new colonies in the East Indies. Hunter, though, faced with the vested interests of cynical governments, found himself unable to control the narrative of Indians'—or his own—life. He had got where he was by virtue of inventing a character in print; now, whether or not that character had originally existed, he found the courage to take the path that it pointed him towards—a path ending in a noble death for the ideal Indian/white community he had long imagined. If he was in fact an impostor, he now vindicated his sincerity by accepting without flinching the ultimate consequences of being the man he claimed to be. He had lived a Romantic role of his choosing—and perhaps of his invention—to the death. It was an end that Byron, had he himself lived to see it, would have honoured.

16

Peter Jones/Kah-Ke-Wa-Quo-Na-By

The shores of Lake Ontario became the home of Joseph Brant, John Norton, and the Mohawks after the loss of their land to the US in 1783. They were also the traditional home of another Indian people, the Six Nations' old enemies, the Ojibwa (Anishinabe: called Chippewa and Mississauga by the British). The Great Lakes Ojibwa were different from the Iroquois: they spoke an Algonquinian language; they reckoned descent in the male, not the female, line. Nevertheless, in the post-1814 period, the two groups drew together in face of their common problems as minorities in a colony rapidly filling with white immigrants.

No one understood these problems or combated them more effectively than Kahkewaquonaby, Peter Jones. Born in 1802 to an Ojibwa mother who was the second wife of his white father, a surveyor of Welsh extraction, he grew up on the Lake's north shore in an Ojibwa band that was disintegrating, plagued by disease, alcohol abuse, and encroachment by white immigrants on their lands. Demoralized and outnumbered 10–1 by whites, who cheated and reviled them, and believing that the Spirit who inhabited their territory had withdrawn, the band declined to no more than 200 by the 1820s. In 1818 and 1820 they 'sold', without understanding what the 'sale' meant under colonial law, all but 200 acres.[1]

Kahkewaquonaby was no longer living among his mother's band by then. In 1816 his father, realizing it faced extinction, took him to live nearby with his family by his first wife on lands sold him by Joseph Brant near the Grand River. There, Jones joined a hybrid society: his father's family was mixed Anglo-Mohawk, like Norton's. Jones learnt English and some Mohawk, was baptized an Anglican, and was schooled in agriculture. It seemed he would follow the path towards 'improvement'

---

[1] This and much other biographical information I take from Donald B. Smith, *Sacred Feathers: The Reverend Peter Jones (Kahkewaquonaby) and the Mississauga Indians* (Lincoln and London, 1987).

and 'civilization' along which Brant and Norton were leading the Grand River community.

Kahkewaquonaby took a different route to the same destination, a route that ultimately made him a leader of the Lake Ojibwas, a visitor to Britain, and a published author. In summer 1823 he went to a Methodist camp meeting and underwent a spiritual upheaval, converting to this highly emotional version of Christianity promoted by US missionaries. He then dedicated his life to the Methodist cause, becoming one of the first Indian missionaries and converting most of the Ojibwa band of his boyhood. For Jones, conversion meant adoption of white lifeways as well as Christian belief: he introduced the Ojibwa to Anglo-style village life and to agriculture, broke the addiction to alcohol, and restored their self-worth.

Like Norton, Jones found himself in conflict with the Canadian authorities. In 1836 the recently arrived Lieutenant Governor of Upper Canada, Sir Francis Bond Head, believing Indians were Romantic primitives who could never be civilized, tried to push them to give up their remaining lands and move to Manitoulin Island, beyond the white settlers' corrupting influence. As Theodore Binnema and Kevin Hutchings have shown, Head was a Romantic author before he came to Canada, who idealized Indians as noble savages. On the basis of his picturesque ideals, imbibed from books, he decided Indians' rightful place was as uncorrupted rustics in a wild landscape. This view, as Head's own prose reveals, was a debasement of Romantic aesthetics, akin to Wordsworth but lacking Wordsworth's insistence on the irreducible human individuality of the rustics whose life he admired. Head's Indians were merely decorative figures in a landscape, valued for their appearance, which completed a picturesque scene. Head's scheme was doubly sentimental. He wanted to save the idealized Indians of his imagination from civilization's corrupting effects, but also wanted to indulge his own romantic yearnings. He wished to group Indians together on the island, in part, so he and other white aesthetes, tired of the cares of business, could refresh themselves by making pastoral excursions. On his plan, Indians would become tourist guides for jaded whites looking for a holiday escape into primitive purity: Head wrote rapturously of being paddled across Lake Huron in scenery 'beautiful beyond all powers of description'. And he raved about the salutary effects of adopting 'Indian habits' and sleeping 'under blankets on the ground'.[2]

---

[2] Sir Francis Bond Head, *The Emigrant* (London, 1846), 127, 126.

Head's plan demonstrates the dangers of Romantic idealism in the hands of a colonial government that combined naivety, paternalist condescension, and power. Head succeeded in pressurizing some Ojibwa bands to cede their rich land on the lake-shore in preparation for a move to the beautiful but barren islands. From Head's point of view, removal was Britain's duty to an inferior race that civilization inevitably destroyed. On Manitoulin Island the Indians could die out in dignified fashion in the wilderness where they belonged. Besides, the lands they would give up would be lucrative to the Crown. The scheme, Head assured the government in Britain, would line whites' pockets as well as salve their consciences—a perfect colonial venture:

I have already stated that this expense will shortly be defrayed altogether by the sale of the lands they have this year liberally surrendered to me; and even if that were not to be the case, I do think that, enjoying as we do, possession of this noble province, it is our bounden duty to consider as heir-looms the wreck of that simple-minded ill-fated race, which . . . is daily and yearly fading before the progress of civilisation.

We have only to bear patiently with them for a short time, and with a few exceptions, principally half castes, their unhappy race, beyond our power of redemption, will be extinct.[3]

What Head did not admit, though Jones and other Ojibwas told him so, was that the island had too little soil to cultivate and few animals to hunt. It abounded only in snakes. Indians sent to live there would indeed soon be extinct: they would starve. Jones opposed the plan vehemently, resisting Head's primitivism by pointing to the achievements Christian Indians had made in agriculture and arts, and campaigning for the grant of full title to their land. Jones even went so far as to gain an introduction to Queen Victoria and to stretch protocol by asking the young monarch a political question—would she ensure the Ojibwa were given secure possession of their land? Lord Glenelg, the Colonial Secretary, who was present at the meeting, indicated the government's assent. The deeds, however, remained unforthcoming.

Head recognized Jones as a major opponent and wrote to Glenelg smearing him. The letter is significant because it reveals the racism that underlaid Head's degenerate Romanticism. For Head, the important thing about Jones was that he was not 'pure' Indian, being of mixed blood. This hybrid identity was distasteful in itself and disqualified him

---

[3] Memorandum printed in Sir Francis Bond Head, *A Narrative* (London, 1839), 13.

as a real Indian: he should not be accepted as a representative of the
Ojibwa. Jones, Head wrote,

is the bearer [of] the double title of *chief* and *missionary* of the Missisauga tribe
of the Chippewa nation of Indians [and] is the son of an American surveyor
who having in open adultery had children by several Indian squaws deemed it
advisable to bring one of them up a missionary!

In this capacity Mr. Peter Jones went some years ago to England where he
was believed to be an Indian. His sallow complexion, his aquiline nose, the
position of his eyes and the phrenological formation of his head, would to any
one acquainted with the red aborigines of America, have at once betrayed his
origin, however, he managed to attract considerable attention in London and
he eventually married a religious lady who followed him out to this Province.[4]

Ironically enough, Head's desire to undermine Jones was so strong
that he used the jargon of racialized anatomy to define white Caucasian
features pejoratively. Glenelg, forewarned of his feelings, if not impressed
by his moderation, nevertheless agreed to meet Jones. The Colonial
Secretary heard Jones's arguments, as well as other reports critical of
Head, and the removal scheme was abandoned and the Lieutenant
Governor returned to Britain.

Jones was exultant at this victory. He was not so successful thereafter,
when he lobbied for the Ojibwa to be given proper financial accounts
of how the Indian Department spent the annuities due to them. He
struggled against official delay to have a manual labour school established, finding that the Indian Department was reluctant to negotiate
with educated Indians who asked awkward questions as equals.

Jones experienced similar tensions to those Brant and Norton had
encountered, as a result of his exceptional position as a hybrid, educated
Indian. Not only did the Indian Department scheme against him,
but his own community feared he was abandoning traditional Indian
ways altogether. When he tried to make the Ojibwa discipline their
children on the Anglo system of rewards and punishments many of
his band withdrew their support. Ojibwa in other locations resisted
a conversion to white ways as absolute as the one Jones stood for.
Pazhekezhikquashkum, chief of the Walpole Island Ojibwa, told Jones
in 1829 that since it was whites who had cheated and sold rum to
Indians, he saw no reason to trust their beliefs: 'the white man's religion

---

[4] Quoted in Theodore Binnema and Kevin Hutchings, 'The Emigrant and the
Savage: Sir Francis Bond Head's Romantic Approach to Aboriginal Policy in Upper
Canada, 1836–8', unpublished paper.

is no better I will hold fast to the religion of my forefathers, and follow them to the far west'.[5] His band did not convert; some Ojibwa who did, in the face of ostracism from traditionalists, lapsed, went mad, or killed themselves.

Nevertheless, Jones was an effective missionary, making hundreds of converts for he, unlike the white missionaries, could speak Ojibwa. He could also write in English, in the tradition of Protestant conversion narratives, demonstrating to a white readership that Indians could become civilized and so promoting the mission, which always needed funds. No Wordsworthian rustics or Byronic patriots filled his pages: he treated his pre-Christian youth as a matter of sin and superstition rather than, as Norton had, justifying Indian customs in their social and spiritual context. For example, Jones saw a vital Ojibwa ceremony through mocking and disillusioned eyes: 'I had the *pleasure* of attending a sacred bear-oil feast, at which each guest had to drink about a gill of what was not any more palatable than castor oil.'[6]

Jones desires to assimilate so completely to the perspective of a self-righteous Biblical fundamentalist that he presents non-Christian Indians with a degree of revulsion and alienation that was rare in most white travel accounts. He has a recent convert's zeal, as if he wanted to prove to his white superiors in the Methodist Conference that he was truly different from his fellow Ojibwa and as narrowly orthodox as the most proper white evangelist.

Jones's career did indeed put him on an assimilationist course, although he was prepared to defy government officials or Methodist ministers who doubted Indians' ability to master white discourses for themselves. And he did master those discourses: his prose, for example, reveals his capacity to sustain the roles of public speaker, campaigner, and author in the metropolis. In 1831 he toured Britain to raise funds, speaking at numerous meetings of evangelical societies. Like Norton before him, he cultivated Britain's religious philanthropists, using for political effect the Indian dress that made him an exotic spectacle in their eyes. They were charmed by this man who so unexpectedly combined Christian orthodoxy with a savage appearance. He was a visible demonstration of what they wanted to achieve—the civilization

---

[5] Smith, *Sacred Feathers,* 110.

[6] *Life and Journals of Kah-ke-Wa-Quo-Na-By (Rev. Peter Jones,) Wesleyan Missionary* (Toronto, 1860), 3.

of Britain's colonial subjects, both for the sake of those subjects and in order to reassure themselves that imperialism was a moral mission not a cruel exploitation.

Unable to be a cultural broker as Brant and Norton had been, because Indian power was so reduced that whites no longer needed their military aid, feared their opposition, or relied upon their trade goods, Jones operated from a much weaker position than previous Indian leaders who had mastered enough of the colonial power's discourses to negotiate with its ministers. Jones posed Britain no threat, and offered it no advantage, and so he could only appeal to people's goodwill and compassion. Dressing in his Indian clothes for chapel congregations, missionary society audiences, and Queen Victoria herself, Jones presented himself as a Romantic figure—an exotic, primitive, child of nature. But he did so knowingly, as one of the few strategies open to him, in order to attract the notice, support, and funding that his community required. His self-Romanticization was no fairground show—no naïve exhibition that placed Indians as curiosities to be condescendingly enjoyed by superior whites. It was part of a calculated diplomatic mission to win hearts and minds, in which Jones alternately impressed Britons by appearing in Anglo dress as a gentleman like themselves, and excited them by appearing in Indian clothes as an Other to their urban and suburban selves. Jones's appearance thus suggested that Indians could retain some of their traditional and exotic difference while embracing much of British, Christian, culture. As a result he made Britons see past the two alternatives that were usually offered as Indians' only possible futures (total assimilation to white ways or extinction as rural primitives). Thus Britons could support Indians' evangelization in the belief it would 'improve' the savages without destroying their function as Romantic rustics—a function that satisfied Britons' sentimental desire that an uncorrupted 'natural man' should somewhere exist as the exotic opposite of their own increasingly commercial and industrial society.

Despite the similar methods they used, Jones's description of his trip is tonally different from Norton's. Jones adopts in apparent sincerity a position so extremely humble that, like Uriah Heep's, it seems both abject and, despite itself, satirical. Thus after an audience with the King and Queen in his 'native costume' he declares himself 'highly gratified with my visit to our great father the King and our great mother the Queen. The King and Queen were dressed very plain, and were very open, and seemed not at all to be proud. . . . Long may they live to be

a blessing to the nation and people!'[7] What Cheryl Walker has argued
of William Apess's 'subjugated discourse' is still more true of Jones: 'the
persona of the "poor Indian" is not presented purely ironically. . . . To
some degree, [the writer] must present himself as a "poor Indian" if he is
to be heard at all'.[8] The effect, for the white liberal reader, then and now,
however, is embarrassment that such submission is embraced—and/or,
according to context, a suspicion that the unself-conscious naivety with
which subjugation is expressed is a covert form of satire. Take, for
example, Jones narrating his visit to Westminster Abbey, centre of a
state Anglican Church he did not subscribe to:

I also saw the place where the Kings of England are crowned, and the royal chairs
they sit on when they are thus crowned. I took the liberty to squat myself down
upon them as we passed by, so that I can now say that I, a poor Indian from
the woods of Canada, sat in the King's and Queen's great crowning chairs.[9]

Is the *lèse majesté* of this anecdote an example of deadpan irony—a
quiet puncturing of pomp of the kind that Indians often made in
council with whites (as witness Bloody Fellow quoted by Norton (see
p. 221))? Probably not, since Jones continues by declaring 'how grateful
and humble I ought to be thus to be honoured by a Christian people!
I do feel thankful for the token of friendship and esteem that has been
shown to me . . . may God bless the English Nation'.[10] It's better seen
as an act of mimicry, stemming from a desire for inclusion: Jones is
genuinely grateful that he, a 'poor Indian', is allowed to sit where the
monarch sat. But this mimicry, loyal as it is, unwittingly exposes the
institutionalization of power in the mind of the subject because Jones
does not quite understand the codes through which Britons express
their loyalty appropriately. Thus he performs, to show his willing
subordination to monarchy, an action that Britons would consider
disrespectful and even rebellious. The colonial subject's embrace of
the colonizer's discourse disturbs its parameters and thus exposes its
artificiality. The British emperor, Jones unconsciously suggests, has no
clothes; his throne is just (in a further, verbal, displacement) a chair.

There was a personal reason for Jones's admiration for the British in
Britain. In 1831 he had met an idealistic Englishwoman, Eliza Field. In

---

[7] *Life and Journals*, 341.

[8] Walker, *Indian Nation: Native American Literature and Nineteenth-Century Nationalisms* (Durham, NC, and London, 1997), 51.

[9] *Life and Journals*, 338.   [10] *Life and Journals*, 346.

1833 she came to America and married him, a highly unusual step, and one that aroused much racist criticism in the US and Canadian press. Jones resented reports such as this:

> Our emotions were tumultuous and painful. A stronger contrast was never seen. She all in white, and adorned with the sweetest simplicity. . . . She a little delicate European lady—he a hardy iron-framed son of the forest. . . . A sweeter bride we never saw. We almost grew wild. We thought of Othello—of Hyperion and the satyr—of the bright-eyed Hindoo and the funeral pile! She looked like a drooping flower by the side of a rugged hemlock! We longed to interpose and rescue her . . . we heard the Indian and herself pronounced man and wife! It was the first time we ever heard the words 'man and wife' sound hatefully.[11]

There were many such racist responses, but also a few that saw the union as a symbol of the superiority of British empire to US republic. The *Niagara Gleaner* argued that 'the Indians and even the Negroes are looked upon and treated as human beings within all the dominions of Great Britain. Not so in the republican states of America . . . to their everlasting disgrace'.[12]

Jones's marriage made him seem a living representative of the colonial romance genre that British poets had popularized. Southey, James Montgomery, and William Lisle Bowles had written verse tales imagining indigenous peoples being civilized by love of and marriage to Christian whites. Jones seemed to be living out their assimilationist fantasies and he was drawn into their orbit because he accessed Britain through the Missionary Societies that they supported. He met Montgomery in 1831, calling him a great poet. Certainly Montgomery, Southey, and Bowles would have approved of Jones's own writings, had they lived to see their publication, since their deep commitment to Christianity, to white culture, and to the Crown exemplified the success of their vision of colonialism as a civilizing mission.

But Jones was a man, not an example, and though he did justify the romanticized vision of colonialism with which Victorians palliated Britain's exploitation of other countries, he also lived on his own individual terms. The colonial governors who advocated Indian assimilation did not welcome Jones's demands for Indians to manage their own affairs any more than Head had done. And when he died, many Ojibwa who

---

[11] *New York Commercial Advertiser*, 12 September 1833, quoted in Smith, *Sacred Feathers*, 141–2.

[12] Quoted in Smith, *Sacred Feathers*, 142.

had resisted his calls for 'whitemanization' attended his funeral. They recognized that he was a valiant, independent man who had refashioned himself and his followers on white people's lines in a genuine—and successful—effort to give an Ojibwa culture devastated by colonization a new self-respect, social structure, and stability. It was a difficult and precarious path that he trod, but Jones, despite the Ojibwas' lack of power, never became alienated from his people, or a tame Romantic savage performing Indianness for the amusement of urban Britons. This in itself was a remarkable achievement in adversity, as the contrasting career of Jones's one-time protégé, George Copway, reveals.

17

John Tanner/Shaw-shaw-wa-be-nase

In the summer of 1827 a middle-aged man, his body scarred by wind, weather, and the wounds of a lifetime spent hunting and fighting, was telling his life story. In the halting English he'd had to relearn in his forties, John Tanner, as white people called him, was explaining to Edwin James, a noted authority on Western Indians, how, as a nine year-old settler's son, he'd been captured by Ottawas in the Ohio valley, and then grown to manhood living among Cree, Assinneboin, and Ojibwa people along the Red River, Canada. Tanner had much to say—how he'd been brought up by a remarkable Ottawa woman, then married and had children, how he'd painstakingly learnt to hunt beavers, bears, and moose, how he'd faced starvation and attempted suicide, how he'd fought the Sioux only to be tomahawked by his own kinsman. Shaw-shaw-wa-be-nase, the Falcon, as the Indians called him, described the daily struggle to survive in haunting detail—the devastating toll of white men's diseases, the withering cold, the destruction wrought by alcohol—all of which broke the tribes into small, ever-shifting bands of orphans and refugees endlessly travelling in search of the disappearing game. He was graphic about the deadly enmities that hunger engendered between Indians—even of the same family—and bitter, too, about the prophets who gained power over the Ojibwas' minds by peddling false hope. He took just as grim a view of the white men of the area, disgusted by murderous 'war' between the rival British fur traders of the North West and Hudson's Bay Company, and revolted by the bestial behaviour of the poor Scots immigrants whose new colony he was hired to assist.

James was riveted by the account, and certain of its veracity. After all, the details of Tanner's capture in 1790 were on record, both the Indians and the traders knew him of old, and when he returned to white society (first in 1818 and then, permanently (or so it seemed), in 1824) his white relatives identified him. Tanner was no hoaxer but indubitably a man who spoke, thought, and felt as an Indian but who happened to be white. His words, rendered into plain, factual, and sober prose by James, were an unparalleled record, from the inside, of what it was like to be an Ojibwa—or rather, in Tanner's significant phrase 'not quite an Ojibbeway'—in the last period in which the Indians of the Great Lakes area still retained much of their territory and most of their traditional lifestyle.[1] James published them in 1830 under the title *A Narrative of the Captivity and Adventures of John Tanner (U.S. Interpreter at Saut de Ste. Marie) during Thirty Years Residence among the Indians in the Interior of North America.* The reviewers immediately accepted their authenticity and their uniqueness—noting that they offered an intimate knowledge that even the best white experts could never achieve. They also commended their romantic power.

What the reviewers did not acknowledge—any more than Tanner himself—was that he was doubly 'not quite an Ojibwa' and that this situation—indeed the whole context in which he lived his life—had come about because of the changing trajectory of white colonialism. Tanner was displaced not once but twice in his boyhood, and then again when he returned to a precarious existence among the whitefolk whom he resembled only on the surface. His first displacement, from white to Ottawa life, occurred as the Indians resisted the encroachment on their lands of US settlers who, emboldened by independence from Britain, were homesteading in the Ohio valley. Throughout the later 1780s and 1790s settlers and Indians were fighting for control of these lands: Tanner's capture from a new white farm was a small incident in a war that lasted till 1794, when the US army decisively defeated the tribes at the Battle of Fallen Timbers. After this victory the Indians were forced to cede land, thus confirming Tanner's second displacement as his Ottawa captors were themselves pushed north and west into lands in which Ojibwa tribes hunted, west of Lake Superior. These lands then came under increasing pressure, as the Ojibwa were themselves gradually coerced into giving up their territories further east and as the Hudson's Bay Company began to settle Scots on the 116,000 square miles it had

---

[1] 'Not quite an Ojibbeway': Tanner's phrase from his *Narrative*. It appears on p. 138 of the best modern edition, from which all further quotations are cited (in parenthesis in the text), *The Falcon: A Narrative of the Captivity and Adventures of John Tanner During Thirty Years Residence Among the Indians in the Interior of North America* (New York and London, 1994).

set aside for the Red River colony (1811).[2] (The situation Jones and Copway grew up in was that experienced by Tanner as a young adult). There was simply not enough game for all the people in the area, vast though it is, and the Ojibwa and the newcomers were forced to hunt new quarry—buffalo—further and further west—bringing them into bloody conflict with the Dakota Sioux.

Tanner's return to white society displaced him again: unlike Hunter he found no influential role as a consequence of being a returned captive. Whereas Hunter had been lionized in Britain, Tanner, although encouraged to cross the Atlantic by no less than Lord Selkirk, nobleman, major shareholder of the Hudson's Bay Company, and driving force of the Red River colony, went not to Britain but to the USA, where he was of little renown, his services to whites having been to the gentlemen of Britain's Canadian territories. Although offered help by government officials, he was soon poverty-stricken, being turned away hungry from the homes of the comfortably off and cheated out of possessions. He experienced conflict and alienation, prevented by his Indianness from adapting to town life and by illness from fetching his children from his Ottawa relations. He tried being a fur trader, a farmer, and an interpreter, moved away from and back to Indian country, and eventually disappeared completely from white people's knowledge. To this day historians do not know what happened to him after 1846.

The narrative that Tanner left behind is remarkable for its difference from most captivity narratives. It does not demonize Indians en masse, does not include sensational stories about their inhuman cruelty, does not treat them as savages. The *American Quarterly Review* was quick to notice this difference, and drew a pointed contrast with Hunter's narrative, published seven years' earlier: 'there is not in the whole of this work', said the reviewer, 'a single incident or observation which is not infinitely stranger and more interesting, than the various fictions with which the public, both of America and England, were gulled a few years since by one of those adventurers, whose temporary success seems always proportioned to the impudence of their impostures'.[3] And, although composed by James—a white explorer and official—from Tanner's

---

[2] Much of the historical information in this chapter derives from John T. Fierst, 'John Tanner's Narrative and the Anishinaabeg in a Time of Change', http://www.archives.gov/ grants/annotation/june_2002/john_tanner_narrative.html.

[3] 'Tanner's Indian Narrative', *American Quarterly Review*, VIII (Sept. 1830), 108–34 (113).

oral testimony, it is also very different from most of the accounts of Indians written by white travellers and historians. It does not generalize about Indian manners and customs, it does not investigate Indians according to a series of well-known categories, it does not occlude the witness's own presence in the events it describes. Tanner's narrative, in fact, disobeys many of the conventions that typically made narratives appear to be reliable sources of fact. It is short on times and dates, skimpy on self-conscious reflection, lacking in thematic organization. Major figures wander out of the story, their relationship to the narrator unconcluded, and never reappear. Yet if this is frustrating, it increases the narrative's authenticity. Its very lack of conventional categorizations and gentlemanly narrative structures, combined with the sheer intensity of its detailed rendition of everyday encounters, gives it a convincing aura of deep immersion in Indian life. It is, of course, a hybrid autobiography, shaped not only by Tanner's own dual identity but also by James's literary method—but this method is one of restraint. James must have decided to preserve Tanner's oral memories, as far as he could, in their own casual order—an order that is only roughly chronological, with omissions, digressions, and unannounced leaps across time and place. What results is a tale that approximates, in its naïve denial of convention and its formal derivation from the organic flow of Tanner's recollections, to the new genre of romantic autobiography. Indeed, it is more deeply romantic than George Copway's account of his life, since its romanticism is a question of a fundamental affiliation, at the level of form, to individual memory, rather than a matter of fashionable poses and choice allusions to English poets.

   Alcohol and disease reappear constantly in Tanner's narrative, two colonial introductions that devastated Indian families, leaving them poor and weak and orphaning scores of children. When these were added to the funnelling of tribes into the area west of the Great Lakes as a result of their displacement from their homelands by white settlement, Indian society began to fragment as groups split into smaller loose bands constantly on the move in search of game animals that were rapidly being hunted out.

   Tanner gradually became a proficient hunter—a slow process of acquiring difficult skills. This proficiency made him admired—he attracted several suitors, took a wife from among them, and supported her, their children, and her family. Yet it also, in the bitterly divided culture produced by hunger and competition for scarce resources, made him envied. In fact, in spring 1813 it almost got him killed, as he related in dramatic terms:

I lived at this time in a long lodge having two or three fires, and I occupied it in common with several other men with their families, mostly the relatives of my wife. It was midnight or after, and I was sleeping in my lodge when I was waked by some man seizing me roughly by the hand and raising me up. There was still a little fire burning in the lodge, and by the light it gave I recognized, in the angry and threatening countenance which hung over me, the face of Wa-ge-tone, the brother of the Little Clam, our principal chief. 'I have solemnly promised,' said he, 'that if you should come with us to this country, you should not live. Up, therefore, and be ready to answer me.' He then went on to Wah-zhe-gwun, the man who slept next me, and used to him similar insolent and threatening language, but by this time, an old man, a relative of mine, called Mah-nuge, who slept beyond, had comprehended the purport of his visit, and raised himself up with his knife in his hand. When Wa-ge-tone came to him, he received a sharp answer. He then returned to me, drew his knife, and threatened me with instant death. 'You are a stranger,' said he, 'and one of many who have come from a distant country to feed yourself and your children with that which does not belong to you. You are driven out from your own country, and you come among us because you are too feeble and worthless to have a home or a country of your own. You have visited our best hunting grounds, and wherever you have been you have destroyed all the animals which the Great Spirit gave us for our sustenance. Go back, therefore, from this place and be no longer a burthen to us, or I will certainly take your life.'

(*Tanner*, 157–8)

The context of this incident is significant. Wa-ge-tone is not abusing Tanner as a *white* stranger stealing Indians' game, but as a displaced Ottawa taking what belongs to the Ojibwa. Wa-ge-tone is fired by traders' rum—a significant cause of violence among the Indians—but his diagnosis is correct. The Ottawas and Ojibwas had moved a hundred miles up the Red River into hunting territory that traditionally belonged to the Sioux: they were in danger. Under this pressure the Indian traditions of hospitality to guests and adopting incomers from other tribes began to crumble: Wa-ge-tone saw Tanner as an enemy because he faced both hunger and loss of authority as a chief's brother if he could not feed his people. On this occasion he was prevented from carrying out his threat; another rival would later attack Tanner successfully.

Hunting on Sioux territory exposed the Ojibwa to violence, which led them to attempt reprisals. Tanner's narrative is valuable because it details this cultural moment from the inside, showing not just what happened, but how it felt to be there. It felt frustrating, it seems, for Tanner experienced at first hand how fragile unity between tribes and bands was. He joined several war expeditions in which the tribes of the region, although divided by language, made common cause against the Sioux. On one such war party, Crees, Ottawas, Ojibwa, and Assinneboins made towards their enemy but, lacking a command-structure, were riven by arguments, desertions, and horse-stealing, until finally so few warriors were left that the party split and returned home. The party had been armed by a white trader, married to an Ojibwa woman, whose father-in-law, a chief, had been killed by the Sioux.

The interwoven nature of the Indian/white relationship appears often in Tanner's text: unlike most accounts written by white visitors to Indian tribes, Tanner understands from the inside that an interdependent culture had sprung up in Indian country, rooted in generations of intermarriage and in the familial ties that this brought. Colonial policies and racial attitudes, on the ground, were inflected by these relationships in complex ways. Likewise, interactions between tribes were never centralized and determined, but differed in different places and times, shaped by local need, and by familial and social factors. Tanner's unparalleled capacity to reveal this knot of influences in play uncovers far more about colonial/Indian life than any formal 'manners and customs' section of a travel account, and gives the lie to racial theorists' supposition that all Indians are similar, being determined by their limited brain size.

Tanner's narrative is immersed in Indians' ways of acting and thinking; it also, however, reveals how many Indians came to resent and reject him. In their own eyes, they had cause. After all, although Tanner suffered badly when epidemics swept through, he had enough immunity not to die. And he was different to the extent that he was culturally resistant to alcohol and this (relative) reluctance to drink himself into a frenzy marked him out as different from many of his neighbours (just as it did Peter Jones, after his conversion to Methodist Christianity). It left him in a less malleable, less exploited relationship to the fur traders who supplied the rum—another source of resentment for Indians who, when sober, resented their dependence on 'firewater' and the shameful deeds it made them do. This difference grew; after Tanner came to manhood he was given special treatment by the traders, who recognized a fellow white, gave him shelter and paid employment and urged him to leave the Indians. For his part, Tanner consulted them whenever things happened that he could not interpret, and, acting on their answers to his queries, became still more distinct from most of his band. Matters came to a head over the new prophets who appeared among the Ojibwa in this time of crisis, the first of them being a representative of Tecumseh's brother, the Shawnee prophet Tenskwatawa.

When we had smoked, he remained a long time silent, but at last began to tell me he had come with a message from the prophet of the Shawneese. 'Henceforth,' said he, 'the fire must never be suffered to go out in your lodge. Summer or winter, day and night, in the storm, or when it is calm, you must remember that the life in your body, and the fire in your lodge, are the same, and of the same date. If you suffer your fire to be extinguished, at that moment your life will be at its end. You must not suffer a dog to live. You must never strike either a man, a woman, a child, or a dog. The prophet himself is coming to shake hands with you, but I have come before, that you may know what is the will of the Great Spirit, communicated to us by him, and to inform you that the preservation of your life, for a single moment, depends on your entire obedience. From this time forward, we are neither to be drunk, to steal, to lie, or to go against our enemies. While we yield an entire obedience to these commands of the Great Spirit, the Sioux, even if they come to our country, will not be able to see us: we shall be protected and made happy.' I listened to all he had to say, but told him, in answer, that I could not believe we should all die in case our fire went out. In many instances, also, it would be difficult to avoid punishing our children; our dogs were useful in aiding us to hunt and take animals, so that I could not believe the Great Spirit had any wish to take them from us. He continued talking to us until late at night, then he lay down to sleep in my lodge. I happened to wake first in the morning, and perceiving the fire had gone out, I called him to get up, and see how many of us were living, and how many dead. He was prepared for the ridicule I attempted to throw upon his doctrine, and told me I had not yet shaken hands with the prophet. ... I did not rest entirely easy in my unbelief. The Indians generally received the doctrine of this man with great humility and fear. Distress and anxiety was visible in every countenance. Many killed their dogs. ... But, as was usual with me in any emergency of this kind, I went to the traders, firmly believing, that if the Deity had any communications to make to men, they would be given, in the first instance, to white men. The traders ridiculed and despised the idea of a new revelation of the Divine will, and the thought that it should be given to a poor Shawnee. Thus was I confirmed in my infidelity. Nevertheless I did not openly avow my unbelief to the Indians, only I refused to kill my dogs, and showed no degree of anxiety to comply with his other requirements. As long as I remained among the Indians, I made it my business to conform, as far as appeared consistent with my immediate convenience and comfort, with all their customs. Many of their ideas I have adopted, but I always found among them opinions which I could not hold.

(*Tanner*, 144–7)

So Tanner, his own suspicions confirmed by the traders' advice, rejected the prophet's authority, even though this isolated him and he was forced to dissemble his conformity. What is striking in his account of the affair is his deference to the traders' opinion—his assumption that whites have superior spiritual knowledge—and the unwitting irony of the supposedly Christian traders declaring that revelation, once made to a poor Jew, would not be made to a poor Shawnee. It is of course a racist statement.

Historians have attributed the popularity of the Shawnee prophet to the need of Indians, who were seeing their old traditions and beliefs collapsing under the pressure of white colonization, to take power into their own hands.[4] Desperate times brought forth radical doctrine—hence a rejection of white men's technologies and of traditional Indian medicine was demanded. Tanner's refusal to be convinced is not simply a result of his affiliation to white culture, but also of his experience of the efficacy of traditional Indian methods. He resented giving up the herbal remedies in his medicine bag, having proved their usefulness; he continued to use his dogs to track and corner game, catching a bear while believers in the prophet, having killed their dogs, starved. And he maintained his own faith in the prior tradition of the medicine hunt, accepting the guiding power of prayers and dreams.

Tanner cannot be written off as a white man simply upholding his birth-society's beliefs. His dilemma and his solution to that dilemma bespeak a deep upheaval in Indian society and reveal a conflict among and within Indians about which aspects of their culture could still be valid as colonial pressure brought blow after blow upon their way of life. Prophecy was one answer, but after a few years, the enthusiasm for the Shawnee prophet waned; it was a local successor, an Ojibwa named Ais-kaw-ba-wis, who proved to be Tanner's bane, because he could no longer contain his derision while his family and band members, on the other hand, became believers. This then made him the target of Ais-kaw-ba-wis's ire, and the prophet used his influence to make Tanner seem a Jonah whose presence cursed the band, or even an

---

[4] See John Sugden, *Tecumseh: A Life* (London, 1999), 113–26. Such prophets arose in emulation of the Shawnee all over Indian country. In 1815 the mestizo Hillis Hadjo undertook to purify the Creeks from the deleterious effects of white culture. Seeking help against the US settlers, he visited London but after his return to Florida was decoyed into American hands and summarily hanged. See J. Leitch Wright, Jr., *The Only Land They Knew: the Tragic Story of the American Indians in the Old South* (New York and London, 1981), 288.

evil spirit working against them. Here is Tanner's account of the
sad affair:

in conversation with my companions, I soon betrayed my want of credulity.
'It is well,' said I, 'that we may be made acquainted with the whole mind
and will of the Great Spirit at so cheap a rate. We have now these divinely
taught instructors springing up among ourselves, and fortunately, such men as
are worth nothing for any other purpose. The Shawnee prophet was far off.
He-zhi-ko-we-ninne and Manito-o-geezhik, though of our own tribe, were not
with us. They were also men. But here we have one too poor, and indolent, and
spiritless, to feed his own family, yet he is made the instrument, in the hand
of the Great Spirit, as he would have us believe, to renovate the whole earth.'
I had always entertained an unfavourable opinion of this man, as I knew him
to be one of the most worthless among the Indians, and I now felt indignant
at his attempt to pass himself upon us as a chosen and favoured messenger
of the Supreme Spirit. I hesitated not to ridicule his pretensions wherever I
went, but notwithstanding that bad luck constantly attended him, he gained a
powerful ascendancy over the minds of the Indians. His incessant beating of the
drum at night scared away the game from our neighbourhood, and his insolent
hypocrisy made him offensive to me at all times, but he had found the way to
control the minds of many of the people, and all my efforts in opposition to
him were in vain.

(*Tanner*, 186)

To Tanner it seemed the prophet made the people poorer and hungrier
in order to exploit their desperation. He saw him attempt to rape a
woman; he saw him stagger, naked and drunk, into his lodge, and was
disgusted to find that he was not held up to justice or ridicule, as would
formerly have been the case. Social structures were dissolving and being
replaced by a personal despotism resting on the peddling of the false
hope that, through their prophet, the Indians could influence the Great
Spirit in their favour. For his part, the prophet recognized a powerful
opponent in Tanner and worked to have him cast out: 'I now,' he said,
'began to experience the inconveniences resulting from having incurred
the ill will of Ais-kaw-ba-wis. He it was who prejudiced the Indians
so much against me, and particularly the relatives of my wife, that
my situation at Me-nau-zhe-tau-naung was uncomfortable, and I was
compelled to return to Red River' (*Tanner*, 192). Tanner went to work
for Lord Selkirk's new Scots colony.

In moving from Indian society to the colony Tanner was not escaping
strife. The Red River scheme intensified years of rivalry between the
two major fur-trading companies, the Hudson's Bay and the North

West. The former operated from the Bay shore, relying on Indians to bring furs to its forts there; the latter was a newer, thrusting concern, stringing a network of posts across the interior at which white traders bought fur which was then canoed to Montreal and the St Lawrence. This more assertive trading policy brought the North West Company huge profits at the Hudson's Bay's expense, since its aggressive inland traders prevented furs reaching the Hudson's Bay Company's coastal forts. But the North West faced the disadvantage of distance: its canoe route was long and cumbersome, and it envied the Hudson's Bay Company's monopoly of waters draining into the Bay. By 1811 a trade war was developing, as the Hudson's Bay Company also tried to move inland, with cheap rum being used to seduce the Indians to change their customary dealing with one side or the other. Thus colonial competition between the white incomers (mostly Scots) had deleterious effects upon the Indians who harvested the natural resources.

The North West and Hudson's Bay traders were rivals, but they agreed on one thing—that the fur harvest should not be disturbed by the arrival of poor white settlers to farm on Indians' hunting grounds. But in 1811 the idealistic young Scots laird Lord Selkirk bought a majority stake in the Hudson's Bay Company, with the paternalist intention of getting a land grant on which to settle the poor clansfolk who were being displaced from their crofts by capitalist agriculture (mostly sheep grazing). Selkirk wanted to do good to the desperate peasants to whom he felt a residual responsibility as hereditary clan chief. As a reader of travel writing, he knew of the supposed affinity between Indian tribes and Scottish clans, knew of the successful intermarriage between the two in the American South, and knew of the relationships Scots traders had formed with Cree and Ojibwa women.[5] He got his land grant, and in 1812 hundreds of settlers began to arrive at the Red River. They met a hostile response: the North West Company did not want them settling across their supply routes; the métis (Indian/French Canadian) did not want them occupying the land from which they got their livelihood; the Indians did not want still more competitors for game. The settlers were soon being harassed and attacked. And they lacked the tools and skills to survive. Tanner was drafted in to keep them from starving—he was employed as a buffalo hunter (competing with the Sioux). He did not

---

[5] For the idealistic plan see Thomas Douglas, Lord Selkirk, *Observations of a Proposal for Forming a Society for the Civilization and Improvement of the North American Indians Within the British Boundary* (London, 1807).

find it a situation that recommended white society to him, for although he fulfilled an important role he was not always treated with respect. He remembered that

> our number was increased to four clerks and about twenty men, the latter employed in bringing in the meat I killed to my lodge, whence it was carried in carts to the settlement. All of these lived in my lodge, but one of the clerks named M'Donald was very abusive to my wife and children. Mr. Hess repeatedly checked him for this conduct, but as he continued it, he complained to Mr. Hanie. . . .
>
> (*Tanner*, 192)

M'Donald was then sent away alone to guard Tanner's kills; the skilled hunter was too essential to annoy, and Tanner was offered a house and land if he would settle permanently. But Tanner was disgusted by many of the settlers, noting that 'Those Scots labourers who were with me, were much more rough and brutal in their manners than any people I had before seen. Even when they had plenty, they ate like starved dogs, and never failed to quarrel over their meat. The clerks frequently beat and punished them, but they would still quarrel' (*Tanner*, 193). Contemptuous over this very un-Indian display of greed, and uncertain that the settlement would survive, Tanner declined the offer of permanent residence. He was, by now, at home in neither Indian nor British-emigrant society, for neither offered a stable home, wracked as each was by the effects of cut-throat colonial competition for land and profit.

Back in Tanner's Indian village, Ais-kaw-ba-wis poisoned minds against him: a relative was sent to call him home, but gave this private warning: 'Do not believe that your father-in-law calls you to Me-nau-zhe-tau-nung, to be at peace, or with any kind intention. When the children were sick, they called Ais-kaw-ba-wis to do something for them, and he having made a chees-suk-kon, said he had called you into his enclosure, and made you confess that you had shot bad medicine at the children, though you were at that time at Red River. He made your father-in-law believe that you had the power of life and death over his children, and he continues to believe, as do most of the Indians of the band, that it was your medicine which killed them. Be assured, therefore, that they call you thither with the design of killing you' (*Tanner*, 193). Tanner was now, whether he stayed or left, to blame for the death of his own children from sickness and hunger. He was trapped.

Ironically enough, although he started at once for his village, Tanner was himself struck down by a white disease caught from the new settlers.

From this point his life became more and more dangerous. He returned to a village full of sadness and death, where his hunting prowess was needed but his supposed spiritual power reviled. Soon, his in-laws began to plot against him, taking his six-year-old son away while he was supervising corn fields. Tanner pursued the kidnapper, confronted him, stabbed his horse, and took back his son. He was not to be cowed. But he found the ill-will stirred up by Ais-kaw-ba-wis was so great in his village that he determined to leave. He then had a bad fall from a tree which nearly killed him. He recuperated at the Rainy Lake trading house of the North West fur traders, but before he fully recovered he returned to the village. It was then that his mother-in-law attacked him. A year after this Tanner's wife and mother-in-law had deserted him. Alienated, he wanted neither to take another wife, as friends suggested, nor remain with other Indians. Instead, he wintered alone with his children, doing all the domestic work and hunting single-handed too. The following spring he brought food to the starving Indians at the village and his wife and mother-in-law returned to him—but little trust now remained.

It was now—in 1816—that Tanner became involved in the strife between the two fur-trading companies. The North West Company sent presents to the Indians to call them to attack the Hudson's Bay Company establishment at the Red River. 'I thought these quarrels between relatives unnatural', Tanner wrote, adding 'I wished to take no share in them, though I had long traded with the people of the North West Company, and considered myself as in some measure belonging to them. Many of the Indians obeyed the call, and many cruelties and murders were committed' (*Tanner*, 209–10). Selkirk's Red River settlement was reduced to ashes and the Indians then went to the outlet of Lake Winnipeg to intercept any Hudson's Bay Company people entering the country that way. Tanner expressed his disdain by staying behind, refusing to participate on either side. He was visited by Mr Harshfield of the North West Company, who tried to persuade him to help track down and kill Lord Selkirk; Tanner refused. As the rival British traders stormed each other's posts, intimidated, kidnapped, and murdered each other, and as Ais-kaw-ba-wis continued to prejudice his family against him, Tanner decided to leave the region and return to the USA. He then went to Rainy Lake trading house and found it had been taken over by 'Captain Tussenon' (Captain d'Orsonnens, employed by Selkirk as head of Hudson's Bay Company forces). The Captain 'succeeded in convincing me that the Hudson's Bay Company was that which, in the present quarrel, had the right on its side, or rather, was that which was acting with the sanction of the British government, and by promising to aid me in my return to the states, by liberal presents, good treatment, and fair promises, he induced me to consent to guide him and his party to the North West Company's house, at the mouth of the Assinneboin' (*Tanner*, 213). Tanner had now become sucked in to a vicious colonial mini-war—on the opposite side to that taken by most of the Ojibwa. He was in receipt of an annuity from Lord Selkirk: however outraged he was, he had abandoned his initial stance of appalled neutrality. Certainly the métis saw him as a Hudson's Bay Company man, for they lurked about his camp with the design of taking him by surprise and killing him.

With the aid of his hired troops and his political clout, Selkirk won the war for the Hudson's Bay Company, and then attempted to impose a renewed paternalist rule across the confused country. Tanner records him making 'one of those long and fatherly speeches so common in Indian councils', telling the Sioux and Ojibwa to make peace as loyal subjects of the King. Selkirk, meanwhile, took a fancy to the white Indian, and invited him to come to live in Britain, to which Tanner replied that 'my attachments were among the Indians, and my home was in the Indian country. I had spent great part of my life there, and I knew it was too late for me to form new associations' (*Tanner*, 222). And so Tanner did not follow in Norton's and Hunter's footsteps as a visitor to London: Selkirk had him escorted back to Lake Winnepeg, where he rejoined the Ojibwa—only to face a winter of starvation.

By now, Tanner was marked out as an enemy of the North West Company, when most of the Indians were their allies, as an Ottawa among Ojibwa and as a white man among Indians. And he was still plagued by the ill-will of Ais-kaw-ba-wis among a people made desperate by hunger and forced to enter Sioux territory. He joined a small band hunting buffalo, which most of his companions, being used to forest game, failed to kill. One, named Waw-bebe-nais-sa, became so envious of Tanner's success that he tried several times to kill him—having first identified Tanner in his mind as a racial other. Tanner writes 'when he came to the fork of my road, with his little son twelve years old, I heard him say to the lad, "stop here while I go and kill this white man"' (*Tanner*, 228). Forewarned, Tanner challenged and faced him down. Later, though, Waw-bebe-nais-sa launched an unprovoked attack on Tanner in Tanner's mother-in-law's lodge—with, Tanner later suspected, her and his wife's connivance. The unprepared Tanner was severely wounded by a tomahawk blow to the head. Although

Tanner does not speculate further on his assailant's motives, it seems that his envy and hatred were fuelled not only by his resentment of his own impotence but also by the conviction that Tanner, as a white man, caused the sickness of the Indians. In this superstitious belief his wife, led by her mother, encouraged him. Their desperation was exacerbated by fear: the band, 'having never hunted in the prairie before now became panic struck at the idea that the Sioux would fall upon their trail and pursue them. I was too weak to travel and moreover I knew that we were in no danger from the Sioux, but my mother-in-law found much fault because I was not willing to start with the Indians' (*Tanner*, 232). And so the wounded Tanner was abandoned by his family; only a friend called Oto-pun-ne-be and his young cousin nursed him; this friend challenged and attacked Waw-bebe-nais-sa in revenge, only to be restrained by the chief of the band and others. The band was locked into strife, divided on various lines—personal, familial, and racial. Behind it all was starvation: Tanner recorded that Oto-pun-ne-be 'to whom I was often under obligation for the kindnesses he bestowed upon me, has since experienced the fate which overtakes so many of all characters and descriptions of people among the Ojibbeways of that country: he has perished of hunger' (*Tanner*, 232).

Tanner's pariah status was cruel because it struck at the core of his internalized social self. As an Indian by adoption since childhood he had no pre-existent white identity to fall back upon when, with an understandable but terrible logic, the Ojibwa blamed him for the toll that white men's vice, lusts, and diseases took upon them. He now recognized that he must leave Indian life, though not for the British fur trade, where the North West Company officials still saw him as a Hudson's Bay Company man. When he told one trader of his intention to go to the US, he replied 'it would have been well ... had you gone long ago' (*Tanner*, 234). And so Tanner did go, in 1819, with a letter from the Indian Agent at Mackinac, to Governor Cass—the very man who had ridiculed Hunter's captivity narrative in the press. Cass had no doubts about Tanner's veracity however, and gave him clothes and promised to send him to his white relatives on the Ohio.

Tanner's assimilation to white society was never complete. He found sleeping in beds and wearing white clothes uncomfortable; he became ill; suffered poverty, chafed at waiting for help from officials. He met his brother and sisters, but could not speak English so as to communicate with them. His share of their parents' property became a matter of legal dispute. Not finding contentment in Kentucky, he went north in 1822 and then returned to the US with some of his children—their mother reluctantly accompanying them because she did not want to lose them, but then turning back. He subsequently returned to Mackinac, putting his children into school there, and then became a trader for the American Fur Company on his old stamping grounds of Lake Winnepeg and Red River. Impeded by his reluctance to sell alcohol to his Indian friends, he concentrated on recovering his children from another wife, whom he had been long separated from even before 1819. This he achieved, with the aid of the Hudson's Bay Company, who offered presents to the chief of the band in which the children lived. But with his wife's connivance, one of the band shot him in his canoe as he travelled with his family. After a long period recovering at the traders' Rainy Lake post, he was forced to return to the US without his daughters, and knowing his wife wanted him dead. He then became an interpreter at Mackinac, went to New York to raise money by publishing his narrative, and engaged at Sault De St Marie as interpreter for Henry Schoolcraft. His narrative ends on a note of paternal frustration—as if all Tanner's despair at the loss of his Indianness was distilled into anguish over his family. His children were the only close loving relatives he had; they were his one responsibility and one hope for a future that would survive him. But there was no place that they could all be at home, and Tanner was left to face a restless yearning:

Three of my children are still among the Indians in the north. The two daughters would, as I am informed, gladly join me, if it were in their power to escape. The son is older, and is attached to the life he has so long led as a hunter. I have some hope that I may be able to go and make another effort to bring away my daughters.

(*Tanner*, 280)

This is an unfulfilled ending, but that is appropriate for a narrative that eschews cliché and sentiment throughout. Tanner reveals the inadequacy of the standard motifs of noble and ignoble savagery by uncovering levels of complexity rarely found in portraits of Indian life. He shows that 'Indian life' is itself a misnomer—there was no unchanging general Indian culture, but rather many varied and shifting human relationships, pushed into change from within but also pressured from without by the numerous ways in which colonial affairs played out on the ground. He reveals the strength of his bond with the way of life he grew up in and with the environment he felt part of—without ever naming the bond as such, let alone idealizing it. It was perhaps in response to this that the reviewer in the *American Quarterly* argued that

there are interspersed through his plain and unpretending Narrative many romantic occurrences, which under the pen of a Brown or a Cooper, and wrought up by their fervent imagination, might lay the foundation of some thrilling passages, like those which are met with in their compositions. It is often from more slender materials than these that the powerful genius of Scott has woven his magic tales ...[6]

But Tanner's story did not need jazzing up by a Brown, Cooper or Scott, for although it was not 'worked-up', it was nevertheless a product of a deep affiliation to a way of living that Tanner never conceptualized or dramatized but that shone through the very achievement of his intense desire to recollect in words a life that was now lost to him. Although it is hardly like *The Prelude* in content or form, Tanner's narrative made him, in this respect, the most Wordsworthian of all those Indians whose words appeared in print. Or, to put it another way, Wordsworth evolved highly self-conscious new literary means to produce in writing the sense of immersion in a rural culture that he dimly remembered feeling in his pre-literate youth; Tanner, on the other hand, because he was severed from rural culture not by his growth into adulthood but by politics and place, still retained its characteristics—one of them being the narrative forms of oral storytelling, which James preserved in his transcription. It was in rendering these forms, and the structures of feeling and thinking that they articulated, that James did Indian speakers a great service—after Tanner's narrative a way of being that differed from white people's reason and logic was now (in at least approximate form) on paper as a fluid, intelligent, and subtle means of interpreting the world.

[6] *American Quarterly Review*, 113.

18

Kah-ge-ga-gah-bowh/George Copway

By the mid-1830s most of the British authors who had come to be called Romantics were dead. Most of the eastern Indian nations were also, if not dead, diminished in number, dominated by US power, and coerced into removal west of the Mississippi. The days of their independence and of their alliance with Britain as military and trading partners, were over.

Romanticism, lived on, however, as the mainstream literary language of middle-class whites. Indian society also lived on, despite the upheavals caused by white colonization. In this final chapter I tell the story of an Indian who came to prominence after Indian Removal, after the end of the Indian-British alliance, after the heyday of Romanticism. George Copway, a Methodist Ojibwa who lectured and published in New York, reveals how Romanticism (or rather a clichéd popular simplification of Romanticism) left Indian authors a difficult legacy that both empowered and limited them, in the new post-Removal era of US dominance.

In 1850 the hopes of the missionary lobby that British culture would civilize grateful Indians seemed to come true when a Native American writer prefaced his English account of Ojibwa beliefs with this quotation:

> 'Tis a story,
> Handed from ages down; a nurse's tale,
> Which children open-eyed and mouthed devour,
> And thus as garrulous ignorance relates,
> We learn it and believe.[1]

The verse is from Southey's 1801 epic *Thalaba* and the Indian author quoting it is George Copway, an Ojibwa of the Rice Lake band (near Lake Ontario), born 1818, who, inspired by Peter Jones, had converted

---

[1] Quoted on p. 95 of George Copway, *The Traditional History and Characteristic Sketches of the Ojibway Nation* (London, 1850). Further quotations are cited in parenthesis in the text, as *History*.

to Methodism, become a missionary, gone to New York, visited Britain, and become a popular lecturer.

Had Southey lived to read it, he would have enjoyed Copway's use of his verse since, in its original context, the extract from *Thalaba* labels the Ojibwa spiritual narratives that follow as the foolish superstition of an old and credulous woman—suitable only for entertaining children. As such, the quotation suggests an Indian author anxious to assimilate to white society, as if Copway wished to present his people's beliefs as tales to amuse white readers with their charming naivety. Clearly, they are not to be taken seriously.

Despite this relegation of his natal culture, Copway does value one aspect of Ojibwa identity—its interdependence with the uncultivated forests, lakes and river, and with the animals and plants that live there. He declares, 'I have stood on one of the mountain peaks and seen a column of snow descending upon the icy waters of Lake Superior, a distance of fifty miles, and it has taken one day and a-half to reach the edge of the lake which lay at the base of the mountain' (*History*, 14). In other words, it is not just the fine view that is worth recording, but the fact that he has traversed the landscape to reach, on foot, what he had seen. Copway establishes his authority as a historian of his nation by demonstrating that he knows the country on and in his body. His sense of its beauty springs from an active participation in, rather than a distanced contemplation of, the place. If this is an aspect of Copway's Indianness, translated into English, it is also a Romantic notion that would have been familiar to readers reared on Wordsworth, Scott, and Byron. In fact, Copway makes his affiliation to Romanticism explicit in the next paragraph when he writes 'the sun rises and sets with beautiful effect. Its rays resting upon the clouds and reflected from them, clothe the whole extent in robes of fire; every hill seems blazing with the glory of the sun. In every ray is seen the spirit of poetry'. (*History*, 14) And lest this poetic spirit seem over-generalized and vapid, he quotes a Romantic poem:

> Land of the forest and the rock—
>   Of dark-blue lake and mighty river—
> Of mountains reared aloft to mock
> The storm's career, the lightning's shock—
>   My own green land forever!
>
> (*History*, 15)

Copway asserts his ownership of the land in English by means of the verse in which intense emotional identification with the landscape is culturally sanctioned. Elsewhere in his writing he quotes British poets Henry Kirke White and Byron to this end; he also cites US renditions of Indian songs and includes lines of his own composition. By these means he can play on white readers' aesthetic responses (their 'finer feelings'), allaying his anxiety about asserting in English what amounts, if expressed in political terms, to a prior claim of land ownership. Loving his country, the Native American is also, as 'one of Nature's sons' and 'ruler of the forest world', its rightful possessor (*History*, 15).

Who was the Indian author who used Romantic poetry in place of explicitly political prose? Copway was an extraordinary, if unreliable, man who became a missionary in Canada, a journalist in the US, a lecturer in Britain, and a peace envoy in Europe. Born in 1818, he grew up in an Ojibwa community crumbling through loss of land, sickness, alcoholism, harassment, and despair. In 1826 his parents, influenced by Peter Jones, converted. By 1834 he was himself a Methodist missionary at Lake Superior; in 1837 the church sent him to the Ebeneezer Manual Labor School in Illinois, where he received his only formal education in English. From here he travelled to the cities of the US east coast, returning to Canada in 1839 where, in an act of the utmost significance for his later career, he married Elizabeth Howell, the daughter of an immigrant farmer from Yorkshire. At this moment Copway had taken a decisive step: he had married a white woman, following Jones's example and attracting a racist reaction. Howell was an educated gentlewoman of literary inclinations with a knowledge of English poetry. Many white Canadians were horrified to think of a refined lady being embraced by a 'savage'.

Copway's path did not run smooth. He annoyed his white missionary superiors because he resisted their authority, and even Jones regretted his hasty and headstrong nature. Worse, in 1845, finding it hard to support his family, he, according to his Ojibwa flock at Saugeen, misappropriated mission funds. The Rice Lake Ojibwa made similar claims and Copway was imprisoned by the British Indian Department. On release he was expelled from the Canadian Conference of the Wesleyan Methodist Church and rejected by his Ojibwa community. He now stood in no-man's-land.

From this point on, Copway had no choice but to improvise roles for himself in white society. He went to the US and, within the year, had become an author. *The Life, History and Travels of Kah-ge-ga-gah-bowh (George Copway)*, published at Albany, went through many reprints before the end of 1847. On the strength of its success, Copway was able to become a popular speaker on subjects including the 'Superstitions and legends' of the Indians and 'America: Its Elements of Greatness and its Scenery'. As Bernd C. Peyer suggests, Copway appeared at the perfect time and place, for East Coast liberals still felt guilty about the removal of Indians west of the Mississippi and were eager to find an Indian who had successfully adopted white ways but who also embodied the ideal of the natural man.[2]

The trickster figure is a feature of Indian society. Changing his shape, altering his voice, the trickster cheats and confuses evil spirits and thus acquires power. Accounts of Copway's speeches suggest that he played this role, shifting his modes of address as he strove constantly to reinvent himself and the Indianness he represented. He needed to fascinate his new community, the fickle community of paying audiences, not simply to get an Indian voice heard but just to live: his words were his currency in the capitalist culture of America's new cities, where most people had never seen an Indian and were curious both to see a 'savage' and to hear that he had become civilized. The lectures brought Copway to the attention of the US literary men who had begun to romanticize the Indian. Cooper, Longfellow, and Schoolcraft took him up only to disengage themselves when Copway borrowed money once too often, or used their names to promote himself too blatantly. As Peyer points out, the position of professional man of letters 'was simply not available to an Indian in antebellum American society'.[3]

In 1850 Copway's efforts to market himself led him to publish an epic poem, *The Ojibway Conquest*. He was later accused of having substituted his own name on the title page for that of its real author, Indian agent Julius Taylor Clark, who had lent him a copy of his manuscript. Also in that year, he got a chance to expand his public when he was invited to speak as the 'Christian Indian of America' at the World Peace Congress being held in Frankfurt. Copway sailed for Britain, where he lectured and was introduced to aristocratic society and then, on 24 August, made his speech at the Congress. It included a spectacular coup de théâtre that shows how cleverly he could work an audience:

His oration was delivered in a grandiloquent style, but its effect was rather on the eye than the ear, the great point being the unwrapping of a mysterious implement

[2] Bernd C. Peyer, *The Tutor'd Mind: Indian Writers in Antebellum America* (Amherst, MA, 1997).
[3] Peyer, *The Tutor'd Mind*, 262. Copway's work is also well assessed in the editors' introductions to George Copway, *Life, Letters and Speeches*, ed. A. LaVonne Brown Ruoff and Donald B. Smith (Lincoln, NE, and London, 1997), 1–60.

which he had carried about, and which in the eyes of the peacemakers looked marvellously like a sword. When he deliberately took off the linen wrapper, and discovered something which looked rather like a cat-o'-nine tails, and which he declared to be an Indian banner of peace, the acclamations were tremendous.[4]

But Copway dissipated the effect by giving a rambling speech that went on too long. Still, his performance won him the admiration of German literary men.

Back in the US, Copway published a narrative of his European tour, *Running Sketches of Men and Places*, largely composed of passages cited verbatim from local tour guides.[5] In 1851 he launched a journal, *Copway's American Indian*, an ambitious venture whose failure left him short of money. From this point on, his novelty having expired, Copway faded from public life and faced poverty and, for a time, separation from his wife and surviving daughter. In 1867 he advertised himself as an Indian healer in Detroit; in 1868 he appeared at a Catholic mission to the Ojibwa and Iroquois near Montreal. The former Methodist missionary was baptized a Catholic and died shortly afterwards in January 1869.

Living beyond the social and spiritual support that Methodism offered in both Ojibwa and white society proved Copway's chief difficulty. Without an actual community to which he belonged he had little consistent sense of who he was representing to whom, yet knew that his popularity depended on his representing more than himself. Rejected by the Methodist Ojibwa, he reinvented himself as a spokesman for Indianness in general, but struggled to articulate in detail what this generic Indian was and where s/he might flourish. In the late 1840s Copway advocated the creation of a pan-Indian state in which Indians could reside unmolested by white settlers and acquire education in English (and not in Indian languages), eventually to become full citizens of the US. He promoted the scheme in lecture and pamphlet but discovered that winning the admiration of liberals did not amount to political leverage, while it was apparent that none of the Indian tribes had chosen to have him as a chief or advocate.

Both Peyer and Cheryl Walker have written astutely about Copway's literary and political arguments.[6] To their accounts I want to add, in

---

[4] *The Times*, quoted in Peyer, *The Tutor'd Mind*, 251.

[5] George Copway, *Running Sketches of Men and Places, in England, France, Germany, Belgium and Scotland* (New York, 1851).

[6] Peyer in *The Tutor'd Mind*; Walker in her *Indian Nation: Native American Literature and Nineteenth Century Nationalities* (Durham, NC, and London, 1997).

the rest of this chapter, a consideration of the use he makes of Romantic discourse, a use I take to be the product of a collaborative authorship with his wife Elizabeth. In 1850 Copway republished his *Life, History and Travels* in amended form for the British market complete with a new beginning in which he presented himself as a sensitive soul, bereft of the joy in nature that he once unknowingly felt when still innocent of sorrow:

Thought recurs to the innocency of childhood, when no care appeared, as foreboding clouds in the distant sky; but when, half-naked, I sent my shout of merry laughter into the distant woods, or mocked the birds which sang over me. A nature as free as the deer, a heart as light as the dawn of day.

Fancy's pictures are not needed in my life to represent the past. The realities stare at me, and the days which I have spent in the forest yet cause a momentary joy, and give life's wheel smoothness in their passage to the grave. Lakes, rivers, wild woods, and mountain peaks, frequented as in youth, arise, and still can I feel the glowing of youth's fires, which then were fanned by the breath of heaven. I drank from the hand of Nature.[7]

Copway offers his sensitivity as a response to landscape and time that he, more than any other Indian, is able to make. And he also offers it as gift made from weakness to the strength of Great Britain:

From a land of wildness and desolate solitude I come, and at the feet of noble Britons drop the tears of pleasure, and pay a humble homage, not to man, but to the greatness of the Palefaces,—or that which makes them great,—science and religion; in presenting myself before them as I do. None of my race have, perhaps, seen the different phases of one man's varied history as I have. The path I have trodden has been here and there rugged, steep, and intricate. Flowers and thorns have clustered in my bosom at the same time, and have left the aching heart to bleed.

(Recollections, 1)

It is a gift designed to reassure his readers that he comes not to argue with them but to share his sorrowfulness, to ask for pity although he never says exactly what causes his grief, save the generic condition of being an Indian separated from his birth and childhood place. He comes to ask them to condescend to be sensitive in terms that demand neither their self-sacrifice nor mental exertion, for they are terms derived secondhand from familiar texts—Wordsworth's 'Immortality Ode', Byron's *Childe Harold*, Shelley's 'Ode to the West Wind'—but stripped of the vigorous

---

[7] Copway, *Recollections of a Forest Life* (London, 1850), 2. Further quotations are cited in parenthesis in the text, as *Recollections*.

self-analysis that these poets undertook. In short, Copway writes the condition of Indianness as a feminized Romantic pose, as a young Werther who falls upon the thorns and bleeds. It is likely that this and other passages of aestheticism derived from Elizabeth, displaying as they do an acute sense of the watered-down and sentimental Romanticism that a number of authors, including Hemans, had made into Victorian Britain's most popular poetic style.

It is not a pose that allows an author an active, adult voice, yet Copway frequently returns to it because it taps into a popular discourse and also because it formulates an aspect of his Indian identity for which he could have no voice in English unless he detailed the shameful circumstances of his exile from Ojibwa society. In effect, Copway narrates what remains of his tribal identity in terms that give it emotional power but avoid revealing that he is severed from it, rejected for his embezzlement of funds. Love of nature occludes social and personal history just as it did when Coleridge and Wordsworth used English landscapes to subsume their guilt over embracing, then abandoning, Jacobin politics:

I am one of Nature's children; I have always admired her; she shall be my glory; her features—her robes, and the wreath about her brow—the seasons—her stately oaks . . . all contribute to my love of her. . . . Is this dear spot, made green by the tears of memory, any less enticing and hallowed than the palaces where princes are born? I would much more glory in this birthplace, with the broad canopy of heaven above me, and the giant arms of the forest trees for my shelter, than to be born in palaces of marble, studded with pillars of gold! Nature will be Nature still, while palaces shall decay and fall in ruins. Yes, Niagara will be Niagara a thousand years hence! The rainbow, a wreath over her brow, shall continue as long as the sun, and the flowing of the river—while the work of art, however impregnable, shall in atoms fall!

(*Recollections*, 10, 11–12)

Like Wordsworth, Copway constantly moves from a 'dear spot' to a generalized Nature. Apparently this is a bid for power since it gives the Indian a privileged intimacy with a natural world with which whites have lost touch. It was an intimacy that whites liked to think they yearned for: Copway's sentimental exclamations certainly reveal his and Elizabeth's desire to conform to, rather than challenge or even modify, fashionable literary style. They may also have arisen from the awkward 'cultural cringe' of one who had abandoned his natal culture twice, once for Methodism, a second time for the technological world of the city. 'Nature' as an abstracted category is a Western, rather than Ojibwa, concept. In affiliating Indians to it as 'Nature's Children', Copway makes them the infantilized descendents of a degenerate popular Romanticism.

And yet, despite the frequent self-undermining acts of mimicry, despite the imitations of white discourse that simultaneously assert and sabotage pride in Indianness, Copway does occasionally succeed in portraying Ojibwa culture as a civilization, a complex society that makes demands and offers fulfilment for adults. He does so only in recollecting his youth, since his own adulthood entailed separation from the society, but he nonetheless achieves more than mere nostalgia. His account of hunting with his father reveals a more subtle and purposeful engagement with the country than his Romanticized Nature allows:

For years I followed my father, observed how he approached the deer, the manner of getting it upon his shoulders to carry it home, &c. The appearance of the sky, the sound of the distant waterfalls in the morning, the appearance of the clouds and the winds, were to be noticed. The step, and the gesture, in travelling in search of the deer, were to be observed.

(*Recollections*, 19)

Copway recounts Ojibwa spiritual practices with verve and describes the Medicine Lodge institution that was a central feature of Ojibwa society. He also includes Ojibwa songs, as if to counter the English poetry he elsewhere cites with Indians' own verse. Yet these too are ambiguous. One turns out to have been composed by Henry Schoolcraft (the US Indian agent for whom Tanner interpreted), though 'suggested' to him by the song of a chief at Fort Des Moines:

I will go to my tent and lie down in despair,
I will paint me with black, and sever my hair,
I will sit on the shore where the hurricane blows,
And relate to the God of the tempest my woes;
I will for a season on bitterness feed,
For my kindred are gone to the mounds of the dead,
But they died not of hunger, nor wasting decay,
For the drink of the white man hath swept them away.

(*Recollections*, 33)

If this evidences Indian poetic achievement, it also reveals their consciousness of their own weakness. That Copway chooses to include it reveals his own need to align with white men's sentimental attitudes (the poem asks for pity but accepts that Indians will inevitably die out) and simultaneously declares his own humiliating awareness that he remains a member of his race. Copway simply cannot find a place to stand:

even his authority-claiming gestures for Indian culture open a mine of abjection and so he oscillates between observing Ojibwas with the detachment of a white traveller, asserting their worth, and condemning their conduct with all the severity of one who needs to prove that he is a true convert to the dialect of an opposing group.

Things are not always so bad. Copway's literary strategies may ultimately fail to establish an authoritative position but they achieve many local effects. These are more prominent in his 1850 publication *The Traditional History and Characteristic Sketches of the Ojibwa Nation*, as when he objects to the US government calling Indians 'children' (forgetting he has used the phrase himself):

The government and its agents style us 'My children.' The Indians are of age—and believe they can think and act for themselves. The term 'My children' comes with an ill grace from those who seem bent on driving them from their father's house.

(*History*, 201)

This is assertive criticism with no hint of residual deference and is typical of the language Copway attains when he remembers the history of paternalist condescension the Ojibwa have endured from the British and US governments. For instance, when he remembers that 'in the year 1818, 1,800,000 acres of good hunting land' was 'surrendered to the British Government' he ventriloquizes the incredulity of a politically innocent reader before providing a sarcastic answer: 'For how much, do you ask? For 2,960 dollars per annum! What a *great sum* for British generosity!' (*Recollections*, 14).

Sarcastic rhetoric proves no more than an occasional resource. Time and again it is poetry, and the uncontroversial emotional depth that poetry is assumed to provide, that Copway uses to claim authority—an aesthetic authority that will not be challenged because it avoids fact in favour of feeling. The process reaches its tragicomic apogee when, as he embarks for Europe, he attempts to tap into US patriotic fervour:

I mounted the long-boat and delivered the following address to my friends on the wharf; which having delivered, I had to throw at them: . . .

> Farewell, my native land, rock, hill, and plain,
> River and lake, and forest home adieu;
> Months shall depart e'er I shall tread again
>   Amid your scenes, and be once more with you.
> I leave thee now; but wheresoe'er I go,
>   Whatever scenes of grandeur meet my eyes

My heart can but ONE native country know,
        And that the fairest land beneath the skies
America! Farewell; thou art that gem,
Brightest and fairest in earth's diadem.[8]

Presumably it is Byron's *Childe Harold* (whom he quotes later in the book) whom Copway imitates. The effect, however, is unintentional comedy, so unconscious does Copway seem of the absurdity of his spouting verse in such ordinary modern circumstances and then in an act of bathetic literalism, throwing the manuscript onto the quayside. Sterne's pompous sentimental traveller, always treating the occasion as a chance to bolster his own ego, rather than Byron's patriot pilgrim, is the hero Copway unwittingly invokes. At the root of the problem is isolation: because Copway is not secure in either Ojibwa or white communities he has little firm sense of what is an appropriate social or literary discourse for the event. He misapplies the codes he has read in books just enough to travesty them. If this hints at their absurdity, the joke is nevertheless on him, as a would-be assimilator too eager to renounce his past for a white culture whose multiple discourses are harder to manipulate than he realizes.

Cheryl Walker has written that 'Copway bespeaks the dilemma of the Indian caught between a traditional culture which is no longer viable in the old sense and an alien culture which is both destructive and empowering at the same time'.[9] Romantic discourse was one of the most empowering yet destructive elements of Victorian culture, a discourse Copway and Elizabeth could never adopt without, at the same time, translating Ojibwa identity into generalized, feminized, infantilized form. This is nowhere better displayed than in the paradox that quoting British poets reveals Copway's adeptness at assimilation and occludes any exploration he might make in his own words. In fact, the frequent recourse to quotation exposes that for Copway even his own words are, to the extent that they are English, foreign. To be a Romantic Indian was a prospect that British literature offered Copway as a better alternative to being a missionary Methodist or a political campaigner. And it gave him emotional power and popular currency. What he could not derive from it was a literary voice able to represent the experience of Ojibwa identity as an adult social and ontological condition. Copway struggled but, limited by irresolvable tensions between the literary

---

[8] *Running Sketches*, 14.   [9] Walker, *Indian Nation*, 108.

discourses available to him, never succeeded in transforming the generic
Romantic Indian that he bespoke from a child into a man. In this
respect he was a prophetic figure—and an admonitory one with whom
to end this book, for in his absorption by a clichéd and sentimentalized
derivative of British Romanticism, he was the forerunner, despite his
genuine achievements, of the later Indians who would find themselves
patronized and infantilized, and their real and complex selfhoods
and histories travestied, by the suffocating power of the mass-market
discourses in which they were represented to the white public. As
Romanticism became a debased popular currency and as Indians became
Reservation curiosities, pulp fiction and Hollywood movies traded time
and again on the cliché which Copway had struggled to turn to his
and Indians' advantage—the brave, hardy, but primitive children of
nature, too simple for civilization but admirable as embodiments of
a oneness with nature that urban whites felt themselves to have lost.
Today, this idealized view is more popular than ever since, while it is
regarded as improper to portray Indians as fearful (though thrilling)
savages (as pre-1960s cinema portrayed them), it more than ever fulfils
white liberals' pastoral fantasies to depict Indians as representatives
of ecological wholeness and natural wisdom. Thus one aspect of the
ambivalent eighteenth-century stereotype of the Indian has recently
become dominant—Indians are, in today's popular culture, noble
primitives and children of nature rather than ignoble savages and fierce
beasts. The audiences of *Little Big Man*, *Dances with Wolves*, and
Unforgiven are invited to sympathize with Indians because they allow
access to such wholeness and wisdom—just as Copway invited readers
of his *Life*. But the invitation is cheap wish-fulfilment, allowing the
audience to feel morally superior (because they sympathize with the
naturally wise Indians who are misunderstood by whites within the
film) without requiring them to question their own implication in
the capitalistic and colonizing process from which they have, in fact,
benefited. Still less are they required by such debased Romanticism to do
anything—either to modify their own practices as capitalistic consumers
of resources and native peoples, or to enter into a relationship with actual
Indians. Instead, they are allowed to rest content with an updated version
of an old sentimental lie. It was to undermine this lie (among others)
that Indians such as Apess and Norton and Britons such as Wordsworth
and Southey used their rhetorical skills to create more challenging,
complex and demanding representations of Indians. It is with the aim of
valuing their achievement, and of undermining modern versions of the

lie, that I have written this history of a rhetorical figure and its varied relationships with the real. If this book goes some way to opening our eyes about the social and literary construction of what many took (and still take) to be a real and natural figure—the Romantic Indian—and if it lets us understand the consequences of that construction, then it will not have been in vain.

Bibliography

Place of publication is London unless otherwise stated.

Adair, James, *The History of the American Indians; Particularly Those Nations Adjoining to the Mississippi, East and West Florida, Georgia, South and North Carolina, and Virginia* (1775).

Adams, Richard C., *The Ancient Religion of the Delaware* (Washington, DC, 1903).

Allen, Robert S., *His Majesty's Indian Allies: British Indian Policy in the Defence of Canada, 1774–1815* (Toronto and Oxford, 1992).

American Anthropologist.

American Quarterly Review.

Anderson, Benedict, *Imagined Communities* (1991).

Annual Register (1778).

Anon., 'Tanner's Indian Narrative', *American Quarterly Review*, 8 (Sept. 1830), 108–34.

The Anti Jacobin Review and Magazine.

Apess, William, *On Our Own Ground: The Complete Writings of William Apess, A Pequot*, ed. Barry O'Connell (Amherst, MA, 1992).

Arnold, Josias, *Poems* (1797).

Augstein, Hannah Franziska (ed.), *Race: the Origins of an Idea, 1760–1850* (Bristol, 1996).

Aupaumut, Hendrick, *A Short Narration of My Last Journey to the Western Country* in *Memoirs of the Pennsylvania Historical Society*, 2 (1827).

Axtell, James, *The School upon a Hill: Education and Society in Colonial New England* (New Haven and London, 1974).

——— , *The European and the Indian: Essays in the Ethnohistory of Colonial North America* (New York and Oxford, 1981).

Ayer MS 654, Newberry Library, Chicago.

Bage, Robert, *Hermsprong; or Man as he is Not*, ed. Peter Faulkner (Oxford, 1985).

Bailyn, Bernard and Morgan, Philip D. (eds.), *Strangers within the Realm: Cultural Margins of the First British Empire* (Chapel Hill, NC, and London, 1991).

Barbauld, Anna Laetitia, *The Poems of Anna Letitia Barbauld*, eds. William McCarthy and Elizabeth Kraft (Athens, GA, and London, 1994).

Barker, Francis et al (eds.), *Europe and its Others*, 2 vols. (Colchester, 1985).

Barlow, Joel, *The Vision of Columbus*, 5th edn. (Paris, 1793).

Bartram, William, *Travels through North and South Carolina, Georgia, East and West Florida, The Cherokee Country ... together with Observations on the Manners of the Indians* (1791).

Bath Chronicle, Thursday 20 December 1804.

Baynton, Benjamin, *Authentic Memoirs of William Augustus Bowles, Esquire, Ambassador from the United Nations of Creeks and Cherokees, to the Court of London* (1791).

Beauchamp, William Martin, *The Iroquois Trail, or Foot-Prints of the Six Nations, in which is included David Cusick's Sketches of Ancient History of the Six Nations. 1826* (Fayetteville, NY,1892; rpt. New York, 1976).

Bellin, Joshua David, *The Demon of the Continent: Indians and the Shaping of American Literature* (Philadelphia, 2000).

Belmonte, Thomas, 'The Trickster and the Sacred Clown: Revealing the Logic of the Unspeakable', in *C. G. Jung And The Humanities: Toward A Hermeneutics Of Culture*, eds. Karin Barnaby and Pellegrino D'Acierno (1990), 45–66.

Berkhofer, R. F., *Salvation and the Savage: An Analysis of Protestant Missions and American Indian Response, 1787–1862* (Westport, CT, 1965, rpt. 1977).

——, *The White Man's Indian* (New York, 1978).

Bernasconi, Robert, 'Who Invented the Concept of Race? Kant's Role in the Enlightenment Construction of Race', in *Race*, ed. Robert Bernasconi (Oxford, 2001), 11–36.

Bhabha, Homi K., 'The Other Question ... the Stereotype and Colonial Discourse', *Screen*, *24/6* (Nov./Dec. 1983), 18–36.

——, 'Signs Taken for Wonders', in *Europe and its Others*, ed. Francis Barker et al, 2 vols. (Colchester, 1985), I, 89–106.

——, 'Of Mimicry and Man: The Ambivalence of Colonial Discourse', in *Modern Literary Theory*, eds. Philip Rice and Patricia Waugh (1989), 234–41.

——, *The Location of Culture* (London and New York, 1994).

Bieder, Robert E., *Science Encounters the Indian, 1820–1880: The Early Years of American Ethnology* (Norman and London, 1986).

Binnema, Theodore, and Hutchings, Kevin, 'The Emigrant and the Savage: Sir Francis Bond Head's Romantic Approach to Aboriginal Policy in Upper Canada, 1836–8', *Journal of Canadian Studies*, forthcoming.

Bissell, Benjamin, *The American Indian in English Literature of the Eighteenth Century* (New Haven and London, 1925).

Black Hawk, *Life of Black Hawk 1834* (rpt. New York, 1994).

Blair, Hugh, *A Critical Dissertation on the Poems of Ossian, the Son of Fingal* (1763).

Blumenbach, J. F., *The Anthropological Treatises of Johann Friedrich Blumenbach*, trs. Thomas Bendyshe (1865).

Bond, Richmond P., *Queen Anne's American Kings* (Oxford, 1962).

Bougainville, Louis Antoine de, *Voyage autour du monde par la frégate du roi La Boudeuse et la flute L'Étoile, en 1766, 1767, 1768 & 1769* (Paris, 1772).

Boyd, Thomas Alexander, *Simon Girty, the White Savage* (New York, 1928).

Breen, T. H., 'Creative Adaptations: People and Cultures', in Jack P. Greene and J. R. Pole (eds.), *Colonial British America: Essays in the New History of the Early Modern Era* (Baltimore and London, 1984).

Brinton, D. G., *The Lenape and their Legends* (Philadelphia, 1885).

Brissot de Warville, J. P., *New Travels in the United States of America 1788*, ed. Durand Echeverria (Cambridge, MA, 1964).

Brown, Dee, *Bury My Heart at Wounded Knee: An Indian History of the American West* (New York, 1972).

Brown, Jennifer S. H., *Strangers in Blood: Fur Trade Company Families in Indian Country* (Vancouver, 1980).

Burke, Edmund, *Reflections on the Revolution in France* in *The Writings and Speeches of Edmund Burke*, gen. ed. Paul Langford, 17 vols. (Oxford, 1981).

Burnet, James (Lord Monboddo), *Antient Metaphysics Containing the History and Philosophy of Men*, 5 vols. (1784).

Butler, 'Orientalism', in *The Penguin History of Literature. Vol 5: The Romantic Period*, ed. David B. Pirie (Harmondsworth, 1994).

Byron, George Gordon, Lord, *Byron's Letters and Journals*, ed. Leslie Marchand, 12 vols. (1973–82).

——, *The Complete Poetical Works*, ed. Jerome McGann, 7 vols. (Oxford, 1980–86).

Calloway, Colin G., *Crown and Calumet* (Norman, OK, 1987).

——, 'Simon Girty: Interpreter and Intermediary', in James A. Clifton (ed.), *Being and Becoming Indian: Biographical Studies of North American Frontiers* (Chicago, 1989), 38–58.

——, *The American Revolution in Indian Country: Crisis and Diversity in Native American Communities* (Cambridge, 1995).

Campbell, Thomas, *Annals of Great Britain from the Ascension of George III to the Peace of Amiens*, 3 vols. (1807).

——, *Gertrude of Wyoming: a Pennsylvanian Tale and Other Poems* (1809).

——, *History of our own Times*, 2 vols. (London, 1843–5).

——, *Life and Letters of Thomas Campbell*, ed. William Beattie, 3 vols. (1849).

Camper, Petrus, *The Works of the Late Professor Camper, on the Connexion between the Science of Anatomy and the Arts of Drawing, Painting, Statuary* (1794).

Carlson, Paul H., *The Plains Indians* (College Station, TX, 1998).

Carver, Jonathan, *Travels through the Interior Parts of North America, in the Years 1766, 1767, and 1768* (1778).

——, *The Journals of Jonathan Carver and Related Documents, 1766–1770*, ed. John Parker (St Paul, MN, 1976).

Cashin, Edward J., *Lachlan McGillivray, Indian Trader: The Shaping of the Southern Colonial Frontier* (Athens and London, 1994).

Castiglia, Christopher, *Bound and Determined: Captivity, Culture-Crossing, and White Womanhood from Mary Rowlandson to Patty Hearst* (Chicago, 1995).

Catlin, George, *Letters and Notes on the Manners, Customs and Condition of the North American Indians*, 2 vols. (1841).

Caughey, John W., *McGillivray of the Creeks* (Norman, OK, 1938).

Charlevoix, Pierre François Xavier, *Letters to the Duchess of Lesdigueres, Giving an Account of a Voyage to Canada, and Travels through that vast Country, and Louisiana, to the Gulf of Mexico* (1763).

Chateaubriand, François-René de, *Atala, René*, trs. Irving Putter (Berkeley and Los Angeles, 1952).

Clark, Robert, 'The Last of the Iroquois: History and Myth in James Fenimore Cooper's *The Last of the Mohicans*', *Poetics Today*, 3/4 (1982), 115–34.

Colden, Cadwallader, *The History of the Five Indian Nations of Canada* (1747).

Cole, Douglas, *Captured Heritage: The Scramble for Northwest Coast Artifacts* (Norman, OK, 1985).

Coleridge, S. T., *Coleridge's Miscellaneous Criticism*, ed. T. M. Raysor (1936).

_____ , *The Collected Letters of Samuel Taylor Coleridge*, ed. E. L. Griggs, 6 vols. (Oxford, 1956–71).

_____ , *Lectures 1795 on Politics and Religion*, ed. L. Patton and P. Mann (London and Princeton, NJ, 1971).

_____ , *Table Talk*, ed. Carl Woodring (London and Princeton NJ, 1990).

_____ , *Samuel Taylor Coleridge: Poems*, ed. John Beer (1993).

_____ , *Aids to Reflection*, ed. John Beer (Princeton, NJ, and London, 1993).

_____ , *The Notebooks of S. T. Coleridge*, ed. Kathleen Coburn, 5 vols. (London and Princeton, NJ, 1957–2002).

_____ , *Poetical Works*, ed. J. C. C. Mays, 3 vols. (Princeton, NJ, 2001).

Coles, Harry L., *The War of 1812* (Chicago, 1965).

Colley, Linda, *Captives: Britain, Empire and the World 1600–1850* (2003).

Copway, George, *Recollections of a Forest Life* (1850).

_____ , *The Traditional History and Characteristic Sketches of the Ojibway Nation* (1850).

_____ , *Running Sketches of Men and Places, in England, France, Germany, Belgium and Scotland* (New York, 1851).

_____ , *Life, Letters and Speeches*, ed. A. LaVonne Brown Ruoff and Donald B. Smith (Lincoln, NE, and London, 1997).

Cooper, James Fenimore, *The Deerslayer* (New York and London, 1987).

_____ , *The Pioneers* (New York and London, 1988).

Cowper, William, *William Cowper: The Task and Selected Other Poems*, ed. James Sambrook (London and New York, 1994).

Crèvecoeur, Michel Guillaume Jean de (afterwards calling himself St John de), *Letters from an American Farmer: Describing Certain Provincial Situations,*

Manners and Customs ... and Conveying some Idea of the Late and Present Interior Circumstances of the British Colonies in North America. Written, for the Information of a Friend in England (1783).

Cross, Stephen J., 'John Hunter, the Animal Economy, and Late Eighteenth Century Physiological Discourse', *Studies in the History of Biology*, 5 (1981), 1–110.

Cusick, David, *Sketches of the Ancient History of the Six Nations* (Lewistown, NY, 1827).

Dannenburg, Anne Marie, ' "Where, then, shall we place the hero of the wilderness?" William Apess's *Eulogy on King Philip* and Doctrines of Racial Destiny', in Helen Jaskoski (ed.), *Early Native American Writing: New Critical Essays* (Cambridge, 1996), 66–82.

Day, Thomas, *The Desolation of America: A Poem* (1777).

———, *The History of Sandford and Merton, a Work Intended for the Use of Children*, 3 vols. (1783–9).

DeLoria, Philip, *Playing Indian* (New Haven and London, 1998).

Dennis, Matthew, *Cultivating a Landscape of Peace: Iroquois–European Encounters in Seventeenth-Century America* (Ithaca, NY, 1993).

Densmore, Christopher, *Red Jacket: Iroquois Diplomat and Orator* (Syracuse, NY, 1999).

Derounian-Stodola, Kathryn Zabelle and Levernier, James Arthur, *The Indian Captivity Narrative, 1550–1900* (New York, 1993).

Digby, Lt William, *The British Invasion from the North: The Campaigns of Gens. Carleton and Burgoyne from Canada, 1776–1777* (Albany, NY, 1887).

Dippie, Brian W., *The Vanishing American: White Attitudes and U.S. Indian Policy* (Lawrence, KS, 1982).

Donovan, Kathleen M., *Feminist Readings of Native American Literature: Coming to Voice* (Tucson, AZ, 1998).

Douglas, Thomas, Earl of Selkirk, *Observations of a Proposal for Forming a Society for the Civilization and Improvement of the North American Indians Within the British Boundary* (1807).

———, *Sketch of the British Fur Trade in North America*, 2nd edn. (1816).

———, *Narratives of Occurrences in the Indian Countries of North America, since the Earl of Selkirk's Connection with the Hudson's Bay Company* (1817).

Dowd, Gregory Evans, *A Spirited Resistance: The North American Indian Struggle for Unity 1745–1815* (Baltimore, 1992).

———, *War Under Heaven: Pontiac the Indian Nations, and the British Empire* (Baltimore and London, 2002).

Drinnon, Richard, *Facing West: the Metaphysics of Indian-Hating and Empire-Building* (Minneapolis, 1980).

———, *White Savage: The Case of John Dunn Hunter* (New York, 1972).

Ebersole, Gary, *Captured by Texts: Puritan to Post-Modern Images of Indian Captivity* (Charlottesville, VA, 1995).

Edinburgh Review.

Edmunds, R. David, *American Indian Leaders: Studies in Diversity* (Lincoln, NE, and London, 1980).

——, *Tecumseh and the Quest for Indian Leadership* (Boston, 1984).

Edwards, Bryan, *The History, Civil and Commercial of the British Colonies in the West Indies*, 2 vols. (1793).

Edwards, Jonathan, *An Account of the Life of the Late Reverend David Brainerd* (Edinburgh, 1765).

Eliade, Mircea, *Shamanism: Archaic Techniques of Ecstasy* (Princeton, NJ, 1964).

Ellison, Julie, 'Race and Sensibility in the Early Republic: Ann Eliza Bleecker and Sarah Wentworth Morton', *American Literature*, 65/3 (Sept. 1993), 445–74.

Eze, Emmanuel Chukwudi (ed.), *Race and the Enlightenment: A Reader* (Oxford, 1997).

Felsenstein, Frank (ed.), *English Trader, Indian Maid: Representing Gender, Race, and Slavery in the New World: An Inkle and Yarico Reader* (Baltimore and London, 1999).

Ferguson, Adam, *An Essay on the History of Civil Society*, 6th edn. (1793).

Ferriar, John, MD, 'Of Popular Illusions, and particularly of Medical Demonology', *Memoirs of the Literary and Philosophical Society of Manchester*, *3* (1790), 23–116.

Fierst, John T., 'John Tanner's Narrative and the Anishinaabeg in a Time of Change', http://www.archives.gov/grants/annotation/june_2002/john_ tanner_narrative.html.

Foreman, Carolyn Thomas, *Indians Abroad 1493–1938* (Norman, OK, 1943).

Foreman, Grant, *Indian Removal: The Emigration of the Five Civilized Tribes of Indians* (Norman, OK, 1932).

——, *Advancing the Frontier, 1830–1860* (Norman, OK, 1933).

Franklin, Benjamin, *Two Tracts: Information to Those Who Would Remove to America*, 3rd edn. (1784).

Freneau, Philip, *Poems Written and Published During the American Revolutionary War*, 2 vols. (Philadelphia, 1809).

Gentleman's Magazine.

Gilbert, Benjamin, *A Narrative of the Captivity and Sufferings of Benjamin Gilbert and his Family who were surprised by the Indians, and taken from their farms, on the frontiers of Pennsylvania in the spring 1780* (Philadelphia and London, 1790).

Giltrow, Janet, 'Westering Narratives of Jonathan Carver, Alexander Henry, and Daniel Harmon', *Essays on Canadian Writing* (Summer 1981), 27–41.

Gisborne, Thomas, *Poems, Sacred and Moral* (1799).

Goldberg, David Theo, *Racist Culture; Philosophy and the Politics of Meaning* (Oxford, 1993).

Goldsmith, Oliver, *The Traveller* (1765).

Goslee, Nancy Moore, 'Hemans's "Red Indians": Reading Stereotypes', in *Romanticism, Race and Imperial Culture 1780–1834*, eds. Alan Richardson and Sonia Hofkosh (Bloomington, IN, 1996).

Gossett, Thomas F., *Race: The History of an Idea in America* (Dallas, 1963 [1975]).

Gould, Stephen Jay, *The Mismeasure of Man* (New York and London, 1981).

Grace, Henry, *The History of the Life and Sufferings of Henry Grace*, 2nd edn. (Basingstoke, Reading and London, 1795).

Gray, Thomas, *Thomas Gray and William Collins: Poetical Works*, ed. Roger Lonsdale (Oxford, 1977).

Graymont, Barbara, *The Iroquois in the American Revolution* (Syracuse, NY, 1972).

Greenfield, Bruce, *Narrating Discovery: The Romantic Explorer in American Literature, 1790–1855* (New York, 1992).

Grim, John A., *The Shaman* (Norman, OK, 1983).

Grinde, Jr., Donald A. and Johansen, Bruce E., *Exemplar of Liberty: Native America and the Evolution of Democracy* (Los Angeles, 1991).

Gustafson, Sandra, 'Nations of Israelites: Prophecy and Cultural Authority in the Writings of William Apess', *Religion and Literature, 26/1* (1994), 31–53.

Halkett, John, *Historical Notes Respecting the Indians of North America* (1825).

Halleck, Fitz-Greene, *Red Jacket*, in *American Poetry: The Nineteenth Century*, ed. John Hollander, 2 vols. (New York, 1993).

Handbook of North American Indians, vol. 15, ed. Bruce G. Trigger (Washington, DC, 1978).

Harrison, Keith, 'Samuel Hearne, Matonabbee, and the "Esquimaux Girl": Cultural Subjects, Cultural Objects', *Canadian Review of Comparative Literature, 22/3–4* (1995), 647–57.

Head, Sir Francis Bond, *A Narrative* (1839).

———, *The Emigrant* (1846).

The Headley Manuscript, MS 13350 New York State Library.

Hearne, Samuel, *A Journey from Prince of Wales's Fort in Hudson's Bay to the Northern Ocean 1769, 1770, 1771, 1772 (1795)*, ed. J. B. Tyrell (Toronto, 1911 [facs. rpt. New York, 1968]).

Hebard, Grace Raymond, *Sacajawea: Guide and Interpreter of Lewis and Clark* (Glendale, CA, 1932 rpt. Minneola, NY, 2002).

Heckewelder, John, *A Narrative of the Mission of the United Brethren Among the Delaware and Mohegan Indians, from its Commencement, in the Year 1740, to the Close of the Year 1808* (Philadelphia, 1820).

Hemans, Felicia, *The Works of Mrs. Hemans with a Memoir by Her Sister*, 7 vols. (Edinburgh, 1839).

———, *Records of Woman with Other Poems*, 2nd edn. (Edinburgh and London, 1828, facs. rpt. Oxford and New York, 1991).

Hemans, Felicia, *Felicia Hemans: Selected Poems, Letters, Reception Materials*, ed. Susan J. Wolfson (Princeton, NJ, and Oxford, 2000).

Herder, J. G., *Outlines of a Philosophy of the History of Man*, trs. T. Churchill (1800).

Home, Henry, Lord Kames, *Sketches of the History of Man*, 4 vols. (Edinburgh, 1788).

Horsman, Reginald, *Expansion and American Indian Policy 1783–1812* (East Lansing, MI, 1967).

——, *The Frontier in the Formative Years 1783–1815* (New York, 1971).

——, 'Scientific Racism and the American Indian in the Mid-Nineteenth Century', *American Quarterly*, 27 (1975), 152–68.

——, *Race and Manifest Destiny: The Origins of American Racial Anglo-Saxonism* (Cambridge, MA, 1981).

Hunter, John Dunn, *Memoirs of a Captivity among the Indians of North America, from Childhood to the Age of Nineteen: With Anecdotes Descriptive of their Manners and Customs. To Which Is Added, Some Account of the Soil, Climate, and Vegetable Productions of the Territory Westward of the Mississippi*, 3rd edn. (1824).

Huntley, Lydia Howard (afterwards Sigourney), *A Sketch of Connecticut Forty Years Since* (Hartford, CT, 1824).

Hutchings, Kevin D., 'Writing Commerce and Cultural Progress in Samuel Hearne's "A Journey . . . to the Northern Ocean" ', *Ariel*, 28/2 (April 1997), 49–78.

Hyde, Lewis, *Trickster Makes This World: Mischief, Myth, And Art* (New York, 1998).

Irving, Washington, *Knickerbocker's History of New York* (1809, revised 1812).

——, *The Sketch Book of Geoffrey Crayon, Gent.* (1820).

Jackson, Helen Hunt, *A Century of Dishonor: A Sketch of the United States Government's Dealings with Some of the Indian Tribes* (Norman, OK, 1995).

Jacobus, Mary, *Tradition and Experiment in Wordsworth's 'Lyrical Ballads' (1798)* (Oxford, 1976).

James, E. Wyn, ' "The New Birth of a People": Welsh Language and Identity and the Welsh Methodists, c. 1740–1820', in *Religion and National Identity: Wales and Scotland, c. 1700–2000*, ed. Robert Pope (Cardiff, 2001), 14–42.

Jameson, Anna, *Winter Studies and Summer Rambles in Canada* (1838).

——, *Sketches in Canada and Rambles Among the Red Men* (1852).

Jaskoski, Helen (ed.), *Early Native American Writing: New Critical Essays* (Cambridge, 1996).

Jefferson, Thomas, *Notes on the State of Virginia* (New York, 1964).

Jennings, Francis, *The Ambiguous Iroquois Empire: The Covenant Chain Confederation of Indian Tribes with English Colonies from its Beginnings to the Lancaster Treaty of 1744* (New York, 1984).

_____ , *Empire of Fortune: Crowns, Colonies and Tribes in the Seven Years' War in America* (New York, 1988).

_____ , *The Founders of America: How Indians Discovered the Land, Pioneered in it, and Created Great Classical Civilizations; How They Were Plunged into a Dark Age by Invasion and Conquest; and How They Are Reviving* (New York, 1993).

Johansen, Bruce Elliott and Mann, Barbara Alice (eds.), *Encyclopaedia of the Haudenosaunee (Iroquois Confederacy)* (Westport, CT, and London, 2000).

Johnson, Samuel, *The Idler, 81*, 3 November 1759.

_____ , *The Works of Samuel Johnson*, gen. ed. John H. Middendorf (New Haven, 1958).

Jones, Edward, *Musical and Poetical Relicks of the Welsh Bards: Preserved by Tradition, and Authentic Manuscripts, from Remote Antiquity; Never Before Published* (1784).

Jones, Eugene H., *Native Americans as Shown on the Stage 1753–1916* (Metuchen, NJ, and London, 1988).

Jones, Peter, *Life and Journals of Kah-ke-Wa-Quo-Na-By (Rev. Peter Jones,) Wesleyan Missionary* (Toronto, 1860).

Jones, Uriah James, *Simon Girty, the Outlaw* (Harrisburg, PA, 1931).

Kalter, Susan, 'Finding a Place for David Cusick in Native American Literary History', *Melus*, Fall 2002. http://www.findarticles.com/p/articles/mi_m2278/is_3_27/ai_94640668.

Kames, Lord, *see* Home, Henry.

Keane, John, *Tom Paine: A Political Life* (1995).

Kelsay, Isabel Thompson, *Joseph Brant 1743–1807: A Man of Two Worlds* (Syracuse, NY, 1984).

Kitson, Peter J., and Lee, Debbie (eds.), *Slavery, Abolition, And Emancipation: Writings in the British Romantic Period*, 8 vols. (1999).

Knight, David, *Ordering the World: A History of Classifying Man* (1981).

Knighton, Lady, *Memoirs of Sir William Knighton*, 2 vols. (1838).

Konkle, Maureen, 'Indian Literacy, U. S. Colonialism, and Literary Criticism', *American Literature, 69/3* (1997), 457–86.

_____ , *Writing Indian Nations: Native Intellectuals and the Politics of Historiography, 1827–1863* (Chapel Hill, NC, 2004).

Krupat, Arnold, *The Voice in the Margin: Native American Literature and the Canon* (Berkeley, 1989).

_____ , *Native American Autobiography; An Anthology* (Madison, WI, 1994).

_____ , *The Turn to the Native: Studies in Criticism and Culture* (Lincoln, NE, 1996).

Kupperman, Karen Ordahl, *Settling with the Indians: The Meeting of English and Indian Cultures in America, 1580–1640* (London, Toronto and Melbourne, 1980).

Kupperman, Karen Ordahl, (ed.), *American in European Consciousness, 1493–1750* (Chapel Hill, NC, 1995).

——, *Indians and English: Facing Off in Early America* (Ithaca, NY, and London, 2000).

Lahontan, Louis-Armand de, *New Voyages to North-America by the Baron de Lahontan*, ed. R. G. Thwaites (Chicago, 1905).

Larson, James L., *Interpreting Nature: The Science of Living Form from Linnaeus to Kant* (Baltimore, 1994).

Lawrence, William, *Lectures on Physiology, Zoology and the Natural History of Man*, 3rd edn. (1823).

Liebersohn, Harry, *Aristocratic Encounters: European Travelers and North American Indians* (Cambridge, 1998).

The Literary Gazette.

London Magazine.

Loudon, Archibald, *A Selection of the most Interesting Narratives of Outrages, Committed by the Indians in Their Wars with the White People*, 2 vols. (Carlisle, PA, 1808, rpt. 1888, facs. rpt. New York, 1971).

Lowes, John Livingston, *The Road to Xanadu: A Study in the Ways of the Imagination* (1978).

Macbeth, Sally, 'Memory, History, and Contested Pasts: Re-imagining Sacagawea/Sacajawea', *American Indian Culture and Research Journal*, *27/1* (2003), 1–32.

MacCormack, Sabine, 'Limits of Understanding: Perceptions of Graeco-Roman and Amerindian Paganism in Early Modern Europe', in *America in European Consciousness, 1493–1750*, ed. Karen Ordahl Kupperman (Chapel Hill, NC, and London, 1995), 79–129.

McCulloh Jr., J. H., *Researches &c Concerning the Aboriginal History of America* (Baltimore, 1829).

Macfarlane, Robert, *The History of the Second Ten Years of the Reign of George the Third* (1782).

McGoogan, Ken, *Ancient Mariner: The Arctic Adventures of Samuel Hearne, the Sailor who Inspired Coleridge's Masterpiece* (New York, 2004).

McKenney, Thomas L., *Sketches of a Tour to the Lakes; of the Character and Customs of the Chippeway Indians &c.* (Baltimore, 1827).

McKenney, James, *The Indian Tribes of North America*, ed. Frederick Webb Hodge and David I. Bushnell Jr., vol. 2 (Edinburgh, 1934: republished East Ardsley, Yorks., 1972).

Mackenzie, Henry, *The Man of the World* (1773, facs. rpt. New York and London, 1974).

Maclaren, I. S., 'Samuel Hearne's Accounts of the Massacre at Bloody Fall, 17 July 1771', *ARIEL: A Review of International English Literature*, *22/1* (1991), 25–51.

_____, 'Exploration/Travel Literature and the Evolution of the Author', *International Journal of Canadian Studies*, 5 (1992), 39–68.

_____, 'Notes on Samuel Hearne's *Journey* from a Bibliographical Perspective', *Papers of the Bibliographical Society of Canada*, *31/2* (1993), 21–45.

McLoughlin, William G., 'Red Indians, Black Slavery and White Racism: America's Slaveholding Indians', *American Quarterly*, *26* (October 1974), 367–85.

McRobert, Patrick, *Tour through Part of the North Provinces of America in 1774 and 1775* (Edinburgh, 1776).

McWilliams, Jr., John P., *The American Epic: Transforming a Genre, 1770–1860* (Cambridge, 1989).

Maddox, Lucy, *Removals: Nineteenth-Century American Literature and the Politics of Indian Affairs* (New York, 1991).

Malone, Patrick M., *The Skulking Way of War: Technology And Tactics Among The New England Indians* (Baltimore and London, 1991).

Marshall, J. P. and Williams, Glyndwr, *The Great Map of Mankind: British Perceptions of the World in the Age of Enlightenment* (London, 1982).

Martin, John, *Animal Magnetism Examined in a Letter to a Country Gentleman* (London, 1790).

Mather, Cotton, *Soldiers Counselled and Comforted: A Discourse Delivered unto Some Parts of the Forces Engaged in the Just War of New England against the Northern and Eastern Indians* (Boston, 1689).

Meek, Ronald L., *Social Science and the Ignoble Savage* (Cambridge, 1976).

Miller, Mary Ruth, *Thomas Campbell* (Boston, MA, 1978).

Monthly Review.

Moon, Randall, 'William Apess and Writing White', *Studies in American Indian Literatures*, *5/4* (1993), 45–54.

Morris, Thomas, *Journal of Captain Thomas Morris*, in R. G. Thwaites (ed.), *Early Western Travels 1748–1846*, vol. I (Cleveland, OH, 1904).

Morton, Samuel George, *Crania Americana, Or, a Comparative View of the Skulls of Various Aboriginal Nations of North and South America: To Which Is Prefixed an Essay on the Varieties of the Human Species* (1839).

Moulton, Gary E., 'John Ross', in R. David Edmunds (ed.) *American Indian Leaders: Studies in Diversity* (Lincoln, NE, and London, 1980), 88–106.

Murray, David, *Forked Tongues: Speech, Writing and Representation in North American Indian Texts* (Bloomington, IN, 1991).

Murray, Laura, 'The Aesthetic of Dispossession: Washington Irving and Ideologies of (DE)Colonization in the Early Republic', *American Literary History*, *8/2* (1996), 205–31.

Namias, June, *White Captives: Gender and Ethnicity on the American Frontier* (Chapel Hill, NC, and London, 1995).

Nash, Gary B., *Red, White, and Black: the Peoples of Early America* (Englewood Cliffs, NJ, 1974).

Nester, William R., *Haughty Conquerors: Amherst and the Great Indian Uprising of 1763* (Westport, CT, 2000).

New Monthly Magazine.

Nobles, Gregor H., *American Frontiers: Cultural Encounters and Continental Conquest* (1998).

Norton, John, *The Journal of Major John Norton 1816*, ed. Carl F. Klinck and James J. Talman (Toronto, 1970).

Owen, William, *Diary of William Owen From November 10, 1824, to April 20, 1825*, ed. Joel W. Hiatt (Indianapolis, IN, 1906, rpt. Clifton, NJ, 1973),

Paine, Thomas, *The Rights of Man*, ed. Henry Collins (Harmondsworth, 1969).

——, *The Thomas Paine Reader*, ed. Michael Foot and Isaac Kramnick (Harmondsworth, 1987).

——, *The Writings of Thomas Paine*, ed. Moncure Daniel Conway, 4 vols. (1896, facs. rpt. 1996).

Parker, Robert Dale, *The Invention of Native American Literature* (Ithaca, NY, 2003).

Parkman, Francis, *The Conspiracy of Pontiac* (1851, rpt. New York, 1962).

Parliamentary History, 19 (1778).

Pearce, Roy H., *Savagism and Civilization: A Study of the Indian and the American Mind* (rev. edn. Baltimore, 1965).

——, *Natives and Newcomers: The Cultural Origins of North America* (New York, 2001).

Peckham, Howard H., *Pontiac and the Indian Uprising* (1947, rpt. Chicago, 1961).

Perdue, Theda, *Cherokee Women: Gender and Cultural Change 1700–1835* (Lincoln, NE, and London, 1998).

Peyer, Bernd C., *The Tutor'd Mind: Indian Writers in Antebellum America* (Amherst, MA, 1997).

Pirie, David B. (ed.), *The Penguin History of Literature. Vol 5: The Romantic Period* (Harmondsworth, 1994).

The Poetry and History of Wyoming: Containing Campbell's Gertrude . . . and the History of Wyoming by William L. Stone (New York and London, 1841).

Pope, Robert (ed.), *Religion and National Identity: Wales and Scotland, c. 1700–2000* (Cardiff, 2001).

Pratt, Lynda, 'Revising the National Epic: Coleridge, Southey, *Madoc*', *Romanticism, 2/2* (1996), 149–63.

Pratt, Mary Louise, *Imperial Eyes: Travel Writing and Transculturation* (London and New York, 1992).

Pratt, Stephanie, *American Indians in British Art, 1700–1850* (Norman, OK, 2005).

Preston, William, *Poetical Works* (Dublin, 1793).

Prucha, Francis Paul, *American Indian Policy in the Formative Years: The Indian Trade and Intercourse Acts, 1790–1834* (Cambridge, 1962).

_____ , *The Great Father: The United States Government and the American Indians* (Lincoln, NE, 1984).

Quarterly Review.

Raynal, Abbé, *A Philosophical and Political History of the Settlements and Trade of the Europeans in the East and West Indies*, trs. J. Justamond, 8 vols. (1783).

Redding, Cyrus, *Literary Reminiscences and Memoirs of Thomas Campbell*, 2 vols. (1860).

Rice, Philip, and Waugh, Patricia (eds.), *Modern Literary Theory* (1989).

Richardson, Alan and Hofkosh, Sonia (eds.), *Romanticism, Race and Imperial Culture 1780–1834* (Bloomington, IN, 1996).

Richardson, William, *Poems Chiefly Rural*, 3rd edn. (Glasgow, 1826).

Richter, Daniel K. and Merrell, James H. (eds.), *Beyond the Covenant Chain: The Iroquois and Their Neighbors in Indian North America, 1600–1800* (Syracuse, NY, 1987).

Ritson, Joseph, *A Historical Essay on National Song in A Select Collection of English Songs*, 3 vols. (1783).

Ritterbush, Philip C., *Overtures to Biology: The Speculations of Eighteenth-Century Naturalists* (New Haven and London, 1964).

Ritvo, Harriet, *The Platypus and the Mermaid and Other Figments of the Classifying Imagination* (Cambridge, 1997).

Robertson, Fiona, 'British Romantic Columbiads', *Symbiosis: A Journal of Anglo-American Literary Relations*, 2/1 (1998), 1–23.

Robertson, William, *The History of America*, 3 vols. (Dublin, 1777).

Robinson, Deane, *A History of the Dakota or Sioux Indians* (1904, rpt. Minneapolis, 1967).

Rousseau, Jean Jacques, *Discourse On the Origins of Inequality (Second Discourse) Polemics, and Political Economy*, vol. 3 of *The Collected Writings of Rousseau*, eds. Roger D. Masters and Christopher Kelly (Hanover and London, 1993).

Rowlandson, Mary, *The Sovereignty and Goodness of God by Mary Rowlandson*, ed. Neal Salisbury (Boston, 1997).

Ruoff, A. LaVonne Brown and Ward Jr. Jerry W. (eds.), *Redefining American Literary History* (New York, 1990).

Rutherford, John, 'Relation of a Captivity', in M. M. Quaife (ed.) *The Siege of Detroit* (Chicago, 1958).

Sarris, Greg, *Keeping Slug Woman Alive: A Holistic Approach to American Indian Texts* (Berkeley, 1993).

Schaffer, Simon, 'Natural Philosophy and Public Spectacle in the Eighteenth Century', *History of Science*, 21 (1983).

Scott, Sir Walter, *Minstrelsy of the Scottish Border: Consisting of Historical and Romantic Ballads, Collected in the Southern Counties of Scotland; with a Few of Modern Date*, 3 vols. (Kelso, 1802).

_____ , *Familiar Letters of Sir Walter Scott*, 2 vols. (Edinburgh, 1894).

Scott, Sir Walter, *The Poetical Works of Sir Walter Scott*, ed. J. Logie Robertson (London, 1926).

Seaver, James, *A Narrative of the Life of Mrs. Mary Jemison, 1824* (New York, 1975).

Selkirk, Earl of, *see* Douglas.

Sheehan, Bernard W., *Seeds of Extinction: Jeffersonian Philanthropy and the American Indian* (New York, 1974).

——, *Savagism and Civility: Indians and Englishmen in Colonial Virginia* (Cambridge, 1980).

Slight, Benjamin, *Indian Researches, or, Facts Concerning the North American Indians: Including Notices of Their Present State of Improvement, in their Social, Civil and Religious Condition; with Hints for their Future Advancement* (Montreal, 1844).

Slotkin, Richard, *Regeneration Through Violence: The Mythology of the American Frontier, 1600–1860* (Middletown, CT, 1973).

Smith, Adam, *The Theory of Moral Sentiments*, 6th edn. (1790).

Smith, Bernard, *European Vision and the South Pacific 1768–1850*, 2nd edn. (New Haven, 1985).

——, *Imagining the Pacific: In the Wake of Cook's Voyages* (New Haven and London, 1992).

Smith, Charlotte, *The Old Manor House*, ed. Anne Henry Ehrenpreis (Oxford, 1989).

Smith, Donald B., *Sacred Feathers: The Reverend Peter Jones (Kahkewaquonaby) and the Mississauga Indians* (Lincoln, NE, and London, 1987).

Smith, James, *A Narrative of the Most Remarkable Occurrences in the Life and Travels of Colonel James Smith During his Captivity among the Indians from the Year 1755, '56, '57, '58 & '59* (Cincinatti, 1870).

Smith, James Edward, *Memoir and Correspondence of the Late Sir James Edward Smith, M.D., Fellow of the Royal Society of London etc.*, ed. Lady Smith (1832).

Smith, Mary, *An Affecting Narrative of the Captivity and Sufferings of Mrs. Mary Smith* (Providence, RI, 1815).

Smith, Samuel Stanhope, *An Essay on the Causes of the Variety of Complexion and Figure in the Human Species to Which Are Added Strictures on Lord Kaim's Discourse on the Original Diversity of Mankind* (1789).

Smith, William, *The Speech of a Creek Indian, against the immoderate use of spirituous liquors; delivered in a national assembly of the Creeks upon the breaking out of the late war. To which are added 1. A letter from Yariza, an Indian maid of the royal line of the Mohawks, to the principal ladies of New York 2. Indian songs of peace 3. An American fable Together with some remarks upon the characters and genius of the Indians, and upon their customs and ceremonies at making war and peace* (1754).

Smollett, Tobias, *The Expedition of Humphry Clinker*, ed. Angus Ross (Harmondsworth, 1967).

Smyth, J. D. F., *A Tour of the United States of America*, 2 vols. (1784).

Snader, Joe, *Caught Between Worlds: British Captivity Narratives in Fact and Fiction* (Lexington, KY, 2000).

Snow, Dean R., *The Iroquois* (Cambridge, 1994).

Sokolow, Jayme A., *The Great Encounter: Native Peoples and European Settlers in the Americas, 1492–1800* (Armonk, NY, 2003).

Sollors, Werner, *Beyond Ethnicity: Consent and Descent in American Culture* (New York and Oxford, 1986).

Sosin, Jack M., *Whitehall and the Wilderness: The Middle West in British Colonial Policy, 1760–1775* (Lincoln, NE, 1961).

Southey, Robert, *The Poetical Works of Robert Southey, Collected by Himself*, 10 vols. (1837–8).

——, *The Life and Correspondence of Robert Southey*, ed. C. C. Southey, 6 vols. (1849–50).

——, *New Letters of Robert Southey*, ed. Kenneth Curry, 2 vols. (New York and London, 1965).

——, *Robert Southey: The Critical Heritage*, ed. Lionel Madden (London and Boston, 1972).

——, *Robert Southey: Poetical Works 1793–1810*, gen. ed. Lynda Pratt, 5 vols. (2004).

Spence, Thomas, *Pig's Meat; or Lessons for the Swinish Multitude*, 2nd edn., 3 vols. (1793–5).

——, *The Reign of Felicity, Being a Plan for the Civilizing the Indians of North America* (1796).

Spencer, Oliver M., *The Indian Captivity of O. M. Spencer* (1834, rpt. Chicago, 1917).

Stafford, Fiona, *The Last of the Race: The Growth of a Myth from Milton to Darwin* (Oxford, 1994).

Stanley, George F. G., *The War of 1812* (Toronto, 1983).

Stone, William L., *Border Wars of the American Revolution*, 2 vols. (New York, 1846).

——, *Life of Joseph Brant (Thayendanagea)*, 2 vols. (Albany, NY, 1864).

Sugden, John, *Tecumseh: A Life* (1999).

Sussman, Charlotte, *Consuming Anxieties: Consumer Protest, Gender, and British Slavery, 1713–1833* (Stanford, 2000).

Sword, Wiley, *President Washington's Indian War* (Norman, OK, 1985).

Szasz, Margaret Connell, *Indian Education in the American Colonies, 1607–1783* (Albuquerque, NM, 1988).

——, (ed.), *Between Indian and White Worlds: The Cultural Broker* (Norman, OK, and London, 1994).

Tanner, John, *A Narrative of the Captivity and Adventures of John Tanner (U.S. Interpreter at Saut de Ste. Marie) during Thirty Years Residence among the Indians in the Interior of North America* (New York, 1830).

Tanner, John, *The Falcon: A Narrative of the Captivity and Adventures of John Tanner During Thirty Years Residence Among the Indians in the Interior of North America* (New York and London, 1994).

Thomas, David Hurst, *Skull Wars: Kennewick Man, Archaeology, and the Battle for Native American Identity* (New York, 2000).

Timberlake, Henry, *The Memoirs of Lieut. Henry Timberlake (Who Accompanied the Three Cherokee Indians to England in the Year 1762)* (1765).

Tobin, Beth Fowkes, *Picturing Imperial Power: Colonial Subjects in Eighteenth-Century Painting* (Durham, NC, and London, 1999).

Todd, Janet, *Sensibility: An Introduction* (London and New York, 1986).

Trio, Karim, 'Denominated "SAVAGE": Methodism, Writing and Identity in the Works of William Apess, A Pequot', *American Quarterly*, 48/4 (1996), 653–79.

Turner, Frederick, *The Frontier in American History* (New York, 1962).

Tyler, Royall, *The Contrast* (1787).

Underhill, Ruth M., *Red Man's Religion: Beliefs and Practices of the Indians North of Mexico* (Chicago and London, 1965).

Van Kirk, Sylvia, *'Many Tender Ties': Women in Fur-Trade Society in Western Canada, 1670–1870* (Winnipeg, 1980).

Vaughan, Alden T., 'From White Man to Redskin: Changing Anglo-American Perceptions of the American Indian', *American Historical Review*, 87/4 (1982), 917–53.

_____ and Richter, Daniel K, 'Crossing the Cultural Divide: Indians and New Englanders, 1605–1763', *Proceedings of the American Antiquarian Society*, 90 (1980).

Voltaire, Francois Marie Arouet, *An Essay on Universal History and the Manners and Spirit of Nations*, 2 vols. (Edinburgh, 1782).

Walker, Cheryl, *Indian Nation: Native American Literature and Nineteenth-Century Nationalisms* (Durham, NC, and London, 1997).

Weld, Isacc Jr., *Travels Through the States of North America and the Provinces of Upper and Lower Canada During the Years 1795, 1796, and 1797* (1799).

West, Elliott, *The Contested Plains: Indians, Goldseekers and the Rush to Colorado* (Lawrence, KA, 1998).

White, Richard, *The Middle Ground: Indians, Empires, and Republics in the Great Lakes Region 1650–1815* (Cambridge, 1991).

Wiget, Andrew, 'His Life in His Tail: The Native American Trickster and the Literature of Possibility', in *Redefining American Literary History*, eds. A. La-Vonne Brown Ruoff and Jerry W. Ward, Jr. (New York, 1990), 83–96.

Williams, Basil, *The Life of William Pitt, Earl of Chatham*, 2 vols. (1913).

Williams, Gwyn A., *Madoc: The Making of a Myth* (1979).

Williams, John, *Farther Observations on the Discovery of America, by Prince MADOG ab Owen Gwynedd, About the Year 1170* (1792).

Williams, Joseph, *Poetical Works* (Shrewsbury, 1786).

Williams, Roger, *A Key into the Language of America*, eds. John J. Teunissen and Evelyn J. Hinz (Detroit, 1973).

Williamson, Peter, *French and Indian Cruelty; Exemplified in the Life and Various Vicissitudes of Fortune of Peter Williamson*, 5th edn. (Edinburgh, 1762, facs. rpt. Bristol, 1996).

Wilson, James, *The Earth Shall Weep: A History of Native America* (1998).

Wind, Astrid, ' "Adieu to all": the Dying Indian at the Turn of the Eighteenth Century', *Symbiosis: A Journal of Anglo-American Literary Relations, 2/1* (1998), 39–55.

Wood, Peter H., Waselkov, Gregory A., and Hatley, M. Thomas (eds.), *Powhatan's Mantle: Indians in the Colonial Southeast* (Lincoln, NE, and London, 1989).

Wordsworth, William, *The Poetical Works of William Wordsworth*, ed. E. de Selincourt and Helen Darbishire, 5 vols. (Oxford, 1940–49).

_____ , *The Prelude 1798–99*, ed. Stephen Parrish (Ithaca, NY, and Hassocks, Sussex, 1977).

_____ , *The Prelude, 1799, 1805*, 1850, eds. Jonathan Wordsworth, M. H. Abrams, Stephen Gill (New York and London, 1979).

Wordsworth, William and Coleridge, Samuel Taylor, *Lyrical Ballads 1798*, ed. W. J. B. Owen, 2nd edn. (Oxford, 1969).

Wright, J. Leitch Jr., *Britain and the American Frontier 1783–1815* (Athens, GA, 1975).

_____ , *The Only Land They Knew: the Tragic Story of the American Indians in the Old South* (New York and London, 1981).

Wyss, Hilary E., 'Captivity and Conversion: William Apess, Mary Jemison, and Narratives of Racial Identity', *American Indian Quarterly*, 23/3–4 (1999), 63–82.

Yellow Bird, Michael, 'What We Want to be Called: Indigenous Peoples' Perspectives on Racial and Ethnic Identity Labels', *American Indian Quarterly*, 23/2 (1999), 1–22.

Zeisberger, David, *History of the Northern American Indians*, ed. Archer Butler Hubert and William Nathaniel Schwarze (Columbus, OH, 1910, rpt. Lewisburg, PA, 1999).

Index